CONFESSIONAL LUTHERAN DOGMATICS

Robert D. Preus, Editor
John R. Stephenson, Assistant Editor

IX

THE CHURCH

AND
HER FELLOWSHIP, MINISTRY, AND GOVERNANCE

by

Kurt E. Marquart

Published by
The Luther Academy
St. Louis, Missouri

Paul T. McCain, Technical Editor
Cover design by Jack Cascione

 Published by The Luther Academy, 15825 373rd Avenue, Northville, SD 57465 (business office)

When not the author's own translation, quotations from *The Book of Concord*, trans. and ed. Theodore G. Tappert, are used by permission of Augsburg Fortress Press; quotations from *Luther's Works*, American Edition are used by permission of Concordia Publishing House and Augsburg Fortress Press.

Library of Congress Catalog Number: 89-84112

ISBN: 0-9622791-9-6 (Volume IX)
0-9622791-0-2 (13-Volume Set)

Printed in the United States of America
Sheridan Books, Chelsea, Michigan

Dedicated to

THE MINISTERIUM OF THE LUTHERAN CHURCH—MISSOURI SYNOD

in memory of

CARL FERDINAND WILHELM WALTHER

Confessional Lutheran Theologian

TABLE OF CONTENTS

Part Three: The Ministry

Part Four: Church Governance

GENERAL INTRODUCTION
by
Robert D. Preus, General Editor
Confessional Lutheran Dogmatics

For some time now those of us in the Lutheran Church who have interested ourselves in the Lutheran Confessions and actually taught them and done research in these great symbolic writings have recognized the need for a dogmatics book based upon the outline and thought patterns of the Lutheran Confessions. Such a book which has never been written before, except for Leonard Hutter's little *Compendium Locorum Theologicorum,* would address the theologians, Lutheran and hopefully others, of our day with a truly confessional answer to the theological issues which we are facing in Christianity and in our Lutheran Zion today. We were in no way interested in replacing in our Lutheran Church—Missouri Synod Francis Pieper's monumental *Christian Dogmatics* as a textbook which has served students in our church body and others for three generations. Such an intention would have been unnecessary and unproductive. The authors of the various monographs, which will appear in this series entitled *Confessional Lutheran Dogmatics,* come at their respective subjects from somewhat different vantage points and backgrounds and personal predilections as they do dogmatics. It was decided, therefore, to issue a series of dogmatics treatises on the primary articles of faith usually taken up in traditional dogmatics since the 16th century. (e.g. the Augsburg Confession; Philip Melanchthon's *Loci communes;* Martin Chemnitz's *Loci theologici,* etc.)

But why the approach from the Lutheran Confessions? Are not these musty old creeds and symbols irrelevant to our day, and would not a series of monographs written from the point of view of confessional Lutheran theology be equally irrelevant to the theological issues confronting the church today? It is because we must respond with an emphatic no to such a question that we presume to issue the forthcoming volumes. The Confessions whose theology is taken directly from the Scriptures are relevant to our day just as the Scriptures themselves which are always "profitable for doctrine, for reproof, for correction, for instruction in righteousness" (2 Tim 3:16). There is a real call and need for just the kind of dogmatics book here proposed, that is, a *Confessional Lutheran Dogmatics*. First of all, there has been no dogmatics book of any kind published by orthodox confessional Lutheran theologians for more than a generation (Elert, Pieper, Hönecke, Hove, etc.). During the same time, however, there has been a renewed interest in the Lutheran Confessions, in their function in giving form to our Lutheran presentation of doctrine and to some extent even in norming that doctrine. I am referring here not merely to the excellent studies of Edmund Schlink, Holsten Fagerberg, Leif Grane, Peter Brunner, Wilhelm Maurer, Friedrich Mildenberger, Hermann Sasse, and others but to many recent books and studies written in connection with centennial observances of the Book of Concord, the Augsburg Confession, etc. Thus, it would appear that there is need not only for a dogmatics text in our day, but one that is strictly and consciously confessional in its presentation of doctrine and its assessment and analysis of modern theological trends throughout the Christian Church. This series, of which the present volume is a part, is written to fill this need, and it is the hope and prayer of the authors that the present volume will to some extent accomplish this aim.

The volumes making up *Confessional Lutheran Dogmatics* are not a theology of the Lutheran Confessions; they are rather a book in *Dogmatics*. However, they differ from other dogmatics books in that they are patterned strictly after the theology of the Book of Concord as they address the issues of today. They follow not only the theology of the Book of Concord, as for instance the texts of Francis Pieper and Adolph Hönecke and other confessional Lutheran dogmaticians have done, but, unlike the former confessional Lutheran dogmaticians, the authors of the present volumes follow the actual pattern of thought (*forma et quasi typus*, ὑποτύπωσις of the Lutheran Confessions. Such a procedure is according to the principle of the Confessions themselves; Creeds and Confessions are indeed a pattern and norm according to which all other books and writings are to be accepted and judged (see FC SD, Rule and Norm, 10). This fact will account for the agreement in both doctrine and formulation that the reader will observe within the present entire dogmatics book; the authors bind themselves not only generally to the theology of the Book of Concord but to its content and terminology (*rebus et phrasibus*, Preface to the Book of Concord, Tappert edition, p. 13).

There is another reason for the doctrinal agreement which will be apparent among the authors of the *Confessional Lutheran Dogmatics*. It is this, that all the authors share the concept of doctrine, unity of doctrine, consensus in doctrine, and purity of doctrine consistently articulated in our Confessions. All of the Lutheran Confessions see doctrine as a singular, organic whole. Christian doctrine is like a body (*corpus doctrinae*) with parts (*partes*) or joints (*articuli*) and ligaments and members (*membra*). The plural "doctrines" is rarely used in the Confessions, as in Scripture, but rather the singular "doctrine." In the Church if one member suffers, the whole body suffers; according to the organic, unitary nature of Christian doctrine, if one article or member fails, the whole body of doctrine is affected adversely. Luther said, "One article is all the articles, and all articles are one."[1]

As a confessional Lutheran dogmatics the present volume will consciously and scrupulously draw its doctrine from Scripture. All the Confessions, beginning with the Creeds and concluding with the Formula of Concord, claim to be and are direct explications of the sacred Scriptures. As such, their purpose is never to lead us away from Scripture nor to summarize the Scriptures in a way as to make further study of the Scriptures unnecessary; but they are written to lead us into the Scriptures. This is exactly what their function has been in the history of the Church, whether we think of the many commentaries written on the early Creeds by the church fathers or the expositions of our Confessions by the Reformers and their successors. The reader will therefore notice the present work in dogmatics engages in much more direct and extensive exegesis than other works in dogmatic theology of our day except the immense *Church Dogmatics* by Karl Barth. This is altogether proper and called for in a *Confessional Lutheran Dogmatics*.

The present work is a kind of *loci communes*, the recapitulation of the main themes of Scripture on the basis of the confessional Lutheran outline and pattern of thought. The Lutheran Confessions themselves never claim to be the final work on the understanding and exegesis of the Scriptures; we recall Luther's statement on *oratio, meditatio, tentatio*[2] with its blasts against theological

1. *WA* 40:II:47.32–33; *LW* 27:38. *Galatians Commentary*, (1535).

know-it-alls and how often this statement of Luther's was repeated by the post-Reformation theologians in their dogmatics works. The Confessions always lead deeper into the Scriptures, especially as new issues arise in new cultures and succeeding generations which must be faced only with theology drawn from the Scriptures and patterned after the Lutheran Confessions.

The forthcoming volumes are dedicated to Dr. Francis Pieper, a great confessional Lutheran dogmatician of our church, in the hope and prayer that they will help to achieve what he did so much to accomplish in his day; namely, doctrinal unity and consensus in the doctrine of the Gospel and all its articles among all Lutherans and a firm confessional Lutheran identity so sorely needed in our day.

---

2. *WA* 50:659.4; *LW* 34:285, *Preface to the Wittenberg Edition of Luther's German Writings,* (1539).

PREFACE

The treatment which follows intends simply to display some of the incomparable evangelical treasures of the Church of the Augsburg Confession, so that these may shine in their own light. The work is frankly animated by the conviction that it is just the characteristically Lutheran "ecclesiology of the cross"—as distinct from the alternative paradigms of Eastern Orthodoxy and Roman Catholicism on the one hand, and of Zwingli/Calvinism on the other—which reproduces the New Testament substance with unique fidelity.

The present arrangement of the material lays no claim of course to being the best, let alone the only, possible one. On the contrary, our presentation cheerfully invites more competent efforts from such as care about what is at stake here. Some complexities and perplexities are of course bound to arise also in connection with the articles of the church and the ministry. Not all problems in this area are really native to it, however. Some seem to spring rather from the perennial temptation to make "theory" fit, rather than correct, an alien and inconsistent practice. This then easily leads to unhappy conceptualizations of the sort compared by Melanchthon—following Socrates—to "an unskilled cook" severing "the member at the wrong place" (Ap. XXIV. 16). The present work attempts to set things out so as to keep the fundamental contours, connections, and issues transparently clear.

Non-Lutheran readers are asked for their indulgence and understanding as they overhear, as it were, a discourse addressed above all to Lutheran pastors and theological students, at a time of crisis over their confessional patrimony. Lutheran readers who may find the references to Victorian Missouriana tedious are of course free to skip over what does not interest them. The documentation is necessary, however, since some popular impressions of, say, Walther's actual position, are one-sided and even inaccurate.

Thanks are of course due to many people, but particularly to the general editor, Dr. Robert Preus, and the assistant editor, Dr. John Stephenson, for their valuable advice and assistance, and to Pastors Paul B. McCain, Paul T. McCain, and Mr. Matt Harrison for compiling the indices, and most especially to Pastor Paul T. McCain, the technical editor, for his painstaking attention to detail.

K. Marquart

Reformation/All Saints, 1990

ABBREVIATIONS

References to the Book of Concord:

AC Augsburg Confession
Ap. Apology of the Augsburg Confession
SA Smalcald Articles
Tr. Treatise on the Power and Primacy of the Pope
SC Small Catechism
LC Large Catechism
FC Formula of Concord
 RN Rule and Norm of the Formula of Concord
 Ep. Epitome of the Formula of Concord
 SD Solid Declaration of the Formula of Concord

References to Editions and Translations of the Book of Concord:

BKS *Bekenntnisschriften der evangelisch-lutherischen Kirche.* 10th ed. Vandenhoeck & Ruprecht, 1986.
Tappert *The Book of Concord,* Minneapolis. Augsburg Fortress Press, 1957.
Bente *Triglot Concordia: The Symbolical Books of the Ev. Lutheran Church, German-Latin-English.* Northwestern Publishing House, 1989.

References to the Book of Concord are to the confession, article and paragraph number.

References to Luther's Works:

WA *D. Martin Luthers Werke. Kritische Gesamtausgabe.* 61 vols. Weimar, 1883–.
WABr *D. Martin Luthers Werke. Briefwechsel.* 18 vols. Weimar, 1930–.
WADB *D. Martin Luthers Werke. Deutsche Bibel.* 12 vols. Weimar, 1906–1961.

WATr *D. Martin Luthers Werke. Tischreden.* 6 vols. Weimar, 1912–1921.

LW *Luther's Works. American Edition.* 55 vols. Jaroslav Pelikan and Helmut T. Lehmann, general editors. St. Louis: Concordia; Minneapolis: Augsburg Fortress Press, 1955–1986.

When citing from Luther whenever possible the translation is cited from *Luther's Works* with the reference to the *Weimar Ausgabe* following. When no translation was available, it was provided by the author or provided from another source indicated after the reference to *WA*.

References to Church Fathers:

MPG *Patrologia Cursus Completus. Series Graeca.* Ed. J. P. Migne. Paris, 1857–1866.

MPL *Patrologia Cursus Completus. Series Latina.* Ed. J. P. Migne, Paris, 1878–1890.

Lightfoot *The Apostolic Fathers.* 2 Parts in 5 volumes. Reprinted Baker, 1989.

Mansi *Sacrorum conciliorum nova et amplissima collectio.* Ed. Johannes Dominicus Mansi. 53 vols. Florence, 1759–1798.

ANF *The Ante-Nicene Fathers of the Church.* A. Roberts, editor. 10 volumes. Reprint. Grand Rapids, 1987.

NPNF *The Nicene and Post-Nicene Fathers of the Church.* First Series: 11 volumes. Second Series: 14 volumes. P. Schaff, editor. Reprint. Grand Rapids, 1988.

FCh *The Fathers of the Church.* New York and Washington, D.C., 1947–.

Other references:

TDNT *The Theological Dictionary of the New Testament.* G. Kittel, editor. G. Bromiley, translator. 10 volumes. Grand Rapids, 1964–1976.

Inst. *The Institutes of the Christian Religion.* J. Calvin. F. Battles, translator. Vol. 20 of *Library of Christian Classics.* Philadelphia, 1960.

THE CHURCH

The church is not merely an association of outward things and rites, like other polities, but it is mainly an association of faith and of the Holy Spirit in men's hearts, which indeed has outward marks so that it may be recognized, namely, the pure teaching of the Gospel and the administration of the sacraments in agreement with the Gospel of Christ.

Apology VII/VIII.5

1

SKETCHING THE CONTOURS

Our world is not "post-Christian," merely post-Constantinian, which is a very different matter. Our age has seen inflicted on Christianity the most sophisticated and brutal assaults it has ever had to endure. Out of the depths of unspeakable dungeons came eloquent confessions, like that of the Lutheresque Romanian Pastor Richard Wurmbrand, who concluded that if Christianity was indeed dead everywhere else, as his tormentors insisted, then he would with Mary Magdalene weep at its tomb until it would rise again.[1] Then there are the life and work of an Alexander Solzhenitsyn, the conversion of a Malcolm Muggeridge, and the broadcast, unprecedented in seventy years of Babylonian Captivity, of the Easter Liturgy over Radio Moscow in the millennial year of Russian Christianity, 1988. What are these if not stunning resurrections of Christianity in the very midst of its enemies (Ps. 110:2)? Let us be done then with self-indulgent prattle about our "post-Christian" age! What is clearly over is the Constantinian Era, even if a few doddering state churches here and there manage to cling to their wonted illusions a little while longer. If the centuries of the intimate church/state embrace appear now as a "kind of collective experience of the far country in which the prodigal spent his inheritance with harlots,"[2] the target of the complaint is not of course the precious gift of God in the conversion of the Roman Emperor, but the abuse and progressive distortion of this gift.

As the church wends her way through the centuries, the ever changing landscape compels her to attend now to this and now to that aspect of her faith. The so-called Enlightenment abruptly changed the very travelling arrangements. Increasingly deprived of Western society's unquestioning support, the churches were forced to look to their own resources, and to ask themselves the most fundamental questions about their warrants and purposes.

1. R. Wurmbrand, *Christ in the Communist Prisons*, 243.

2. Fr. Robert Adolfs in D. Martin and P. Mullen, *Unholy Warfare: The Church and the Bomb*, 192.

John Henry Newman put it starkly in the first of the *Tracts for the Times*: "... should these secular advantages [i.e. those of social and legal establishment] cease, on what must Christ's ministers depend?"[3] The Oxford Movement's answer was to stake the legitimacy of the Anglican Church chiefly on the so-called "apostolic succession" of its bishops. Newman himself moved on to Roman Catholicism, which at the First Vatican Council in 1870 anchored its ecclesiology in the extremist version of papal infallibility passionately advocated by another ex-Anglican, Cardinal Manning.[4]

The Lutheran churches, too, were compelled to look to the rock whence they had been hewn. The ravages of rationalism and historicism had undermined all stable positions. As Troeltsch was to put it in a famous lecture: "Gentlemen, everything is tottering!" More particularly, however, the radical abrogation of the Lutheran Confessions involved in the forced union with Calvinism in Prussia and elsewhere, in the nineteenth century, created a deep crisis of confessional identity for the Lutheran churches there, and ultimately everywhere. The mass emigrations to America and Australia are the well-known symptoms of that crisis. It was only natural that the ecclesiastical turmoil placed ecclesiology into the very forefront of theological interest and discussion. For Lutherans this meant a salutary struggle for their Reformation roots, and particularly for the dogmatic and practical recovery of their evangelical Magna Charta, the seventh article of the Augsburg Confession.

The trouble with state-church establishment had been its very comfortableness. Assured of their temporal well-being, the churches did not have to bother about the transcendent grounds and aims of their existence. They grew soft, flabby, and compliant. It was as if a vertebrate organism had been strapped for centuries into an artificial external skeleton, leaving its own backbone to atrophy from disuse. How dearly the churches have had to pay in our time—and are still paying—for their soggy backbones!

In the New World the transplanted Lutherans at last had the opportunity—denied their forbears in Europe—to let the church among them shape itself according to its own inner dynamic, and to stand on its own feet. Some floundering was of course to be expected, and sometimes took extravagant forms, e.g., Kavel's

3. J. Kent, *End of the Line*, 63.
4. C. Butler, *The Vatican Council 1869–1870*, 32–33, 108, 144, 172, passim.

biblicistic "apostolic church order" in Australia,[5] and the Stephan/Grabau clericalism in America. C.F.W. Walther's work in St. Louis[6] undoubtedly represents the high-water mark of a sober and balanced Lutheran ecclesiology. Steeped in Luther, well-versed in the post-Reformation dogmatic tradition, and compelled by circumstances to devise workable structures for various levels of church-life, Walther was easily the greatest Lutheran ecclesiologist in America. He was a churchman in the best sense of that word. What is meant by "churchmanship" nowadays is often a sad caricature, reflecting the tyranny of pragmatism in the surrounding mass-culture.[7] There is no escape from the strangle-hold of this form of "culture Christianity" except by a perennial return to first principles in the matter of church and ministry. In respectful parody of the Catechism one may say that while ecclesiology is indeed crucial in itself, it must be crucial among us also.

5. T. Hebart, *Die Vereinigte Ev.-Luth. Kirche in Australien*, 59ff. Also A. Brauer, *Under the Southern Cross*,. 99–101, 108–117.

6. When one considers Walther's great trilogy on the church, *Church and Ministry*, *True Visible Church*, and, *Proper Form*, together with his hitherto untranslated *Pastoraltheologie*, it is difficult to understand E. Clifford Nelson's judgment that "no thoroughgoing study [of the relationship of the Lutheran doctrine of the Church to the historical, empirical structures of the Church in the world] was undertaken" in America and that "no Lutheran bodies seriously addressed the ecclesiological problem." E. Nelson, "Ecclesiology as Key to the Lutheran Future," 10.

7. For a case-study see L. Loetscher, *The Broadening Church*. A careful study of the rise of unbelief in Victorian America suggests that this rise may owe more to overanxious accommodation to cultural trends on the part of religionists than to the latters' supposed resistance to change. See J. Turner, *Without God, Without Creed: The Origins of Unbelief in America*.

2

THE CHURCH AND CHRIST

The vocabulary of the New Testament repeatedly shows a preference for the bland word, that is, the one least encumbered with preemptive semantic freight (e.g., "ἀγάπη" as the main word for "love"). So the colorless, secular "ἐκκλησία" ([political] assembly) came to designate the new reality of the church.[1] The term had been coopted already by the LXX, as a translation of the Hebrew "*qahal*." However, "*qahal*" is also rendered "συναγωγή" in the LXX. The latter term was well established by NT times as the normal designation for the Jewish religious assembly. "Συναγωγή" could also designate the earliest Jewish-Christian gatherings—in the NT only at Ja. 2:2—but the irreversible rift between church and synagogue was soon reflected by the standard use of "ἐκκλησία" for the one and "συναγωγή" for the other. The two terms also carried *inclusive* (men, women, and children; Jews and Gentiles; any number over one, Mt. 18:20) and *exclusive* (at least ten circumcised men) overtones, respectively. The semantic terrain staked out by "ἐκκλησία" stands in conscious contrast not only to that of "συναγωγή," but especially also to the implications of the "religious language" of paganism: ". . . Christians avoided the cultic words θίασος, ἔρανος, σύνοδος, σύλλογος, etc., and preferred instead to fill a secular term with their own peculiar meaning, making the term sacred for ever afterwards."[2]

Already the secular meaning of "ἐκκλησία" as "assembly" included the idea of "invited" or "regularly convened," and differed decisively in this respect from the shapeless "ὄχλος" (crowd or mob). According to Acts 19:32.39.41, an ἐκκλησία, or public meeting, must conform to certain standards. The Hebrew "*qahal*," possibly related to "*qol*" (voice),[3] can mean "call-up" in its secular use,

1. See K. Schmidt, "ἐκκλησία," in *TDNT*, III:501–504.
2. N. Turner, *Christian Words*, 70.
3. L. Koehler and W. Baumgartner, *Lexicon*, II:829.

but as *"qehal Yahwe"* clearly implies the initiating and constituting activity of God (Deut. 23:2 ff.).

The New Testament church is altogether the salvific workmanship of God, the Blessed Trinity (Eph. 4:4–6). As the Father sent the Son, so the Son—Who as the Second Adam (Rom. 5:12–21; I Cor. 15:45) is both church and ministry "in embryo"—sends His Apostles, having equipped them with the Holy Spirit for the mission to forgive and retain sins (Jn. 20:22.23). The church is the outcome, the object, the medium, and the aim of this evangelical mission of the Triune God, for she is the spiritual building which, from its apostolic-prophetic foundation (Eph.2:20), "grows into a holy temple in the Lord [Jesus], . . . for a residence of God in the Spirit" (v. 22).

The church is part and parcel of the "mystery of Christ" (Eph. 3:4; 5:32; Col. 4:3). The Christian mysteries (I Cor. 4:1) are the very opposite of all mystagogical mumbo-jumbo. They are not a secret doctrine muttered darkly among the few in the know. They are rather the saving secrets of God, utterly inaccessible to all human ingenuity, yet freely revealed and publicly (Mt. 10:27) proclaimed in the "mystery of the Gospel" (Eph. 6:19; cf. Mt. 13:11; Eph. 1:9; 3:9; Col. 1:26.27).

This church is both the (collective) body of Christians and the (mystical) body of Christ (Rom. 12:4.5; I Cor. 12:12–27; Eph. 1:23; 4:4 ff.; 5:30; Col. 2:19). Although the Christians vastly outnumber Christ, He completely "outweighs" them. The dependence is not mutual, but entirely one-sided. Life flows from the Head to the members (Col. 2:19), and from the Vine to the branches: "For without Me you can do nothing" (John 15:5). What is alone decisive and constitutive for the church is Christ and genuine union with Him. In this sense "ecclesiology is simply Christology and vice versa."[4]

Like Christ Himself (Jn. 6:38; 8:23), His church is also from "above" (Gal. 4:26). The modern notion of the church as a religious club—or a federation of such clubs—formed by the voluntary banding together of like-minded individuals, is a secular caricature. The church is created from above, by her Head, not from below, by her membership. The church is "the mother that begets [!] and bears every Christian through the Word of God" (LC Creed, 42). It is this vertical dimension which alone creates and shapes the horizontal. Here the evangelical ecclesiology of Luther

4. *TDNT*,III:512.

and the religious individualism and subjectivism traceable to Schleiermacher part company, radically and irreconcilably.[5]

When the New Testament, appropriating a rich Old Testament theme (e.g. Is. 62:4–5; Jer. 2:2; Hos. 2:21–22), further teaches that the church is the Bride and Wife of Christ (Jn. 3:29; II Cor. 11:2; Eph. 5:23 ff.; Rev. 19:7; 21:9), this is meant not to "put distance" between Christ and His church, but on the contrary, to stress their closeness and oneness (Eph. 5:28–32; cf. I Cor. 7:4). Ennobled by her union with the κύριος (Lord), the church is κυρία (Lady) [II Jn.1], for He withholds nothing from her who is "the fullness of Him who fills all in all" (Eph. 1:23). The self-identification of Christ with His church can hardly go farther than Acts 9:4: "Saul, Saul, why do you persecute Me?"

Given the reference to Genesis 2 in Eph. 5:31, one may at least draw attention to the parallel between the creation of Eve and the "new creation" (II Cor. 5:17) of the church. As Adam's bride was taken out of his side while he slept, so the Second Adam's Bride is brought into existence by means of the spirit, the water, and the blood (I John 5:8), which correspond verbatim to what issued from His sacred body when He began His three days' sleep of death (Jn. 19:30.34). John Gerhard, following illustrious ancient Fathers whom he cited, saw the Sacraments of Holy Baptism and of the Lord's Supper prefigured here.[6] For Luther it was self-evident that the spirit, the water, and the blood of I John 5:8 refer to the evangelical preaching office [*Predigtamt*], Baptism, and the Holy Supper.[7] John 6:63, "The words which I have spoken to you are spirit and are life," supports Luther's identification of "spirit" with Gospel-proclamation.

Since the church is of a piece with Christ, she must share His earthly fate: "As He is, so are we in this world" (I Jn. 4:17; cf. Jn. 15:18–21). "He has become one cake with us by faith" (Luther).[8] This means that "everything that happens with Christ forms a prefiguration for the church."[9] Luther is not pursuing allegorical will-o-the-wisps here. On the contrary, he decisively overcame the

5. W. Elert, *Eucharist and Church Fellowship*, 1–14.

6. J. Gerhard, *Harmonia Quatuor Evangelistarum*, II,2052–2053. Luther used similar imagery in a sermon he preached at the baptism of Bernhard von Anhalt in 1540, cf. *LW* 51:325; *WA* 49:132.15–22.

7. *WATr* IV:519–520, # 4799.1–2. *"der Geist, das ist, das Predigamt; 2. das Wasser, das ist, die Taufe; 3. das Blut, das ist, das Abendmahl des Herrn."* See also *LW* 30:316; *WA* 20:781-782, *Commentary on 1 John*, (1527).

8. *WA* 17:II:329.21–22, *Ein ander Sermon am Christtag*, (1527).

9. F. Hahn, cited in A.-E. Buchrucker, *Wort, Kirche und Abendmahl bei Luther*, 122.

vagaries of the "fourfold sense"[10] by seeing precisely the "historical-grammatical" sense as truly "spiritual," that is, as one Christ-bearing whole. The entire Bible, he had come to see, aims at our salvation and "deals only with Christ everywhere, if it is looked at inwardly, even though on the face of it it may sound differently."[11]

Christ quite deliberately rejected the high road of easy popularity, and chose the low road of the cross, thus reversing the choice of Adam (Mt. 4:1–11; cf. Gen. 3:1–7). That too is the way of His church. Just as Christ's divine nature and glory were not self-evident to common sense (Jn. 6:42), so also His church and her dignity are hidden under "weaknesses, sins, errors, and various offenses and forms of the cross. . . that it is not evident to the senses anywhere."[12] Unlike the Scarlet Woman of Rev. 17, the humble maid of Christ gives herself no airs (Rev. 12). Relying only on the blessing and protection of the God-Man, the pilgrim church cheerfully shares His ignominy "outside" the camp—until her pilgrimage is consummated in the glorious City of God (Heb. 13:11–14). "And blessed is he whoever is not offended in Me" (Mt. 11:6).

---

10. It is surely fanciful to argue with Gregory the Great, who cites Augustine, that Mk. 13:32, "that day neither the Son nor the angels know," refers to Christ "with respect to His body, which we are" *NPNF* (2:XIII/II:48).

11. *LW* 25:405; *WA* 56:414.15–17, *Commentary on Romans* (1515–1516).

12. *LW* 27:84; *WA* 40:II:106.21–22, *Commentary on Galatians* (1535).

3

FOUR BASIC TYPES OR "MODELS" OF ECCLESIOLOGY

In ecclesiology everything hinges on a few crucial distinctions, and the most crucial distinction of all is that between the church as the interior fellowship of faith and the church as the exterior fellowship in the means of grace. In Christology, if one lets either sight or reason override faith, one will end up denying either the divinity or the humanity of the God-Man. Faith, resting on God's Word alone, is not offended by the lowliness of Christ's servant form (Phil. 2:5 ff.), but confidently embraces in it the eternal Son of God. Something analogous is true of the church, the mystical body of Christ. It is difficult to imagine a greater contrast than that between the "one holy catholic and apostolic church" of the Creed, and the Christendom which we daily experience as a bewildering extravaganza of competing factions—some zealous, many sluggish, and a few quite mad. Nor is this shocking contrast of recent origin. It can be found already in the New Testament. The turbulent church of Corinth, for example, faction-ridden and racked by moral and emotional excesses, was hardly convincing even only as an icon of the "holy temple in the Lord" (Eph. 2:21) and the "glorious church, not having spot, or wrinkle, or any such thing" (5:27)—let alone as that reality itself.

The tension between appearance and reality came to a head in connection with the church's oneness or unity, which is indeed where this paradox is still felt most keenly. For over a millennium the creedal adjectives—one, holy, catholic, and apostolic—sufficed as a dogmatic definition of what the church had to say about herself. Even the centuries-long rivalries over "primacy," which led to the fateful rupture between East and West, did not precipitate more detailed dogmatic definitions of the church. "Curiously enough," writes Eastern Orthodox theologian John Meyendorff, "the ecclesiological problem was never formally posed as a real issue in the medieval debate between Constantinople and Rome."[1] A. Schmemann remarks that the Eastern rejection of the papal pretensions "was due to an Orthodox 'instinct' more than to a positive ecclesiological doctrine."[2]

The Western church settled, more or less comfortably, into the notion of the papacy as visible center and guarantee of the church's unity. Confidence in this panacea, however, was badly shaken already a century before Luther, when no fewer than three rivals claimed to be pope at once, and were replaced by yet a fourth at the Council of Constance in 1417. This spectacle had been preceded by the ignominious "Babylonian Captivity" of the papacy in Avignon (1309–1377). Forced by circumstances to see how illusory were all structural, administrative safeguards of truth and unity, the Reformation had to dig down to the roots of the matter. The result was the first explicit dogmatic definition of the church, embodied in Augsburg Confession VII:

> It is also taught that at all times there must be and remain one holy Christian church, which is the assembly of all believers, among whom the Gospel is purely preached and the holy sacraments are given in accordance with the Gospel [German].
>
> Likewise they teach that the one holy church is to remain forever. But the church is the congregation of saints, in which the Gospel is purely taught and the sacraments are rightly administered [Latin].

The later, Reformed (Calvinist) confessions reflect this definition, but also differ from it significantly. Rome's modern ecclesiology also developed in reaction to that of the Reformation. Until very recent times Eastern Orthodoxy's attitude to the Reformation was strongly influenced by Roman Catholic polemics, owing, perhaps, in part, to the trauma of Ecumenical Patriarch Cyril Loukaris' (1621–1638) "conversion" to Calvinism.

We have arrived here at the parting of the ways of the major Christian confessions. Exotic movements like Pentecostalism aside, there are four great alternative paradigms or "models" of the church, among which one must decide: the Eastern Orthodox, the Roman Catholic, the Lutheran, and the Zwingli-Calvinist or "Reformed" (including Arminian derivatives). These four basic types may in turn be arranged into two sets of two. Although Roman Catholicism and Eastern Orthodoxy do have important differences, they tend to look alike when viewed from a Lutheran, and especially from a Calvinist perspective. Conversely, Roman

1. J. Meyendorff, *The Orthodox Church*, 209.
2. A. Schmemann, "The Idea of Primacy in Orthodox Ecclesiology," 37.

Catholic and Eastern Orthodox observers are likely to perceive Lutheran and Calvinist theologies as tweedledee and tweedledum, despite the great gulf which divides Wittenberg and Geneva, historically and confessionally.

Is it possible to discern a pattern in the ecclesiologies of these major versions of Christianity? Without oversimplifying unduly, we may say that traditional Roman Catholicism (before Vatican II) particularly, but also Eastern Orthodoxy, *externalize* the church, while Calvinism *spiritualizes* her. Lutheran theology, by its innermost logic, understands the church *incarnationally*. To put this in Christological terms, the traditional Roman ecclesiology tends toward "Eutychianism," in that it confuses Christ's mystical body with the visible organization headed by the pope. Calvinist ecclesiology is "Nestorian" in letting an "invisible church" and a "visible church" stand side by side, without any real integration or bonding between them. The "Chalcedonian" approach of Lutheran ecclesiology distinguishes—without separating!—the church as inward communion of faith and as outward participation in the means of grace. Since the external Gospel and sacraments are the indispensable, God-given source, foundation, and sustenance of all faith and spiritual life, these means of grace bind in one the two "modes" of the church, and keep them from flying apart into two churches.

Since it is inconvenient to keep repeating phrases like "inward communion of faith" and "outward communion in the means of grace," the terms "invisible" and "visible" have established themselves as theological shorthand for these two aspects of the church. Traditionally the Roman Catholic and Eastern Orthodox churches have rejected the invisible/visible distinction, while the Lutheran and the Calvinist churches have affirmed it, but—this must be stressed—*in different senses*. The terminology may of course vary. Unlike Luther, who repeatedly spoke of the church as "invisible," the Lutheran church's official symbolical books do not use that language. Instead, the Apology in Art. VII/VIII speaks of the church "properly so called" [*proprie dicta*] (28,29), and "loosely so called" [*large dicta*] (10), and of being the church or being in the church "in name alone" [*nomine tantum*] or "in fact and in name" [*re et nomine*] (10,11,12). It is just this and not any Calvinist surrogate that all orthodox Lutheran theologians since John Gerhard have meant when they spoke of the church in terms of "visible" and "invisible." Gerhard specifically rejects the canard that the Lutherans have invented two churches, one visible and one invisible. Rather, says Gerhard, "we say that one and the same church is in different respects visible and invisible."[3]

If the terminology may vary, what is the dogmatic content of the proposition that "the church in the proper sense of the word is invisible" (C.F.W. Walther)?[4] As Walther's proof-texts show, the dogmatic substance of the assertion is twofold: (1) Only those who by Spirit-given faith participate interiorly in the life of Christ, that is, only believers, belong to the church properly speaking; (2) only God therefore sees and knows the true extent of the church's membership. The "invisibility" of the church then refers not to the obvious fact that we cannot presently see the church triumphant in heaven,[5] but to the hiddenness of the church here on earth, because faith or spiritual life "is hidden with Christ in God" (Col.3:3). But of course this hidden church has public, visible marks, by which she may be recognized with certainty: the holy Gospel and Sacraments of Christ, purely preached and rightly administered.

3. J. Gerhard, *Loci*, X.XXIII.VII.81. Quenstedt says the same in *Systema Theologicum*, III.xv.1632.

4. C.F.W. Walther, *Church and Ministry*, 38.

5. Schmemann speaks oddly of "the Protestant divorce between a visible and human Church which is contingent, relative and changing, and an invisible Church in heaven" (*The Idea of Primacy*, 36).

4

THE CHURCH AND HER MARKS OF IDENTIFICATION (*NOTAE*)

The first 29 paragraphs of the Apology's article on the church are devoted to the distinction between the church as hidden fellowship of faith and the church as public fellowship in the means of grace. Since the Apology here cites most of the main biblical images of the church, these will provide a natural approach to the Scripture-proof.

The Church as Hidden Fellowship of Faith

Ap. VII/VIII.5–8 appeals to Eph. 1:22.23 and 5:25–27, which describe the church as the *body* and the *holy bride* of Christ. The conclusions are drawn that "those in whom Christ is working nothing by His Spirit are not members of Christ" (German), and that "this church alone is called the body of Christ, which Christ renews, sanctifies, and governs by His Spirit." Even K. L. Schmidt, the author of the ἐκκλησία article in Kittel's *TDNT*, remarks, despite a strong bias against the visible/invisible distinction:

> In terms of a sociologically defined concept of society one can never grasp the nature or meaning of the assembly of God in Christ. The decisive point is fellowship with Christ. Epigrammatically, a single individual could be—and would have to be—the ἐκκλησία if he has fellowship with Christ. . . . In face of all sociological attempts to understand the question of the Church, it must be considered that in Paul, in his disciples, and then in the Fourth Evangelist ecclesiology is simply Christology and vice versa.[1]

This church-defining "fellowship with Christ," however, must include not only the objective offer of it in the means of grace, but also the subjective reception and appropriation of it in Spirit-wrought faith. "And if anyone does not have the Spirit of Christ,

1. *TDNT* III:512.

he does not belong to Christ [οὐκ ἔστιν αὐτοῦ]" (Rom. 8:9). One is and can be "in Christ" only "through faith" [διὰ τῆς πίστεως] (Gal.3:26; Eph. 3:12.17), because justification and salvation are out of [ἐκ] or through [διά] faith, Rom. 1:17; 3:22; 4:16; 9:30; Gal. 2:16; 3:8.11.14.22.24; Eph. 2:8; 3:17. There is no difference at all here between the great justification epistles (Rom. and Gal.) and Paul's "encyclical on the church" (Eph.). And if it is true also of the "Fourth Evangelist" that for him "ecclesiology is simply Christology," then faith will have the same central and constitutive significance there. That this is indeed the case is suggested already by the statistical fact that although the Gospel of John never uses the noun "faith," the verb "believe" occurs there nearly twice as often as in the entire Pauline corpus! One of the chief Johannine "parallel expressions" for the church—instances in which the word "ἐκκλησία" may not be used "and yet the thing itself is under discussion"[2]—is "the Vine" (John 15:1 ff.). Clearly the branches which "remain" in the Vine and "bear fruit" (vv.2.4.5.7.8) can refer only to *believers* in Christ. While the Savior's life-giving, external Word is the instrument through which He makes people "clean" (v.3), that object is not attained in the individual until the Word has engendered the appropriating response of faith: " 'You are clean, but not all of you.' For He knew His betrayer" (Jn. 13:10.11). The image of the Flock (Jn. 10) will be discussed later.

The church is not a corpse, but the living body of Him over Whom death can no longer exercise any rule (Rom. 6:9). Just as God is not a God of the dead but of the living (Mt. 22:32), so His church bears Him not dead but living children "by the power of the Spirit" (Gal. 4:29). To speak, as *The Roman Catechism* does, of "dead members"[3] of the living body of Christ is self-contradictory. Dead "members" are no members, just as dead "faith" is no faith (Ja. 2:17.19.20.26). It is true of course that "hypocrites and evil men" participate in the outward fellowship of the church. "But when we come to define the church, we must define that which is the living body of Christ and is the church in fact as well as in name" (Ap.VII/VIII.12). As the body and bride of Christ the church is of course also holy (Eph. 5:25–27)—first and foremost by virtue of justification, but secondly also by way of sanctification:

2. *TDNT* III:517.
3. *The Roman Catechism*, 102.

> That is why they are called a Christian people and have the Holy Spirit, who sanctifies them daily, not only through the forgiveness of sins acquired for them by Christ (as the Antinomians foolishly believe), but also through the [putting away], the purging, and mortification of sins, on the basis of which they are called a holy people.[4]

The exact meaning of the "communion of saints" in the Creed will be discussed later under the head of church fellowship. The phrase is reflected in the Augsburg Confession's definition of the church, and is expressly appealed to in the argumentation of the Apology (Ap. VII/VIII.7, 8).

Paul addresses his letters either to "the saints" [holy people, ἅγιοι] (Eph. 1:1; Phil. 1:1) or to the "church" or "churches" in those places (Gal. 1:2; I Thess. 1:1; II Thess. 1:1), or he combines both expressions directly (I Cor. 1:2; II Cor.1:1) or indirectly (Rom.1:7, cf. 16:4.16; Col. 1:2, cf. 4:16). The terms describe exactly the same reality. In I Cor. 1:2 "the ἐκκλησία is identified with 'them that are sanctified in Christ Jesus.' "[5] Further, the "saints" of I Thess. 3:13 and II Thess. 1:10 are clearly believers and only believers. It is naive to assume that since Paul was writing to clearly identifiable congregations, therefore he defined "saints" and "church" in the sense of outward membership and participation, regardless of faith. The inspired Apostle can hardly have had less theological acumen than his faithful pupil Martin Luther, who wrote in his classic book against Erasmus, *The Bondage of the Will*:

> I call them saints and regard them as such; I call them and believe them to be the Church of God; but I do so by the rule of love, not the rule of faith. For love, which always thinks well of everyone, and is not suspicious but believes and assumes the best about its neighbors, calls anyone who is baptized a saint; . . . But faith calls no one a saint unless he is declared so by a divine judgment, because it is in the nature of faith not to be deceived.[6]

There follows shortly Luther's famous epigram: "Out of sight is the church, the saints are hidden" (*abscondita est ecclesia, latent sancti*).[7]

In Ap. VII/VIII.4 there is a brief reference to the church as God's *Temple* [ναός]: "Paul also predicts that Antichrist will 'take his seat in the temple of God' (II Thess.2:4), that is, that he will rule and hold office in the church." Since the church is the "temple of the

---

4. *LW* 41:143–144; *WA* 50:624.30–33, *On the Councils and the Church* (1539). See also *LW* 41:113–115; *WA* 50:598–600.

5. *TDNT* III:507.

6. *LW* 33:88; *WA* 18:651.34–652.1–7, *The Bondage of the Will* (1525).

7. *LW* 33:88; *WA* 18:652.23, *The Bondage of the Will* (1525).

living God" (II Cor. 6:16) or the "holy temple in the Lord" (Eph.2:21), she can, properly speaking, consist only of believers, for "what harmony is there between Christ and Belial? What does a believer have in common with an unbeliever? What agreement is there between the temple of God and idols?" (II Cor. 6:15, 16. See also I Cor. 3:16–17; 6:19, and the Christological connection in Jn. 2:19–21).

Just as it is possible to be "in" the world (Jn. 17:11; I Jn. 4:17), yet not "of" it (Jn. 15:19; 17:14.16; I Jn. 4:5), so it is possible to be "in" the church, and hold office in it, without really being "of" it, i.e., when saving faith is absent. The offices of the church and their ministrations of the means of grace do not lose their validity and/or efficacy on account of an incumbent's unbelief. That is the anti-Donatist burden of AC VIII. The distinction between being "in" the church externally and being "of" it internally, is found already in I Jn. 2:19: "They went out from us, but they were not of us [ἐξ ἡμῶν]."

Other designations of the church, synonymous with "temple," are God's "building" (I Cor. 3:9; Eph. 2:21) or "house" (I Tim. 3:15; I Pet. 2:5). The Petrine text speaks expressly of a "spiritual house," made up of "living stones," which in context can refer only to believers. These Christians in turn are members [οἰκεῖοι] of God's very household and family (Eph. 2:19; Gal.6:10).

The church as the *"People* [λαός] *of God"*—the image rediscovered and made central at Vatican II—is succinctly described in Ap. VII/VIII.14: ". . . Paul distinguishes the church from the Old Testament people by the fact that the church is a spiritual people, separated from the heathen not by civil rites but by being God's true people, reborn by the Holy Spirit." A modern biblical scholar makes the same point: "That which most decisively marks the Church off from the old Israel, and which stamps it as the eschatological community, is its common possession of the Spirit."[8] This means that ecclesiology is Pneumatology as well as Christology. The mystery of the church is Trinitarian.

Behind the term "People of God" lies the whole wealth of the Old Testament experience of the nation formed and fed by God

8. J. Robinson, *The Body*, 72. While this book rightly combats a false spiritualism, it tends to the opposite extreme, and so fails to do justice to the spiritual nature of Christ's Body. The author's bias becomes clear in his blatantly political Introduction, and in this statement, which borders on the grotesque: "It is almost impossible to exaggerate the materialism and crudity of Paul's doctrine of the Church as literally now the resurrection *body* of Christ" (p. 51). A Roman Catholic ecclesiologist, A. Dulles, *The Catholicity of the Church*, 40, calls this "an exaggeration."

through prototypes of Baptism and the Eucharist (I Cor. 10:1–4). From Genesis (12:2; 17:4), Exodus (19:5.6; 24:8), and Leviticus (26:12), through the great prophets, Isaiah (6:5 ff.; 40:1; 43:1 ff.; 53:8; 66:10 ff.), Jeremiah (7:23; 29:14; 31:31 ff.), and Ezekiel (37:1 ff.), down to Micah (4–6) and Malachi (1:1 ff.; 3:1 ff.), the theme of God's People is rich and all-encompassing. All this is now concretely embodied in the New Testament People of God described in that grand sequence of appositions: "You are a chosen race [γένος], a royal priesthood, a holy nation [ἔθνος], a people [λαός] of God's very own [εἰς περιποίησιν]" (I Pet. 2:9). This is the church He has acquired [περιεποιήσατο] "with His own blood" (Acts 20:28).

As God's new people, who once were no people but now are *the* People of God (I Pet. 2:10), the church is the true "Israel of God" (Gal. 6:16). To qualify for membership in this New Israel, it is not enough to belong to the "Israel according to the flesh" (I Cor. 10:18), for "not all who are descended from Israel are Israel" (Rom. 9:6). "Understand then that those who believe are children of Abraham" (Gal. 3:7). Only by faith does anyone belong to the olive tree of the real Israel, while unbelief entails being broken off (Rom. 11:20). "A man is not a Jew if he is only one outwardly [ἐν τῷ φανερῷ], nor is circumcision merely outward and physical. No, a man is a Jew if he is one inwardly [ἐν τῷ κρυπτῷ]; and circumcision is circumcision of the heart, by the Spirit, not by the written code" (Rom. 2:28.29. Cf. Gal. 4:21:31).

For the Apology it is self-evident that the church is the *Kingdom of Christ*:

> If we were to define the church as only an outward organization embracing both the good and the wicked, then men would not understand that the kingdom of Christ is the righteousness of the heart and the gift of the Holy Spirit, but would think of it as only the outward observance of certain devotions and rituals" (VII/VIII.13).

In our day, by contrast, it has become fashionable to argue that "kingdom" and "church" are quite different entities. The confusion seems to arise from an indiscriminate lumping together of God's power, grace, and glory. We shall return to this subject in detail in connection with the distinction of the "Two Kingdoms." It is enough here to point out that if it is true that the church is the People or Israel of God, then it must be true that she is His kingdom, for He is the King of Israel (Is. 44:6; Zeph. 3:15. Compare Ex. 15:18; I Sam. 12:12; etc.). Specifically of course the church, as the New Israel, is the kingdom of "great David's greater Son" (Ps. 2:6;

24:7; 110:1 ff.; Jer. 30:9; Mic. 4:6–8; Zech. 9:9; Jn. 18:36.37). Christ was proclaimed King in the Annunciation (Lk. 1:32.33), given royal and divine honors by the Magi (Mt. 2:1–11), acclaimed as King in the *Benedictus Qui Venit* (Jn. 12:12–15), which still welcomes Him in the Sacrament of the Altar, and was condemned and crucified on this very charge (Jn 19:14–22). "The royal banners forward go . . . O Tree with royal purple dight!" From His victory and coronation (Eph. 1:20–23; 4:8–10; Phil. 2:9–11; Col. 2:15; Heb. 2:9) there issues the fullness of the Spirit of Pentecost (Jn. 7:39), whence the mighty river of salvation flows to the uttermost parts of the earth (Ps. 1:3; 46:4; Rev. 22:1.2).

It is interesting to note that in the Gospels we find the word "church" used only in Mt. 16:18 and 18:17, while the word "kingdom" [βασιλεία] occurs repeatedly in almost every chapter of the Synoptics. Yet in the Epistles "kingdom" is rare and "church" very frequent. This suggests either that Wellhausen and von Harnack were right in saying that Paul fundamentally altered the original message of Jesus,[9] or else that the post-Pentecost church really is the concrete embodiment of Christ's kingdom of grace. Only the latter possibility is of course theologically tenable. Since the church is the body of Christ, it is also the embodiment of that kingdom which has "come near" in Jesus (Mk. 1:15). Specifically, the church is a royal priesthood or a priestly kingdom (I Pet. 2:9, cf. Ex. 19:6; Rev. 1:6; 5:10), because her Head is King-Priest of the order of Melchisedek (Heb. 7, cf. Gen. 14:17–20).

The parables of the kingdom, moreover, often stress the hiddenness of that kingdom in the present age (*"cruce tectum,"* hidden under the cross, Ap. VII/VIII.18), a theme suggested by the very term "mysteries of the kingdom" (Mt. 13:11). A classic text is Lk. 17:20.21: "The Kingdom of God does not come visibly [μετὰ παρατηρήσεως, with observation]. Neither shall they say, Look here, or there. For look, the Kingdom of God is among you." Two things are clear: (1) The "ἐντός" in v. 21 must be translated "among" and not "within," since the persons addressed are the Pharisees. (2) The Kingdom is not a matter of the remote future, but is present [ἔστιν, v. 21] already now, even in the midst of anguish and oppression (Rev. 1:9). As for "visibility," even Robinson says in connection with II Cor. 4:18 that the Body of Christ "is not among the things that are seen [τὰ βλεπόμενα, i.e. the σάρξ]

9. A. von Harnack, *What is Christianity?*, 178.

and belong to this age only (πρόσκαιρα), but is αἰώνιον, belonging to the age to come (v. 18)."[10]

Paying heed to the precise wording of the Parable of the Tares, the Apology sets out its manifest intent: "He clearly says in Mt. 13:38 that 'the good seed means the sons of the kingdom, the weeds are the sons of the evil one.' *The field, he says, is the world, not the church*"(VII/VIII.19, our emphases). On the other hand, in the parables of the net (Mt. 13:47) and of the ten virgins (Mt.25:1 ff.) "Christ is talking about the outward appearance [*specie*] of the church. . . He teaches us that the church is hidden under a crowd of wicked men so that this stumbling block may not offend the faithful" (par. 19). To conclude with par. 17: "But why belabor the obvious? If the church, which is truly the kingdom of Christ, is distinguished from the kingdom of the devil, it necessarily follows that since the wicked belong to the kingdom of the devil, they are not the church."

On this bedrock of divine, evangelical truth—*sola fide*!—all millennial/chiliastic fantasies about Palestinian real estate, or about political clout and grandeur, must inevitably founder (see AC XVII.5).

"This church is properly called 'the *pillar of truth*' (I Tim. 3:15), for it retains the pure Gospel and what Paul calls the 'foundation' (I Cor. 3:12), that is, the true knowledge of Christ and faith" (Ap. VII/VIII,20). Here the church's objective foundation comes to the fore.

Although the Good Shepherd chapter (Jn. 10) is referred to in the concluding, ecclesiological paragraph of Ap. IV, the classic treatment is that of the Smalcald Articles (III.XII):

> Thank God, a seven-year old child knows what the church is, namely, holy believers and sheep who hear the voice of their Shepherd. So children pray, "I believe in one holy Christian church." Its holiness does not consist of surplices, tonsures, albs, or other ceremonies of theirs which they have invented over and above the Holy Scriptures, but it consists of the Word of God and true faith.

Since the Shepherd calls His own sheep by name (Jn. 10:3), since they know His voice (v. 4) and will flee from and not follow anyone else (v. 5), and since He knows His own and His own know Him (v. 14), it is perfectly clear again that only believers belong to His *holy flock*, the church. See also I Pet. 5:2–4.

In sum, the biblical, evangelical "*sola fide*" holds also for the

10. Robinson, *The Body*, 76.

doctrine of the church.[11] The alternative is to speak with the Council of Trent of "the faithful [!] who are 'fornicators, adulterers, effeminate, liers with mankind, thieves, covetous, drunkards, railers, extortioners' (I Cor. 6:9 ff.)."[12] But this is a burlesque on biblical language and teaching.

The Church as Public Fellowship in the Means of Grace—the Marks of the Church

The last two biblical images particularly give clear and direct expression to that saving truth of the Gospel which is the source and foundation of faith and therefore of the church. The "truth" of I Tim. 3:15 and the "voice" of the Good Shepherd in Jn. 10:4 are what the Apology calls the "marks" (*notae*) of the church: "the pure teaching of the Gospel and the sacraments" (VII/VIII.20). However, the other images of the church also mention or imply this vital element. The church as the body of Christ would be a lifeless torso were it not for the gathering, integrating, life-giving Head, acting through His saving truth (Eph. 4:4–6.15.16; cf. 1:10.22; 5:23). That the life-giving evangelical truth includes also the sacramental form of that truth comes to expression for instance in Eph. 4:4–6, and very specifically in Eph. 5:26, where "the washing of water with the word" is the means by which the divine Bridegroom purifies His Bride, the church. One should also refer again to I Jn. 5:6–8. Then, as the Temple of God, the church stands squarely on its apostolic-prophetic foundation (Eph. 2:20). The People and Kingdom of Christ correspond to the glorious Gospel of His Kingdom (Mt. 24:14, cf. 26:13) and to the New Testament in His blood (I Cor. 11:25, cf. 10:1–4; II Cor. 3–4, and all of Hebrews).

Why and in what sense are these means of grace, or better, means of salvation (*media salutis*), the "marks of the church"? The English "mark," which translates the Latin "*nota*," is not particularly evocative. The German equivalent, "*Zeichen*"[sign],[13] at once

11. K.L. Schmidt remarks quite correctly that "a true conception of the Church, the community, the assembly of God in Christ, stands or falls with a true conception of justification" (*TDNT* III:512). He seems to have forgotten this when he defines the church as a "*corpus mixtum*"(p. 534), that is, a mixed body consisting both of believers and unbelievers. As for Luther, it has been well said that he "has no 'doctrine of justification,' for which one could muster some understanding, or which one might perhaps even find 'correct,' while one at the same time regards him as less felicitous in the doctrine of church and ministry. If one wants the one, one must take the other into the bargain" (L. Grane, *Modus Loquendi Theologicus*, 190, our translation).

12. H. Denzinger, *The Sources of Catholic Dogma*, 256.

13. Ap. VII/VIII.5, 7, 12, 20, 28. In the last two paragraphs the Latin has "*signum*."

links up with the rich NT "σημεῖον" [sign]. O. Cullmann has argued that in John's Gospel particularly we are meant to see the sacraments as the true counterparts today of the miracles ("signs") of Jesus: "Clearly the sacraments mean the same for the Church as the miracles of the historical Jesus for his contemporaries."[14] Against Pentecostalism one may therefore put it like this: the "full Gospel" is not proclamation plus healings, etc., but proclamation plus sacraments. As Jesus spoke and acted in His earthly ministry, so His church now speaks and acts in His name. But the risen Savior has, in His means of salvation, given His church even "greater" (Jn. 14:12) things to do than the physical healings and other miracles which were "signs" of His saving Lordship, inviting absolute trust and confidence in Him. Since Baptism, for instance, communicates eternal life itself (Rom. 6:4; Tit. 3:5,etc.), it is "greater" than the raising of Lazarus (Jn. 11), which restored only his earthly life, and that temporarily.

Circumcision is called a "sign" in Rom. 4:11. It is quite biblical therefore to apply this term also to the greater New Testament reality of Baptism, of which circumcision was a type or shadow (Col. 2:11.12, cf. v. 17). However, the NT sacraments are not *mere* signs, but they are powerful, efficacious signs, which actually do and give what they signify: "the sacraments were instituted not only to be signs by which people might be identified as Christians, but . . . they are signs and testimonies of God's will toward us for the purpose of awakening and strengthening our faith" (AC XIII.1).

Also suggestive is the "sign" given the dumbfounded shepherds by the Christmas angels: "You will find the Baby wrapped in swaddling-clothes, lying in a manger" (Lk. 2:12). Without some such sign, how could the shepherds have been expected to find the newborn Savior? And without some analogous signs, how could people to-day be expected to locate His church, and to distinguish her from frauds and counterfeits?

Not all signs of course carry the same weight. Whether in medical diagnosis or in theological judgment, some signs and indications are more compelling than others. So Luther could on occasion list all sorts of vital signs of the church, such as prayer, the Ten

14. O. Cullmann, *Early Christian Worship*, 70.

Commandments, suffering, hope of eternal life, etc.[15] But the most basic, unfailing (Is. 55:11), and therefore infallible marks of the church are the pure Gospel and sacraments. They are marks of recognition precisely because they are first of all powerful "signs and testimonies of God's will," by which faith, hope, love, and in short all spiritual and churchly life are created and sustained. There is even a certain hierarchy among these marks themselves (I Cor.1:17):

> Truly the Gospel is the one most sure and noble mark of the church, much surer than Baptism and the Bread, because [the church] is conceived, made, nurtured, borne, trained, fed, clothed, adorned, armed, and preserved only through the Gospel. In short, the church's whole life and being consists in the Word of God [*tota vita et substantia ecclesiae est in verbo Dei*].[16]

Or:

> For the pulpit can and must alone preserve Baptism, Sacrament, doctrine, articles of faith, and all estates in their purity.[17]

It is the creative Gospel-word which is the "active ingredient" in the sacraments, so that otherwise inert elements like water, bread, and wine, themselves become "active" or instrumental in communicating to us regeneration in one case, and the life-giving body and blood of Christ in the other. Herein lies the inherent priority of the Word, which, in St. Augustine's famous phrase, "comes to the element, and it becomes a sacrament."[18]

The question now arises how these marks of the church relate to the church's attributes (oneness, holiness, catholicity, and apostolicity). The Counter-Reformation made these four attributes into the "marks of the church."[19] Oneness and catholicity in particular, understood in terms of the visible papal regime and its world-

---

15. For example in *On the Councils and the Church* (1539) Luther lists as vital signs, "the possession of the holy Word of God," (*LW* 41:148; *WA* 50:628.29–30); "the holy Sacrament of Baptism," (*LW* 41:151; *WA* 50:630.21–22); "the holy Sacrament of the Altar," (*LW* 41:152; *WA* 50:630.21–22); "the Office of the Keys exercised publicly," (*LW* 41:153; *WA* 50:631.36–37); "the fact that it consecrates or calls ministers," (*LW* 41:154; *WA* 50:632.35–36); "the holy possession of the sacred cross," (*LW* 41:164; *WA* 50:641.35–642.1). Luther concludes that "in addition to these seven principal parts there are other outward signs . . ." (*LW* 41:164; *WA* 50:643.6). Luther goes on to list all manner of good works noting that "these signs [works] cannot be regarded as reliable as [those] noted before since some heathen too practice these works and indeed at times appear holier than Christians" (*LW* 41:167; *WA* 50:643.27–29). A similar list is found elsewhere in Luther, for example see *Against Hanswurst* (1541), *LW* 41:194–198; *WA* 51:479–485.

16. *WA* 7:721.12. English version cited in Walther, *Church and Ministry*, 70.

17. *LW* 28:62; *WA* 36:485.14–15, *Commentary on I Corinthians 15* (1532–1533).

18. *"Accedit verbum ad elementum, et fit Sacramentum . . .", Sermons on the Gospel of John*, 80.3, *MPL* 35:1840; *NPNF* 1:VII:344.

19. *The Roman Catechism*, 104–109.

wide extent, were pressed as distinguishing marks of the one true church, against the claims of the Reformation. Modern Roman Catholics freely acknowledge the wrong-headedness of this approach: "There was little basis in Scripture or in the early tradition for understanding unity, holiness, catholicity, and apostolicity as visible marks of an organized society."[20] It is clear that if the pure Gospel and Sacraments of Christ really are the true marks, which authentically identify the church, then these same marks also identify and define the church's authentic unity, holiness, catholicity, and apostolicity. This matter will be taken up again under the head of unity and fellowship.

In what sense then do the marks identify the church? It is self-evident that the external marks define, constitute, and identify the church as outward fellowship in the means of grace. This outward fellowship, however, is not another or a different church from the inward fellowship of faith: it is that self-same church, in its visible "mode."[21] That unbelieving hypocrites, who do not belong to the church, are nevertheless indistinguishably mixed up with the believers in their outward gathering round the means of grace, is of course a fact. We have here a sort of "complementarity principle": We can determine exactly *who* the church is and *where* it is, but we can never combine the two into an identification of the believing individuals in any given place. When we talk about *who* the church is, we must define it as the believers, whom we cannot observe or identify as such anywhere. And when we talk about *where* the church is, we must locate it by its public marks, but we cannot tell who the individual believers are. In other words, the marks always tell us where the believers are to be found, but they can never identify particular persons as believers (except of course by the rule of love, which is often deceived). The marks attach to the church, not to individuals.

The one conclusion that must *not* be drawn is that there are two churches. It is precisely "*this* church," that is, the one church "made up of true believers and righteous men scattered throughout the world," and not some mere outward surrogate, which is recognized and grasped in "its marks" (Ap. VII/VIII.20). So long

20. A. Dulles, *Models of the Church*,120. See also A. Dulles, *The Catholicity of the Church*, 13–16; 131ff.

21. "*Propter confessionem coetus Ecclesiae est visibilis. . . Ex confessione cognoscitur Ecclesia* [On account of the confession the gathering of the church is visible. . . From the confession the church is recognized]"(*WA* 39:II:161.8.14). Also: "It will be visible to all who believe, but invisible to unbelievers"(*WA* 31:I:506.17).

as the internal and external aspects or "modes" of the church are kept together, it does not matter much whether we talk about them as "the church in the proper and the wide senses," or as "the church invisible and visible." The one church is invisible in respect of the "who," and visible in respect of the "where."

The trouble is that the "visible/invisible" terminology is used also in Calvinism, where however it means something quite different. There the outward marks define only the "visible" church, with the result that there are in effect two churches. The Westminster Confession (1647), for instance, defines as follows:

> I. The catholic or universal Church, which is invisible, consists of the whole number of the elect...
>
> II. The visible Church, which is also catholic or universal under the gospel ... consists of all those, throughout the world, that profess the true religion, and of their children...
>
> III. Unto this catholic visible Church Christ hath given the ministry, oracles, and ordinances of God...
>
> IV. This catholic Church hath been sometimes more, sometimes less visible...[22]

Calvin himself, in his *Institutes*, speaks of "the former church, invisible to us," in contrast to "the latter, which is called 'church' in respect to men."[23] Although he can speak as though there really were efficacious means of grace, and can therefore echo the Augsburg Confession's definition of the church,[24] his "invisible church" of the elect is ultimately devoid of external marks altogether. In his *Geneva Catechism* (Latin, 1545) Calvin puts it like this:

> There is indeed also a visible Church of God, which he has described to us by certain signs and marks, but here we are properly speaking of the assemblage of those whom he has adopted to salvation by his secret election. This is neither at all times visible to the eye nor discernible by signs [*nec signis dignoscitur*].[25]

The reason for this strong disjunction between a visible and an invisible church is the prior disjunction between the external Gospel and faith. If Christ redeemed not all mankind, but only a part of humanity, the elect, then there can be no such thing as objective means of grace, efficaciously offering salvation to all. In a revealing sentence, Calvin says: "Yet since we see that not all indiscriminately embrace that communion with Christ which is offered

22. P. Schaff, *Creeds of Christendom*, 3:657–658.
23. J. Calvin, *Institutes of the Christian Religion*, IV,I.7, vol. 2, 1022).
24. Ibid., IV,I.9, p. 1023. Note the comments in H. Sasse, *Here We Stand*,128–136.
25. J.Calvin, *Tracts and Treatises on the Doctrine and Worship of the Church*, tr. H. Beveridge, 51–52.

through the gospel, reason itself [!] teaches us to climb higher and to examine into the secret energy of the Spirit, by which we come to enjoy Christ and all his benefits."[26]

Not the outward sign but the inner experience of the Spirit is the ultimate ground of faith here.[27] The characteristic cleavage in Calvin—inherited from neo-Platonism through a one-sided reading of St. Augustine—between inward and outward, infinite and finite, Spirit and sign, shows up in ecclesiology as the fateful schism between an invisible and a visible church. To avoid suggesting this Calvinist dilemma of two churches it may be best when using the adjectives "visible" and "invisible," to place them after the noun, i.e. "church visible" and "church invisible." This linguistic device more readily conveys the idea that what is being described is not two churches but one and the same church in different respects.

Lutherans themselves have often paid insufficient attention to what the Apology actually teaches in VII/VIII.5. This crucial sentence does *not* say that the church is not a fellowship of outward things and rites,etc. Rather it says this: "The church is not *only* a fellowship of outward things and rites, like other polities, but it is *chiefly* a fellowship of faith and of the Holy Spirit in the hearts. . ." (our emphases). The same church is both. This is because the "outward things and rites" meant here are not, as in Calvinism, mere symbols of internal spiritual operations which may or may not accompany them. Rather, they are powerful, faith-creating means of grace, which really convey forgiveness, life, and salvation. Without them therefore there can be no "fellowship of faith and of the Holy Spirit in the hearts" at all.

The strong link between faith and the external means which engender it, entails an equally strong link between the "fellowship of outward things and rites" and the "fellowship of faith and of the Holy Spirit." To do justice to the bi-polarity or "complementarity" involved, we speak, with our Confessions, of the church in the proper sense (the believers as such) and of the same church in the wide sense (the believers gathered round the means of grace, plus the unbelieving hangers-on). In this way the doctrine of the church in its own way reflects the great incarnational and sacramental dimensions which shape the whole biblical evangel.

26. *Institutes*, III,I.1, (1:537).
27. Ibid., III,XXIV, 965–969; 973–975; 985; IV,XIV,1281–1294.

5

"ONE, HOLY, CATHOLIC, AND APOSTOLIC"

The oneness of the church means both her unicity (numerical, quantitative oneness), and her unity (qualitative oneness or harmony). There is only one church because there is only one Lord (Jn. 10:16; Eph.4:4–6; see also Rom. 5:15–19 and I Jn. 5:11.12)—and He is not polygamous (Eph.5:23.32). The all-embracing unity that reigns within this church is not a mechanical, egalitarian uniformity, but a rich harmony-in-diversity befitting the organic integration of a living body. Individual characteristics and differences are not "overcome" or abolished (Gal.3:28; see I Cor. 7:17–24 and I Pet. 2–3), but reconciled where necessary (Eph. 2:11–22; Col. 3:15), and adapted to ordered mutual service in the one body (Rom. 12:4–8; I Cor. 12–14; Eph. 4:1–16). Distinctions of grace, analogous to those of the created order, will in fact endure to eternity (I Cor. 15:41.42).

The unity of the church is given in her indissoluble union with Christ, and is therefore also an article of faith, not of sight. Confessional and sacramental unity in the pure Gospel is of course outward and visible, but only faith can see and understand such appearances as expressions and manifestations of the real unity of the church. The interplay of visibility and invisibility here reflects the same dialectic which, as we have seen, governs the church herself.

The unity of the church, furthermore, is closely related to the other three Creedal attributes, holiness, catholicity, and apostolicity. Certainly the holiness of the church is due entirely to her salvific unity with Christ, not to any imagined eruptions of excellence from within the "human material" of Adam's fallen race (Rom. 5; I Cor. 15). The unity with Christ and with others in His body, moreover, is mediated by His holy and "holy-making" instruments of salvation. Elert and others have argued that the *sanctorum communionem* we confess in the Apostles' Creed was originally meant as the "participation in the holy things," which latter in turn referred specifically to the sacramental body and blood of

Christ.[1] This in no way implies that Luther's version, "communion of saints," which had been traditional since Augustine, is "wrong." That the church is indeed the communion of saints, that is, of those who are holy by faith in Jesus, is of course absolutely true. The question is only the historical one: what in fact did the phrase *sanctorum communionem* mean originally? The sublime bond between the holy things and the holy people is expressed in the sacramental invitation of the Greek Liturgy: "The holy things for the holy people." More will be said about this *"sanctorum communionem"* in connection with church fellowship. Suffice it to note at this point that the holiness of the church—both as imputed "alien righteousness" and as "inherent righteousness" or renewal—is effectively communicated through the "holy things" of the Gospel, culminating in the New Testament Holy of Holies, the very body and blood of the Lord. These same *"sancta"* or holy things constitute the unity of the church (Eph. 4:4–6; see AC VII).

The pre-theological, purely linguistic gist of "catholicity" is simply wholeness or completeness ("καθ' ὅλης," Lk. 4:14; 23:5; Acts 9:31.42;10:37; or "καθ' ὅλην," Lk. 8:39). Applied to the church, catholicity is above all a qualitative wholeness or integrity, and only secondarily and accidentally does it refer to universality[2] or extension throughout the inhabitable world ("οἰκουμένη," hence "ecumenical"). The reason for this is that Christ is indivisible. Where He, the Head is in the midst of His "two or three" (Mt. 18:20), there His body is in its wholeness.[3] Each local church is the whole, i.e. catholic, church at that place, not a mere fragment or splinter. The connection between this wholeness and the oneness of the church becomes especially clear when we consider catholicity in time as well as in space. When Thomas Aquinas and Luther[4] both trace

1. W. Elert, *Eucharist and Church Fellowship in the First Four Centuries*, 6–14; 204–223. The customary Augustinian interpretation is argued in J. Kelly, *Early Christian Creeds*, 388–397.

2. This interpretation may be traced to the fourth century struggle, in the Western church, against the Donatists and their "geographical provincialism,"G.V. Florovsky, *"Sobornost,"* in E. Mascall, ed., *The Church of God*, 57.

3. ὅπου ἂν ᾖ Χριστὸς Ἰησοῦς ἐκεῖ ἡ καθολικὴ ἐκκλησία. Ignatius, *Epistola ad Smyrnaeos* VIII.88; Lightfoot II:2:311. "wherever Jesus Christ is, there is the catholic church." As the editors of *FCh* (I:21) note: "The expression καθολικὴ ἐκκλησία appears here for the first time in Christian literature."

4. *Against Hanswurst* (1541), *LW* 41:194; *WA* 51:477.31ff. Luther is probably referring to Augustine's *City of God* where we find the following description of the two cities: "It is recorded of Cain that he built a city, but Abel, being a sojourner, built none. For the city of the saints is above, although here below it begets citizens, in whom it sojourns until the time of its reign arrives, when it shall gather together all in the day of the Resurrection; and then shall the promised Kingdom be given to them, in which they shall reign with their Prince, the King of the Ages, time without end" (*City of God*, XV.1; *MPL* 41.437–438; *NPNF* 1:II:284).

the church back to Abel, they stand on common patristic ground.[5] In this sense catholicity is but the oneness of the church throughout time and space. The church triumphant in heaven and the church militant on earth are one festal throng or ἐκκλησία (Heb. 12:23).

In keeping with its qualitative thrust, the term "catholic" came quite naturally to designate the true or "orthodox" church, as distinct from heretical and schismatic[6] groups. Now, "orthodoxy" is usually taken to mean "right opinion." However, the Greek word "δόξα" can mean "praise, glory" as well as "view, opinion." Syriac and Slavonic do in fact translate "orthodoxy" as "right praise" (Russian: *"pravoslavie"*).[7] That the two meanings of "orthodoxy" are not as far apart as might be thought is clear from the Athanasian Creed: "And the catholic faith is this, that we worship one God in three Persons. . ." Luther's Small Catechism makes exactly the same connection in the first petition: "God's name is kept holy when the Word of God is taught in its truth and purity, and we, as the children of God, also lead holy lives according to it."

With these considerations we have arrived at the last of the four attributes of the church, that of apostolicity. Since the one holy church is "built on the foundation of the apostles and prophets" (Eph. 2:20), apostolicity is clearly a decisive criterion for what is church and therefore also for what belongs to the true unity of the church. An agreement, union, and cooperation may be ever so intimate, but if it runs counter to the church's apostolic-prophetic foundation, it is a false, deceptive, and illicit unity.

In the course of church history and still today quite different answers have been and are given to the question of just what it is that links the church in various times and places to its one and only "foundation of the apostles and prophets." All must agree of course that the genuine Gospel, including the sacraments, is crucial. Yet this evangelical content is variously embroidered and en-

5. "The second-century *Shepherd of Hermas* portrays the Church as a very old woman, created before all things; and Greek Fathers of the next few centuries, such as Origen, Athanasius, Eusebius, Gregory Nazianzen, and John Chrysostom, regularly allude to the pre-existence of the Church as being, next to Christ, the first-born of all creation. Ambrose speaks of Abel as a type of the Church, and Augustine, particularly in his controversial works against the Manichaeans, develops the theme of the Church having existed from the time of Abel" (A. Dulles, *The Catholicity of the Church*, 88–89).

6. αἵρεσις, originally had the neutral meaning of "party" or "school," but acquired pejorative connotations by NT times, *TDNT*, I:180–182. In later ecclesiastical usage "heresy" designates a deviation from Christian doctrine, which is necessarily church-divisive, whereas a "schism" is a separation over personal and other differences which should not divide the church.

7. D.J. Chitty, "The Communion of Saints," 158n.

meshed in juridical/liturgical formalities like dependence on the Roman bishop, or on General Councils, or simply on bishops properly ordained by other bishops. To a greater or lesser extent the *content* of the Gospel is in all such schemes judged by extraneous *formalities*, and is therefore inevitably distorted. The *Lima Statement* ("Baptism, Eucharist, and Ministry," 1982) may serve as an object lesson here. This ambitious attempt to stitch together an ecumenical consensus devotes as much space to the Ministry as to Baptism and the Eucharist combined, lacks any adequate definition of the Gospel, and leaves major sacramental questions open; yet it does not fail to urge "the sign of the episcopal succession" and "openness" about the ordination of women! In such nests of self-contradictions formalistic misunderstandings of apostolicity eventually avenge themselves.

There is of course a true apostolic succession, but it has little to do with external connections (Mk. 9:38–40!) to privileged places, persons, or hands.[8] Instead it has everything to do with the faithful transmission of evangelical, sacramental substance—and only with that. Already Jerome wrote: "The church consists not in walls but in the truth of her teachings. The church is where the true faith is."[9] What, we may ask, are the "traditions" (παραδόσεις) which Paul "handed on," and in which we are to become his "mimics" as he was Christ's (I Cor. 11:1.2)? We have clear and concrete answers in I Cor. 11:23 and 15:3—Paul transmits, exactly as he himself has received it, the saving evangel (15:1) of the cross and resurrection of Jesus, including His holy Supper. So long as this content remains undiminished and unfalsified (Gal. 1–2) Paul welcomes its proclamation, even if a particular proclaimer's motives are bad (Phil. 1:15–18).

Precisely this genuine apostolicity is the standpoint of the Augsburg Confession:

> For this is enough for the true unity of the Christian church, that the Gospel be preached there unanimously according to its pure understanding, and the sacraments be administered in accordance with the divine Word. And it is not necessary for the true unity of the Christian church that uniform ceremonies, instituted by men, be observed everywhere, as Paul says to the Ephesians, chapter fourth: "One body, one Spirit, as you are called to one and the same hope of your calling, one Lord, one faith, one Baptism" (VII.2–4).

8. See H. Sasse, "Apostolic Succession," in *We Confess the Church*, 84–107.
9. On Ps. 133, cited in C.F.W. Walther, *Church and Ministry*, Thesis V, p. 75.

In the nature of the case therefore the irreducible criterion of apostolicity is content, substance, truth, never mere form, appearance, or technicality. Apostolic truth is divine, Dominical truth (Lk. 10:16; Jn. 8:31–32; 16:12–15; 17:6–8). Now Christ's salvific gift of Himself to us in His Gospel and sacraments is efficacious and complete. It does not need to be supplemented with "biblical" pseudo-connexions like Jordan River water, "the Robe," "the Shroud," Pentecostal flames, sounds, quakings, and the like. The absence of such things is no loss, and their presence would be no gain; indeed, if anything, their absence is gain, for "blessed are those who have not seen and yet have believed" (Jn. 20:29). Similarly, true apostolicity exists wherever the apostolic Gospel and sacraments hold sway in their truth and purity. Antiquarian trappings, outward continuity with ancient Christian sees, supposed links to II Tim. 1:6 by way of unbroken chains of ordaining hands, and, for that matter, misguided attempts to imitate apostolic miracles (II Cor. 12:12), are in and of themselves as irrelevant to genuine apostolicity as handkerchiefs traceable to Paul (Acts 19:12), should such "relics" turn up. In their place, good ancient customs are of course valuable as symbols, badges, and reminders of continuity with apostolic truth. They must never be allowed to carry independent weight, however, which can then be exploited against the truth. Once apostolic truth has been ascertained, then no incantations to the contrary of "Church! Church!" by mitred dignitaries or democratic mobs may be allowed the slightest standing. That is Luther's true, evangelical apostolicity and catholicity or "*sobornost.*"[10]

The Reformation itself is of course the classic test-case here. At no other point in church history did there occur such a massive head-on collision between the apostolic Gospel, on the one hand, and official trappings and institutions with impressively apostolic pedigrees, on the other. Is it possible to be certain of apostolic truth even when the apparently apostolic trappings and prestige of "official channels" are arrayed against it? An affirmative answer to this deciding question is nowadays taken for granted even by responsible Roman Catholic churchmen. Consider this noble paragraph from a speech given at Vatican II:

> It is a certain historical truth that at the beginning of our divisions, those who took the initiative had no desire to act primarily and unconditionally against unity, but began by seeing that certain truths

10. See Luther's *On the Councils and the Church* (1539) and *Against Hanswurst* (1541) in *LW* 41:3–178; *WA* 50:509–653 and *LW* 41:179–256; *WA* 51:469–572.

> were fundamental in divine revelation; for instance, the apostolic rights of the Churches, in the schisms of the eleventh century, or again, in the sixteenth-century Reformation, the dogma of justification by faith in the Lord Jesus our Saviour, which had been defined at the First Council of the Apostles in Jerusalem. On the other side of the ledger, what scholar well versed in the history of those two periods would dare to doubt or deny that some Christians, perhaps many of them, and even Pastors of our Catholic Church, made light of these truths at that time (though they are certain truths) and sinned in various ways against those who bore witness to these truths?[11]

In the last analysis there is no reliable test of apostolicity except the apostolic truth itself, as it is laid down in the apostolic-prophetic Scriptures of God. Everything else is ambiguous and may be counterfeited. Scripture, too, may of course be misinterpreted, but to seek correctives and guarantees against such misinterpretation outside the sacred text itself is to take refuge in that "enthusiasm" which is "the source, strength, and power of all heresy, including that of the papacy and Mohammedanism" (SA III/VIII,9). God's church is under, not over, His Word.[12] "For the Gospel, which is the wisdom and power of God, constitutes the church and does everything."[13] Or: "Where God's Word is pure and certain, there everything else must be: God's kingdom, Christ's kingdom, the Holy Spirit, baptism, the sacrament, the office of the ministry, the office of preaching, faith, love, the cross, life and salvation, and everything the church should have. . ."[14] In other words, apostolic appearances apart from apostolic doctrine are a hollow mummery. They differ from true apostolicity as the fossil of a fish differs from a fish. But the apostolic doctrine, that is, the Gospel, is full of healing and regenerating powers for the church of all times and places, and also creates fitting external vessels for itself.

Regrettably, the Reformation's exuberant joy and confidence in the confession of the divine truth alarm modern theologians more than does Pontius Pilate's convenient sneer, "What is truth?" Insistence on dogmatic integrity is decried as an "intellectualistic" warping of the Gospel. Yet it was just the orthodox "Old Lutherans" who prized faith as something vastly more than cerebral exercises! "The Gospel," wrote C.F.W. Walther, "is not a philosoph-

11. L. Elchinger, Coadjutor Bishop of Strasbourg (France), in Y. Congar, *Council Speeches of Vatican II*, 146.

12. See H. Sasse, *Holy Church or Holy Writ?*, 24.

13. *Lectures on Romans* (1515), *WA* 56.156.26, *LW* 25:145.

14. *The Private Mass and the Consecration of Priests* (1533), *LW* 38:196; *WA* 237.11–14.

ical system, but a fruit-bearing power of God."[15] The real reason for the modern hatred of the Reformation's zeal for truth must be sought elsewhere: "The historical-critical relativism and scepticism of Erasmus have defeated [Luther] in his own church." So wrote the distinguished Reformation scholar W. Maurer.[16]

Those who would belittle the Reformation as but one tinny pipe within the many-voiced organ of the church's corporate confession, ought to ponder this pre-Reformation testimony, which speaks with clairvoyant prescience to our "pluralistic" age:

> When you shall see the wicked heresy, which is the army of Antichrist, standing in the holy places of the church, then let those who are in Judea head for the mountains, that is, those who are Christians should head for the Scriptures. For the true Judea is Christendom, and the mountains are the Scriptures of the prophets and apostles, as it is written: "Her foundations are in the holy mountains." But why should all Christians at this time head for the Scriptures? Because in this period in which heresy has taken possession of the churches there can be no proof of true Christianity nor any other refuge for Christians who want to know the truth of the faith except the divine Scriptures. Earlier we showed in many ways which is the church of Christ, and which heathenism. But now there is for those who want to know which is the true church of Christ no way to know it except only through the Scriptures. Why? Because heresy has everything just like the church. How, then, will anyone who wants to know which is the true church of Christ know it in the midst of this great confusion resulting from this similarity, except only through the Scriptures? The Lord, therefore, knowing that there would be such a great confusion of things in the last days, commands that Christians who... want to gain steadfastness in the true faith should take refuge in nothing else but the Scriptures. Otherwise, if they look to other things, they will be offended and will perish, because they will not know which is the true church, and as a result they will fall into the abomination of desolation which stands in the holy places of the church.[17]

15. Western District, LCMS, Essay, 1870.
16. E.-W. Kohls and G. Muller, eds., *Kirche und Geschichte*, I:20.
17. M.Chemnitz, *Examination of the Council of Trent*, I:156, attributes this to John Chrysostom. However, this 49th Homily, on Mat. 24, belongs to a work not written by Chrysostom, although it was attributed to him for centuries *before* the Reformation, and was quoted as his in the standard commentary, the *glossa ordinaria*. Our particular quotation, whoever may have composed it, is thoroughly in the spirit of the great Chrysostom.

EXCURSUS

"INVISIBILITY" IN PURSUIT OF PRECISION

It should not be assumed that once the Calvinist sense of the visible/invisible distinction is excluded, the remaining use of that terminology is unambiguous. The nineteenth century struggles on this very score among would-be confessional Lutherans tell another story.[1]

Some objections to the church's invisibility, to be sure, are based simply on misunderstandings. Take A. Schlatter's oft-repeated but ill-considered argument that "People are the church, and people are not invisible."[2] "People," however, are the church not simply as people, but only as believers, and as such they are precisely not visible. Brutus and the rest of Caesar's assassins were certainly visible enough as people, but their conspiracy was invisible, and as such indistinguishable from other people. Another well-entrenched fallacy is the claim, usually presented as self-evident, that the church is not a "Platonic republic" (Ap. VII/VIII.20) and therefore not invisible. In the Apology, however, the "Platonic republic" argument turns, for the Lutherans at least, on existence or non-existence, not on visibility or invisibility: "We are not dreaming about some Platonic republic, as has been slanderously alleged, but we teach that this church actually *exists*, made up of true believers and righteous men scattered throughout the world." Even Brutus' conspiracy, though invisible, did have real, concrete existence in this world—unlike Plato's republic, which remained an unrealized ideal.

In view of the language just cited from the Apology, it is astounding to read in a would-be Lutheran pronouncement: *"The Church is a visible body of believers*. It is not a scattered selection of

1. H. Fagerberg, *Bekenntnis, Kirche und Amt in der deutschen konfessionellen Theologie des 19. Jahrhunderts*, 121-131, passim.

2. H.G. Pöhlmann, *Abriss der Dogmatik*, 241.

individuals known only to God."[3] If it is held that the word "assembly" in AC VII suggests a "visible body," it must be remembered that behind the AC lie formulations like that of Luther's *Great Confession* of 1528: "Thus this Christian Church is physically dispersed among pope, Turks, Persians, Tartars, but spiritually gathered [assembled] in one gospel and faith, under one head, i.e. Jesus Christ."[4]

That this is the consistent position precisely of the mature Luther may be illustrated by quotations like these, arranged chronologically:

> 1535: Therefore we correctly confess in the Creed that we believe a holy church. For it is invisible, dwelling in the Spirit, in an "unapproachable" place (I Tim. 6:16).[5]
>
> 1541: The church is a high, deep, hidden thing which one may neither perceive nor see, but must grasp only by faith, through baptism, sacrament, and word.[6]
>
> 1545: This article, "I believe one holy Christian church," is as much an article of faith as the rest. This is why natural reason cannot recognize it, even if it puts on all its glasses. The devil can cover it over with offenses and divisions, so that you have to take offense at it. God too can conceal it behind faults and shortcomings of all kinds, so that you necessarily become a fool and pass false judgement on it. Christendom will not be known by sight, but by faith. And faith has to do with things not seen, Hebrews 11 [:1].[7]

Buchrucker's *Wort, Kirche und Abendmahl bei Luther* (1972) gives a particularly lucid, comprehensive, and well-documented account of Luther's position. A valuable feature also is the overview of the Luther-scholarship of the last hundred years, as it pertains to ecclesiology.[8] One is tempted to say that the Luther scholars have made complicated, even convoluted, what for Luther himself

3. *Lutheran Unity: Material for Study, Discussion, and Response*, 8.

4.*Confession Concerning Christ's Supper* (1528), *LW* 37:367; *WA* 26:506.38–40. Earlier Luther had written: "Thus the essence, life, and nature of Christendom is not a physical assembly, but an assembly of hearts in one faith, as Paul says in Ephesians 4 [:5], 'One baptism, one faith, one Lord.'... For if Christendom were a physical assembly, one could tell by looking at every single body whether or not it is a Christian, a Turk, or a Jew, just as I can tell by looking at someone's body whether it is a man, a woman, or a child, black or white... But I cannot tell at all whether or not he believes. Therefore, whoever does not want to err should remember clearly that Christianity is a spiritual assembly of souls in one faith, and that no one is regarded as a Christian because of his body. Thus he should know that the natural, real, true, and essential Christendom exists in the Spirit and not in any external thing, no matter what it may be called" (*Against the Papacy in Rome, Against the Most Celebrated Romanist in Leipzig* [1520] *LW* 39:65–69; *WA* 6:293–296).

5. *Galatians Commentary* (1535), *LW* 27:84.

6. *Against Hanswurst* (1541), *LW* 41:211; *WA* 51:507.31–33.

7. *Preface to the Revelation of St. John* (1546), *LW* 35:410; *WADB* 7:419.36–420.1–4; *LW* 27:84.

8. Pp.59-81.

was obvious and straightforward. Yet that would not be quite fair. The trouble is that the apparent simplicity of Luther's language can mislead badly when that language is applied in terms of the distinctions and categories of a later time. So it is possible, for example, to take Luther's statements, cited above, about the invisibility of the church, and to infer from them a false contrast between an invisible church and a visible one, without noticing that Luther says nothing of the sort. Modern readers are almost bound to read such a duality into Luther's occasional talk of "two churches."[9] But in a most trenchant remark Buchrucker singles out the Norwegian theologian C.F. Wislöff as being one of the few to have recognized "that the counterpart to the one church in Luther is the pseudo-church, hence not the visible side of the invisible church, consisting of many churches."[10] Both the true and the false churches exist in outward, palpable embodiments, to be judged by the criteria of the church's marks.

Nineteenth century German Protestant theology had its own reasons for stressing the invisibility of the church. Although Luther was of course always appealed to, the real dynamic here was a force-field shaped by rationalism, romanticism, pietism, the Prussian Union, and the theology of F. Schleiermacher. These influences made a quite un-Lutheran understanding of the church—one steeped in subjectivity and bereft of confessional and sacramental substance—seem self-evident, and even self-evidently "Lutheran." This aberration in turn gave rise to the oddity of Lutherans thinking that they had to give up Luther in order to find a less marshmallowy doctrine of the church than the one

9. In his treatise, *On the Papacy in Rome, Against the Most Celebrated Romanist in Leipzig* (1520), Luther wrote, "For the sake of better understanding and brevity, we shall call the two churches by two distinct names. The first, which is natural, basic, essential, and true, we shall call 'spiritual, internal Christendom.' The second, which is manmade and external, we shall call 'physical, external Christendom.' Not that we want to separate them from each other; rather, it is just as if I were talking about a man and called him 'spiritual' according to his soul, and 'physical' according to his body" (*LW* 39:70; *WA* 6:296.37–297.1–6). But in 1541, in his treatise, *Against Hanswurst*, Luther expressed himself on this subject more carefully and less one-sidedly after his encounter with the fanatics and sacramentarians than before. He wrote: "For there are two kinds of churches stretching from the beginning of history to the end, which St. Augustine calls Cain and Abel. The Lord Christ commands us not to embrace the false church; and he himself distinguishes between two churches, a true one and a false one, in Matthew 7:[:15] . . ." (*LW* 41:194; *WA* 51:477.30–33).

10. Buchrucker, 131,n.39.

commonly offered in his name.[11] A contributing factor no doubt was the pervasive developmentalism—it was the time of Hegel, Darwin, and Marx—which made it easy to assume that several doctrines in the Book of Concord had been left "unfinished," and so in need of completion.[12]

The 20th century has tended to favor an understanding of the church as basically visible. Among possible reasons for this one may cite the success of the Ecumenical Movement, with its stress on outward, historical institutions, and its growing orientation to social, political activism. A related factor no doubt is the abiding influence of Troeltsch's distinction between the "church-type" and the "sect-type,"[13] a distinction expressive of a sociological, externalistic notion of the church. It is safe to surmise also that the decidedly materialist, physicalist bent of the prevailing culture has played its part—and of course the *Zeitgeist*, like Radon gas, is rarely detected until the damage is done, if then.

Luther-interpreters, too, are now reluctant to talk about the church's invisibility, even though Luther himself, as we have seen, used that term. Buchrucker's on the whole splendid treatment noticeably de-emphasizes Luther's express "invisibility" language, and counters it with instances of "visibility," even though the latter are mostly derived by inference rather than directly from Luther's own usage.[14] If past mischief has become so ingrained in the terminology that "invisibility" today almost automatically suggests a contrast with a second, "visible" church—something which never entered Luther's head—then the allergic aversion to that language is understandable. Still, it would seem best to let Luther keep his plain and straightforward speech, and to add whatever comments might be needed to safeguard his meaning.

---

11. For example, A. F. O. Münchmeyer, *Das Dogma von der sichtbaren und unsichtbaren Kirche*. See the two reviews, one pro and the other con, in the Rudelbach/Güricke *Zeitschrift für die gesammte lutherische Theologie und Kirche*. Münchmeyer apparently followed Delitzsch (*Vier Bücher von der Kirche*, 1847) in defining the church as the baptised, rather than as the believers. W. Elert's somewhat strained argumentation in *Der Christliche Glaube*, 409–412, follows the same general line.

12. Even the great churchman W. Löhe took this view (Hebart 232–241, passim). For the larger context, see Fagerberg, *Bekenntnis, Kirche, und Amt*, 149–183, and M. Hein, *Lutherisches Bekenntnis und Erlanger Theologie im 19 Jahrhundert*, 122-177. Hebart's sympathetic but not uncritical treatment credits Harless and Löhe with having been the first among the newly awakened confessional Lutherans to tackle the visible/invisible distinction (121). Löhe maintained the old distinction, but without the usual fallacies. On the other hand he departed from the Reformation in wishing to make of the church an article of sight and not only one of faith (131).

13. E. Troeltsch, *The Social Teaching of the Christian Churches*.

14. Buchrucker, *Wort,Kirche und Abendmahl bei Luther*,120-142.

Buchrucker himself sums up his discussion of Luther's position by suggesting the formula: "*simul abscondita et visibilis* [at the same time hidden and visible]."[15] What this means is spelt out by Sasse, to whom Buchrucker also refers:

> The Christians in Corinth had to believe that they were God's people and that in, with, and under their visible assembly the spiritual body of Christ was present—just as they could not see, taste, or feel that the consecrated bread and the consecrated wine in the Lord's Supper were the true body and the true blood of Christ. They had to believe that.[16]

To a hiddenness so understood—and why not call it "invisibility"?—to an invisibility of the church in, with, and under the visible assembly round the Gospel and sacraments of Christ, surely there can be no valid objection in the name of Luther's Reformation. To believe and prize God's promise and institution beneath the unlikeliest of appearances (LC, Baptism 8–9)—that is the ecclesiology of the cross.

The irony is that just when Lutherans were becoming diffident about the church's invisibility, Roman Catholicism was rediscovering it. It turns out that Robert Bellarmine's famous pronunciamento about the church being as visible as the Kingdom of France and the Republic of Venice was exaggerated Counter-Reformation rhetoric. Centuries earlier Thomas Aquinas had stressed the church as interior participation in the life of grace.[17] *Lumen gentium,* the dogmatic constitution on the church, and undoubtedly the major achievement of Vatican II, broke dramatically with the past when the proposed wording that Christ's church "is the Catholic Church" was changed to say instead that this church "subsists in the Catholic Church."[18] "Thus the one Church of Christ can also be present outside the Catholic Church, and it is present, and also, indeed, visible, in so far as factors and elements which create unity and therefore the Church are effective here"(W.Becker).[19]

Lumen gentium is couched in biblical and patristic (rather than scholastic or juridical) language, the opening chapter being enti-

---

15. Ibid., p.142.

16. H. Sasse, *We Confess the Church,* 47.

17. "Thomas, influenced by the Augustinian doctrine of the mystical body, sees the Church primarily from its inward aspect. One becomes a member of the Church through union with Christ, the head of the mystical body. This union is not placed in visible ordination towards the Church, but in participation in the grace of Christ. Hence, in Thomas, the invisible aspect of the Church predominates over the visible" (A. Grillmeier in H. Vorgrimler, *Commentary,* I:172).

18. Ibid., 149-150.

19. Ibid., II:69.

tled "The Mystery of the Church." That very phrase gave rise to misgivings, as A. Grillmeier reports: "Many Fathers feared that the title might open up the way to abandoning the truth of the visible Church for the ideology of an invisible Church. The truth was that an effort was being made to arrive at a more adequate view of the complex reality of the Church than had hitherto been current." A little later Grillmeier comments, in language that might have been borrowed from Gerhard, Quenstedt, or Sasse: "Visible and invisible Church are not to be understood as two separate, distinct and completely different entities but as one complex reality composed of a divine and a human element (8:1). The whole reality of the Church can never be fully visible on earth, it can only be accepted for the moment in faith."[20]

On the face of it we have here a remarkable convergence to Reformation ecclesiology,[21] and to the extent that this represents a genuine evangelical resurgence within modern Roman Catholicism, one can only thank the Lord of the church, Who sustains His own everywhere. It was not an evangelical stream, however, but a latitudinarian undertow which controlled Vatican II, and shaped its posture of accommodation to modern secular culture. That becomes clear in the optimistic evaluation of non-Christian religions as being also vehicles of salvation.[22] Karl Rahner, probably the single most influential thinker behind the Second Vatican Council, put it like this: "The Council. . . says that even someone who regards himself as an atheist, if only he follows his conscience, is united to the paschal mystery of Christ; that every human being in a way known only to God is in touch with God's revelation and can really believe by an act that is salutary in a theological sense."[23] Actually this position is not as revolutionary as it may seem, having been foreshadowed already at Trent.[24]

Ultimately it is a question of the right distinction between Law and Gospel. Where that distinction is denied in principle or abolished in practice, the church will either be reduced legalistically to a particular visible, juridical structure, or else it will evaporate into

20. Ibid., I:138–146.

21. The brevity of the above excerpt makes the convergence seem closer than it really is. In context "visible church" for Grillmeier has reference not simply to the gathering about the Gospel and sacraments, but above all to the "society furnished with [divinely instituted] hierarchical organs," that is, the priesthood culminating in the episcopacy and the papacy.

22. *Lumen Gentium*, II:16 and the *Declaration on the Relation of the Church to Non-Christian Religions*, in *The Sixteen Documents of Vatican II with Commentaries by the Council Fathers*, 126.255–260.

23. K. Rahner, *Concern for the Church*, 100.

24. M. Chemnitz, *Examination of the Council of Trent*, I:426.

an abstract, universalistic invisibility, projecting upon mankind, in a false magnanimity, the cruel illusion of salvation through Law, natural knowledge, and sincere self-disposition.[25] By contrast the true import of the church's essential invisibility has always been the *sola fide*, the very quintessence of the evangelical confession. This means that no visible structure, least of all a "Lutheran church," may pretend to be co-extensive with the mystical body of Christ. On the other hand, since faith is totally dependent on Christ's Gospel and sacraments, these objective, visible moorings keep the church's invisibility from being dissipated into a gaseous habitat for flutter-spirits.

25. K. Rahner: "It is obvious to us that the Church and the Churches do not consist merely of what belongs to them in their character as historical, social entities. We know that their real theological essence means the Spirit and grace; and that for them the decisive things are the faith, hope and love which in them come to fruition—indeed that these realities are to be found beyond the Churches themselves, wherever a person overcomes his own nature and listens to the voice of conscience" (*Jesus, Man, and the Church*, 183).

CHURCH FELLOWSHIP

It is sufficient for the true unity of the Christian Church that the Gospel be preached unanimously according to the pure understanding of it and that the sacraments be administered in accordance with the Divine Word.

Augsburg Confession VII.2

6

THE NATURE OF CHURCH FELLOWSHIP

The nature and basis of church fellowship cannot of course be separated—each decisively shapes and determines the other. Nonetheless it will be helpful to distinguish the two aspects, mainly in order to clarify at the outset *what sort of thing* fellowship really is. This is necessary because of the unchurchly and unbiblical perspectives of modern individualism and pietism which routinely dominate and distort the subject.

To begin with, there is no such thing as a "doctrine of fellowship." There is only a doctrine of *church* fellowship, which is part and parcel of the doctrine of the church. This fact has far-reaching implications. It means, for instance, that it is beside the point to invoke a naive philologism, as though everything could be settled by studying the biblical usage of "κοινωνία" and related words, important as these are. The main linguistic contribution to the right understanding of church fellowship is the fact that the "κοινωνέω/κοινωνία/κοινωνός" word group comes from "κοινός"(common) and denotes a sharing or common participation in something (Mt. 23:30; Lk. 5:10; Rom. 15:27; I Cor. 10:16–20; II Cor. 1:7; I Tim. 5:22; I Pet. 4:13; 5:1).

Church fellowship is the fellowship of the church. It is first of all a "vertical" but then also a "horizontal" relationship among holy persons, mediated by "holy things." All the constitutive elements come together in I John 1:1–3: Our fellowship (κοινωνία) is with the Father and with the Son—also of course with the Holy Spirit, II Cor. 13:13, cf. I Jn. 5:6–8—as well as with one another, and this fellowship is brought about by the proclamation of the Word of that Life which the apostles themselves heard, saw with their eyes, and touched with their hands. And blessed are those who not having seen in that way, have yet believed (Jn. 20:29)!

Unlike all the relationships and sociabilities we know from human nature and culture, the fellowship of the church is uniquely shaped by the unity of the Divine Persons within the

Holy Trinity (*cf.* Jn. 17:21–24). It is through the Word-made-flesh, full of grace and truth (Jn. 1:14), and in Whom dwells all the fullness of Godhood bodily (Col. 2:9), that we actually become "partakers of the divine nature [θείας κοινωνοὶ φύσεως]" (II Pet. 1:4). Since God is love (I Jn. 4:8.16), the fellowship of the church arises out of the divine love and grows towards ever fuller participation in it and ever greater mutual exercise in that responding love which the divine love kindles in us (I Jn. 1:5–9; 4:7–21; Jn. 15:9.10; I Cor. 13; Eph. 3:14–4:16; II Pet. 1:3–7).

All these sublime realities of the church's life are ours by faith (*sola fide*, cf. Gal. 5:6). Yet although these mysteries "spill over" into the practicalities of daily life, and become embodied there, we have no direct, experiential access to their inner nature and splendor. Here too the principle applies that our "life is hid with Christ in God" (Col. 3:3). We must concentrate therefore on those blessed, God-given means by which the fellowship is brought about and sustained.

> Fellowship is founded in Baptism and finds its concrete expression in the Sacrament of the breaking of bread. That corresponds exactly to the usage of Paul: God has called the believers "into the fellowship of His Son, Jesus Christ our Lord." "By *one* Spirit we were all baptised into *one* body. . . and all were made to drink of *one* Spirit" (I Cor. 1:9; 12:13). The connection with the Lord's Supper becomes quite clear (I Cor. 10:16f.). The κοινωνία of the body and blood of Christ coincides with the κοινωνία of the church.[1]

When we speak of "church fellowship," therefore, in the sense of something to be granted or refused, practiced or not practiced, we mean not the whole inexpressible "width and length and depth and height" (Eph. 3:18) culminating in the Divine Society[2] of the Blessed Trinity, but only that "tip of the iceberg," as it were, that presents itself to our observation and judgment.[3]

Church fellowship then is common participation in the salvific goods or treasures of the church. St. Lawrence's well-known little joke on the Roman prefect, which brought him the martyr's crown

1. H. Sasse, *We Confess the Sacraments*, 141. This essay is also found, in a different translation, as an appendix in H. Sasse, *This Is My Body*.

2. The Latin Bible translates "κοινωνία" in the personal sense of I Jn. 1 not with "*communio*" but with "*societas*."

3. Luther: "The Latin word *communio* means 'fellowship,' and this is what scholars call the holy sacrament. . . Fellowship is of two kinds. . . . The first kind of fellowship is inward, spiritual, and invisible, for it is in the heart. It means that through faith, hope, and love a man is incorporated into the fellowship of Christ and all the saints—as signified and given in the sacrament. . .The second fellowship is outward, physical, and visible. It means that a man is allowed to participate in the holy sacrament, to receive it and to partake of it together with others" (*A Sermon on the Ban* [1520], *LW* 39:7–8; *WA* 6:63–64).

in the year 258, established the profound saying that the poor were the treasures of the church. Yet Luther saw even more deeply when in his 95 Theses he allowed only relative validity to this definition:

> 59. St. Lawrence said that the poor of the church were the treasures of the church, but he spoke according to the usage of the word in his own time.
>
> 62. The true treasure of the church is the most holy gospel of the glory and grace of God.[4]

Behind this understanding lies the fundamental distinction between Law and Gospel, love and faith, sanctification and justification. The divine, faith-creating treasures from which the church comes into being and lives must not be confused with anything less, not even with their own precious fruit of mutual love and help. The Large Catechism's debunking of the popular notion of the "relic" ("*Heiligtum*") as concentrated sacrosanctity, applies in principle to all rivals of the Gospel:

> The Word of God is the true holy thing [*Heiligtum*] above all holy things. Indeed, it is the only one we Christians acknowledge and have. Though we had all the bones of all the saints or all the holy and consecrated vestments gathered together in one heap, they could not help us in the slightest degree, for they are all dead things that can sanctify no one. But God's Word is the treasure that sanctifies all things. By it all the saints themselves have been sanctified (Third Commandment, 91).

God's Gospel-Word, which lavishes upon His church the treasures of salvation, includes of course also the holy sacraments. Because the Sacrament of the Altar is the communion (κοινωνία, I Cor. 10:16) of Christ's body and blood, the very Holy of Holies of the New Testament, it expresses *the* communion or fellowship of the church *par excellence* (v. 17. Compare the whole context of vv. 14–21 and II Cor. 6:14–18; also Heb. 13:10). The Sacrament is not a silent mummery, however, like some Masonic "landmark," which requires only outward observance, without any precise understanding and confession of what it means. It is, on the contrary, embedded in the matrix of the "apostles' doctrine" (Acts 2:42) and is itself the very essence of Gospel proclamation and confession (I Cor. 11:26). "For the ceremony of the Mass or of the Supper . . . was instituted for the sake of preaching" (Ap. XXIV.35, German). Altar fellowship then *is* church fellowship, and of course presupposes and includes baptismal and pulpit fellowship:

4. *The Ninety-Five Theses* (1517), *LW* 31:30–31; *WA* 1:236.16–17, 22–23.

> The fellowship created by Word and sacraments shows itself fundamentally in pulpit and altar fellowship. It can show itself in many other ways, some of which, like prayer and worship and love of the brethren, the church cannot do without; others of which, like the holy kiss or the handshake or the reception into one's house, vary from place to place and from time to time. In whatever way the fellowship created by Word and sacraments shows itself, all visible manifestations of fellowship must be truthful and in accordance with the supreme demands of the marks of the church. The "sacred things" (*sacra*) are the means of grace, and only by way of them is anything else a "sacred thing" (*sacrum*).[5]

This language echoes the necessary distinction between *communio/communicatio in sacris* (fellowship in sacred things) and *cooperatio in externis* (cooperation in externals). These "externals" can indeed be very spiritual, namely when they express mutual love and care in Christ (I Jn. 3:15–18). Such sharing of "externals" too is "fellowship" (κοινωνία, Acts. 2:42; Rom. 12:13; 15:26; Gal.6:6; Phil. 1:15; 4:15.16; Heb. 13:16) in the double sense of the *sharing* in whatever things are involved, and also of the deeper *sharing* of which the outward activity is an expression. But love's duty of rendering bodily help extends also beyond the circle of faith (Gal. 6:10). And there are circumstances when even "externals" can signal wrongful participation or fellowship in evil (II Jn. 10.11, cf. I Tim. 5:22).

To repeat, church fellowship is not about just anything for which the word "κοινωνία" (fellowship) could possibly be used, but is completely bound up with the public functioning of the means of grace in a relationship for which also other words, beside the κοινωνία-group, are used in the New Testament (I Cor. 10:16–21; II Cor. 6:14–16). Church-fellowship is concerned most directly not with what *follows and flows from* love, but with what *precedes and brings about* faith—and to that "everything must yield—love, an apostle, an angel from heaven, etc.!"

"O blest communion, fellowship divine," we sing in R. Vaughan Williams' stirring "For All the Saints," echoing the Collect for All Saints' Day: "O almighty God, Who hast knit together Thine elect in one communion and fellowship in the mystical body of Thy Son. . ." Fellowship is communion. But what of the *communionem sanctorum*, the "communion of saints" in the Apostles' Creed? On

5. Thesis 12 of *Fellowship in Its Necessary Context of the Doctrine of the Church*. These 13 theses comprised the "Statement of the Overseas Committee" presented to the Synodical Conference in 1961 in an effort to resolve the deadlock among the member synods on church fellowship. *Proceedings of the Recessed Forty-sixth Convention, Lutheran Synodical Conference*, 1961, 9–13. We shall be citing this important document as *Overseas Committee Statement,1961*.

the familiar interpretation customary in the Western church, the reference is masculine, *sancti*, holy people. This is also how Luther takes it in the Large Catechism. It is also possible, however, that the neuter, *sancta*, is meant, in which case the reference would be to the Lord's body and blood in the sacrament. As Elert, Sasse and others contend, this was the original meaning of that expression in the Creed.[6] Dogmatically there is no contradiction here but only complementarity. Nor does the doctrine of church fellowship depend on this one way or the other. The question is purely the historical one: what *originally* did *communio sanctorum* mean? If "holy things" are confessed in the Creed, it would mean that in addition to the New Testament Temple consisting of the "holy persons" in Christ (Eph. 2:21), we would have also a specific reference to its "holy of holies" (τὰ ἅγια, Heb. 9:12). We could then view the mystical body of Christ stereoscopically, as it were, together with its ontological foundation in the body once and for all sacrificed on the Cross and now distributed till the end of time in the Sacrament of the Altar (cf. Heb. 13:10). The κοινωνία of the mystical body of Christ finds its supreme objective expression in the κοινωνία of His sacramental body (I Cor. 10:16.17).

The objective understanding of church fellowship as pulpit and altar fellowship stands in sharp contrast to the subjectivism that followed in the wake of Schleiermacher.[7] For the latter fellowship arises from below, by the banding together of like-minded religious individuals. This fellowship as religious sociability or camaraderie creates the church. Everything is topsy-turvy here. The individual comes first, the church second. Fellowship as human inter-personal relations defines the nature of the church rather than being derived from the prior nature of the church and understood therefore as common participation in the church's goods. The results of such thinking, incubated for over a century in sentimentality and secularization, are today everywhere in evidence as a full-blown pathology: the church and her fellowship are expected to abdicate their own supernatural priorities, and to make themselves useful instead as emotional "support-groups" compet-

6. In *Eucharist and Church Fellowship*, Elert shows that even in the West the meaning of "holy things" in the Third Article is well attested, e.g. an early twelfth century French version, which has "*la communiun des seintes choses*" (p. 10). Also: "Abelard correctly refers the *sancta* to the Eucharist, and the ancient Irish text scarcely permits any other interpretation. . ." (p.11). For the traditional Augustinian interpretation see Kelly, *Early Christian Creeds*, 388–397.

7. We rely here on Elert's trenchant characterization of the contrast between Schleiermacher and Luther. *Eucharist and Church Fellowship*, 1–8.

itively servicing the "felt needs" of autonomous individuals/consumers, who in turn pursue their own inalienable right to self-determined "self-fulfillment". In such circumstances, and under the lash of pragmatism, it becomes in principle impossible to distinguish any longer between services and circuses, edification and exploitation, faithfulness and fraudulence, love and lunacy.

The terminal stages of this church-dissolving individualism do not of course appear overnight and without warning. Herein may well lie, for North American Lutherans, the true significance of the ignominious dissolution of the Synodical Conference. That body had been founded in 1872, precisely as a vehicle for orthodox church fellowship, and having for its high aim "the consolidation of all Lutheran synods of America into a single, faithful, devout American Lutheran Church."[8] Not quite a century later the Synodical Conference broke up—over the same issue on which it had been founded, that of church fellowship. *Post mortem* findings must focus on the clear-sighted diagnosis supplied by the Overseas Committee on Fellowship, which comprised some of the leading spirits in communion with the Synodical Conference abroad: "Since the premature turning off into the byway of fellowship has led to a dead end, it would seem best, first of all, to return to the [traditional highway of the doctrine of the church] and there move forward together guided only by the marks of the church."[9]

By the premature "byway of fellowship" was meant the tendency to think of fellowship in terms of isolated individuals or "Christians," rather than in those of the church and of churches. But church fellowship is by definition something to do with churches. It cannot "compute" footloose individuals except by derivation from and connection to churches. The normative marks, after all, attach to and identify not individuals but the church. Focusing simply on individuals derails the whole discussion into the trackless wastelands of subjectivism. That, oddly enough, was the trouble with both the "Missouri" and the "Wisconsin" documents on fellowship at that time, even though on the face of it the two approaches seemed diametrically opposed.[10] Both synods were being recalled by their confessional brothers overseas not to some new-fangled academic construct, but back to

8. R. C. Wolf, *Documents of Lutheran Unity in America*, 196.

9. *Overseas Committee Statement, 1961.*

10. The Wisconsin Synod defined its "unit concept" thus: "Church fellowship is every joint expression, manifestation and demonstration of the common faith in which Christians on the basis of their confession find themselves to be united with one another." The weak-

their own great common roots and heritage, as embodied in men like Walther, Hoenecke, and Pieper, who were held, if anything, in even higher esteem overseas than in America.

The presentation of the Missouri Synod's Theological Commission, "Theology of Fellowship," was criticized severely. See *European Supporting Documents*, pp. 17–29. The Europeans also endorsed the stringent criticisms of both the Wisconsin and the Missouri documents transmitted officially by representatives of the Australian sister church (ELCA). The essential flaw of the Missouri document was put thus by the Australians: "The tendency throughout—and it is intentional—is not to speak of churches, but to speak of individuals. For with them, in accordance with the subjective πρῶτον ψεῦδος at the basis of the whole presentation, we can. . .distinguish those who are plainly not of Christ. . . and those who are true Christians. . ." The application of the biblical texts forbidding false fellowship is rendered problematical in this way, if not virtually impossible—except in the cases of manifest heresiarchs, most of them safely dead. Regarding joint prayer in this context one can hardly improve on the judiciously framed final thesis of the Overseas Committee of 1961:

> Prayer is not one of the marks of the church and should not be co-ordinated with Word and sacraments, as though it were essentially of the same nature as they. As a response to the divine Word, it is an expression of faith and a fruit of faith, and when spoken before others, a profession of faith. As a profession of faith it must be in harmony with and under the control of the marks of the church.

Unlike preaching and the sacraments, prayer is not necessarily an official act of the church as such, but is something which individuals may do in private. Such private acts and situations are governed fundamentally by familial and other social relations and obligations, and do not necessarily commit and compromise the church. On the other hand, such considerations are overridden

---

ness here, despite the best intentions, was twofold: (1) The starting point was the faith of individuals and their *de facto* agreement, rather than the church's objective marks. This introduced a certain subjectivism into the premises. (2) The definition, "*every* joint expression,etc.," was too sweeping. It overlooked, among other things, the distinction between the two kingdoms. Taken literally, therefore, it would forbid joint political action against abortion, for instance, by Roman Catholic, Baptist, and Lutheran citizens, since, if they were all motivated by the love of Christ, their action would be a "joint expression" of faith, and so would constitute church fellowship. For detailed analysis and critique see *European Supporting Documents*, Part III, pp. 3–13, in the files of Concordia Historical Institute, St. Louis, Mo., and the public letter of 15 July 1961 from Doctors W. M. Oesch and M. Roentsch to President O. J. Naumann of the Wisconsin Synod (31 pp.).

when and to the extent that churches act officially, normally through and with their public ministers.[11]

Between the lines drawn by these "pure types" lies a not inconsiderable "mixed" or grey area, in which judgments will differ, and in which—other things being equal—such differences of judgment must be borne in mutual charity. The existence of such a zone of ambiguity—under the church's overarching missionary imperative, with its summons to faithful confession in resourceful mobility—is suggested by apostolic precedent and example (Acts 2:46–3:1; 21:24–26; 24:11.12).[12] Joint prayers, also by church leaders, for divine blessing and guidance, in the immediate context of genuine efforts to overcome doctrinal divisions under the Word of God, clearly fall within the evangelical constraints so well defined by the Lutheran Church of Australia in its *Theses of Agreement*:

> When joint prayer shows the marks or characteristics of unionism, it must be condemned and avoided. Such marks and characteristics of unionism are:
>
> a) failure to confess the whole truth of the divine Word (*in statu confessionis*);
>
> b) failure to reject and denounce every opposing error;
>
> c) assigning to error equal right with truth;
>
> d) creating the impression of unity in faith or of church fellowship where it does not exist (II,2).

Given the current climate of rampant subjectivism and sentimentalism, it has been necessary in this discussion to stress above all the objective nature of church fellowship as joint, public participation in those supernatural riches which create and shape the church. Our main foil was and is the popular misconception—for which the name of Schleiermacher may serve as a convenient identification code—that church fellowship is religious togetherness or chumminess or friendly "sharing" among individuals. Once this shapeless and secularizing caricature has been put aside, however, it is also necessary to guard against a false objectivism—as though we were in the means of grace or the marks of the

11. *European Supporting Documents*: "Wisconsin and the Norwegians are right in urging that we cannot pray together with those who *represent* divisions and offenses contrary to the doctrine which we have learned (Rom. 16:17 and all parallels). . . . The Lutheran Symbols, all Lutheran doctrine and practice in orthodox times including the Synodical Conference synods in past decades, as well as the ancient church have insisted that unity and continuity of pure doctrine demands that we do not pray together with gainsayers" (p. 13). See also *infra*, Ch. 8, n.21.

12. "Paul feels free, according to Acts 21:24 ff., to let himself be purified, together with certain Jewish Christians of Jerusalem, in the temple, which surely did not happen without the prayers of such priests as did not personally confess Christ" (Oesch/Roentsch letter, p. 27).

church dealing with impersonal, vaguely occult entities. That would be magic, and is the opposite of everything the church confesses. No, the living God Himself confronts and deals with us in His holy Word and sacraments. He does not send "sheriffs and bailiffs" (Luther), but comes to us Himself, together, to be sure, with "angels and archangels and with all the company of heaven." No Buddhist absorption or transcendence of personality here! By the holy mysteries of His saving Gospel the Trinity of Persons in the unity of substance draws us into a personal communion so intimate and sublime as to surpass all human understanding. The church is "the brotherhood" (I Pet. 2:17); and by virtue of the Incarnation she is the Brotherhood of God and man (Mt. 12:46–50; Jn. 20:17; Heb. 2:11–17).

7

THE BASIS AND CRITERIA FOR CHURCH FELLOWSHIP

Once the *nature* of church fellowship has been clarified, it is relatively easy to set out the *basis* or *criteria* for God-pleasing pulpit and altar fellowship. This matter was unavoidably broached already in our treatment of joint prayer in relation to church fellowship. In brief, the criteria for fellowship are precisely those that define "the true unity of the church."[1] According to the Augsburg Confession, this means unanimity in the pure proclamation of the Gospel and in the right administration of the sacraments. And as we have seen in our consideration of the church's unity, apostolicity is the decisive criterion here. The Gospel is "purely" taught and the sacraments are "rightly" administered if and only if they conform to the apostolic norm. Whatever is not apostolic is apostatic. Proclamations contrary to the apostolic norm are for that reason and to that extent pseudo-gospels (Gal. 1:1–12), to be shunned and excluded (Rom. 16:17; Tit. 3:10). In short, they are church-divisive.

Simple and axiomatic though the above may be and indeed is, a number of rather basic issues arise here which require some discussion. They may perhaps be treated most economically in connection with questions to do with the real import of AC VII.

Gospel, Doctrine, Articles.

It is sometimes suggested that "doctrine of the Gospel" in the Augsburg Confession is not the same thing as "the doctrine and all its articles" in the Formula of Concord (Ep.X.7;SD X.31). Instead, the AC supposedly sees "the gospel as one article among

1. "The outward unity of the Church as 'the fellowship of outward ties and rites' must rest upon the same basis on which the spiritual unity of true believers rests and depends, viz., upon the marks of the One Church: the pure teaching of the Gospel and the right administration of the Sacraments. Where there is truth, there is unity" (Lutheran Church of Australia, *Theses of Agreement*, V,21).

those making up 'the doctrine and all its articles.' "[2] This is quite impossible. No sixteenth century Lutheran could have thought of the Gospel as one among many other articles! Such a trivialization rests entirely on modern misconceptions. One begins by assuming that the Gospel is simply the article of justification, and ends up rather quickly and painlessly with a few harmless slogans thought to document "agreement in the Gospel" and so to provide a "sufficient" excuse for any desired church-fellowship.

The Reformation knows no such "mini-gospel." AC VII is based largely on the 12th of the *Schwabach Articles* (1529), which has this language: "This church is nothing else than believers in Christ, who hold, believe and teach the above-mentioned articles and parts, and for this suffer persecution and martyrdom in the world; for where the Gospel is preached and the Sacraments used aright, is the holy Christian church. . ."[3] The Augsburg Confession says nothing different. To preach the Gospel purely is to preach it correctly in all its constituent articles, in harmony, in other words, with *all* the doctrinal articles of the Confession—otherwise what would have been the point of confessing them all? Justification is *the* "chief article" (Ap.IV.2), but not the only article, not even the only "chief article"[4] of the Gospel. This means that the article of justification integrates all the articles of faith into one organic whole, so that to deny any one of them is to distort justification itself:

> The article of justification cannot be rightly taught where the great articles of the Apostles' and the Nicene Creed are not kept. The denial of the Virgin Birth leads to a false doctrine of the incarnation. A false doctrine of the incarnation leads to a false understanding of justification and of the sacraments. Thus the article of the standing and falling of the church keeps together all articles of the Christian faith and illuminates them. For Lutherans the consensus required should always be regarded as the doctrinal content of the Book of Concord.[5]

The contrast in AC VII, it must be remembered, is not between the Gospel and other articles of doctrine, but between the Gospel, all of it, and "human traditions or rites and ceremonies instituted by men."

2. H. George Anderson, "Gospel and Doctrine," in *The Function of Doctrine and Theology in Light of the Unity of the Church* [hereinafter: *FODT*], 62. Anderson adds: "This usage would also suit the terminology of the Confession, where justification—the fullest definition of 'gospel'—is one of 28 articles."

3. M.Reu, *The Augsburg Confession: A Collection of Sources*, 43.

4. For *"Hauptartikeln"* (chief articles) or *"fürnehmbsten Artikeln"* (*"de praecipuis articulis"*) in the plural, see AC, Conclusion of 1st Part, and FC SD, Intro. 3, *BKS*, 83d and 830.

5. H. Sasse, "Theses on the Seventh Article of the Augsburg Confession," 16. See also H. Sasse, *Here We Stand*, 110–152.

A little attention to the terms will go a long way here. It is a well-known fact that the NT words διδασκαλία and διδαχή—both of which can, like the Latin *doctrina*, denote both the activity and the content of teaching—appear in the plural only when referring to the false doctrines of men or of demons (Mt.15:9; Mk. 7:7; Col. 2:22; I Tim. 4:1; Heb. 13:9). Falsehoods are many—the truth is but one. It is best therefore to speak of the various aspects of the one evangelic truth or doctrine not as "doctrines" but as "articles" or "parts." The Latin "*articulus*" means a joint or small member, such as the joint of a finger.[6] An article is by definition something which, incomplete in itself, is part and parcel of a larger organic whole. "Articles of faith and doctrine" (heading of AC I–XXI) therefore does justice both to the multiplicity of aspects and to the oneness of the whole.

Most instructive is the usage of the Large Catechism. The Gospel as distinct from the Law there is not the Second Article of the Creed, against all the rest, but the whole Creed [German: *Glaube*=faith], which "is a very different teaching from the Ten Commandments" (II.67). This (Apostles') Creed used to be divided into twelve articles, but resolves itself much more naturally into the three articles corresponding to the Creed's Trinitarian structure. Yet these three could "be treated more fully and divided into as many parts as there are words" (II.12). So the Second Article, for instance, consists in turn of several "parts" or sub-articles, i.e., "such articles as the birth, passion, resurrection, and ascension of Christ," which are preached about in detail at their own special times in the church year (II.31–32). This Second Article is "very rich and far-reaching" (II.26); indeed, "the entire Gospel that we preach depends on the proper understanding of this article. Upon it all our salvation and blessedness are based, and it is so rich and broad that we can never learn it fully" (II.33).

The Gospel, then, is neither a bloodless abstraction (see Mt. 26:13!) nor a content-free "kerygmatic" gushing. The whole idea of an undogmatic Gospel or of a rift between "κήρυγμα" and "δόγμα" is a modern myth. In keeping with its incarnational/paschal core, the Gospel is a substantive and sacramental communication of revealed divine truth or doctrine. This truth is in principle the same whether confessed in the embryonic form of the simplest NT Creed, "Jesus is Lord" (Rom. 10:9; I Cor. 12:3; Phil. 2:11), or in the ancient and Reformation symbols which spell out

6. Therefore Melanchthon can, following Plato, compare botched distinctions to the failure of clumsy cooks to sever bones properly, at the joints. Ap. XXIV.16.

the Trinitarian and soteriological import of the Lordship of Jesus. The whole Book of Concord is nothing but the unfolding, in response to changing circumstances, of the dogmatic content already "nested" in the formula, "Jesus is Lord." For the Reformation, as in the Scriptures, the Gospel is not a safe, placid commonplace commanding the assent of all reasonable people. It is rather the saving wisdom of God in its human servant form (I Cor. 1:18–2:16), and for that very reason presents itself to us as a many-faceted, sharp-edged, irreducible dogmatic content, against which men and devils rage, and which therefore is and remains embattled and controversial (Lk. 2:34!) in the present age.

"Gospel" in Wide and Narrow Senses

The strict and wide senses of "Gospel"—this explicit distinction occurs not in the AC but in FC V—differ only in the exclusion or inclusion of the Law respectively. Since the church and her unity are created and preserved entirely by the Gospel, and not by the Law, the Gospel in AC VII is the Gospel in its proper or narrow sense. The Law, after all, is not unique to or distinctive of the church, since it is found, in some form, also in the synagogue, in the mosque, and even in natural man (Rom. 2:14.15). It is the Gospel that is the church's distinctive mark and "secret," and from her even the "principalities and powers" must learn it (Eph. 3:10). "These articles of the Creed, therefore, divide and distinguish us Christians from all other people on earth" (LC II.66).

"These articles of the Creed" include, as we have seen, all their constitutive parts or sub-articles. This language further highlights the precise identity of the AC's unanimity in the purely taught Gospel with the Formula's agreement "in the doctrine and in all its articles" (SD X.31)[7]—all the more so as both expressions in their respective settings are paired with the right administration of the sacraments. Nor is this stress on the many-articled Gospel as distinct from the Law a theological novelty. It was clearly articulated,

7. D. G. Truemper argues that when the AC "speaks of 'articles' it is not. . . speaking of doctrinal formulations, but of the parts of the confession" (*Cresset*, Feb. 1980, 29). On the face of it we have here a distinction without a difference, for what could the various "parts of the confession" possibly be other than "doctrinal formulations"? The context shows, however, that "doctrinal formulations" here is code for "doctrinal content." The claim then is that by "articles" the AC means not the various aspects of the evangelic truth, but the literary units or sub-divisions of the AC itself! The demonstrable fact is that any such self-reference in the AC is strictly secondary and derivative. What is primary and decisive is the standard pre-Reformation notion of *"articuli fidei"* (articles of faith) as the component parts of the one Christian faith or creed. When the Schwabach Articles, one of the AC's main sources, define the church as "the believers in Christ, who hold, believe, and teach the above-mentioned

for instance, by F. Pieper, in 1888: "The expression 'articles of faith' designates a quite definite concept: the doctrines of the Gospel in contrast to the Law."[8]

Yet a moment's consideration will show that though utterly *distinct*, Law and Gospel can never be *separate* in practice: "Although the Law therefore does not belong within faith and therefore also not within the definition of faith, acceptance of the Law is nevertheless a necessary presupposition of unity in faith."[9] God's "alien work" of smashing all smugness and self-righteousness by His Law is done not for its own sake, but for the sake of God's "proper," life-giving work through the Gospel (Ap. XII.51–58). The

---

articles and parts," surely no one imagines that the "articles and parts" are the Schwabach document's own paragraphs, rather than the controverted components of the Christian faith. Or consider the very first of Luther's *Propositions Against the Whole Synagogue of Satan* . . . , which arrived in Augsburg a week after the Confession had been presented: "The church of God has no power to make up a single article of faith, just as she has never made up any, nor will ever make up any" (*WA* 30:II:420.6–7). In the AC itself, dissenting "about [*de*] no article of faith from the catholic church" (Intro. to XXII-XXVIII) cannot refer to a portion of the AC's own text. Elsewhere Truemper undertakes to explain FC SD X.31, agreement "in the doctrine and in all its articles," as not meaning "full agreement in all the larger and smaller parts of Christian doctrine" ("The Catholicity of the Augsburg Confession: CA VII and FC X on the Grounds for the Unity of the Church," 12). He rightly observes that "the term 'doctrine' in article X of the Formula of Concord is primarily and essentially an equivalent term for the 'gospel,' " but wrongly opposes the singularities "gospel" and "doctrine" to agreement "in a whole range of doctrinal formulations" (p. 14). Having failed to account for the FC's plural, "all its articles," Truemper simply drops the subject, but not the false claim. There is a clear-sighted purpose behind all these apparent muddles: if the straightforward reading of the FC prevails, "then Missouri's insistence upon full, or at least very substantial, doctrinal agreement as a precondition for church fellowship would be shown to have the support of the Book of Concord" (*Cresset*, p. 29). Or: "If the Formula of Concord is understood as a kind of commentary on the Augsburg Confession (which in some sense it must be), and if 'the doctrine and all its articles' i[s] the authoritative interpretation of the 'it is sufficient' of AC VII (which is at issue here), then the inevitable consequence is current LCMS fellowship policy" (D. Truemper, "How Much Is Enough?"). One can only concur in this candid judgment.

8. "Thus the Lutheran Church has understood the divinely willed unity in the faith. She defines the 'true unity of the Christian church' so in the 7th article of the Augsburg Confession: 'that the Gospel be preached unanimously according to its pure understanding and the holy sacraments are administered according to the Gospel'. . . Here [FC Ep. X.7] our church declares that by true unity she understands agreement 'in the doctrine and in *all* its articles,' not merely in some of them. . .Also in the [above] thesis only the Gospel is meant. When we speak of 'articles of the Christian doctrine,' this is to be understood as the revelation and preaching of Christ. . . . The Law does not come into consideration here. The foundation on which the Christian church is built is Christ, the Gospel. . .The Law does not create the church, neither does the Law unify the church. Only the Gospel does that. Therefore the Law does not belong into a definition of Christian unity or unity in the faith. . . . When it is said: we believe the Law, the word 'believe' is taken in a totally different sense than when one speaks of the Christian faith. The expression 'articles of faith' designates a quite definite concept: the doctrines of the Gospel in contrast to the Law" ("Of Unity in the Faith," 6–13. Our translation).

9. Ibid., 13.

Law prepares the way for the Gospel, and the Gospel presupposes that the Law has done, and is doing, its work. In *practice*, therefore, it comes to the same thing whether the Gospel in AC VII is taken in its narrow or wide sense. Taken in the narrow sense, the rightly preached Gospel presupposes the rightly preached Law. If the latter is distorted, so, correspondingly, is the former. And taken in the wide sense the Gospel cannot be purely preached except in the "especially brilliant light" (FC SD V.1) of the Law/Gospel distinction, by which the whole Scripture (*universa scriptura*) "is to be divided into these two chief topics: into the law and the promises" (Ap. IV.5).

Is *Doctrina* the Activity of Teaching or the Content?

Even that archetypal scholastic, Thomas Aquinas, could use *"doctrina"* (teaching) as equivalent to *"praedicatio"* (preaching), and generally meant by it "both the act of teaching and the knowledge communicated in teaching."[10] Since the German of AC VII.2 speaks of the activity of preaching, and since the "teaching [*doctrina*] of the Gospel" is syntactically coordinated with the "administration of the sacraments," it is clear that the *"doctrina"* in AC VII is the activity of teaching. The complete phrase, however, is *"doctrina evangelii,"* with the evangelium or Gospel supplying the dogmatic content. Hence the argument about the word *"doctrina"* by itself is really a red herring. The Latin ("to agree [*consentire*] about the teaching of the Gospel and the administration of the sacraments") means nothing other than the parallel German text ("the Gospel be preached unanimously according to its pure understanding and the sacraments be administered in accord with the divine Word"). There is no escaping the thoroughly dogmatic nature of the *"doctrina evangelii,"* since "the Gospel is never *mere* proclamation devoid of doctrinal content but is always doctrine."[11] Furthermore, R. C. Schultz has, following W. Elert,[12] drawn attention to the *"doctrina evangelica"* of the Edict of Theodosius I, which had been basic Imperial law since the fourth century, and which

10. Per Erik Persson, *Sacra Doctrina: Reason and Revelation in Aquinas*, 43–44.

11. R. Preus, citing the standard commentators, Fagerberg and Schlink, in "The Basis for Concord," 21.

12. W. Elert, *The Structure of Lutheranism*, 274.

Melanchthon probably meant to echo in AC VII.[13] Schultz's conclusion is that "the meaning of the doctrine of the gospel (*evangelic doctrine*) becomes more obviously defined in terms of the entire doctrinal section of the Augsburg Confession itself." Still, attempts to turn AC VII into an attractive ecumenical slogan by jettisoning unwelcome dogmatic ballast, continue unabated. A case in point is the subtly argued but extremely radical scheme of Gerhard Ebeling, which, with adaptations by Wenzel Lohff, decisively shaped the Leuenberg Concord.[14] Ebeling's "Word-theology" re-interprets "Word" (or "Word-event"), "Gospel," and "faith" along existentialist, "hermeneutical" lines, so that whatever else they may now mean, dogma or doctrine in the old sense they are not. Unlike American retailers of such ideas,[15] however, Ebeling does not purport to be reproducing the historic position of the Reformation. He freely admits that for Luther and the Reformation the "Word" meant doctrine, even "pure doctrine," recognizable as such.[16] This, however, according to Ebeling, "rests on a presupposition which we cannot possibly make our own any more." Rather, we must distinguish much more radically than did the Reformers between the Word, the Bible, and doctrine! Ebeling concludes this essay on the significance of doctrinal differences with a revealing pronouncement from Bonhoeffer: "The antitheses between Lutheran and Reformed. . . are no longer genuine."

The "True Unity of the Church" is Not a Domain of Pure Inwardness

AC VII, about the church and her true unity, was held by the official theology of the Prussian Union Church to apply to the "invisible" church.[17] Ebeling, in his own way, follows suit.[18] "But," as Sasse points out, "the *teaching purely* and *rightly administering the*

13. *FODT*, 55. An expanded version appeared as "An Analysis of the Augsburg Confession Article VII,2 in its Historical Context, May & June, 1530." *Sixteenth Century Journal*, XI, 3 (1980), 25-35. The essay is illuminating despite the "even deeper conclusions than [Elert] or Maurer would have been likely to draw" (p. 28), which serve the cause of reunion with Rome.

14. See T. Mannermaa, *Von Preussen Nach Leuenberg*, esp. 41–102.

15. Note, for instance, D. Truemper's astonishing assertion that both AC VII and FC X demand for true unity only "the actual preaching of the gospel and the actual administration and reception of the sacraments—and not a doctrine or doctrines about the gospel and about the sacraments" ("The Catholicity of the Augsburg Confession," 12.) If only Zwingli had thought of this at Marburg, how many centuries of heartache might not the church have spared herself!

16. G. Ebeling, *Word and Faith*, 174–177.

17. H. Sasse, *Was Heisst Lutherisch?*, 15, n. 2.

18. Ebeling, op. cit., 166, 181–186.

sacraments takes place in the 'visible' church."[19] The invisible bonds of faith which unite the church to Christ, and so also within herself, cannot of course be traced by us. The pressing problem at Augsburg, however, was that true unity of the church which could be outwardly grasped and registered, and concerning which the adherents of the papal party were making false claims and impossible demands. That is the focus of AC VII, and therefore orthodox Lutheran theologians have always correctly understood and applied this article as directly setting out the criteria for external church fellowship.[20]

It is a spiritualizing misunderstanding to cite against the above Ap. VII/VIII.31: "We speak of the true, that is, spiritual unity, without which it is not possible for faith to exist in the heart or the righteousness of the heart before God." The German expressly defines this "spiritual unity" as "believing in one Christ, having one Gospel, one Spirit, one faith, the same sacraments." Unlike saving faith itself, its objective basis in the one Gospel, faith (=creed), and sacraments comprises publicly manifest entities. And if these entities are truly the glorious power of God for salvation and the ministration of Spirit and life (Rom. 1:16; II Cor. 2: 12–3:18), then one cannot belittle common participation in such means of salvation as merely "outward" and therefore not really "spiritual." The internal and external aspects of the church's unity or fellowship may be split into two unities no more than the church invisible and visible may be torn asunder into two churches. Calov, therefore, in his great commentary on the Augsburg Confession, taking for granted that true unity includes outward communion, rightly observes that "for the spiritual unity of the church interior gifts are required no less than external fellowship."[21]

Orthodoxy: the Paramountcy of Truth

Outward unity is created and normed by the truth, not truth by unity. Any "paramountcy of unity" which makes truth secondary,

19. Sasse, op. cit. See also H. Sasse, "Theses on the Seventh Article of the Augsburg Confession,", 14 ff., and K. Marquart, "Augsburg Confession VII Revisited,", 17–25.

20. This includes of course the great Missouri Synod standard-bearers, C.F.W. Walther (*True Visible Church*, Theses 8, 12, 18 D, 24, and other works) and F. Pieper (*Das Grundbekenntnis der evangelisch-lutherischen Kirche*, 98–99). By contrast, see A. C. Piepkorn, "What the Symbols have to say about the Church," 750, 751, 759, for a confused and unwarranted dichotomy of "*unitas*" (AC VII) and "*concordia*" (FC X), when the German has "*Einigkeit*" for both.

21. A. Calov, *Exegema Augustanae Confessionis.*

is pseudo-ecclesial. For the true unity of the church the pure Gospel and sacraments are "sufficient"—but also necessary—whereas uniformity in man-made ceremonies is neither necessary nor sufficient. This absolute primacy of the evangelical truth has been put nowhere more starkly than in Luther's extended commentary on Galatians:

> We are surely prepared to observe peace and love with all men, provided that they leave the doctrine of faith perfect and sound for us. If we cannot obtain this, it is useless for them to demand love from us. A curse on a love that is observed at the expense of the doctrine of faith, to which everything must yield—love, an apostle, an angel from heaven, etc.!. . .We can be saved without love and concord with the Sacramentarians, but not without pure doctrine and faith. . . Doctrine is heaven; life is earth. . . Therefore there is no comparison at all between doctrine and life. "One dot" of doctrine is worth more than "heaven and earth" (Matt.5:18); therefore we do not permit the slightest offense against it. But we can be lenient toward errors of life. For we, too, err daily in our life and conduct; so do all the saints, as they earnestly confess in the Lord's Prayer and the Creed. But by the grace of God our doctrine is pure; we have all the articles of faith solidly established in Sacred Scripture.[22]

This is not of course an ontological argument about the relative importance of divine truth and love—such speculation could be nothing but presumptuous absurdity. The point rather is a very practical one: given our situation and the divine arrangements for our salvation, truth lies closer to the surface, as it were, and is therefore more easily identified than love. Divine love has chosen to make itself known to us through the divine truth of the Gospel. We have therefore a reliable instrument by which to gauge truth-claims. We have no comparable controls by which to test love-claims as such. If we are to distinguish nonetheless between true love on the one hand and demonic pretences or silly sentimentalities on the other, as indeed we must, then the only way to do this safely is by way of the revealed truth (I Cor. 13:6).

What has been said about love applies in principle also to unity. According to M. Dummet, Wykeham Professor of Logic in the University of Oxford, the "paramountcy of unity" is a principle "held in common by [Roman] Catholic and [Eastern] Orthodox, and rejected by Protestants." This principle means "that it is enjoined on us, whatever the provocation, never to take any step to disrupt the unity of the church." Prof. Dummet is concerned chiefly with the self-contradictions in which those involve themselves who publicly profess the Christian faith but then deny the

22. *Galatians Commentary* (1535), *LW* 27:38–42; *WA* 40:II:47–52.

most basic elements of that faith. Prof. Dummet's incisive observations on this score should be welcomed by honest churchmen everywhere. It is irrefutably true, for instance, that if Jesus

> did not believe himself divine, then we have no ground to do so, and hence commit idolatry in praying to him. If he knew nothing of the Trinity, then we know nothing of the Trinity, and have no warrant whatever for supposing that there is a Trinity. If he intended to found no community, then the church has no standing and is an impostor institution.[23]

If it is indeed true, however, as Prof. Dummet argues, that the growing "liberal consensus" along the above lines is gaining dominance also in Roman Catholic seminaries, and so is "helping to transform [that] church into something distinctly fraudulent," then what becomes of the "paramountcy of unity"? The scandalous dogmatic self-contradictions, says Dummet, ought "to be tolerated no longer: not if there is to be a rationale for belonging to that church." What then if they are tolerated, what if the crisis continues to deepen? Must not the time come to apply the principle so admirably formulated by Dummet himself: "If the church is a fraud there can be no justification for belonging to it: no justification for complicity with fraud"?[24] At this point one must either bid farewell to the "paramountcy of unity" and embrace the paramountcy of truth, or else surrender one's conscience and integrity unconditionally to an institution which is thereby granted absolute power to corrupt absolutely. "Doctrine is heaven; life is earth." And fraud is hell!

Orthodoxy as a Whole vs. the Dividedness of Heterodoxy

There is only one church, as there is only one faith and one Gospel (Eph. 4:4.5). Orthodoxy—that is doctrinal and sacramental conformity to this one faith—is the divinely willed condition of the church (Jn. 8:31.32; 17:17; Eph. 2:20). Heterodoxy, on the other hand, opposes other teachings to the one doctrinal, sacramental truth, and so disfigures the one faith according to alien and illicit patterns (Rom. 6:17; 16:17; I Tim. 6:3–5; II Tim. 1:13; 4:3). Such false teachings and teachers are to be clearly renounced and abandoned (Mt. 7:15; 15:9–14; 16:5–12; Jn. 10:5; Rom. 16:17; Gal. 1:6–9; Tit. 3:10). If instead they are harbored and acknowledged as legitimate, there arises that tragic self-contradiction, the "heterodox

23. M. Dummet, "A Remarkable Consensus," 424ff.
24. Idem.

church," with which the orthodox church cannot practice church fellowship without thereby surrendering the truth and becoming heterodox itself (Gal. 5:9; I Tim. 5:22; II Jn. 10.11; Rev. 18:4).

Since church fellowship (pulpit and altar fellowship) requires and presupposes unanimity in the pure Gospel and sacraments of Christ, the exercise of such church fellowship is a solemn, public, and reciprocal profession and acknowledgement of one another's orthodoxy (Gal. 2:9).[25] The Reformation's understanding that "church fellowship is equivalent to doctrinal fellowship and confessional fellowship,"[26] expresses nothing other than what was self-evident in Christian antiquity:

> By his partaking of the Sacrament in a church a Christian declares that the confession of that church is his confession. Since a man cannot at the same time hold two differing confessions, he cannot communicate in two churches of differing confessions. If anyone does this nevertheless, he denies his own confession or has none at all.[27]

It follows that church fellowship is not an optional[28] matter—like diplomatic recognition—which might be granted or refused at

25. ". . . Church fellowship, that is, mutual recognition as brethren, altar and pulpit fellowship and resultant co-operation in the preaching of the Gospel and the administration of the Sacraments, presupposes unanimity in the pure doctrine of the Gospel and in the right administration of the Sacraments. . . We declare that wherever continued co-operation in the preaching of the Gospel and the administration of the Sacraments and worship exists, there we have a witness to the world of unity in the faith and a profession of church fellowship" (Lutheran Church of Australia *Theses of Agreement*, V:26–28).

26. Buchrucker, *Wort, Kirche, und Abendmahl bei Luther*, 175 (our translation). Also: "to acquiesce in the other's doctrine, that is church fellowship. For church fellowship is doctrinal fellowship, which exists for Luther only where sameness [*aequitas*] of doctrine obtains" (Ibid., n.70).

27. W. Elert, *Eucharist and Church Fellowship*, 182.

28. It is seriously inadequate, theologically, to counter false and unacceptable "models" of external unity in the church (i.e. conciliarity, "reconciled diversity," and selective fellowship) not with the true evangelical, biblical "model," but with an improvised construct which is admittedly "neither divinely ordained nor Scripturally mandated" (*The Nature and Implications of the Concept of Fellowship*. A Report of the Commission on Theology and Church Relations of The Lutheran Church—Missouri Synod, 1981, 42). The fault here lies in the definition of the preferred "model" as "ecclesiastical declarations of altar and pulpit fellowship based on agreement in doctrine and practice." Now, of course, "ecclesiastical declarations," in the sense of formalities of parliamentary procedure, are things indifferent, mere *adiaphora*. But such official "declarations" are neither essential to nor distinctive of the correct practice. (After all, even the unacceptable "models" have to be implemented by some sort of "ecclesiastical declarations"). What is essential and distinctive is "altar and pulpit fellowship based on agreement in doctrine and practice"—and that IS "divinely ordained" and "Scripturally mandated," to use the language of the document. The reliance on mere *adiaphora* in so vital a matter as church fellowship avenges itself in the conclusion of the *Nature and Implications* document, which compensates for the shortfall of divine authority by appealing to strictly human authority, viz., Synodical regulations and procedures "mutually agreed-upon" (p. 46). F. Pieper: "All government of the Church which does not bind the consciences of Christians to Christ's Word, but to the word of men, is pseudo-government" (II:394).

will, depending on all sorts of prudential considerations. Rather, church fellowship exists and must be recognized wherever orthodoxy prevails.[29] On the other hand, where heterodoxy reigns, or is given equal rights with orthodoxy, church fellowship must be refused.

What is also clear is that church fellowship is by its very nature indivisible—it is either granted whole or refused whole. It does not come in bits and pieces. Two churches are either in communion or they are not in communion. There is no third possibility. And if two churches enter into fellowship or communion, they thereby become one communion or church, regardless of administrative differences. To imagine otherwise, to think for instance that pulpit and altar fellowship is only a harmless courtesy, while organizational amalgamation is the much weightier "real thing," is to confuse substance and shadow, and to substitute church politics for the rightful reign of the Gospel.

If the proper nature and basis of church fellowship are taken seriously, the resultant either/or is profoundly distasteful to the whole modern temperament. It seems rather like regarding divorcees as either totally innocent or totally guilty—and we are all too sophisticated for that. It is perfectly true, moreover, that there are believers, dear children of God, in heterodox churches, if only the Gospel is still somehow "getting through" to create and sustain faith. It is also true that there are hypocrites in the orthodox church. Given these realities, is it not counter-intuitive, indeed Pharisaical, to draw church fellowship boundaries so strictly, as though one ecclesial communion—and a small one at that!—had a monopoly on all true Christians? And since there will be Christians from all sorts of churches in heaven, had we not better get used to them here on earth? That is how the matter strikes many people today, and that is why the issue is at once pressing and delicate.

One way out of this dilemma is to attempt to break up the stark either/or into a graded series of both/and's. Even Roman Catholicism at the Second Vatican Council entered cautiously upon this "ecumenical" path with an imaginative "ecclesiology of ele-

29. "If there is a church in Australia—and, thank God, a church which agrees with us in the true faith exists there—then we must maintain fellowship of confession and of love also with that church. Were we to deny a church-body which agrees with us in the faith, that is, confesses Christ's name in all articles, then we should be denying Christ Himself in such a church-body," (F. Pieper, *Vorträge*, 191. Our translation).

ments."[30] Instead of the notion of membership, Vatican II employs the idea of being linked to the church in various degrees or at different levels, including that of unbaptized unbelievers. Given Rome's confusions of natural religion and the Gospel, and of divine and human authority in the church, the new scheme is probably as resourceful and effective an adaptation to modern conditions as can be expected on those premises. It certainly liberates modern Roman Catholics from the embarrassing old absolutism,[31] which for all practical purposes identified the visible institution headed by the papacy with the Mystical Body of Christ. While granting some *communicatio in sacris* to Eastern Orthodoxy, and to individuals of other churches in emergencies, Vatican II did not expressly adopt the "sliding scale" of the World Council of Churches' Faith and Order Commission (Lund, 1952), which ranges from "closed communion" and "limited open communion" through "intercommunion" with or without "intercelebration" all the way to "full communion."[32] Such a terracing of church fellowship, however, is based on arbitrary criteria apart from and beyond the pure Gospel and sacraments, and is therefore biblically indefensible. If "intercommunion" is warranted biblically, then so are "intercelebration" and "full communion," and if not one then also not the others. With the Gospel one cannot distinguish among them. If such artificial gradations and a piecemeal communion are nevertheless assigned fundamental validity and significance, then this is the work of man-made regulations and bureaucratic legalisms. Church fellowship by degrees[33] in effect quantifies the Gospel. Yet the Gospel and therefore orthodoxy is at bottom holistic, and calls for qualitative, not quantitative judgments:

> For the sectarians who deny the bodily presence of Christ in the Lord's Supper accuse us today of being quarrelsome, harsh, and

---

30. J. Feiner, "Commentary on the Decree" [on Ecumenism], in Vorgrimler, *Commentary on the Documents of Vatican II*, II, 80; Also A. Grillmeier, *Commentary*, I:168ff.

31. J. Feiner rightly observes: "The Decree on Ecumenism recognizes in non-Catholic communities more than Calvin does in the papal Church, more than mere scanty 'vestiges' or miserable 'relics'; it sees in them essential structural elements of the Church" (*Commentary on Vatican II*, II, 74). Luther, incidentally, was even more generous in seeing under the papacy "the very choicest Christendom and many pious and great saints" (*WA* 21:147f. The translation in *LW* 40:232 is weak).

32. *Commentary on Vatican II*, II:106.

33. "There are even those who suppose that they can establish degrees of unity. The degrees match the level of agreement reached so far in the discussions. The consensus one tries to read out of Article VII is in all such cases a purely human arrangement. . . . Not agreement in doctrine. . . but only the consensus in the *pure* doctrine and in the *right* administration of the sacraments is the consensus demanded in the Augsburg Confession" (H. Sasse, *We Confess the Church*, 67).

> intractable, because, as they say, we shatter love and harmony among the churches on account of the single doctrine about the Sacrament. They say that we should not make so much of this little doctrine. . . This is especially so because they agree with us on other articles of Christian doctrine. . .To this argument of theirs we reply with Paul: "A little yeast leavens the whole lump" [Gal. 5:9]. In philosophy a tiny error in the beginning is very great at the end. Thus in theology a tiny error overthrows the whole teaching. . .For doctrine is like a mathematical point. Therefore it cannot be divided; that is, it cannot stand either subtraction or addition. On the other hand, life is like a physical point. Therefore it can always be divided and can always yield something. . .Therefore doctrine must be one eternal and round golden circle, in which there is no crack; if even the tiniest crack appears, the circle is no longer perfect. . .If they believed that it is the Word of God, they would not play around with it this way. . . and they would know that one Word of God is all and that all are one, that one doctrine is all doctrines and all are one, so that when one is lost all are eventually lost, because they belong together and are held together by a common bond. . .Therefore if you deny God in one article of faith, you have denied Him in all; for God is not divided into many articles of faith, but He is everything in each article and He is one in all the articles of faith.[34]

Only from this perspective is it possible to make sense of the harsh condemnations of false doctrine in the New Testament, which modern readers find so perplexing. It has been argued, for instance, that Rom. 16:17, "Mark those who cause divisions and offenses contrary to the doctrine which you have learnt, and avoid them," forbids church fellowship only with outright unbelievers, not with erring Christians, since v. 18 adds: "they that are such serve not our Lord Jesus Christ, but their own belly."[35] As if we could determine who really believes and who does not! Since believers exist in all churches which are still somehow Christian, the Romans text could then be applied to no heterodox church whatever. Clearly Paul was talking about objective criteria, not subjective imponderables, when he referred to "the doctrine which you have learnt." One should note also the "kiss of peace" in v. 16, which suggests a Eucharistic context.

It is difficult to imagine a subjectively more benign and well-meant error than Peter's misguided solicitude for his Lord's safety and welfare in Mt. 16:22. Yet the objective effect of his sentimental intervention coincided precisely with the devil's intent to deflect

34. *Galatians Commentary* (1535), *LW* 27:36–39; *WA* 40:II:45–48.

35. Within the Missouri Synod the best-known example is Thesis Five of *A Statement* of 1945 (*Speaking the Truth in Love*). The classic response to this argumentation is R. Hoerber, *A Grammatical Study of Rom. 16:17*.

the Savior from His path to the Cross (Mt. 4:1 ff.). Therefore, having a few verses before called him "blessed," the Lord turns on Peter with a quite unexpected severity and says: "Out of my sight, Satan! You are a stumbling block to me; you do not have in mind the things of God, but the things of men" (16:23, NIV). Other New Testament condemnations of error, including Rom. 16:17 ff. are mild by comparison. But, it may be objected, the Lord did not deny Peter the equivalent of church fellowship. True, but then Peter did not persist in his error either. It is just the nature of heterodox communions, on the other hand, that they do persevere in their heterodoxy. That is the very reason for their continued separate existence. Nor must it be imagined that the heretics of Paul's day simply rejected the New Testament, root and branches. On the contrary, the Judaizers no doubt accepted the Lordship of Jesus, Baptism, etc., but only insisted on a few "little" extras in addition, like mandatory circumcision—on which see Gal. 5:2–12. H. P. Hamann therefore wrote:

> Surely one must see that the true counterpart in our day to the false teachers of the New Testament age are the heterodox church-bodies themselves. . . For in them heterodoxy, false teaching, heresy, is given a habitation and a name; it is given respectability; it is given perpetuity—and all this under the protection of the blessed name "Church"! The false teachings given a refuge in heterodox bodies are every whit as bad as the false teachings known in the New Testament. . . And the New Testament condemnation of false teachers should be applied to them directly and without any softening of the rebuke.[36]

Unvarnished falsehood is easy to detect and not nearly so dangerous therefore as a seductive melange of truth and error. It is just such a mixture of incompatibles that actually characterizes heterodoxy and heterodox churches. This radical doubleness of heterodoxy—may we call it "schizopneumia," on the analogy of "schizophrenia"?—flies the flags both of Christ and of Belial, of light and of darkness, of faith and of unfaith, of God's temple and of idols (II Cor. 6:14.15). This calls for two complementary postures towards heterodox churches. Two modern analogies can help to illustrate this. Consider a cancer patient. The whole ingenuity of medical technology is deployed to attack the cancer in such a way as to maximize the damage inflicted on the cancer cells, while minimizing injury to the rest of the body. It is just this concern

36. H. P. Hamann, in the Evangelical Lutheran Church of Australia's official critique of the LCMS' CTCR's "Theology of Fellowship," 1961.

which Luther expresses in his 1528 letter "Concerning Rebaptism."[37] The fanatics attack the papacy in a blind fury, without regard for the Christians who are held captive there. Luther, on the contrary, recognizes under the papacy the continued existence of the body of Christ, with the "true Spirit, Gospel, faith, baptism, sacrament, keys, the office of the ministry, prayer, holy Scripture, and everything that pertains to Christendom."[38] Correspondingly, he holds of the Protestant enemies of the sacraments that "we must admit that the enthusiasts have the Scriptures and the Word of God in other doctrines. Whoever hears it from them and believes will be saved, even though they are unholy heretics and blasphemers of Christ."[39]

When the fanatics therefore rage indiscriminately on the principle, "whatever is in the papacy we must have and do differently,"[40] they re-enact a tragedy that had taken place in the Thuringian forest: A man, trying to help his brother who was being mauled by a bear, missed the bear and accidentally stabbed the brother. So the fanatics "attack the temple of God and miss the Antichrist who sits therein, just as the blind, who grope after water, take hold of fire."[41] The moral is worth quoting in full:

> They take a severe stand against the pope, but they miss their mark and murder the more terribly the Christendom under the pope. For if they would permit baptism and the sacrament of the altar to stand as they are, Christians under the pope might yet escape with their souls and be saved, as has been the case hitherto. But now when the sacraments are taken from them, they will most likely be lost, since even Christ himself is thereby taken away. Dear friend, this is not the way to blast the papacy while Christian saints are in his keeping. One needs a more cautious, discreet spirit, which attacks the accretion which threatens the temple without destroying the temple of God itself.[42]

Regard for captive Zion, however, must not weaken one's resolve in resisting the oppressor, Babylon. This suggests another modern analogy, that of one nation, part of which is free, under a benign and civilized government, while another part has been conquered by brutal terrorists with designs on the rest of the country. In these circumstances the "good" government would, as long as it existed, clearly represent the true interests of the entire nation,

---

37. *Concerning Rebaptism* (1528), *LW* 40:229–262; *WA* 26:144–174.
38. Ibid., *LW* 40:232; *WA* 26:147.37–39.
39. Ibid., *LW* 40:251; *WA* 26:164.5–7.
40. Ibid., *LW* 40:233; *WA* 26:148.23–24.
41. Ibid., *LW* 40:233; *WA* 26:148.31–32.
42. Ibid., *LW* 40:233–234; *WA* 26:148.38–149.

no matter how much of its actual territory had been annexed by the neighboring concentration camp. Patriots of that nation would then do all in their power to deprive the robber regime of any tokens of legitimacy, and this not from hatred or contempt of their compatriots in captivity but precisely from loyalty to them. Nor would public shows of friendship and hobnobbing with the oppressors be taken as indications of esteem for the oppressed. The latter themselves would not wish to see their oppressors legitimized, and would regard any moves in that direction as adding insult to injury. Now, of course political and spiritual government differ so fundamentally, that all analogies between them are bound to be misleading. Our sole point here is the crucial distinction between the heterodox "regime" or system as such, and its victims. Opposition to the former must never mean hostility to the latter. On the contrary, it is just genuine love for the whole church, and especially for those parts of it languishing under the Babylonian Captivity of heterodoxy, that demands unremitting, uncompromising, and exclusive fidelity to the genuine evangelical and ecumenical banner, that is, to the pure marks of the one church. "For we cannot do anything against the truth, but only for the truth" (II Cor. 13:8). All false banners, regimes, doctrines, systems and the like, under whatever name, must be roundly repudiated as illegitimate, that is, as misrepresentations of the one Lord and His one church. That is what it means to refuse church fellowship to heterodox churches as such. Refusal of church fellowship does *not* mean excommunication:

> By their exclusion from the celebration of the Holy Supper in communion with the Lutheran Church, members of erring communions are not being excommunicated, much less declared to be heretics and condemned, but they are merely being suspended until they shall have reconciled themselves with the orthodox church by renouncing the false communion (or fellowship) in which they stand (C.F.W. Walther).[43]

The lines of church fellowship, it will be remembered, run not directly between individuals, but by way of the uniting center, that is, the church's pure marks. Individuals are in fellowship with one another by way of their pulpits and altars. They do not first come to know each other as brothers in the faith, and then form a common relationship to the church. Rather, the mutual acknowledgement hinges on the prior mutual participation in the common faith of the church. One's spiritual identity is shaped not so much by

43 Walther, *Theses Concerning Communion Fellowship with Those Who Believe Differently*, 11.

personal verbal professions of the moment, as by the public doctrine of the altar and pulpit at which one regularly confesses (Acts 2:42; I Cor. 10:17; 11:26). The old Lutheran theologians always cited II Sam. 15:11, about the two hundred men who followed Absalom "quite innocently, knowing nothing about the matter," to illustrate the situation of sincerely misguided believers, trapped in heterodoxy. Their personal sincerity warrants church fellowship with them as little as the naivete of Absalom's two hundred once meant that making common cause with them was no longer treasonable.

Neither sentimental simplifications nor urbane universalisms like those of the World Council of Churches and of Vatican II really take into account the whole trans-human, demonic dimension involved in heterodoxy. Forbidding marriage and certain foods, for instance, may strike us as a simple case of overdone asceticism. Paul, however, brands such prohibitions "doctrines of demons" (I Tim. 4:1). Satan, the arch-liar and arch-murderer, is also "the father of lies" (Jn. 8:44). He and his minions take grim pleasure in donning churchly trappings and angelic disguises (II Cor. 11:14) in order to entice and seduce as many as possible away from the saving truth of God (II Thess. 2:9–12). It is not enough, therefore, to understand heterodoxy only or mainly psychologically, in terms of human ignorance, ambition, illusion, or even malice. These are trifles compared to the super-human malignities that lurk behind and exploit them in constant counter-thrusts against the saving work of God (I Pet. 5:8.9). Not flesh and blood are the real enemy, but "principalities and powers," against which no human ingenuity avails, but only the armory of God (Eph. 6:10–18). Physical persecutions, inquisitions, and crusades against heresy are inversions and mockeries of the ways of God (Mt. 5:3–12;I Pet. 2:13–4:19). The church's battles are fought not with worldly weapons but with spiritual ones alone (II Cor. 10:3–6). Responsible theological identification and exclusion of heterodoxy by means of the church's marks calls not for personal meanness and enmity, but for a modest sobriety and charity of mind (Rom. 12:17–21; Gal. 6:1–10; Phil. 4:5). It is just because "the love of Christ constrains us" (II Cor. 5:14) that we dare not yield "for a moment" (Gal. 2:5) to any corruption of the Gospel. "To dissent from the consensus of so many nations and to be called schismatics is a serious matter"—but divine authority demands it (Tr. 42).

We can now appreciate the profound simplicity of Augsburg Confession VII. To common sense it may well seem that one must choose between the whole church and the whole truth. The more people are to be included, the more the truth will have to be diluted to what they hold in common. On the other hand, the more truth is to be salvaged, the more people will have to be defined out of the church. But this inverse proportion is deceiving. AC VII defies the illusion by keeping the whole church firmly anchored in the whole truth. That of course is biblical. Since there is only one Gospel, one truth, and one faith, and since faith is in every case the work and gift of the Holy Spirit, it follows that the Spirit works the same faith in all believers. To the extent that we are Christians at all, we are true Christians. Whatever is in us above, beyond, or against the one faith, comes not from the Spirit of truth (Jn. 16:13), and is therefore not faith but a mere conceit of the flesh (Mt. 16:23; Rom.7:14–25; 16:18). By faith the newly baptised baby and the aged saint have the same Christ—all of Him. Just as in the Sacrament "one receives and a thousand receive—and the many as much as the one,"[44] so in Christ all participate in the fullness of one and the same divine truth. Faith is always a theological reality, not a psychological phenomenon. It is not accessible therefore to direct human inspection. This means that disturbances, confusions, and disfigurements at the surface level of empirical human appearances in principle negate the underlying oneness of faith no more than does the infant's or the comatose believer's inability to verbalize any of it.

Mention must be made in this connection of the distinction between *"fides qua"* (faith by which) and *"fides quae"* (faith which). The former is the personal, subjective faith by means of which the individual receives and appropriates the treasures of salvation in the Gospel. The latter is the objective content of the faith which is believed. Only mischief and confusion result when this distinction is pressed into "ecumenical" service, with the suggestion, for instance, that all Christians have the same *"fides qua,"* or saving faith, but differ about the *"fides quae,"* that is, the doctrine in all its articles. This suggests that the *"fides qua"* is a sort of core-excerpt from a larger *"fides quae,"* so that agreement in this mini-faith is enough for salvation, while full agreement in the maxi-faith of Christian doctrine is not so essential. The simple truth of the matter is that *"fides qua"* is not a sort of shrunken version of *"fides quae,"* a rival, but smaller content. It is, rather, the act of believing, while the *"fides quae"* is the content. These two therefore are and can be in competition no more than food and eating. And since the

44. *"Sumit unus, sumunt mille: Quantum isti, tantum ille,"* from Thomas Aquinas' famous Eucharistic hymn, *Lauda Sion Salvatorem*, often quoted by the old Lutheran theologians.

smallest faith takes hold of the whole Christ, since the Holy Spirit bears witness to the whole truth, and since the one baptism is into the one Lord and the one faith, therefore all *"fides qua"* takes hold of one and the same *"fides quae."* The contrary appearance of some disarray at the cognitive level does not alter the reality. This consideration does not in the least excuse or mitigate the evil of false proclamation in the church, for all attacks on the *"fides quae"* in principle imperil the *"fides qua."* It is simply a matter of taking due account of the Holy Spirit's work at the "receptor's," or we might say, the "victim's," end of the garbled communication—in accord with the ancient adage that "the ears of the people are holier than the mouths of the priests."

It is the humble grandeur of the orthodox church that she represents and confesses the faith of all Christians, also of those who cannot speak for themselves. She embodies the true interests of all believers, for she teaches that pure Gospel and administers those holy sacraments through which alone Christ builds His church—even under contrary appearances. Her cause therefore is not a narrow, sectarian one, "but the cause of Christ and the church" (Ap. XII.90). Under changing historical forms and names, her fate registers and reflects the titanic struggles till the end of days between Abel and Cain, Isaac and Ishmael (Gal. 4:29), Jacob and Esau (Rom. 9:13), the narrow way and the broad way (Mt. 7:13.14), the woman and the dragon (Rev. 12): ". . . the true doctrine and church is often so oppressed and forlorn, as happened under the papacy, as though there were no church, and it often appears as though she had quite perished" (Ap. VII/VIII.9, German).

It is perfectly correct to call the orthodox church "the true visible church," as opposed to false or erring visible churches. That is the traditional terminology. Its denotations are unexceptionable, but its connotations may in today's context needlessly prejudice some. In this chapter we have restricted ourselves to the simpler terms "orthodox church" and "heterodox church," in order to avoid as much as possible any unnecessary disputes about words. Heterodox churches are churches and sects at the same time. They are churches insofar as they still retain such essentials of the Gospel and sacraments as will allow people to be converted and become children of God. But heterodox churches are sects insofar as they deviate from the evangelical truth and so divide the church and by their errors threaten the faith of Christians.[45] Or, as Car-

45. Our language here follows closely that of F. Pieper in *Christian Dogmatics*, III.423.

pzov put it: "Insofar as the church is impure, she is no church, though the true and pure church is within her, as regards certain members known to God, who lie hidden there."[46]

In conclusion, the Gospel and sacraments of Christ, insofar as they are the marks of the church, distinguish the church from all that is not church; and insofar as these marks are pure, they distinguish the orthodox church from heterodox churches. In and of themselves, of course, the marks are always pure—for to the extent that impurities or disfigurements are added, these are not the church's marks at all but alien features. "Another gospel" is as such precisely "no gospel" (Gal. 1:6.7). Those who do not believe that revealed divine truth is concretely accessible in the church, will of course find this discussion in particular—and traditional theology in general—hopelessly arrogant and fanciful. Their objections cannot be considered here in detail. That is a task for Prolegomena. In the doctrine of the church the truth of the faith once delivered to the saints (Jude 3) is a given, no, *the* given. To suppose otherwise, to imagine that truth and error cannot be reliably distinguished, is to embrace ecclesiological deism. The church of Christ, on the contrary, is "the pillar and foundation of the truth" (I Tim. 3:15). Luther:

> But whatever wavers or doubts cannot be truth; and what would be the use or need of a church of God in the world if [she] wanted to waver or be uncertain in [her] words, or wanted to say something new every day, now asserting this, now rejecting that?[47]

Orthodoxy Does *Not* Mean Theological Perfection

In chess one may learn the basic rules in five minutes, but this does not make one a grand master. Similarly, orthodoxy is a bare minimum, a starting point, a floor, not a ceiling. It means keeping all the articles of faith straight, and not allowing anything to contradict them. At the same time an orthodox teacher may be quite wrong in his understanding of this or that biblical text—indeed, where is the theologian whose mind is entirely free of eccentric notions? Not every mistake is at once heretical or church-divisive. On the basis of I Cor. 3:11–15 the Apology teaches a very necessary leniency in this regard (VII/VIII.20–21, compare IV.231–243).

Gerhard and the other old Lutherans chided the Jesuits for maintaining that every biblical statement was an article of faith, therefore also the item that the apocryphal "dog of Tobit wagged

46. Cited in a slightly different translation in C.F.W. Walther, *The True Visible Church*, 24.
47. *Against Hanswurst* (1541), *LW* 41:213; *WA* 51:511.24–27.

its tail."[48] The Lutherans, on the contrary, distinguished between articles of faith, which were necessary for salvation, and other, supporting biblical details and ramifications about which one might be ignorant or even wrong without direct detriment to faith. Of course, once one recognized that something was presented as a fact in Scripture, one was not free to deny it, for then one would be opposing the inspiration and authority of God's holy Word—a major article of faith indeed. That is the point of Hunnius' remark: "He indeed is a heretic who denies an article of faith; but not only he, but also he who denies a historical narrative of the Holy Ghost."[49]

The founders of the Missouri Synod shared this position, and are therefore unjustly lampooned today as perfectionists, who could tolerate no disagreement about anything. Walther, for instance, was convinced that the prohibition of interest-taking was a biblical teaching. When pressed, however, he insisted that it was not an article of faith, so that if someone were sincerely wrong only on this sort of thing, no grounds would exist for refusing church fellowship. Everything depended, Walther said, on whether those who rejected the point at issue did so from sincere misunderstanding or from stubborn resistance to what they recognized to be biblical teaching. If the latter, it would of course be a case of attacking the foundations, and hence would be church-divisive.[50]

Those who caricature orthodoxy as a demand for theological perfection do so in order to discredit the demand by appealing to Luther's *"simul justus et peccator"* (at the same time righteous and sinner). The idea is that to require orthodoxy is to require a certain degree of sanctification, and that in turn is to confuse Law and Gospel. This whole approach, however, rests on a category-mistake, and reflects puritanic/pietistic moralism rather than the evangelical, confessional marks-of-the-church orientation. The church and her fellowship rest not on faith but on its objective source: the pure Gospel and sacraments. Orthodoxy in this sense therefore has nothing to do with sanctification (an orthodox office-bearer may turn out to be personally a hypocrite [AC VIII]). The point is not anyone's personal quality or worthiness, but the

48. Cited in C.F.W. Walther, *True Visible Church*, 105.

49. Ibid., 106.

50. See lengthy citation in R. Bohlmann, "The position of the LCMS on the Basis for Fellowship," *FODT*, 37. In support Bohlmann cites *1969 LCMS Convention Workbook*, p. 505, n. 25. The original source is*Der Lutheraner*, 27 (May 1871), 131. See also Brobst's *Theologische Monatshefte*, 4 (September 1871), 272–273.

alone-saving truth of the Gospel, which is prior to all faith, love, and sanctification. Unlike love and sanctification, which are always piecemeal, incomplete, subject to the Law's calibrations (Rom. 13:10), the Gospel of justification does not work by halves, sevenths, or tithes, but by wholes (Rom. 8:31ff.; II Cor. 1:19.20). Church-fellowship turns on this holistic, utterly prior Gospel, not on sanctification or on anything else which is "in us," and so subject to fluctuation by degrees.

Orthodox Confessions as Pure Gospel (Pure Marks) in *Practice*

If Holy Scripture is the inexhaustible gold mine of divine truth, the creeds and confessions of the church are the minted coin of evangelical currency. For the Book of Concord truth is not an abstraction, but a concrete given. It is the divine, evangelical truth as revealed in Holy Scripture and faithfully confessed in the Apostles', Nicene, and Athanasian Creeds, as well as in the Augsburg Confession and its associated documents (FC SD, Rule and Norm). Orthodox creeds and confessions are truth-preserving, and therefore divide as well as unite. By identifying decisive elements of the biblical teaching, such creeds call and gather the faithful to the standards of authentic proclamation. On the other hand, by pin-pointing the differences, the creeds distinguish true biblical teaching from counterfeits and misunderstandings, thereby warding off rival, heterodox teachings, and excluding their persistent adherents. Creeds and confessions therefore embody the church's marks in concrete, concentrated form.

This confessional spirit of the Church of the Augsburg Confession is fundamentally at odds with the anti-confessional outlook which animates the Reformed (Zwingli-Calvinist) churches. The latter, as Karl Barth has rightly seen, ultimately know no such thing as "Reformed doctrine." Instead of the Lutheran insistence on the *properly understood* Scripture, the Reformed churches maintain a basically abstract *sola Scriptura* principle, that is, a "timeless appeal to the open Bible and to the Spirit which from it speaks to our spirit." Barth continues:

> Our fathers had good reason for leaving us *no* Augsburg Confession, authentically interpreting the word of God, *no* Formula of Concord, *no* "Symbolical Books" which might later, like the Lutheran, come to possess an odor of sanctity. They left us only *creeds*, more than one of which begin or end with a proviso which leaves them

> open to being improved upon in the future. The Reformed churches simply do *not* know the word dogma, in its rigid hierarchical sense.[51]

The decisive impulse here, evident already in Calvin but stronger in Barth, is a deeply Platonic, anti-incarnational spiritualism, which decrees an eternal *apartheid* between finite and infinite, temporal and eternal, human and divine. Absolutes in this anti-sacramental scheme must hover permanently beyond the reach of concrete, historical embodiment, which latter is exiled to a shadowy underworld of the relative and the provisional. Trendy Lutherans have drunk deeply from these post-Barthian, anti-confessional wells.[52] However, Lutheran writers often feel obliged to appeal to the Confessions in the very process of attacking them. One technique is to isolate FC Ep. RN.8, so as to suggest that orthodox creeds and confessions can be *no more than* "merely witnesses and expositions of the faith, setting forth how at various times the Holy Scriptures were understood in the church of God by contemporaries with reference to controverted articles,etc."[53] What the Epitome says here of extra-biblical writings applies to them only in comparison to the sacred, inspired text itself. In other words, only Scripture is ultimate norm, *norma normans*. It is complete fabrication, however, to suggest that therefore orthodox creeds are not normative in the sense of *norma normata*, but are "merely witnesses." On the contrary, the Formula lists all the documents of the Book of Concord as forming, together with the Sacred Scriptures of God, "the Summary Formulation, Basis, Rule, and Norm, Indicating how all Doctrines should be Judged in Comformity with the Word of God and Errors are to be Explained and Decided in a Christian Way."[54]

The Solid Declaration expressly states that the *sola scriptura* principle does not involve rejection of the normativeness of the Symbolical Books:

> Our intention was only to have a single, universally accepted, certain, and common form of doctrine which all our Evangelical churches subscribe and from which and according to which, because

51. K. Barth, *The Word of God and the Word of Man*, 229–230.

52. It is difficult to think of a better example than V. L. Eckstrom, "Pluralism and Lutheran Confessionalism," 109–149.

53. A variant of this approach is to exempt the Augsburg Confession itself, but to claim that the FC "allocates to all other writings the status of witnesses to the way in which 'at various times the Holy Scriptures were understood in the church of God by contemporaries'" (D. Truemper, "The Catholicity of the Augsburg Confession," 13).

54. Tappert, 503.

> it is drawn from the Word of God, all other writings are to be approved and accepted, judged and regulated.[55]

Not an abstract "timeless appeal to the open Bible" is decisive, but the concrete confession of the properly, evangelically, understood Bible.

As the church's pure marks in concrete, concentrated form, the orthodox confessions define the basis and limits of church fellowship. Where these confessions are contravened in doctrine and practice, there the Gospel is not being purely preached, and the Sacraments are not being rightly administered. In this sense the Augsburg Confession and its associated documents in the Book of Concord "distinguish our reformed churches from the papacy and from other condemned sects and heresies" (FC SD RN.5). These boundary-markers against major falsifications of Christian truth stand also against kindred errors among nominal Lutherans, who pay lip-service to the Augsburg Confession but whose "teachings are contrary to the expressed Word of God and cannot coexist with it" (Preface to the Book of Concord). Indeed the pseudo-Lutheran errors "are of such a nature that the opinions of the erring party cannot be tolerated in the church of God, much less be excused and defended" (FC SD Intro.9).

As bearers of the public marks of the church, the Confessions demand actual practice and implementation, not formal pedantries of any sort. If the Gospel is being purely preached and the sacraments are being rightly administered, then orthodoxy and church fellowship in fact obtain, even if not all orthodox creeds and confessions are formally named in church constitutions or ordination vows.[56] On the other hand, solemn professions of loyalty to the entire Book of Concord count for nothing if they are confined to the "patient paper" of formal documents, while in practice pulpits, seminaries, and publications disseminate also teachings contrary to the Book of Concord. If confessions do not actually confess, they are play-confessions, toy tokens in a sacrilegious game of "church."

"The unity of the Church does not consist in subscription to the

55. FC RN 10, Tappert, 506.

56. F. Pieper: "If the Lutheran Confession were not mentioned at all in a congregation's constitution, but if the teaching in that congregation were in all points in accord with the Word of God, then that would be an orthodox Lutheran congregation. And if a congregation were to say ten times in its constitution that in this congregation the preaching was to be Lutheran, yet if in reality the preaching were not Lutheran but Methodist, Baptist, synergistic, etc., then that would not be a Lutheran congregation, despite its declaration in its constitution" (*Vorträge*, 185).

same Confessions, but in the acceptance and teaching of the same doctrines."[57] And of course "a church does not forfeit its orthodox character through the casual intrusion of errors, provided these are combatted and eventually removed by means of doctrinal discipline."[58] It is of the very nature of the Gospel, and therefore of the evangelical Reformation, that content takes precedence over form, and reality over appearance.

It is in church fellowship above all that confession or denial takes place. When church fellowship is limited to churches with which there is genuine consensus in the Gospel and sacraments, as defined in the Book of Concord, then these Confessions are being implemented in accordance with their whole thrust and intent.[59] When on the other hand nominally Lutheran churches officially practice or tolerate pulpit and altar fellowship with churches and ministers whose doctrine is in conflict with that of the Book of Concord, then the Confessions are thereby abrogated, despite continued lip-service to them from church-political motives. By coalescing with non-Lutheran churches at their altars and pulpits, Lutheran churches cease to be Lutheran and become syncretistic sects.

It is certainly conceivable that occasionally some Lutheran theologians or even a larger group of them and their followers could find that they have lost their former convictions, and no longer believe, teach, and confess as does the Book of Concord. If this were then publicly admitted, and the proper consequences drawn, no one could object to the integrity of the proceedings. What is intolerable, and destructive of all churchly integrity, is the continued pretence of confessional loyalty when the reality is demonstrably otherwise. So for example one cannot without perjury ac-

57. H. E. Jacobs, "The General Council," 94.

58. LCMS, *Brief Statement*, 29. This so-called "doctrinal discipline" must not be confused with "church discipline" in general, which is an additional mark of the church for the Reformed, but not for Lutherans (FC SD XII, 34). If anti-evangelical teaching is granted equal rights with the truth in pulpits, seminaries, and publications, this is no mere lapse in discipline. It is rather a church-divisive and church-destructive attack on the Dominical and apostolic foundations of the church, Eph. 2:20. A necessary corollary of the above is Walther's thesis: "True Evangelical Lutheran particular and local churches or congregations are only those in which the doctrine of the Evangelical Lutheran Church, as set out in her Symbols, is not only legally recognized, but also holds sway in public preaching" (*True Visible Church*, 133. The translation given there is slightly inaccurate). On the basis of Jer. 8:8 Walther adds that the lip-service of "nominal Lutherans" to the orthodox Confessions—when in fact false doctrine prevails among them—"must be rejected as vain boasting."

59. "For Lutherans the consensus required should always be regarded as the doctrinal content of the Book of Concord, which does not necessarily mean agreement in theological terminology" (Lutheran Church of Australia, *Theses of Agreement*, V,22).

cept pulpit and altar fellowship with Episcopal and Presbyterian churches,[60] and also claim that one still abides by one's ordination vow and subscription to the Book of Concord, which confesses with Luther:

> I reckon them all as belonging together (that is, as Sacramentarians and enthusiasts), for that is what they are who will not believe that the Lord's bread in the Supper is his true, natural body, which the godless or Judas receive orally as well as Peter and all the saints. Whoever, I say, will not believe this, will please let me alone and expect no fellowship from me. This is final (FC SD VII.33).

The historic confessional position was put like this by C.F.W. Walther: "The Evangelical Lutheran Church rejects every fraternal or ecclesiastical fellowship with such as reject its Confession, either in whole or in part."[61] Nor was this a "Missourian" peculiarity. The "centrist" *Minneapolis Theses* (1925) stated:

> Church fellowship, that is, mutual recognition, altar and pulpit fellowship, and eventually co-operation in the strictly essential work of the Church, presupposes unanimity in the pure doctrine of the Gospel and in the confession of the same in word and deed. Where the establishment and maintenance of church fellowship ignores present doctrinal differences or declares them a matter of indifference, there is unionism, the pretense of union which does not exist. [The Galesburg Rule] is not only in full accord with, but necessarily implied in, the teachings of the divine Word and the Confessions of the evangelical Lutheran Church. This rule, implying the rejection of all unionism and syncretism, must be observed as setting forth a principle elementary to sound and conservative Lutheranism (III,1.2).

---

60. The reference here is to the "interim Eucharistic sharing" between several U.S. Lutheran bodies and the Episcopal Church since 1982, and the terms of Lutheran-Reformed altar-fellowship agreements documented in J. E. Andrews and J. A. Burgess, eds., *An Invitation To Action. The Lutheran-Reformed Dialogue Series III 1981-1983.* In direct contradiction to FC SD VII *An Invitation* claims that "those churches that have subscribed to the Reformed Confessions have always taught and still teach the real presence of Christ in the Eucharist," and that the difference is simply about the "mode" of Christ's presence, which should not be divisive (114–115). Only rarely is this anti-confessional revolution admitted, and then much too guardedly to enlighten the general membership. For example, *Lutheran and Presbyterian-Reformed Agreement 1986: A Study Guide,* released by The Office of the Presiding Bishop of The American Lutheran Church, stated: "In the same way Lutherans who adopt the Leuenberg Agreement have modified their confessional stance by agreeing that condemnations in the Reformation Confessions are inapplicable to those churches with which they now find consensus (cf. *Invitation To Action,* 69–70). Three Batak churches in 1984 took another historic step by joining forty-eight Christian churches in adopting documents establishing what Lutherans call 'pulpit and altar fellowship.' Among these churches are Pentecostals, Methodists, Mennonites, and the Reformed. Thus Lutherans cannot deny that in effect they are producing new Confessions by the way old Confessions are being used in new situations and by new situations to which they commit themselves" (11).

61. *True Visible Church,* 128.

Even Franklin Clark Fry once wrote, on behalf of the United Lutheran Church in America: "Insistence upon agreement in doctrine as a precondition for church fellowship is the distinguishing mark of Lutherans among all Protestants and should never be relaxed."[62]

To see the subsequent abandonment of doctrinal, confessional, and sacramental consensus as the proper basis for church fellowship simply in cultural terms, as a relaxation of outdated rigidities, is to mistake the true significance of this development. What it really means, theologically, is the summary abrogation of the Lutheran Church's Symbolical Books. If these Symbols are no longer allowed to govern church fellowship, then they may still be fussed over as ethnic or cultural heirlooms of a by-gone age, but they cannot in that case be taken seriously as confessions of the pure Gospel and Sacraments of Christ. The Confessions have then in fact been quietly pushed aside and pensioned off, like senile relatives who must be gently but firmly got out of the way of progress. On this score at least there appear to be few illusions in the upper echelons of the "Lutheran" World Federation:

> Thus the fundamental principle, "church fellowship is a fellowship of common confession," which has been rather rigidly maintained on the Lutheran side in the past, no longer applies today—at least in its exclusive form... Today, however, it is in theory at least, no longer possible to maintain, as was the case from the end of the 16th century, that Lutheran churches can be "identified" as "Lutheran" because they accept the historical confessions as their confession. . .Indeed, the Lutheran church is no longer the same. First, it is undeniable that *delimitation* from the Reformed church and the Reformed confession was an essential aspect of Lutheranism's self-understanding in the past. Second, it is prepared to re-interpret *its own confession* on certain important points. . . If we think of the previous Lutheran insistence on *CA Invariata* [Unaltered Augsburg Confession] and of the "doctrinal basis" of the LWF, then it should become clear that we are not dealing here with a minor issue or splitting hairs. Thus one must interpret the outcome of the Lutheran/Reformed dialogue by saying that "Lutheran confessionality" and "Reformed confessionality" can certainly still be distinguished from one another, but can no longer be regarded as divided and divisive. . .What I plead for is to do away with a static and timeless notion of confessional identity. Confessionality is open for, and exposed to, modification and change...[63]

62. R.C. Wolf, *Documents of Lutheran Unity in America*, 547.
63. Harding Meyer, "The LWF and its Role in the Ecumenical Movement," 23, 28–29, 31.

8

THE ECUMENICAL MOVEMENT: CHARMS AND CHALLENGES

It cannot of course be our aim here to present a comprehensive treatment of the Ecumenical Movement. Our limited objective is only to sketch out, in broad strokes, certain dogmatically significant inter-connections, so as to display the acute and continuing relevance of Augsburg Confession VII. It would be a great mistake to underestimate the powerful religious appeal of ecumenism both as an idea and as institutionally embodied in such organizations as the World Council of Churches (WCC) and the Lutheran World Federation (LWF). It would be equally mistaken to attempt to confront this appeal simply with negatives, or prohibitions, without adequate theological analysis and the counter-appeal of a more substantive ecclesiology. Our discussion will pursue two converging lines of development, one associated with the WCC, the other with the LWF.

From Lambeth (1888) to Lima (1982)

At its Chicago Convention in 1886 the Protestant Episcopal Church in the United States adopted a plan for Christian re-union, which recalled all churches "to the principles of unity exemplified by the undivided Catholic Church during the first ages of its existence." The "substantial deposit of Christian Faith and Order committed by Christ and His Apostles to the Church" was specified in four points, which, in slightly amended form, were adopted by the international Anglican Lambeth Conference in 1888:

> (a) The Holy Scriptures of the Old and New Testaments, as 'containing all things necessary to salvation,' and as being the rule and ultimate standard of faith.
>
> (b) The Apostles' Creed, as the Baptismal Symbol; and the Nicene Creed, as the sufficient statement of the Christian faith.
>
> (c) The two Sacraments ordained by Christ Himself—Baptism and

the Supper of the Lord—ministered with unfailing use of Christ's words of institution and of the elements ordained by Him.

(d) The Historic Episcopate, locally adapted in the methods of its administration to the varying needs of the nations and peoples called of God into the unity of His Church.[1]

This Lambeth Quadrilateral, or more formally, Chicago-Lambeth Quadrilateral, has since then represented the Anglican ecumenical platform—first as a "floor" and later (e.g. the Church of South India, 1947) more as a "ceiling." That is to say that a clergy uniformly ordained by bishops within the "apostolic succession" of the "historic episcopate" is acceptable to Anglicanism as a destination aimed for rather than as a precondition to be fully met already from the outset of re-union. The Anglican Communion, moreover, has "come to occupy, in some ways, a central position in ecumenical developments and to exercise greater influence than its comparatively small numbers might seem to entitle it to claim."[2] The political and cultural eminence of the British Empire during the formative years of the modern Ecumenical Movement no doubt played its part.

It was a U.S. Anglican missionary (Philippines) bishop, Charles Brent, who moved his own church to seek a conference for the consideration of those "questions touching Faith and Order,"[3] which had been excluded from the agenda of the 1910 World Missionary Conference in Edinburgh. The result was the Faith and Order movement, which merged with the parallel Life and Work movement to form the World Council of Churches in 1948. The International Missionary Council joined the WCC in 1961.

In the early years of Faith and Order genuine efforts were made to document the precise areas of agreement and disagreement among the churches, and this resulted in the publication of valuable studies.[4] There was a scrupulous avoidance of agitation for union, although the Faith and Order discussions understandably helped to create a climate of opinion favorable to the union of churches.[5] Later a more impatient spirit developed, fuelled no doubt also by the social-political agitations of which the World Council was very much a part. By 1982 the WCC's Faith and Order

1. R. Rouse and S.C. Neill, eds., *A History of the Ecumenical Movement 1517–1948*, 265. The American version, typically, had formulated the first point more strongly, defining the Holy Scriptures "as the revealed Word of God."

2. H. R. T. Brandreth, O.G.S., in Rouse and Neill, *A History*, 265–266.

3. Ibid., 407.

4. e.g. W. T. Whitley, ed., *The Doctrine of Grace*; and R. Dunkerley and A.C. Headlam, eds., *The Ministry and the Sacraments*.

5. Rouse and Neill, op. cit., 440–441.

Commission and Secretariat were able to formulate "significant theological convergence" in *Baptism, Eucharist, and Ministry,* known also as the *Lima Text.* The document admits that "although the language of the text is still largely classical in reconciling historical controversies, the driving force is frequently contextual and contemporary." The document understands itself, to be sure, not as "full consensus," but only as one of "various stages" on the way to that goal. Yet it formally requests all churches to begin a process of "reception," and to indicate "at the highest appropriate level of authority," the extent to which they "can recognize in this text the faith of the Church through the ages." This unprecedented appeal stands in dramatic contrast to the spirit if not to the letter of the earlier policy "not to commend any particular scheme of union."[6]

There is of course much to be commended in the document, particularly when one considers the non-creedal and non-sacramental nature of many WCC member churches, and the "ecumenical" tendency to neglect theological questions in favor of socio-political ones. Nevertheless, the crucial sacramental issues are left undecided. "Commentary (12)" recommends recognition of the falsely contrasted "infant baptism" and "believers' baptism" as "equivalent alternatives." Regarding the sacramental presence *BEM* says that "the bread and wine become the sacramental signs of Christ's body and blood" (15). "Commentary (13)" reports that some churches "while affirming a real presence of Christ at the eucharist, do not link that presence so definitely with the signs of bread and wine," and then leaves it up to the churches to decide "whether this difference can be accommodated within the convergence formulated in the text itself." Finally, "Commentary (28)" calls for "further study" of the opinion held in some areas that in place of bread and wine "local food and drink serve better to anchor the eucharist in everyday life."

On the sacraments, then, it is difficult to see in *BEM* more than a certain accommodation of High Calvinism—as distinct from Low Zwinglianism—to traditional, patristic language. In light of FC VII.2–8, however, one may well regard a bluntly Zwinglian way of speaking as less confusing than the biblical-sounding rhet-

6. Ibid., 441. A curt response to Lima from a committee of theologians of the Church of Greece sees this development as "an alteration of the constitutional base" of the WCC, and "considers not only of no value but even harmful any type of official or non-official ecclesiastical reply" (Max Thurian, *Churches Respond to BEM,* V:3. Six volumes of responses have been published at this writing).

oric of Calvin. It is just the latter, of course, that nourishes the illusion of "convergence."[7]

Both the Church of England and the Orthodox Church in America[8] raise the question of the objective *content* of the faith confessed in the sacraments. That of course lies at the heart of the ecumenical problem. If that problem, however, is seen as one of "faith *and* order," then "faith" may come to be eclipsed by "order," in a way curiously reminiscent of the economic law that bad money drives out the good. *BEM* is a perfect case in point: "faith" is confined to an equivocal treatment of the sacraments, and "order"—that thorny thicket of ministry and church government—completely overshadows everything else, even in terms of the space devoted to it.[9] This state of affairs is no accident. It is deeply rooted in the nature of our Christian divisions. In contrast to AC VII, leading Reformed (Calvinist) confessions insist that there is such a thing as a divinely prescribed church polity or pattern of organization.[10] The heirs of these confessions, however, have themselves divided over whether Holy Scripture prescribes a congregational, a presbyterian, or an episcopal polity. Like some Nordic Lutheran churches (e.g. the Church of Sweden), Anglicanism has retained the traditional episcopate, and has, especially in the wake of the Oxford Movement, come to stress "apostolic succession." This latter point has thrust Anglicanism into the role of an ecumenical bridge and catalyst, drawing together East and West, Reformation and Counter-Reformation. Historically, however, and according to its Thirty-Nine Articles, the Anglican Church is a Reformed communion. Yet its Calvinism is moderate and mild, so much so that the Church of England has even been called a "Lutheranizing church."[11]

---

7. Specifically on the sacramental presence, it is noteworthy that churches like the Church of Scotland (Reformed) and the Presbyterian Church (USA) declare themselves satisfied with *BEM* (*Churches Respond* I:91; III:195), while the Roman Catholic and the Russian Orthodox Churches, for example, firmly dissent (VI:22,38; II:8). (The non-member Lutheran Church—Missouri Synod also expressly criticizes *BEM* on this score, III:137). The Church of England acquiesces in the *BEM* wording, apparently even preferring it to the admittedly stronger language of the Anglican/Roman Catholic (*ARCIC*) agreement (III:45–46).

8. Ibid., 32–33; 16–18, 20.

9. "The subject of the ministry divides the churches more strongly than baptism and eucharist and consequently the ministry section of the text is longer and more discursive" (Church of England's Response, Ibid., 49).

10. See the discussion in H. Sasse, *Here We Stand*, 131-136.

11. P. Schaff, *Creeds of Christendom*, I:218. The Anglican Thirty-Nine Articles are clearly "Lutheranizing" on the subject of Baptism (XXVII), but equally clearly Calvinist on that of the Lord's Supper (XXVIII, XXIX).

Despite the intertwining histories of the English and the Continental Reformations,[12] Anglican and Lutheran ecclesiologies differ fundamentally. The true unity of the church and the problem of Christian re-union are understood quite differently. If we compare the Anglican Quadrilateral with the Lutheran "ecumenical platform" of AC VII, the differences become very clear. The first two "planks" of the Anglican platform (Scripture and Creeds) correspond to the AC's purely preached Gospel, and the third (the sacraments) parallels the rightly administered sacraments in AC VII. The fourth Anglican "plank" is the "historic episcopate." Here we have a direct contradiction to AC VII, which insists on the pure Gospel and sacraments as being "enough." The Confession expressly adds that agreement and uniformity in human traditions and ceremonies is "not necessary for the true unity of the Christian church." And by the modern Church of England's own account the "historic episcopate" is not a divine institution but a human tradition.[13]

The Anglican understanding of "Faith and Order" shares a stress on "order" in general with Calvinism, and on the episcopate in particular with Roman Catholicism and Eastern Orthodoxy. Therein lies no doubt much of Anglicanism's ecumenical appeal and importance, reflected also in Lima's commendation of "the sign of the episcopal succession"(M 53).[14] The Lutheran church goes another way in principle.

On the one hand, then, the Anglican Quadrilateral demands more than the "Lutheran Bilateral" (pure Gospel and sacraments), and is therefore the narrower of the two. On the other hand, however, the Quadrilateral's formal professions of Scripture and Creeds do not require adherence to any particular understanding of them. (This is no doubt why the Church of England could cheerfully endorse Lima's language about "the obstinacy of unjustifiable confessional oppositions within the body of Christ,"[15]

12. For a brief, popular account of the significant cultural and theological ties between Lutheranism and British institutions see E. George Pearce, *The Story of the Lutheran Church in Britain Through Four Centuries of History*.

13. "This estimate of the threefold order as not prescribed by Holy Scripture and yet desirable for unity is a position members of the Church of England will welcome. It is in line with the reflections of the Doctrine Commission of 1938" (*Churches Respond*, III:53).

14. Church of England's Response: "What is important is the implication that both episcopal and non-episcopal churches are lacking unless their faithfulness to the apostolic tradition in life and teaching is linked to a common sign of that faithfulness in a single ministerial succession. We consider that the Lima Text is moving in a significant direction and in line with what Anglicans will understand as the faith of the Church through the ages" (Ibid., 56).

15. Ibid., 48.

while the generally irenic response of the Orthodox Church in America energetically objected at that point).[16] AC VII, as we have seen, prescribes no formalities, but concentrates entirely on the substantive requirement that Christ's holy Gospel and sacraments be purely taught and rightly administered, and this unanimously. What this means concretely is spelt out in the rest of the Augsburg Confession, and then in the whole Book of Concord, and may indeed have to be spelt out still further in the future. In this sense the "Lutheran platform" is undoubtedly narrower and more rigorous than the Anglican. The true unity of the church, however, demands that we be narrow where the Gospel is narrow and broad where the Gospel is broad. It is not a virtue either to exceed or to fall short of the Gospel.

This means that when modern Lutherans enter into negotiations about "mutual recognition of ministries," they thereby accept alien premises and adopt pseudo-problems. The Lutheran church has never denied the "validity" of the ministries of the historic Trinitarian churches, the Roman Catholic, Eastern Orthodox, and Reformed. On the contrary—and unlike the proselytizing sectarians—confessional Lutherans acknowledge such ministries as valid though heterodox, do not re-ordain their incumbents when they turn to the service of the orthodox faith and church, and do not sneak about among parishioners behind the backs of their rightful clergy. Nor does the Lutheran church question the validity of the holy means of grace administered in other Trinitarian churches, except that the Zwingli-Calvinist churches, which reject the bodily presence of Christ in the sacrament, are regarded as having "only bread and wine, for they do not also have the Word and instituted ordinance of God but have perverted and changed it according to their own imagination."[17]

The Roman Catholic and Eastern Orthodox churches, on the other hand, think of the "historic episcopate" as integral to a valid ministry, and of the Eucharist in particular as dependent on the validity of the celebrant's ministry. Anglicanism follows this general pattern, but less rigorously. While the Faith and Order "Lima Text" certainly embodies and reflects other influences besides the Anglican, its ecumenical significance for confessional Lutherans is most directly apparent by way of the Anglican/Lutheran contrast. Over a decade before Lima, G. Wingren, the author of several

16. Ibid., 19–20.
17. FC SD VII, 32. Tappert, 575.

deservedly acclaimed publications, compared the Anglican and the confessionally Lutheran ecumenical "platforms," and advanced the astounding thesis that both are equally contrary to AC VII![18]

The argument amounts to the claim, attributed to Wingren's fellow-Swede, A. Nygren, that "the historically transmitted bishop's office and the historically transmitted confessional writings both" are "human traditions," uniformity in which is "not necessary" according to AC VII. In clinging to their respective traditions, both confessional Lutherans and Anglicans belong to the forces which "are blocking the striving for unity." Indeed, according to Wingren, "Lutheran confessionalism" represents "the greatest obstacle to a forceful application of that openness which is the core of AC VII and its short, but far-seeing sentences about the unity of the church."

To see the creeds and confessions of the orthodox church as human "ceremonies" rather than as biblical substance, is theologically and historically indefensible. The reader is reminded only of Luther's incomparably high estimation of "doctrine" and of its absolute primacy.[19] Wingren seeks to bolster his case by highly selective and so misleading citations from the Formula of Concord. His attempt to refine a divinely uniting set of "actual" Gospel functions free of the divisive dross of man-made confessional formulations (="ceremonies"), avenges itself by turning, ironically, into this ultimate formalism: the mere reading of the text "validates" the sermon as evangelical! This melt-down of the very idea of doctrine and confession is supposed to lay bare the neglected but potentially revolutionary "ecumenical capital" of AC VII.

Wingren does, however, draw attention to an ecumenical problem which, as he rightly sees, lies deeper even than the traditional divisions among the churches. He means the conflict between the historical-critical type of biblical scholarship and what he chooses to call "fundamentalism." Yet this radical division over Holy Scripture—which, as Wingren does not say, is really about Christ

18. G. Wingren, *"Ein ungenütztes oekumenisches Kapital," Evangelische Kommentare,* 701–706. This impossible demotion of the Confessions to the status of "human ceremonies" is echoed in E.W. Gritsch and R. W. Jenson, *Lutheranism,* 133, 174, *passim,* and in D. G. Trumper's debunking of "doctrine" and especially of "theological formulations," in "The Catholicity of the Augsburg Confession: CA VII and FC X on the Grounds for the Unity of the Church," 12,14,16,19.

19. Buchrucker, *op. cit.*

and the truth of the Incarnation[20]—has generally not disrupted church fellowship. So the "Lutheran fundamentalist" is not in altar fellowship with his Reformed fellow-fundamentalist, with whom he cooperates in various ways. Instead, he practices altar fellowship with a demythologizing, Bultmann-oriented "fellow-Lutheran," whom he otherwise vigorously combats! Wingren is quite right to detect here "a dash of inner inauthenticity."

Wingren holds that the conflict over Scripture is "a dispute *in* the church, it is not church-divisive, but it surpasses older conflicts, being deeper than they." The solution, it seems, is to drop all demands for doctrinal agreement beyond the level of local pulpits and altars, where rote repetition of preaching texts and words of institution "validates" what are alleged to be the actually functioning Gospel and sacraments. Any "ecumenical capital" discoverable by such means in the Augsburg Confession has about it all the genuineness of Joseph Smith's fabled plates of gold.

From Union Liturgy (1817) to Leuenberg (1973) and the Lutheran World Federation's "Reconciled Diversity" (1977)

Had the crypto-Calvinists in 16th century Wittenberg succeeded, there would have been no Formula of Concord. This would have meant the fudging of Lutheran/Calvinist differences— and so the surrender of the Sacrament of the Altar, and the end of the Church of the Unaltered Augsburg Confession, at least in the land of the Reformation. What stealth had failed to achieve in Saxony, brute force accomplished two and a half centuries later in the Prussian Union. The fateful consequences of this calamity have continued to expand, like concentric shock-waves, and today all but engulf world Lutheranism.

The joint Lutheran-Reformed Communion Service arranged by Frederick William III of Prussia for October 31, 1817, was not as widely imitated as the king had hoped. There followed the royal union liturgy of 1821, which replaced the Lutheran distribution formula, "Take, eat, this is the true body of Christ. . .," with biblically camouflaged weasel-words: "Take, eat. Our Lord Christ said, 'This is my body'. . ." It was left to each communicant's own imagination or religious preference to decide what Our Lord Christ might have meant by His words. In this way the Reformed

20. For an unusually candid discussion of what is involved, see T. Sheehan, *The First Coming*.

king of a largely Lutheran populace hoped to bridge the confessional gap between the two churches and to unite them into one. When persuasion failed, the king resorted to stronger measures, and finally to outright persecution against the conscientious Lutherans in his realm. Thousands of the latter left ultimately for America and Australia, where they founded confessional churches.

The irreducible essence of the Prussian Union became very clear in the 1834 "order-in-cabinet," which tried to pacify the opposition with assurances of moderation:

> The Union intends and means no surrender of the confessions of faith [in force] heretofore, nor was the authority which the confessional writings of both evangelical confessions have had till now voided by it. Entry into [the Union]merely expresses the spirit of moderation and mildness, which will no longer allow the difference in particular points of doctrine of the other confession as grounds for the refusal to [that confession] of external churchly fellowship.[21]

Peter Brunner regarded this government proclamation as a full retreat from the earlier (1817) demand for complete confessional amalgamation in favor of a "confederative" structure, which would preserve the respective confessions. It is clear, however, that even the 1834 document envisaged not a purely external administrative relationship but actual church fellowship across confessional boundaries. Open rejection of the orthodox confession proved church-politically counter-productive. The Union achieved its purpose by pretending that both sets of confessions would remain intact, and then sidetracking them so that they could not control church-fellowship. Thereby the Lutheran confession at any rate has been annulled just as surely as if it had been formally repudiated. A confession which is no longer a binding—and therefore church-divisive—proclamation of evangelical truth is not a confession in the sense of the New Testament or of the Book of Concord. One cannot honestly subscribe to the Book of

21. *Lutherisches Bekenntnis in der Union. Festgabe für D. Peter Brunner*, 105. Despite clear premises, some of Brunner's argumentation is hazy and halting, justifying a certain amount of pulpit and altar fellowship with the Reformed after all (pp. 110 ff.). The illusions fostered by question-begging definitions of "federation" are disallowed by a clear-headed, churchly consistency: "Federation excludes every *communicatio in sacris*, thus pulpit and altar fellowship. The question when and under what circumstances joint prayer is possible cannot be answered with certainty. Only this can be said, that the solemn prayer of the church's liturgy as the prayer of the Body of Christ belongs from time immemorial to the *communicatio in sacris*, as is shown in the custom of the ancient church, in which this prayer was held in connection with the Eucharist behind closed doors, for which Mt. 6:6 was invoked. The purpose of federation is first of all *cooperatio in externis*" (H. Sasse, *In Statu Confessionis*, II:240).

Concord and then grant equal rights in the church to opinions which the Book of Concord solemnly rejects as heretical. By neutralizing and relativizing the Lutheran Confession the Union effectively neutered the Lutheran Church in the territories affected and turned it into a harmless school of thought, one current among others in the same stream. Confessional differences, over which ordinary believers had once risked life and limb and endured exile, now became "technical details" to be disposed of to their own satisfaction by professorial and church-political elites. That certainly spelt the end of confessing as Luther had understood it.

The shock of the Prussian and other, similar unions galvanized serious Lutherans both in Europe and in the New World into a quest for confessional renewal and solidarity. Still, "more than half of Germany's Lutherans were siphoned off into territorial 'Union' churches."[22] This proportion proved fateful, at first in Germany and later world-wide. It created a "gravitational field" which favored the Union. In the long term this "weak force" prevailed over the "strong" confessional forces which operated only spasmodically and then under the constraints of "responsible churchmanship"—a euphemism for sentimentality and pragmatism.

A posture of resolute confessional opposition[23] might have "quarantined" and—given the right circumstances—ultimately dismantled the Union. Such circumstances, favorable to ecclesiastical freedom of action, arose with the structural collapses in Germany in 1918 and again in 1945. Yet both times the (territorial) Lutheran churches banded together with Union churches in joint structures which increasingly legitimized the Union. There is little doubt that considerations of national solidarity played their part.

It is customary to see the fatal flaw of the German Evangelical Church (DEK) of 1933, with "Imperial Bishop" Müller at its head, in its ties to the Nazi regime. This, however, is to measure churchly entities with a secular, political yardstick. H. Sasse saw past the surface to the heart of the matter—and without benefit of several

22. E. Clifford Nelson, *The Rise of World Lutheranism: An American Perspective*, 33–35.

23. The General Evangelical Lutheran Conference (AELK), founded in 1868 in alarm over the expansion of Prussia, with its Union Church, had not admitted Lutherans from Union churches into full membership. In 1907, when Ihmels became President, the AELK decided to admit Union Lutherans, which split the AELK. (B. Wadensjo, *Toward a World Lutheran Communion*, 17–36). Originally confessional and trans-national in intent (Wadensjo, p. 19), the AELK drifted into a more mediating course ("Ihmels' theology . . . implied an apparent deconfessionalization," Wadensjo, p. 30), and came to be buffeted by the nationalist waves of the First World War era. Ihmels' 1925 statement, "We believe in the cause of Germany, Christianity, and the Reformation" (Wadensjo, p. 81), was actually mild, though, compared to some of the religious war hysteria on the other side (Wadensjo, pp. 53–55).

decades' hindsight—when he declared in 1933 that the DEK was in fact the extension of the Union to the whole of Germany.[24] All the territorial Lutheran, Reformed, and Union churches had become signatories to the DEK's constitution on 11 July of that year. Nor, in Sasse's view, was that damage undone by the famous Barmen Synod and Declaration of 1934. On the contrary, Barmen had blithely taken over the basic constitutional provisions of the DEK, which implied the equal value of "the confessions of the Reformation" as bearers of "the Gospel of Jesus Christ." Indeed, Karl Barth, the leading spirit of Barmen, had himself declared that he took the Lutheran-Reformed differences "seriously," but that this conflict must be subordinated to the more pressing battle about the very First Commandment. The historic confessional difference must therefore "become a still serious, but no longer separating, no longer church-divisive contrast of the theological *school*."[25] That of course was just what the Union was all about: "The decisive principle on which the Prussian Union Church was based had been the conviction that there was no real difference between the Lutherans and the Reformed. They were both considered to be parts of the same German Evangelical Church."[26] Let Sasse describe the next step in the escalating drama:

> Then came the day when Hitler's thousand-year *Reich* came to an end. It was the last occasion when the Lutheran bishops in Germany might have confessed with their deeds. They missed also this opportunity, and their churches were swallowed up in the new union called the Evangelical Church in Germany (*Evangelische Kirche in Deutschland [EKiD]*). In Eisenach, at the foot of the Wartburg, the Lutheran Church in Germany was buried in 1948. Löhe's nightmare of the Lutheran Church being buried by its own pastors became a reality.[27]

When E. Clifford Nelson calls Sasse's words "biblically prophetic and evangelically confessional" as well as "prescient,"[28] the reference is not to any of the above, but only to Sasse's brave attack on the Nazi platform's religious plank. In keeping with its ecumenical-triumphalist perspective, Nelson's account concen-

---

24. H. Sasse, *In Statu Confessionis*, I:265.
25. Ibid I:281, 273.
26. Wadensjo, op. cit., 32.
27. H. Sasse, *We Confess the Church*, 59. See also his 1948 paper, "*Das Ende der lutherischen Landeskirchen Deutschlands*," *In Statu Confessionis*, I:303–308.
28. E. Clifford Nelson, *The Rise of World Lutheranism*, 314–315.

trates on the anti-Nazi "church struggle," and spares its readers the trouble of coping with Sasse, the anti-Union prophet.[29]

Sasse's prophetic perception of the post-War Evangelical Church in Germany (EKD) as the extension of the Prussian Union to the whole of Germany has been fully vindicated by the formal declaration of mutual pulpit and altar fellowship in the Leuenberg Concord of 1973. This document finally provided a semblance of theoretical justification for the *de facto* Lutheran-Reformed-Union fellowship within the EKD.[30] The projected scope of the Leuenberg Concord was not of course simply Germany but the whole of Europe. Not to be overlooked is the major part played in these proceedings by the Lutheran World Federation's Geneva office and its Institute for Ecumenical Research in Strasbourg, the initial impetus having come from the WCC's Secretariat of Faith and Order.[31]

Leuenberg was clearly a product of church-political urgencies, not of rigorous theological reflection. Or perhaps one should say that the demand for union and the loss of clear confessional contours had a common theoretical source: the historical-critical attitude to Holy Scripture. That approach relentlessly levels confessional differences, simply because it relativizes and devastates all theological content. Not surprisingly then, joint commitment to

29. Nelson's second-hand treatment of Sasse's objections to Barmen (p. 332) is totally inadequate. While maintaining a certain journalistic "even-handedness," Nelson is clearly impatient with what he calls "Sasse's defensive confessionalism." For a posthumously published review by Sasse of E. Clifford Nelson, ed., *The Lutherans in North America* (1976) see *Lutheran Theological Journal* (August, 1976), 57-61.

30. The immense complexities involved in the ecclesiastical reconstruction after 1945 may be gathered from H. Brunotte, *Bekenntnis und Kirchenverfassung*, 98–148. Brunotte rejects Sasse's critique of Barmen, but himself shows that theologically Barmen was a muddle (pp. 149–175). As one of the chief architects of EKD's constitution, Brunotte of course defends his handiwork. He also describes the tenacity with which the Lutherans in 1948 resisted the other side's demand for a constitutional provision for full inter-communion within EKD. They had to settle in the event for what amounted to limited inter-communion. No one can doubt the sincerity of these men in resisting overt union, or their genuine agonies of soul as they acquiesced in lesser evils in order, as they thought, to spare their churches greater ones. Yet with the benefit of hindsight one cannot avoid a certain impression of temporizing and ineffectual hand-wringing, of tactical cavilling and strategic retreat. Brunotte's own vacillation about "church" and "federation"—EKD was supposed to be a mere federation, but called itself a church—reflects a basic fuzziness which could not support long-term resistance to the enormous pressures for the Union. Brunotte defends EKD as *more* than a mere external federation—which latter might be possible "even with the free churches and with the Roman Catholic church" (p.145)—on the grounds of a special relationship between German Lutheran and Reformed churches, said to be closer than that between any other two "denominations" (143–149, 159)! Given such conceptions, Leuenberg and the ultimate victory of the Union are virtually predestinated.

31. Marc Lienhard, *Lutherisch-reformierte Kirchengemeinschaft heute*, 32. *Ecumenical Relations of the Lutheran World Federation*, 50, 57.

historical criticism was a decisive element in the Leuenberg "breakthrough."[32] However, as Marc Lienhard has frankly pointed out, historical criticism also raised new problems of its own, "as became apparent for instance at Arnoldshain" [a precursor of Leuenberg], "where it was no longer possible to connect the institution of the Supper with the night in which he was betrayed."[33] Lienhard also informs us that by "the collapse of traditional thought-forms"[34] Leuenberg meant "the two-natures doctrine and the doctrine of the communication of attributes."[35]

One can of course put a pretty face on Leuenberg and talk about how the "Lutheran concern" was met there even without the traditional language.[36] It is more realistic and therefore more honest to conclude with the LWF's Harding Meyer, that the acceptance of Leuenberg signals a major change in "Lutheran confessionality."[37] Just how radical a debunking of the very nature of doctrinal confession is involved, becomes clear in Helsinki University Prof. T. Mannermaa's "historical-critical" study, which for the first time traced the real theological pedigree of the Leuenberg text.[38] The

32. The 1971 text referred to "historical-critical Scripture-research," which became the innocuous "development of Scripture-research" in the final version of 1973.

33. Lienhard, op. cit., 54.

34. So the 1971 text. This became the "historically conditioned nature of received thought-forms" in 1973 (# 22).

35. Lienhard, op.cit., 107.

36. *Ecumenical Relations of the Lutheran World Federation*, 14–16. This Report, however, after stressing that "the LWF welcomes" local efforts towards church union, "is ready to support its member churches in such negotiations," and urges upon them "the importance of not bypassing fundamental theological problems," states pointedly: "But the LWF has also found it necessary in this context to stress that a rigid adherence to the Lutheran tradition and fellowship can complicate and retard local union efforts" (3).

37. H. Meyer, "The LWF and its Role in the Ecumenical Movement," 30. Leuenberg "can only mean that both churches no longer hold to the same position on certain points which had for a long time been considered important" (28). This means also that the Altered Augsburg Confession of 1540 "can be considered again as a legitimate possibility of Lutheran understanding of the eucharist," as opposed to "the previous Lutheran insistence on the Unaltered Augsburg Confession"(29)!

38. T. Mannermaa, *Von Preussen Nach Leuenberg*. The author traces the background and development of the *theological method* that resulted in the Leuenberg formula. As his very title indicates, he rightly situates Leuenberg within the context of the Union. In 1967 talks resumed among the Lutheran, Reformed, and Union churches of the German EKiD, as the latter was evolving irresistibly towards full and official church-hood. (Wölber: "The sociological fate of German Protestantism is the pragmatic Union. . .," p. 52). A sea-change occurred, Mannermaa shows, when the theological leadership of the Lutheran party fell to W. Lohff. In a programmatic essay Lohff pointed out that despite the incredible efforts devoted to the inter-confessional talks for nearly 30 years, hardly any real progress could be registered. He also noted that the only consistent line in these talks had been Werner Elert's insistence on real confessional unity, that is, express consensus in doctrine, as precondition for church fellowship. Lohff's conclusion, which formed the premise of his whole subsequent approach: "Inter-confessional conversations are pointless, if they want to take up

whole thing must also be seen in connection with the ecumenical program of "Reconciled Diversity," as promoted by the Lutheran World Federation, to which we now turn our attention. The Lutheran World Federation was founded in Lund in 1947,[39] one year before the formation of the World Council of Churches. Its predecessor, the Lutheran World Convention (1923), had been intended, at least by its American and German organizers, as a selective gathering of confessionally-minded, rather than liberal and unionistic forces.[40] The spirit of Lund, in 1947, was very different. The difference was due, among other factors, to the necessary concentration on the enormous relief problems in the aftermath of World War II, but also to the official participation of the established European churches as such, with their "open" university theology.[41]

From the very beginning the LWF was troubled by the problem of its own nature. Was it a churchly fellowship, or was it purely a forum or conference for external co-operation and for the pursuit of common interests, such as theological discussions?[42] The question was pressed by the United Evangelical Lutheran Church of Australia (UELCA), which belonged to the LWF, but was engaged in merger negotiations with the Evangelical Lutheran Church of Australia (ELCA). The latter church shared the Missouri Synod's objection to the LWF as in fact involving a "union in spiritual matters" without doctrinal unity.[43]

---

again the doctrinal disputes of Reformation times in order to decide them" (55). The solution is to be found in a distinction between the "ground" of fellowship—the Augsburg Confession's "it is enough"—and its "formulation" (*Ausgestaltung*) or expression—the AC's "it is not necessary" (64). "Doctrine" and "confession" here tend to slide down the slippery slopes of mere "expression," leaving behind a content-free "Gospel" as "ground" of fellowship. The spirit is akin to that of the fluttery Barthian "Word-theology," and is reminiscent of H. J. Iwand's remark: "Better with the Gospel among enthusiasts, than let the Gospel become dependent on Confessional writings" (160). The above can only convey a few brief glimpses of the labyrinthine turns of argument painstakingly pursued by Mannermaa. See also U. Asendorf and F.W. Künneth, eds., *Von der wahren Einheit der Kirche* and *Leuenberg—Konkordie oder Diskordie?*

39. B. Wadensjo, *Toward a World Lutheran Communion*, tells the pre-history up to 1929, and E. C. Nelson, *The Rise of World Lutheranism: An American Perspective* (Philadelphia, 1982), describes events up to and including Lund, 1947.

40. Wadensjo, op. cit., 134ff.,165ff.

41. Wadensjo repeatedly stresses the conflict between American confessionalism and the cultural "openness" (read: secularization) represented by the established churches of Europe and their university theology. Given the organizational trends of developing "world Lutheranism," the scales almost inevitably tipped in favor of "openness"—a development hastened no doubt by the towering presence and influence of Sweden's Archbishop Söderblom.

42. The question had troubled already the Lutheran World Convention, since especially the Iowa and Ohio Synods had qualms about anything more than a free conference. Even "federation" was too strong at that time (Nelson, *The Rise*, 219ff., 249, 253, 257, 260–261, passim).

43. *LWF Proceedings*, 1957 (Minneapolis), 159.

The issues raised by the Australian church went "to the very heart of the nature of a federation and particularly the nature of the L.W.F."[44] The next LWF Assembly in Helsinki (1963) was torn in opposite directions on this point. On the one hand, expert opinions both in theology and in "church-law" had made it crystal clear that the LWF was theologically already a church, and was becoming more so also organizationally.[45] Moreover, in the lecture which received by far the most tumultuous and prolonged applause of any in Helsinki, E. C. Nelson (ALC) argued that the various Lutheran churches of the world by virtue of their common confession made up a "Lutheran World Church," and should simply "*declare* themselves to be in fellowship," such a declaration being "long over-due."[46] On the other hand, "the church-political motive of facilitating a hoped for membership of the Lutheran Church—Missouri Synod in the LWF influenced the whole debate" at Helsinki.[47] The result was a down-playing of the LWF's churchly nature, and the adoption of minor constitutional amendments designed to stress the federative, instrumental nature of the LWF. Such church-political dissimulation, or "prudential concern," as Nelson's Helsinki essay described it more elegantly, had evidently been a policy of long standing:

> No doubt the leaders of the Lutheran World Convention and the Lutheran World Federation felt they were acting wisely in making disclaimers of intentions to being or becoming "a church" in a constitutional sense. But, that organized world Lutheranism was an expression of the *ekklesia* had already been recognized (Jorgensen: "It is a Church"). Nevertheless, a prudential concern dictated then that

44. Idem.

45. See P. Brunner, "The Lutheran World Federation as an Ecclesiological Problem," 237–256, and various responses in the same number of *Lutheran World* [Dec. 1960]. Also S. Grundmann, "An Opinion regarding the Study Document of the Commission on Theology," and H. Liermann, "The Legal Nature and Constitution of the LWF" [April 1964] 172–185, and 185–200, respectively. Amid the general agreement among the Germans, Liermann's comments are particularly striking: The LWF "represents a type of church answering to the demands of the modern world, and with a quite new character, but rich in promise for the future. . . [The time of church empires] has been replaced by a period of the formation of church commonwealths, which permit the emergence of world churches of a new sort. Among these is the Lutheran World Federation" (199–200). The first of the three "specialists in church law, or church polity" whose opinions had been requested by the LWF's Executive Secretary, was C. Bergendoff of the U.S.A. His very brief paper (201–203) pleaded for constitutional changes in the interests of accomodating the Missouri Synod and its sister churches. However, his general conclusion and argumentation seemed naive *vis-a-vis* those of Grundmann and Liermann: "The simple fact that [LWF's] nature is defined as a 'free association of Lutheran Churches' prevents it from being a church."

46. "The One Church and the Lutheran Churches," 284–287.

47. G. Gassmann, "The Self-Understanding of the Lutheran World Federation." 9. On the basis of the German original we have changed "churches' political" to "church-political."

> haste be made slowly, in order to dissipate anxieties and to avoid shattering by precipitous action what had already been achieved.[48]

In the event the tactical retreat proved in vain. The Missouri Synod did not join the LWF, and the Australian UELCA was actually obliged to withdraw from the LWF for the sake of church fellowship (1965) and amalgamation (1966) with the ELCA into the Lutheran Church of Australia (LCA). The LCA's Document of Union spelt out the basic "ecclesiological problem" with exemplary clarity: "Can a federation with a specific doctrinal basis act in essential church work (*in sacris*) on behalf of its member Churches without itself assuming the character of Church in the New Testament sense?"

This way of putting the matter cuts through the confused shadow-boxing about whether or not the LWF is a "superchurch." To define "church" in terms of power to compel or chains of command is to follow Roman Catholic or possibly Anglican models. For Lutherans it should be clear that the LWF need not be a "superchurch" in order to be a church. In fact the anti-superchurch constitutional provision of 1963—that the LWF, as "agent" of its member churches, "shall not exercise churchly functions on its own authority"—actually documents the LWF's churchly nature: "For the first time in the history of the Federation the Constitution clearly admits that the Federation exercises churchly functions."[49]

On the basis of the biblical and confessional teaching about church-fellowship one can only agree that "wherever continued co-operation in the preaching of the Gospel and the administration of the Sacraments and worship exists, there we have a witness to the world of unity in the faith and a profession of church fellowship."[50] This necessarily means also that whether something is "church" or not depends not on what it calls itself or on assorted

48. LWF *Proceedings*, 1963 (Helsinki), 285.

49. S. Hebart in "Helsinki and the Nature of the LWF—Documents," 210.

50. Lutheran Church of Australia, *Document of Union*, 7, or *Theses of Agreement*, V, 28. Originally the sentence had included the word "normally," which prepared the way for the next statement: "8. We recognize, however, that such co-operation in periods of emergency, and sporadic co-operation in various aspects of the work of the Church, are not necessarily a witness to a unity in faith." This was unacceptable. The final version dropped "normally," and replaced the original sentence in (8), as well as an equally unacceptable interim version, with this: "8. There are, however, forms of co-operation between Churches not in church-fellowship that are not necessarily a witness to unity in faith." Thereby genuine, orthodox agreement had been formulated on the doctrine of church fellowship. Had he carefully attended to these facts, Pastor G. L. Winter, of a small break-away group in Australia, could have spared himself and his readers the intemperate talk about "complete capitulation under pressure," and his general misconceptions of these events in *How Are The Mighty Fallen: A History of the Events Leading to the Downfall of the ELCA and Formation of the ELCR*, 129–139.

legal formalities, but on what it actually does. If it does what only the church can do then it thereby lays claim to being church in the New Testament sense. To argue, "It is not a church because it is a federation," is rather like saying, "This is not money because it is paper." The terms simply move on different semantic tracks. "Church" says something theological, while "federation" only specifies an organizational form. There is no reason why a church (e.g. a Lutheran church independent of the state) cannot be organized in the shape of a federation of congregations, indeed that is often the case. For Lutherans, only realities, not formalities, decide whether something is or is not church.

Already at Helsinki, it was perceived to be a shocking anomaly for any member-church of the LWF to refuse church fellowship to any other member. The move to ask member churches in that situation "to indicate their reasons,"[51] was aimed particularly at the ALC, which had for church-political reasons (fellowship prospects with Missouri) not declared fellowship with the LCA, although such fellowship was practiced "without restraint."[52] In preparation for the next Assembly (Evian, 1970), E.C. Nelson urged that it was time "not merely to declare fellowship but to declare that the LWF is itself an ecclesiological reality. It makes no pretension to being a 'super-church' (after all what and where is a 'super-church'?), but simply declares itself to be the Lutheran *church* on an international level."[53] The trend culminated at the 1984 Assembly, which entrenched in the LWF's constitution the provision: "The member churches of the Lutheran World Federation understand themselves to be in pulpit and altar fellowship with each other."[54] Despite the absence of the Missouri Synod and a few others, the LWF now appears before the world as the "Lutheran Communion." Its members "have officially spoken of themselves as Lutheran communion and of the LWF as an expression and instrument of their communion. So the churches *are* a communion and are on the way *toward* ever fuller and deeper realization of what that means."[55]

---

51. LWF *Proceedings*, 1963 (Helsinki), 393.

52. ". . . it was apparent that [the resolution] was aimed solely at the ALC. . . . Because of [Missouri's] fears we had deferred declaring official fellowship with the LCA, but meanwhile practiced it without restraint" (F. Schiotz, "Observations on Parts of Dr. Nelson's *Lutheranism in North America, 1914–1970*," 165–166).

53. Editorial, *Lutheran World*, XV, 4 (1968), 323.

54. LWF *Proceedings*, 1984 (Budapest), 264.

55. E.L.Brand, "Toward a Lutheran Communion," 90.

The reason always cited in support of the increasingly insistent demands for unrestricted church-fellowship within the LWF has been the common acknowledgement, in the LWF's constitution, of the same Lutheran Confessions. The argument runs: *Major*: Wherever there is confessional agreement (pure Gospel and sacraments) altar and pulpit fellowship must be granted, according to AC VII. *Minor*: All LWF member churches are in confessional agreement by virtue of their subscription to the confessional paragraph of the LWF's constitution. *Conclusion*: Therefore all LWF member churches must grant each other altar and pulpit fellowship. The argument is perfectly valid, and would be sound, if both premises were true. No Lutheran should of course dream of denying the major premise. It is the minor premise which is patently false. "Confessional agreement" is here reduced to a church-political fiction made up from threadbare constitutional formalities. No amount of harping on the major premise can hide the impossibility of the minor. And without the minor premise the conclusion fails.

A perfect case in point is Brand's significant and wide-ranging essay mentioned above. It repeatedly invokes, almost as an incantation, "the *cantus firmus*: confessional communion is ecclesial communion."[56] Yet Brand expressly denies that this "confessional communion" means "correct theology" or "detailed doctrinal or theological agreement." That, according to Brand, would be "destructive of ecclesial communion both confessionally and ecumenically." Brand opposes his and the LWF's "ecclesiological" approach to the "theological" one of the Missouri Synod, which demands agreement in doctrine and therefore apparently qualifies for Vajta's epithet of "unionism neurosis."[57] The General Synod—ULCA—LCA line is commended for simply taking for granted agreement and fellowship with all bodies "calling themselves Evangelical Lutheran and subscribing to the Confessions," and for being "less exclusivistic" about fellowship with Reformed sects. Indeed, argues Brand, "communion not only encompasses the Lutheran churches into one fellowship; it declares that fellowship

56. Ibid., 70 and passim.

57. Ibid., 31, 78, 111n. Compare Theodore Kaftan's disdain for those who wanted a truly confessional church in Germany after World War I: "Those who could not accept [the fact of theological differences due to different temperaments] were referred to the Missouri Synod which was said to represent a Roman Catholic [!] form of Lutheranism. Kaftan drew the line very sharply at the Missouri Synod: 'Here, however, it is not a case of theological differences but of different religions' " (Wadensjo, *Toward a World Lutheran Communion*, 76). So then every shade of opinion has a right to the Lutheran name—except such as insist on the Lutheran Confessions!

open fundamentally to all Christian communities."[58] To claim warrants for such notions of "confessional communion" in the Augsburg Confession or the Book of Concord is to engage in fantasy.

In 1953 the Executive Committee of the fledgling LWF stated that the Federation "while having a doctrinal basis, has as such no doctrine of its own."[59] If so, this would have provided instant liberation from the confessional commitments of the LWF's constitution.[60] Yet, as P. Brunner pointed out later, the LWF was constantly having to teach, or to take doctrinal decisions, for instance in ruling on the confessional eligibility of churches applying for membership.[61] In admitting the Evangelical Church of Pomerania, for instance, which is in church fellowship with Union and thus also with Reformed churches (this prior to Leuenberg), the LWF by that very act declared recognition of its doctrinal basis compatible with church fellowship with Union churches.[62] This practical surrender of the Confessions, moreover is not exceptional, but has long been endemic.[63] It is not a question of anyone's personal

58. Ibid., 28, 30, 72, 95n, 96n.

59. U. Duchrow, *Conflict Over the Ecumenical Movement*, 248.

60. In an Open Letter to LWF President H. Lilje, Prof. W. M. Oesch pointed out that in this way the LWF had "circumvented the confessional question with modern elegance," the upshot being that the LWF wanted credit for honoring the Confessions, while refusing to take any responsibility for actual doctrine. *Lutherischer Rundblick*, June 1956, 34–39.

61. "Thus there can be no question that the World Federation as such not only has a doctrinal basis, but also actually teaches. . . When it teaches it is undoubtedly acting as a church" (P. Brunner, "The Lutheran World Federation as an Ecclesiological Problem," 245).

62. LWF "has therewith decided that church fellowship with Union churches does not annul the fact of recognition of the doctrinal basis of the World Federation. By the simple fact of receiving this church the World Federation made this undoubtedly far-reaching decision. . . And the decision is this: 'It is possible for a church to recognize the doctrinal basis of the World Federation and still remain in church fellowship with Union churches' " (Ibid., 247).

63. "The Lutheran territorial churches of Germany have been dissolved into the 'Evangelical Church in Germany,' whose Council has just decided that in every member church, all members of the EKiD, without regard to their Confession, must be admitted to the Lord's Supper. The Churches of Sweden and Finland are in intercommunion with the Church of England. . . For good measure the Church of Sweden has now solemnly introduced intercommunion with the Church of Scotland, which is practiced also by Denmark and Norway. How all this works out in the formerly Lutheran mission fields, above all in Africa and India, is well known. The Church of the Palatinate has solemnly accepted intercommunion with the Congregational Union of England and Wales and the related American sects, but demands that all German Lutherans moving into the Palatinate communicate at the Reformed Communion Table of the Church of the Palatinate. In Holland, altar fellowship between the Lutheran and the Reformed territorial churches has been solemnly confirmed. France will follow. And no one takes offence at this. The German professors go from Tübingen to Zurich, from Zurich to Göttingen, from Bonn to Erlangen, from Erlangen to Mainz. For 'the Confessional Age is over,' as they assure us. That their students must some day swear an Ordination vow does not interest them" (H. Sasse, *In Statu Confessionis*, II:268).

"sincerity," but of facing up to the plain fact that most of these churches have long ago ceased being Lutheran in the sense of doctrinal and sacramental conformity to the Book of Concord.

The last remnants of Confessional constraints on church union and fellowship were officially thrown to the winds in 1977 with the endorsement[64] of the notion of "reconciled diversity." This formula stands for "genuine church fellowship" among the various churches, which at the same time grants "the legitimacy of the confessional differences and therefore the need to preserve them."[65] The notion of unity in "reconciled diversity" —sometimes regarded as an LWF counter to the WCC's goal of "conciliar fellowship"—actually arose out of consultations between the WCC and "World Confessional Families," initiated by Faith and Order.[66] Given the radical relativism which regards all confessions as equally legitimate,[67] why bother about them at all? We glimpse here that fundamental "untruthfulness" which is the "sickness at the heart of the Lutheran World Federation," reducing even the

---

64. Taking up an uncommonly cautious egg-walking—not to say levitating—posture, the Assembly did not wish to present "reconciled diversity" as "a detailed and final description of the goal. . . Nor could it be said that, at this present juncture, when various concepts of unity are being considered, the LWF has officially adopted this concept of unity." Yet it officially adopted the document promoting "reconciled diversity" and stating: ". . . we believe that at the present stage of the ecumenical movement the following deliberations on 'reconciled diversity' could function as guiding principles; and adopt the following statement as guidelines for the future ecumenical efforts of the Federation" (LWF *Proceedings*, 1977 [Dar-es-Salaam], 173-174).

65. The LWF's 1984 statement on "The Unity We Seek" described this further as a "communion in the common and, at the same time, multiform confession of one and the same apostolic faith. . . In recognizing these diversities as expressions of the one apostolic faith and the one catholic church, traditions are changed, antagonisms overcome, and mutual condemnations lifted. The diversities are reconciled. . ." (LWF *Proceedings*, 1984 [Budapest], 175).

66. G. Gassmann, "The Unity of the Church," 8–9. Gassmann and Meyer labor to show that "reconciled diversity" and "conciliar fellowship" are complementary, not contradictory or competitive. The 1984 LWF Assembly took the same view (*Proceedings*, 211–220).

67. Behind all the lip-service enshrined in "confessional paragraphs" on patient paper, the reality is this: "Lutheran identity and Lutheran fellowship cannot, however, be defined always and for ever simply by reference to the letter of the traditional confessions. . . This is a necessary consequence of the contingent character of the traditional confessions . . . It points to something which, while appearing in the Lutheran confessions, is not simply identical with their formulations and literal content. To maintain 'substantial agreement' with the Lutheran confession . . . means, therefore, gratefully to endorse the historical form of this confession while at the same time using it in Christian freedom for witnessing and confessing responsibly in the historical context in which God has placed us. . . The role of the historical confessional documents here is that of a theological introduction, not that of a legalistic norm" (*Ecumenical Relations of the Lutheran World Federation*, 32–33). What this can mean even for the very central core of the Confessions is best seen quite concretely in something like the candid group discussion report from Helsinki, where it proved impossible for "world Lutheranism" to agree on a statement on justification: "Is the doctrine of

Confessions to "a tool of church politics."[68] Absent any serious belief in the objective truth of some confessions as distinct from others, "reconciled diversity" may plausibly be taken as "reconciled tribalism," and as a scheme to insure bureaucratic self-perpetuation for the LWF and other "World Confessional Families."[69]

In sum, the LWF's "reconciled diversity" is the ultimate triumph of the Prussian Union—this time world-wide, and embracing not only the Reformed churches, but also the Roman Catholic.[70] All the old confessions may be kept, but they are no longer to be regarded as divisive. Instead of being the sentinel and boundary-marker of evangelical truth, and therefore of pulpit and altar fellowship, the Book of Concord has become one dear old tribal totem among others. The former confessional churches are dissolved, or to be dissolved, into confessional movements[71] or schools of thought within one and the same church and fellow-

---

justification still crucial as the *articulus stantis aut cadentis ecclesiae*? Yes, provided it is understood, not just forensically [!], but inclusively as the renewal [!] of the whole man. Yet it is not the doctrine which is crucial, but that for which the doctrine is the time-limited expression. The great need is for expressing the doctrine in relevant terms. The doctrine of justification is only *one* way of expressing the Gospel" (1963 LWF *Proceedings*, 442). The point is not of course that everyone in the LWF says this sort of thing, but that everyone is expected to put up with it by way of church-fellowship.

68. H. Sasse, *We Confess the Church*, 63.

69. So U. Duchrow, *Conflict Over the Ecumenical Movement*, 284–297. This book "exploded like a bomb in LWF circles" (E.L.Brand, *Toward a Lutheran Communion*, 59). And "what is the real difference in principle between the 'family' of the Lutheran churches and the 'families' of Anglicans, Reformed, Congregationalists, and Quakers?" (H. Sasse, *In Statu Confessionis*, II:271).

70. When the wording, "full ecclesial communion as sister churches," was challenged with reference to Roman Catholicism, G. Gassmann insisted that the phrase "expressed the exact meaning of 'reconciled diversity'" (LWF *Proceedings*, 1977, 201).

71. "Lutheranism is a confessional movement within the larger church," cites H. Meyer in "The LWF and its Role in the Ecumenical Movement," 31. The phraseology echoes the ex-Missouri Synod "AELC's" constitution, which defined "Lutheranism to be a confessional movement within the total Body of Christ rather than a denomination with institutional walls of separation." That language was in turn borrowed from the ill-fated "Mission Affirmations" of 1965, the chief author of which, M. L. Kretzmann, has officially documented their origins in a thoroughly confused and unionistic ecclesiology (LCMS *Proceedings*, 1965 [Detroit], 79–81; 113–140). The contemporary U.S. "Lutheran" cave-in to Leuenberg is documented in J. E. Andrews and J. A. Burgess, eds., *An Invitation To Action: The Lutheran-Reformed Dialogue Series III 1981–1983*. In objective effect this volume is equivalent to the following congratulatory message sent in 1845 by the General Synod (USA) to the Prussian Union—except that the latter has the advantage of more honest and straightforward language: "In most of our church principles we stand on common ground with the Union Church of Germany. The distinctive doctrines which separate the Lutheran and the Reformed Churches we do not consider essential. The tendency of the so-called Lutheran party seems to us to be behind the time. Luther's peculiar views concerning the presence of the Lord's Body in the Communion have long been abandoned by the majority of our ministers" (S.E. Ochsenford, *Documentary History of the General Council of the Evangelical Lutheran Church in North America*, 63).

ship. Behind this massive confessional relativism lies the systematic destruction of Biblical authority by means of historical-critical skepticism[72]—but that whole topic belongs to *Prolegomena*. We may conclude here that the gravitational pull of the Prussian Union, though less dramatic than stronger, more radical forces, has grown into a vast "black hole," which has by now swallowed up most of world Lutheranism.

The Point of it All: Faith or Sight?

No one can doubt that genuine benefits have flowed to Christendom also from the Ecumenical Movement. For example, no major Christian communion to-day any longer simply equates its own visible form with the one, holy, catholic and apostolic church, outside of which there is no salvation. All have been challenged to do more than repeat mechanically past positions. Old misunderstandings and misrepresentations have in many cases given way to a new sense of fairness in historical and dogmatical judgments. Practical day-to-day co-operation and friendship—"grassroots ecumenism"—have replaced ancient suspicions and hostilities, festering in so-called "non-theological factors." Millions of the world's helpless have been rescued from crisis and catastrophe by veritable angels of mercy in the form of relief workers and supplies from co-operative Christian agencies.

No one can fail to acknowledge such things with gratitude.

Yet it is in the great question of truth that the ecumenical movement has—despite promising beginnings in Faith and Order and the undoubted personal integrity of many good men and true—failed dismally and tragically. Given the devastation of biblical authority that attended the churches' general retreat before historical criticism, matters could hardly have turned out otherwise. Anyone not hypnotized by unctuous ecclesiastical cant must welcome an honest journalist's impression:

> The Church of Christ has to stagger on under the guidance of those who increasingly sympathize with, when they do not actually

---

72. E. Käsemann's essay, "The Canon of the New Testament and the Unity of the Church" argues for doctrinal diversity within the New Testament canon and hence for a corresponding diversity within the church. The argument was echoed in official U.S. Lutheran discussions. *The Function of Doctrine and Theology in Light of the Unity of the Church*, 14, 76–81, 89–93.The discounting of confessional differences as variant surface expressions of the same deeper truth is also akin to the so-called Symbolo-Fideism of A. Sabatier, who influenced Nathan Söderblom's ecumenical outlook. B. Sundkler, *Nathan Söderblom: His Life and Work*, 44–49; C. J. Curtis, *Söderblom: Ecumenical Pioneer*, 46. See also D. Hedegard, *Ecumenism and the Bible*, 240.

> countenance, every attack on its doctrines, integrity and traditional practices. By one of our time's larger ironies, ecumenicalism is triumphant just when there is nothing to be ecumenical about; the various religious bodies are likely to find it easy to join together only because, believing little, they correspondingly differ about little. I look forward to the day when an Anglican bishop in full canonicals will attend a humanist rally on the South Downs, or a Salvation Army band lead a procession of Young Atheists to lay a wreath on Karl Marx's grave in Highgate Cemetery. It cannot be long delayed, if it has not happened already.[73]

One must in the end choose between two alternatives. We may think of the "ecumenical equation" as containing two variables, "Gospel" and "Church." We can solve the equation for the one, if we know the value of the other. The ecumenical movement takes "Church" as the known, that is, as the sum total of the visible, historical church bodies. On this assumption the imperative of union is paramount, and any opposition to it is seen as thwarting "what God is doing today." Any "Gospel" calculated from this formula, i.e. the consensus of all church bureaucracies, will be just the thin sort of theological gruel familiar from Lima and Leuenberg.[74]

The other alternative is to start with the Gospel as the given, and proceed to the church from there. Where Christ is with His Gospel, there the church is also, even if only "two or three" appear to be present. But where the Gospel is contradicted, even in Christ's name, there we must register a Babylonian invasion and captivity, although millions may be cheering. The way of true ecumenicity can and must "know what the true church is, lest we be offended by the outward prestige of the false church" (FC SD XI,50). To take this way is with the Augsburg Confession to confess and serve the one church and her true unity. It is to walk by faith, not by sight.

---

73. Malcolm Muggeridge, *Jesus Rediscovered*, 38.

74. "This false ecumenicity changes the article of faith about the church into an article of sight. . . And it seeks to manufacture this unity by laboring to realize the *one* Faith, the *one* Baptism, the *one* Sacrament of the Altar as a compromise made up of various forms of faith, or different conceptions of Baptism, and of different understandings of the Holy Supper" (H. Sasse, *In Statu Confessionis*, II:244–245).

THE MINISTRY

To obtain such faith, God instituted the preaching office to give Gospel and Sacraments. Through these, as through means, he gives the Holy Spirit, who works faith, when and where he pleases, in those who hear the Gospel.

Augsburg Confession V.1–2

9

There are three major options in respect of the public ministry: (1) Roman Catholicism, Eastern Orthodoxy, and for all practical purposes Anglicanism, have traditionally treated the three-tiered hierarchy of deacons, presbyters/priests, and bishops, as divinely-instituted. This is the approach of traditionalism. (2) Calvinism seeks to restore or repristinate the allegedly God-given church-structure and offices found in the New Testament. This is biblicism. (3) The Lutheran Church, following its evangelical hermeneutic, recognizes one God-given New Testament office, which is charged with the proclamation of the Gospel and the administration of the sacraments.[1] Questions of ranking and organization then belong to the realm of Christian liberty.

To obtain an accurate "fix" on this matter it is most economical to proceed by way of three basic distinctions or contrasts: (1) priesthood and ministry, (2) the one Gospel-and-sacraments ministry or office, and auxiliary ministries or offices, and (3) the distinction of the two realms or kingdoms, which will be treated in a later section.

PRIESTHOOD AND MINISTRY

The Reformation rightly gloried in the common spiritual dignity of the whole church as the "royal priesthood" (I Pet. 2:9). It is characteristic of the New Testament that it reserves "priestly"[2]

---

1. ". . . strictly speaking only the Lutherans have a doctrine of the ministry [*Amt*, office], while at the corresponding place the Calvinists treat of ministries [offices], and the Roman Catholics and the Orthodox, as well as in their own way the Anglicans, of the hierarchy....*Lutheranism*, with its doctrine of the preaching ministry [*Predigtamt*] as 'the' office, forcefully underscores the position of the Gospel as the life-giving center of the congregation..." (E. Schott in *Die Religion in Geschichte und Gegenwart*, I:338–339).

2. Etymologically, to be sure, the English word "priest" comes from the Greek "πρε-σβύτερος." What counts, however, is that semantically "priest" and "priesthood" stand for "ἱερεύς (sacerdos)" and "ἱερατεία/ἱεράτευμα (sacerdotium)" respectively.

language for the whole People of God (I Pet. 2:5.9; Rev. 1:6; 5:10; 20:6), using other terms for the various office-bearers of the church.[3] Luther: In I Pet. 2:9 "St. Peter calls all Christians priests. . . Scripture calls those who are now called priests not priests or *sacerdotes* but *ministri, presbyteri, episcopi,* that is, 'servants,' 'elders,' and 'guardians.' "[4] This is conceded also within modern Roman Catholicism:

> *Office and Priesthood.* Today's exegesis has confirmed Luther's claim that the whole New Testament grants the predicate 'priest' (sacerdos) and 'priestly' only to Christ and the whole people of God, but not to a special ministerial office.[5]

It is against this background of the common royal and priestly family status[6] of the whole church of Christ, that the doctrine of the church's ministry must be seen. Everything depends on preserving intact this bipolarity: "A Priest is not identical with Presbyter or Minister—for one is born to be priest, one becomes a minister."[7] All are priests, not all are ministers. There is a priesthood and there is a ministry. They are not the same, yet both are God-given, and there exists between them a contrapuntal relationship.

This organic equilibrium is wrecked by the levelling slogan: "Everyone a minister."[8] In that case the distinction between priesthood and ministry vanishes, and the difference between the ministry of "everyone" and that of "some" becomes, by implication, one of degree, not of kind. The whole topic has turned in recent decades into a veritable nest of confusions. The latter should not be

---

3. The seeming exception is Rom. 15:16, "rendering priestly service [ἱερουργοῦντα] to the Gospel of God," which expression, however, is shaped and dominated by the sacrificial analogy on a grand scale, i.e. "the offering of the Gentiles."

4. *Dr. Luther's Retraction of the Error Forced upon Him* (1521), *LW* 39:229 *WA* 8:247.13–16. See also *The Private Mass and the Consecration of Priests* (1533), *LW* 38:188; *WA* 38:230.13–17: "For this reason also the Holy Spirit diligently prevented the name sacerdos, priest or cleric, from being given to any apostle or to various other offices, but it is solely the name of the baptized or of Christians as a hereditary name with which one is born through baptism."

5. W. Stein, *Das Kirchliche Amt bei Luther*, 216. This meticulously researched monograph appeared as vol. 73 of a series of publications by the *Institut für Europaeische Geschichte, Mainz, Abteilung für Abendlaendische Religionsgeschichte*, under the general editorship initially of Joseph Lortz.

6. Luther's royal family analogy is well known: "It is like ten brothers, all king's sons and equal heirs, choosing one of themselves to rule the inheritance in the interests of all. In one sense they are all kings and of equal power, and yet one of them is charged with the responsibility of ruling" (*To The Christian Nobility of the German Nation* [1520], *LW* 44:128; *WA* 6:407.32–34).

7. *Concerning the Ministry* (1523), *LW* 40:18; *WA* 12:178.9–10.

8. For a careful analysis and critique see A. J. Boehme, "What's 'THE' Fuss All About?"

blamed on the well-known fluidity of the biblical terminology, since that state of affairs is hardly a recent discovery.

A simple linguistic quirk may well account for much of the confusion among English-speaking Lutherans. So long as the concise term *Predigtamt* [literally: preaching office], used in the German AC V, was common coin, its meaning was reasonably self-evident and therefore stable. Since English, however, does not readily string nouns together into compounds, and since the Latin of AC V ("the ministry of teaching the Gospel and administering the sacraments") is far too long for standard reference, a "shorthand" term had to be found, and that term was of course "the ministry."[9] This usage, entrenched in English since at least 1571 (English edition of the Thirty-Nine Articles), governed phrases like "holy ministry," "sacred ministry," and "public ministry." The standard Latin dogmatic locus, among Lutherans, was *"De Ministerio Ecclesiastico"*[10][Of the Ecclesiastical Ministry, or the Ministry of the Church].

This was well and good so long as it was taken for granted that the term "the ministry" here did not stand generically for all sorts of "service," but functioned quite specifically as place-holder for the precise sense of the *ministry* of *preaching* or *teaching* the Gospel and *administering* the sacraments (AC V). Then along came the modern Bible translations, and rendered Eph. 4:12: "for the equipping of the saints for the work of ministry. . ." That "repunctuation"[11] of the text became the rallying cry of the populist/activist program to make "everyone a minister." Since then discourse about "the ministry" in many Lutheran quarters has fallen into a confusion of tongues, in which "pastoral," "lay," "ordained," "commissioned" and other such "ministries" swirl about each other without much theological rhyme or reason. Any semblance of order must then be supplied bureaucratically, that is, arbitrarily. The rise of that utterly oxymoronic locution, "lay-pastor," signals the loss of all categories.

Actually, the traditional practice of saying "ministry," when the fuller "Gospel ministry" or "Word and Sacraments ministry" is meant, reflects New Testament usage better than might at first be

9. Tappert's "office of the ministry" (p. 31) is not a happy translation of *Predigtamt*, since the phrase in effect says *"amt"* twice and *"Predigt"* not at all.

10. This is the Latin heading of AC V. See also C.F.W. Walther, ed., *Joh. Guilielmi Baieri Compendium Theologiae Positivae* III:683 ff. J. Gerhard's locus has the same title (Cotta edition, XII.II.1), as does Quenstedt's *Systema Theologicum*, III:1497.

11. J. H. P. Reumann, *Ministries Examined*, 72.

surmised. Our English "ministry" is of course the Greek διακονία, by way of the Latin *ministerium*. Now, St. Paul repeatedly uses simply "minister" and "ministry" (Acts 20:24, cf. 21:19; Rom. 11:13; I Cor. 3:5; II Cor. 4:1; 6:3.4; 11:23; Eph. 6:21; Col. 1:7; 4:7.17; I Thess. 3:2; I Tim 1:12; 4:6; II Tim. 4:5.11) for what is elsewhere described more fully as the ministry or ministers of "the Word" (Acts 6:4), "the Spirit" (II Cor. 3:8), "righteousness" (II Cor. 3:9), "reconciliation" (II Cor. 5:18), "the New Testament" (II Cor. 3:6), "the Gospel" (Eph. 3:7; Col. 1:23), and "the church" (Col. 1:25).

The other relevant sense of the διακονία-group of words is the very specific one of "deacon" and "diaconate," which no doubt grows out of the word-group's main sense of "service," especially food service, and therefore also provision of bodily support generally. The details need not concern us till the next section. The point is, however, that the interpretation of Eph. 4:12 which ascribes a "work of ministry" to Christians generally would, if true, be untypical. "Ministry" stands generally for concrete offices and services in the church. It is not an umbrella to cover the functions of the "royal priesthood." Rather, it is this "priesthood" that truly expresses the status and appropriate activities of all Christians as such. The "ministry" is the distinct responsibility of a smaller circle within the universal priesthood. Christians generally are told to serve (δουλεύετε, Gal. 5:13) and submit to (ὑποτασσόμενοι, Eph. 5:21, cf. 4:32) one another. If Eph. 4:12 is to be translated "equipping the saints for the work of ministry," then the reference must be to this general mutual helpfulness or "ministration" (NIV: "works of service"), not to the ministry of the Gospel. However, the old translation, "for the perfecting of the saints, for the work of the ministry, etc."[12] is favored by the phrase "ἔργον διακονίας"

12. This understanding is embodied in Tr. 67, while the German version skips the phrase "εἰς ἔργον διακονίας," no doubt because the Luther-Bible had applied the phrase to the saints: *"dass die Heiligen zugerichtet werden zum Werk des Amts"* [that the saints might be fitted to the work of the office]. Luther's construction here is the same as that of the new English translations, but the meaning need not be. See *On Psalm 110* (1535), *LW* 13:332; *WA* 41:209, and *Galatians Commentary* (1535), *LW* 27:103; *WA* 40:II:132.11–15, for examples where Luther applies εἰς ἔργον διακονίας to the Office of the Ministry.

G. Stoeckhardt comments: the teachers of the church "are given and appointed for 'the work' or 'the business of the service,' and this service is 'the upbuilding of the body of Christ,' the church, and consists just in doctrine and preaching. The preaching of the divine Word is the only means by which the church of Christ is built. But the purpose of this service is 'the readying of the saints,' the *consummatio* (Vulgate), the perfecting of the saints" (*Kommentar über den Brief Pauli an die Epheser,* 199. Our translation).

For a critique of the "equipping of the saints" view, see H. P. Hamann, "The Translation of Eph. 4:12—A Necessary Revision," 42–49.

(work of [the] ministry). This wording suggests not informal arrangements but an actual office (note the expressions "καλοῦ ἔργου" [of a good work, with reference to the bishop's office], I Tim. 3:1, and "ἔργον ... εὐαγγελιστοῦ" [work of an evangelist], II Tim. 4:5; cf. Eph. 4:11).

The harmonious equipoise of the priesthood of all and the ministry of some inevitably degenerates into secular "class-warfare" when it is misconstrued in socio-political terms. That aspect of the 19th century discussion[13] continues to haunt us.[14] It was perhaps inevitable that the political turmoil of the time should have been reflected in the disputes about church and ministry. The priesthood of believers came then to be seen as a stalking horse for democratism and populism, while conservative forces took refuge in the "divine right" of a clerical elite, guaranteed by and in turn guaranteeing the established order. It was a piece of naive romanticism to imagine, for instance, that the terrible tides of secularism could be stemmed by concentrating all control in the hands of the clergy. Much more realistic is Sasse's judgment, made in view of the abject acquiescence by Lutheran leaders in Prussia's suppression of their church's confession: "But such are the theologians: for every kick administered them by some officer's boot they at once have a theological rationale."[15]

Priesthood and ministry each have their own sphere and orientation. Competition between them is as pathological as conflict between lungs or feet and the rest of the body. The essence of our common spiritual priesthood, according to I Pet. 2:9, has rarely been put as well as in these words of Luther's: ". . .as Christ himself was a priest and sacrifice, so all of us too as Christians are truly a holy priesthood and the sacrifice itself, as Paul elucidates in Romans 12 [:1], where he teaches that we should sacrifice our bodies as a priestly sacrifice."[16]

---

13. The important 19th century debates are traced in J. H. Pragman, *Traditions of Ministry*, 127–153, briefly characterized in J. H. P. Reumann, *Ministries Examined*, 38–48, and fleetingly alluded to in R. A. Harrisville, *Ministry in Crisis*, 53, 65. For background see H. Fagerberg, *Bekenntnis, Kirche und Amt in der deutschen konfessionellen Theologie des 19. Jahrhunderts*. Also W. Maurer, *Pfarrerrecht und Bekenntnis, 9–26*.

14. J. Heubach shows the urgent need to "liberate" the priesthood of believers from a false and unfortunate confrontation with the ministry. "Das Priestertum der Gläubigen und das Amt der Kirche," 291–300.

15. H. Sasse, *In Statu Confessionis*, I:313–314.

16. *Dr. Luther's Retraction of the Error Forced Upon Him* (1521), *LW* 39:235; *WA* 8:252.31–34.

The precise form of this sacrifice differs of course according to one's particular calling and circumstances, such as those of housewife, farmer, pastor, soldier, and so on.[17] The task of the public ministry of the Gospel is also clear: public preaching and teaching, granting and withholding absolution, and administering the holy sacraments (I Cor. 4:1; see AC V, XIV, XXVIII). In sum, priestly sacrifice and evangelical-sacramental ministry are governed in principle by the most perfect symbiotic harmony. Conflicts arise solely from that wicked self-seeking with which we defile both priesthood and ministry and all other good and precious gifts of God.

Ministers are not of course proprietors of the salvific treasures of the church but are rather stewards of them. Nor have they a monopoly of the faithful teaching, confession, and transmission of the evangelic truth. The ministry's public proclamation is supported by and in turn supports that ceaseless "publishing" (ἐξ–αγγείλητε) of God's "virtues," which is the priestly duty and delight of all who live in and by "His wondrous light" (I Pet. 2:9). The ways in which this happens are as manifold as life's providential opportunities and responsibilities (Mt. 5:16; Acts 8:4; 18:26; Eph. 5:19; 6:4; II Tim. 1:5; 3:15; I Pet. 2:12–15; 3:1.15). Every house-father and house-mother is to be bishop and bishopess "that you help us exercise the preaching office [*Predigtamt*] in [your] houses, as we do in the church."[18] Indeed, the Gospel as the power of salvation makes of believers not only priests but also kings and victors over Satan. In this sense—the context illustrates the unselfconscious interplay of formal and informal, priestly and ministerial teaching—Luther even calls the teaching Christian [*Christianus docens*] "the true God on the face of the earth."[19] This easy interplay between official and unofficial, public and private proclama-

---

17. Heubach warns against the "unfruitful confrontation of ministry and 'general' priesthood," as though the latter were vague and generic, when in fact it is gloriously definite and concrete: "To be a Christian is to be a priest." This great and true dignity of the church as a nation of priests is short-circuited by "the *activistic misunderstanding*. The priesthood of believers is something very active. But it is a mistake to imagine that the more the so-called 'laymen' are involved and activated with churchly tasks, the better for the realization of the priesthood of believers" ("*Das Priestertum*," 292–293). Far greater and better than all the "religious" good works of modern, pietistic or bureaucratic forms of monasticism, is faithfulness in the ordinary duties of daily life, at home and at work, according to the Ten Commandments. See especially AC XXVI.8–11; Ap. XV.25,26; XXVII.38; LC Ten Commandments, 311–318.

18. *Sermon on the First Commandment* (1528), *WA* 30:I:58.8–10; *LW* 51:137.

19. *Commentary on 1 John* (1527), *WA* 20:683.11–12; *LW* 30:261.

tion of the Gospel is not due to looseness of thought or language. It is rooted in the twofold communication of the Keys of the Kingdom, to the whole church (Mt. 18:18; cf. II Cor. 2:10; Tr. 24) and to her public ministry (Jn. 20:23; cf. Mt. 16:19; Tr. 60–61). But this two-foldness is not symmetrical. The priesthood and the ministry possess the Keys, that is, the liberating, life-giving Gospel, in different modes and respects. The priesthood is the church, the bride of Christ, who as "house-mother of Christendom" possesses all the salvific treasures lavished upon her by her Bridegroom—especially the ministry of the Gospel (Eph. 4:7–13; I Cor. 3:21.22; Tr. 69). The ministry, in turn, administers and distributes the common treasures of God and of the church (Mt. 18:20; Rom. 8:17.32; 10:6–15; I Cor. 4:1; II Cor. 2:14–5:21), and this clearly not in the sense of a pragmatic human arrangement, but by divine mandate, institution, and appointment (AC XXVIII.5–6).

We must be done then with false antitheses like, "Is the minister the servant of Christ or of the congregation?" Obviously he is the servant of both: Christ's servant for the benefit of the congregation, and the congregation's servant in the name and on behalf of Christ. Since Christ and the church are Groom and bride, the ministry is "His and hers." St. Paul puts it admirably: "For we do not preach ourselves, but Jesus Christ as Lord, and ourselves as your servants [δούλους, slaves!] for Jesus' sake" (II Cor. 4:5). It must be remembered that "congregation" and "church" are quite the same thing—theologically no distinction between them can be allowed. The minister of the Gospel then is the "servant of the congregation" to serve not people's wants or whims but their needs (I Cor. 4:3; Gal. 1:10; I Thess. 2:4—but see also I Cor. 9:22 and 10:33), and this in accordance with Christ's own directions, and in mutual submission to Him (Rom. 15:1–3; Phil. 2:1–11; I Tim. 4:11–16). H. Sasse put it all in perspective like this:

> It is therefore in fact impossible in the New Testament to separate ministry and congregation. What is said to the congregation is also said to the office of the ministry, and vice versa. The office does not stand above the congregation but always in it. . . Of all Lutheran churches there can hardly be another in which the office of the ministry is so highly honored as in the Missouri Synod, where the congregation is so much the center of churchly thinking and activity. Office and congregation are piped together. The life of the one is also the life of the other. If the office falters, so does the congregation. If the congregation falters, so does the office.[20]

---

20. H. Sasse, *We Confess the Church*, 78–79.

To say that the office is "in" the congregation or priesthood is to average out, as it were, the respects in which each is "over" and "under" the other. St. Paul confesses for himself and all his fellow-ministers: "We have this treasure in earthen vessels [NIV: jars of clay]" (II Cor. 4:7). It is axiomatic that the treasure is always "above" the vessel. In this respect not only the congregations but also the incumbents of the ministry themselves are for their own persons "under" their office. And the gold and silver built on the true foundation by the "living stones" of the priesthood (I Pet. 2:5) are infinitely "above" the hay or straw contributed by unworthy and erring ministers (I Cor. 3:12.13). The holy church of Christ is not at the mercy of the arbitrary fantasies of her ministers, nor are the latter subject to the tyranny of those they must serve. Both ministers and people are strictly accountable to Christ, and in Him to each other, in mutual submission to His alone-saving Word (Rom. 14:4.7–14; I Pet. 5:2–4).

Four points from the *Treatise* will sum up the foregoing:

(1) I Pet. 2:9 applies "to the true church which, *since it alone possesses the priesthood*, certainly has the right of electing and ordaining ministers" (Tr. 69);

(2) "On this Rock" (Mt. 16:18) means "on this ministry [*ministerium, Predig und Predigampt*]," so that "the church is not built on the authority of a man but on the ministry of the confession which Peter made. . . . Christ addresses Peter as a minister" (Tr. 25);

(3) According to Mt. 18:19.20, the Keys are bestowed "especially [*principaliter*, principally] and immediately on the church" (Tr. 24);

(4) "In I Cor. 3:4-8 Paul places ministers on an equality and teaches that the church is above the ministers" (Tr. 11).[21]

So then the church, having the priesthood, has the Keys directly or immediately, and through her Christ commits their public exercise to His and her public ministry, to which in that sense she is subject. In publicly transmitting the office the church acts of course normally through her public ministry [see Latin of Tr. 72], a point to be addressed in detail later.

One may not with W.Löhe dismiss this teaching as Luther's or Melanchthon's "individual" view.[22] It is, as Walther's classic on

21. Tappert, 331, 324, 321.

22. Löhe's position has been thoroughly examined in S. Hebart, *Wilhelm Löhes Lehre von der Kirche, ihrem Amt und Regiment* (1939). Despite his mistakes, Löhe emerges as a truly great pastor, churchman, missionary, and confessor in an age of confessional and sacramental disintegration. Yet Löhe's aberrations are not overlooked. (If we draw attention to some of them here, then only because they are relevant at this point, and with the painful realization that this discussion cannot do justice to Löhe's over-all orientation as a deeply

Church and Ministry has demonstrated, the settled doctrine of the Book of Concord, and of the dogmatic "tradition" that issues from it.

---

devout and courageous evangelical and churchly man of God). Hebart repeatedly registers "un-Lutheran" (300, 304, 309), Romanizing (303) elements in Löhe's doctrine of the ministry and of church-government. Löhe's "most dangerous" (275) aberration was the idea that only the minister can impart actual forgiveness, while in the mouth of a layman any absolving words have "only the force of a consolation," not that of forgiveness itself! In light of the above one is at a loss to understand Hebart's judgment that Löhe's break with Missouri was due to the latter's "false and unhistorical dogmatism"(226) and "bigoted orthodoxism"(240). Löhe did not regard the differences as church-divisive, and held to the notion of "progress in doctrine," believing that the doctrine of the church and the ministry wasn't "finished" yet (226, 278–279). One of the questions he regarded as still unsettled was "whether the office is really a condition for the validity and power of the sacrament" (233)! One can hardly blame any heir of the Reformation for regarding such things not as progress and legitimate development, but as crippling retrogression and surrender. Walther, incidentally, did not in the least deny "that the doctrines of the church and the ministry are capable of further unfolding, as are all other doctrines of Scripture." Such development, however, is a mere pretense "if it does not return to and begin with the place where our church has left off" (1852 Preface, *Church and Ministry*, 8). Luther's consistent theology of church and ministry may *not* be dismissed as merely his "individual" view: "Dr. Luther is rightly to be regarded as the most eminent teacher of the churches which adhere to the Augsburg Confession and as the person whose entire doctrine in sum and content was comprehended in the articles of the aforementioned Augsburg Confession and delivered to Charles V, therefore the true meaning and intention of the Augsburg Confession cannot be derived more correctly or better from any other source than from Dr. Luther's doctrinal and polemical writings" (FC SD VII, 41).

EXCURSUS

LUTHER AND THE *"ÜBERTRAGUNG"* (CONFERRAL) OF THE MINISTRY

The term *"Übertragungstheorie"* ("transfer theory") may sound satisfyingly precise, but really it is not. It has become a handy bugaboo, almost as sinister when deprived of its xenophobic overtones by translation into English, as in the original German. Actually the word *"übertragen"* need not mean precisely "transfer." The context sometimes demands the less pointed sense of "convey," "bestow," or "confer." In the doctrine of the ministry the argument is not about *whether* something is conveyed (*übertragen*), but about *how* and *by whom* this is done. Since, as nearly all agree, those who at some point become ministers were not such before, they must obviously have the ministry conveyed to them somehow and by someone. This is all that the word *"übertragen,"* in and of itself, means in this context. The whole argument is about how and through whom this happens.

It is interesting that S.P. Hebart's classic 1939 Löhe-interpretation, despite its anti-Missouri tenor, repeatedly described Löhe's own position in terms of the office being *"übertragen,"* conveyed, not indeed "by the local congregation, but by Christ through men."[1] Nor is this all. Hebart pointed out that according to Luther and the Confessions the Gospel office is properly conferred [*übertragen*] by the church even without the particular forms of

---

1. S. Hebart, *Wilhelm Löhe's Lehre*, 158, 159, 162, 265. Hebart is here citing according to sense, not exact terminology. Löhe in fact does not use the term *"Übertragung"* in *Haus-, Schul- und Kirchenbuch* I, 1st ed., 104, referenced in Hebart, p. 158n. However, Hebart's citation on his p. 265, does capture a genuine instance of Löhe's use of *"Übertragung"* to describe the office being conveyed by ordained office-holders with prayer and the laying on of hands (W. Löhe, *Aphorismen über die neutestamentlichen Ämter und ihr Verhältnis zur Gemeinde*, 72). Höfling also used the term in *Grundsätze evangelisch-lutherischer Kirchenverfassung*, 38, 39, 42. Most interesting is his use of the word on p. 46 to characterize a Löhe-like position, which is then rejected.

ordination regarded as divinely instituted and necessary by Löhe.[2] It is also noteworthy that the Löhe-oriented Iowa Synod's Davenport and Toledo Theses and other documents, while attacking Missouri's supposedly erroneous notion of *"Übertragung"* (conferral), themselves spoke about the preaching office being *"übertragen"* (conferred) by way of a proper Call.[3] Even modern Roman Catholicism can speak quite freely of a *"Theologie der Amtsübertragung"* (theology of the conferral of the office).[4] W. Stein's painstaking monograph also does not hesitate to describe Luther's position in terms of the *"Übertragung"* of the office.[5] Indeed, K. H. Rengstorf speaks of the *"Übertragung"* of the apostolate on Matthias in Acts 1.[6] There is clearly nothing in the word *"Übertragung"* itself therefore to warrant any jumping to conclusions about a particular "theory." A word is not yet a theory.

It was Höfling who, in his reaction to Löhe, framed what may indeed be called a particular *theory* of "conferral," or even of "transfer." According to him, the only divinely established office is that of the priesthood of all believers. The concrete office of Word and Sacrament does not arise out of a direct divine command and institution. Rather, it emerges by an inner necessity out of the priesthood itself, that is, by the latter's delegation [*Übertragung*] of its individual members' spiritual rights and powers to one of themselves, for the sake of good order. Höfling's later attempts to make this scheme add up to a divine institution of the concrete preaching office [*Predigtamt*] after all, were really only cosmetic.

The real point at issue was whether the church's concrete office of Gospel proclamation rested on a direct divine institution, or whether it arose simply out of the needs and decisions of the priestly community, the church. One can only endorse Schlink's judgment, therefore, that it is—"despite excesses in the opposite direction"—to their "abiding church-historical credit" that Löhe,

---

2. S. Hebart, *Wilhelm Löhe's Lehre,* 300, 301, 303. H. Lieberg's superbly documented *Amt und Ordination bei Luther und Melanchthon* also describes Luther's position in terms of *"Übertragung,"* and this in a section stressing the divine institution of the concrete office, pp. 105, 108.

3. G. J. Fritschel, *Quellen und Dokumente zur Geschichte und Lehrstellung der ev.-luth. Synode von Iowa u. a. Staaten,* 278.

4. P. Bläser, "Amt und Eucharistie im Neuen Testament," 209 and *passim.*

5. W. Stein, *Das Kirchliche Amt bei Luther,* 142.

6. "ἀποστέλλω, etc." in G. Kittel, ed., *TWNT,* I:437.

Kliefoth, Vilmar, Dieckhoff, "and despite everything also Stahl," took a stand against *this* still popular "*Übertragungstheorie.*"[7]

It is a great mistake, however, to lump C.F.W. Walther and the early Missourians together with Höfling, as if they meant the same thing by "*Übertragung.*" By insisting on the divine institution of the office as something distinct from the priesthood of believers, Walther parted company with Höfling at the decisive point. For Walther, the office [*Predigtamt*] is "an office distinct from the priesthood of all believers" (Thesis I), and is "not a human institution but an office that God Himself has established" (Thesis II). It is this divinely established office which "is conferred [*übertragen*] by God through the congregation as the possessor of all ecclesiastical power, or the power of the keys, by means of its call, which God Himself has prescribed" (Thesis VI).[8] Mueller's rendering of the u-word as "conferred," which we have followed here, is much to be preferred to Pragman's and Reumann's "transferred," which then leads to misleading associations of the Missouri Synod with a "transfer theory."[9]

For Höfling, the ministry comes into existence by the *transfer* of the spiritual powers of the individual priests. For Walther, the ministry is a divinely instituted and mandated office, which the priesthood does not originate, but which it receives, ready-made, from God, and in turn *confers* on or *transmits* to the incumbent. Not

7. E. Schlink, *Theologie der lutherischen Bekenntnisschriften*, 330n. The translation by P. F. Koehneke and H. J. A. Bouman, *Theology of the Lutheran Confessions*, 244n, omits the phrase "despite excesses in the opposite direction."

8. C.F.W. Walther, *Church and Ministry*, 21–22.

9. J. Pragman, *Traditions of Ministry*, 144, 145, 149; J. Reumann, *Ministries Examined*, 45, 67, 73, 201. Reumann finds especial significance in *The Ministry: Office, Procedures, and Nomenclature*, issued in 1981 by the Missouri Synod's Commission on Theology and Church Relations. He writes: "It clearly rejects the 'transference theory' in its Thesis 1: 'The office of the public ministry. . . is distinct from the universal priesthood of believers' and 'is not derived from it'; there is rather a 'divine constitution of the office'" (p. 73). Since Reumann had elsewhere identified the "transference theory" with Walther and the Missouri Synod, the misleading impression is given that the 1981 document repudiates Walther's position. The present writer, having been a member of the theological Commission at that time, can personally vouch for the fact that, despite some conceptual muddles in the document, nothing was further from the intentions of that Commission. In fact, Walther's classic *Theses on the Ministry* were appended to the Commission's document "not merely as a matter of historical interest, but as a testimony to the theological and practical consistency of The Lutheran Church—Missouri Synod in its view of the ministry" (*The Ministry*, p. 45). Indeed, if the 1981 statement "clearly rejects 'the transference theory,'" is it not equally clear that Walther's own, completely parallel statements about the divinely instituted office also reject that theory of Höfling's?

As for the term itself, here is an explanation given in a District essay at a convention at which Walther was personally present: "What else do we want to say with the expression '*Übertragung*' than: we receive the office from the congregation through the vocation?" (LCMS Northwest District Report, 1875, 34).

the terms "transfer" or "confer" matter ultimately, but the question of what it is that is transferred or conferred: individual powers, or a divine office?

The Höfling-party over-emphasized the spiritual priesthood at the expense of the office. The Löhe-party did the reverse. It was the ecclesiological greatness of Walther that he held to both divine givens, without yielding or short-changing either. This realization lies behind Pragman's depiction of Walther and some others as occupying "middle ground,"[10] a view for which Pragman has been unjustly faulted.[11] In any case, Pragman's judgment was not original with him; he probably got it from Fagerberg.[12] Now, when it comes to Luther's understanding of the ministry, it is just the right relation between the spiritual priesthood and the public ministry of Word and Sacrament which is the crux. More precisely put, the question is how to combine Luther's strong insistence on the possession of all spiritual powers by the priesthood of believers, with his equally strong insistence on the divinely instituted Gospel office, distinct from the priesthood. Stressing one of these poles at the expense of the other distorts Luther's position.

It is not possible to "layer" the two principles sequentially, as though one represented Luther's "earlier" writings, and the other his "later" ones. Luther's position has about it a remarkable inner consistency, and the "bipolarity"[13] of priesthood and ministry is there from the outset.[14] There are of course in Luther well-known changes of accent or emphasis. Luther was after all first and foremost a preacher, not a "theoretician". And he is a poor preacher indeed who does not adapt his preaching to the particular needs of the time and place. Perhaps the most telling example of Luther's shift of emphasis in respect of the public ministry is the dramatic switch in his interpretation of I Cor. 14:26–31, to which already C.F.W. Walther drew attention.[15] In 1523 Luther took the

10. J. Pragman, *Traditions of Ministry*, 140.
11. J. Reumann, *Ministries Examined*, 67.
12. H. Fagerberg, *Bekenntnis, Kirche, und Amt*, 111–114.
13. H. Lieberg, *Amt und Ordination bei Luther und Melanchthon*, 235–238; 385–387; *passim*.
14. This is lucidly shown in R. Prenter, "Die göttliche Einsetzung des Predigtamtes und das allgemeine Priestertum bei Luther," 321–325.
15. In a letter to Pastor J. A. Ottesen (Norwegian Synod) of 29 December 1858 Walther dealt in some detail with Luther's change of mind. The contradiction, said Walther, is only an apparent one and is certainly not a change in doctrine. In that Luther "remained completely consistent until his death. As earnestly as Luther fought on the one hand against the papistic doctrine of a special priestly *estate* [*PriesterSTAND*] and its consequences, just so earnestly he fought against the enthusiasts for the biblical doctrine of the *order* of the preaching office [*PredigtamtsORDNUNG*]." Although Walther did not use the term "bipolar-

persons referred to in I Cor. 14 to be Christians generally.[16] But in 1532, in his letter about "Infiltrating and Clandestine Preachers," he wrote:

> Undoubtedly some maintain that in I Cor. 14, St. Paul gave anyone liberty to preach in the congregation, even to bark against the established preacher. . . In this passage Paul is speaking of the prophets, who are to teach, not of the people, who are to listen. . . He is not commanding the congregation to preach, but is dealing with those who are preachers in the congregations or assemblies. . . From this it is clear that "sitting by" refers only to authorized prophets or preachers. . . In this chapter [I Cor. 14] St. Paul, thus, often refers to the "congregation," clearly distinguishing between prophets and people. The prophets speak, the congregation listens. . . It should be clear that he is commanding the congregation to listen and build itself up, and is not commissioning it to teach or preach.[17]

Although Luther emphasized "order" as a reason why the church's Gospel office must be committed to particular men for its public exercise, he meant by this not a man-made, ceremonial, ritual order—as Höfling misunderstood the matter later—but an order established by divine mandate, that is, a divine order.

How then are the two divine institutions, the priesthood and the ministry, to be kept from falling apart into rival factions? One must beware of a mechanical side-by-side of rigidly separated functions. The whole point is that office and priesthood fundamentally share the same functions—but in complementary and

---

ity," his brief characterization of Luther's stand in 1523 expresses the reality admirably: "The Keys or the Office the whole church has originally and immediately, that is, all believers [have them]. But God has made the order [*Ordnung*, ordinance] within the church, that this Office be administered only by those specially called to it, who are competent to teach, and who now act [*auftreten*, appear] in a special sense by virtue of their Office in the Name and by the authority of Christ or in His stead. But because the church has the Office originally, therefore every Christian can and ought to use this privilege where its order is not overturned, for example, among the heathen, or where an emergency abrogates the order, when for example no preacher is there to baptize a child near death, or where within the church a wolf opens his mouth, whom to contradict every Christian then has the power, yes the duty and obligation. This doctrine. . . runs through the whole Luther, and there exists no pronouncement by him, from an earlier or later time, which would contradict it" (*Briefe von C.F.W. Walther*, I:115–116. Our translation. C.S. Meyer, ed., *Walther Speaks to the Church*, 57–59, omits some paragraphs from this letter, including some material given above).

16. *That a Christian Assembly or Congregation Has the Right and Power to Judge All Teaching and to Call, Appoint, and Dismiss Teachers, Established and Proven by Scripture* (1523), *LW* 39:310–311, *WA* II:412.30–34–413.1–6. Also *Concerning the Ministry, LW* 40:22–23, *WA* 12:181.11–22. In the former document particularly Luther already stressed the importance of the call for the public exercise of the church's office, and his main application is "that the congregation which has the gospel may and should elect and call from among its members someone to teach the word in its place."

17. *Infiltrating and Clandestine Preachers* (1532), *LW* 40:388–391; *WA* 30:III:522–525. See also W. Stein's excursus on Luther's use of I Cor. 14,*Das Kirchliche Amt bei Luther*, 130–139.

inter-penetrating modes[18] or spheres. As R. Prenter put it, against Höfling's sort of *Übertragung*:[19]

> The functions of the spiritual office are priestly. Therefore they can and ought to be exercised—in case of emergency—by every Christian by virtue of his participation in the universal priesthood. (Another case— beside that of emergency—for which the same holds, is the life of the individual and of families in the non-public, private domain . . .). Just for this reason—that is, *because* they pertain to all Christians equally—those functions may be exercised in public worship only by those who are called to the special office. This does not at all mean, however, that when the universal priesthood in case of emergency or in the private domain exercises the same priestly functions as the office, and when through the calling of the office-bearer in God's name it acts in the service of the office, then it brings forth or produces from within itself, the special office . . . [rather] the right of the office draws the boundaries for the exercise of the priestly functions by the universal priesthood, and not vice versa . . . Only through the working of the office can the universal priesthood endure. The office can proclaim only the Gospel given as a gift to the universal priesthood.

Although Luther's "bi-polar" doctrine was in principle such from the beginning,[20] it is clear that, like all conscientious preachers, Luther also himself grew and matured in the exercise of his office. His changes of accent therefore reflect also this growth, and not merely his accommodation to his hearers and their changing circumstances. The general direction of Luther's development may be glimpsed from his comments on Gal. 1:1:

> Therefore we who are in the ministry of the Word have this comfort, that we have a heavenly and holy office; being legitimately called to this, we prevail over all the gates of hell (Matt. 16:18). . .Thus you see how necessary it is to boast and glory in our ministry in this way. In the past, when I was only a young theologian and doctor, I thought it was imprudent of Paul in his epistle to boast of his call so

18. W. Stein speaks of "modalities" (*Das Kirchliche Amt bei Luther*, 163) and draws attention to several senses in which Luther uses the terms *ministerium/Amt/Dienst* (162–163).

19. R. Prenter, "Die göttliche Einsetzung," 326, 330. Most illuminating is Prenter's orientation of the bi-polarity to the central article of justification. The functioning of the office corresponds roughly to justification and faith, and that of the priesthood (of justified sinners!) to sanctification and love: "Where the *sinner* is *to become* righteous through the Gospel, the office is necessary. Where the sinner *has become* righteous through the Gospel, the functions of the office will out of free love find ever new ways outside its domain. Certainly there are here two domains for one and the same activity [*Wirken*], but there is no conflict and no competition between what is done here and there in a different way and by different persons" (pp. 330–332).

20. See also "Priesthood and Ministry: Luther's Fifth Means of Grace," in B. A. Gerrish, *The Old Protestantism and the New: Essays on the Reformation Heritage*, 90–105, which, despite its title, is generally sound and well-informed.

> often. But I did not understand his purpose, for I did not know that the ministry of the Word of God was so weighty a matter. . . When we boast this way, we are not looking for prestige in the world or praise from men or money, or for pleasure or the good will of the world. The reason for our proud boasting is that we are in a divine calling and in God's own work, and that the people need to be assured of our calling, in order that they may know that our word is in fact the Word of God. This, then, is not a vain pride; it is a most holy pride against the devil and the world. And it is a true humility in the sight of God.[21]

Finally, it is vital to note that "when Luther lets the office act on behalf of or in the name of the universal priesthood, he wants thereby to say something not about the origin of the office—what he has to say about the origin of the office treats of its divine institution—but rather something about the meaning of the office."[22] This communal possession and transmission of the office by the church has nothing to do with a "social contract" or other secular ideologies. Here is the church of God, in which Christ "has become one cake with us,"[23] so that all heavenly treasures are held in common. This κοινωνία (fellowship, communion, participation), weakly reflected in the κοινωνία of earthly goods (Acts 2:42; 4:32), transcends all creaturely limits in making Christians κοινωνοί (partakers) of the very divine nature (II Pet. 1:4). It is in this context that Luther sees the ministry of the Gospel and sacraments as gifts belonging to the church, and so to all Christians (I Cor. 3: 21.22; Eph. 4:8.11). But: "what is the common property of all, no individual may arrogate to himself, unless he is called."[24] It is not a matter of "many individual rights, which the many delegate to particular Christians. Luther maintains the exact opposite: what is the common property of all, to that no individual has a right."[25] By her call, the church does not gather individual functions into one cumulative bouquet. Rather, she conveys the public administration of her common possessions, that public administration being itself a divinely instituted office, and as such also part and parcel of the church's treasures.

---

21. *Commentary on Galatians* (1535) *LW* 26:20–21, *WA* 40:I:62–63.

22. R. Prenter, "Die göttliche Einsetzung," 326.

23. *WA* 17:II:329.22.

24. *"Quod enim omnium est communiter, nullus singulariter potest sibi arrogare, donec vocetur," The Babylonian Captivity of the Church* (1520), *LW* 36:116; *WA* 6:566,30–31. See also *To the Christian Nobility of the German Nation* (1520), *LW* 44:129; *WA* 6:408.9–25.

25. W. Stein, *Das Kirchliche Amt bei Luther,* 90. See also Stein's detailed discussion of Luther's understanding of *"potestas/Gewalt"* (power) in light of the theological and historical context, 80–105.

It was just this, and not any Schleiermacher/Höfling version of the "social contract," that Luther's faithful pupil, C.F.W. Walther, expressed in his 7th Thesis on the Ministry: "The holy ministry [*Predigtamt*, preaching office] is the power, conferred by God through the congregation as the possessor of the priesthood and of all church power, to exercise the rights of the spiritual priesthood in public office on the communality's behalf."[26] Today the "Lutheran" thesis "that Word and sacrament are assigned to the whole church and are performed [*vollzogen*] by the priestly people communally [*als Gemeinschaft*, as fellowship, communion, community]," is, despite confessional variations, becoming an ecumenical commonplace, being represented "with emphasis" also within Roman Catholicism.[27]

26. Walther's "*von Gemeinschaftswegen*" is not correctly translated "in the name of the congregation" (*Church and Ministry*, 268). Our "communality" is admittedly awkward, but "commonwealth" would have sounded too political. The idea is that of a community of goods, of a common and corporate possession.

27. W. Stein, *Das Kirchliche Amt bei Luther*, 214. See his impressive references to Roman Catholic theologians. The Lima *Baptism, Eucharist, and Ministry* document has a section entitled "The Calling of the Whole People of God," but the text is diplomatically inclusive and therefore theologically nebulous.

10

THE ONE GOSPEL MINISTRY [*PREDIGTAMT*] AND AUXILIARY OFFICES

At first sight the New Testament features a luxuriant and irreducible variety of offices. The various terms—like ἀπόστολος, προφήτης, διδάσκαλος, διάκονος, ἐπίσκοπος, κῆρυξ, πρεσβύτερος, ποιμήν, οἰκονόμος—should be studied in detail in Kittel's *Theological Dictionary of the New Testament*. They were treated comprehensively already by, for instance, John Gerhard, in the splendid "Onomatologia" which opens his discussion of the ministry.[1]

"Διάκονος/διακονία" (minister/ministry) is perhaps the most generic and colorless among these terms. Yet as we have seen in the previous section, the term stands already in the New Testament as short-hand for the crucial ministry "of the Word" (Acts 6:4), "of the New Testament" (II Cor. 3:6), or "of the Gospel" (Eph. 3:7; Col. 1:23). Behind the appearance of multiformity, there is one basic ministry, for the church has not several life–principles but only one: Christ's alone-saving Gospel (which always includes the sacraments). From this one and only divine fount and source flows all life and salvation upon the church and, through her, upon mankind (Is. 55; Lk. 8:5; Jn. 6:63; Rom. 1:16;10:17; I Cor. 1:21; II Cor. 2:14–5:21; Gal. 3:2.5; Eph. 3:5–7; I Pet. 1:23–2:3; I Jn. 5:7.8).

It is this one Gospel-ministry which is confessed to be divinely instituted in AC V. The German calls it the *Predigtamt* (literally: preaching office), "to give Gospel and sacrament," while the Latin speaks of the *ministerium docendi evangelii et porrigendi sacramenta* (ministry of the teaching of the Gospel and of administering the sacraments).

Modern eyes, distracted by endless wars over technical—though by no means unimportant—details, are likely to find quite odd and naive the Apology's Scripture-proof for the proposition: "The ministry of the Word has God's command and glorious

1. *Loci Theologici*, XII.XXIV.4–38.

promises" (XIII.11).[2] Only Rom. 1:16 and Is. 55:11 are cited! Yet that no mere "ministry in the abstract" is meant is clear from the very next paragraph, which says without further biblical proof: "The church has the command to appoint ministers."

The divine institution of the ministry simply was not at issue here or anywhere else in the Book of Concord. Much more pressing was the question of the real nature and task of that ministry. Had God perhaps established an order of rightly qualified transubstantiators and mass-sacrificers, with absolute hierarchical control over faith and life to boot? It was against this grotesquerie that the Apology registered the evangelical sea-change of the Reformation: the ministry is for the distribution of Gospel-treasures and for that alone, because it is from that alone that the church lives.[3]

Not oversight or want of care was at work here but that laser-like concentration on Gospel-essentials[4] which is so characteristic of the Lutheran Confession. It is just the seemingly bland "διακονία/*ministerium*" (service), or even "*Predigtamt*" (preaching office) which captures the evangelical essence of the New Testament office, without narrowing it down too quickly to but one particular aspect of that office. In defining the one divinely established office the Augsburg Confession does not begin by fastening upon New Testament "bishops" or "presbyters" or other particular offices, in order to derive from them a divinely prescribed set of offices and structures, in the manner of Calvinism. Instead, it sees "in, with, and under" the variety of offices like those listed in Eph. 4:11 (apostles, prophets, evangelists, pastors, teachers) the one

2. Tappert, 212.

3. R. Prenter's contrary remarks are thoroughly wrong-headed: "Neither Luther nor Melanchthon are of the opinion that the proclamation of the Gospel and the administration of the sacraments are the *foundation* of the church, on which its existence rests. That becomes clear already in the concept 'mark of recognition' *(nota)*" (R. Prenter, *Das Bekenntnis von Augsburg*, 100. Our translation). To cite only one counter-example: "it is certain that the church is not built on the authority of a man but on the ministry of the confession which Peter made. . . Therefore Christ addresses Peter as a minister and says, 'On this rock,' that is, on this ministry" (Tr. 25, Tappert, 324). The pure Gospel and sacraments are *marks* (*notae*) precisely because through them faith—and therefore the church—is created. Nor can one at all accept the logic of Prenter's further argument: "According to the opinion of the Lutheran Reformers it is not the case, as one so often hears it said, that the church is 'created' through the Gospel. . . Then the church would be there only in the segregated moments (thus *not* 'perpetua'[*sic*], without interruption) in which 'the Word' is being proclaimed and heard" (100–101). Were sun, moon, and stars only "there" at the "segregated moments" when they were being created?

4. Although such an orientation is generally lauded in theory, there is much less enthusiasm for the practical consequence that in that case there isn't much margin for "ecumenical" bartering and maneuvering. Where there's only lean meat to begin with, there is no fat to be trimmed.

great office of the Gospel and sacraments, distributing forgiveness, life, and salvation. Because there is one Gospel, there is fundamentally one ministry to serve it, and this one ministry is just as much a divine institution as are the means of salvation themselves.[5]

Later Lutherans would have done well to retain, with Lutheran Orthodoxy, the traditional term "ministry of the church" (*ministerium ecclesiasticum, Predigtamt,* from the Latin and German headings of AC V) for the one divinely established office of the Gospel. Going too directly to, say, "πρεσβύτερος" [elder],[6] foreshortens the grand, evangelical sweep of both Scripture and Confessions, and short-circuits the real linkage to the divine institution.

As for the term "pastor" (ποιμήν, shepherd), it is of course perfectly biblical. Nor could one wish for better, more evangelical evocations (Ps. 23; Jn. 10; 21:15–17). Nevertheless, the modern Lutheran talk about "pastoral ministry,"[7] though perfectly satisfactory for most practical purposes, can mislead, if pressed theologically. On the one hand, the term can give the impression that "pastoral ministry" is simply one species among others of the same genus, "ministry," so that "pastoral ministry," "teaching ministry," "social ministry," and the like, all make up the one divinely coached "team ministry"! On the other hand, if the "pastoral" aspect is pressed as the decisive, divinely instituted feature, then the discussion is too easily derailed into questions of authority, supervision, and ranking, which are precisely the wrong issues. What is divinely instituted, according to Scripture and the Confessions, is not some particular pecking order (Lk. 22:24–27!),[8] but the glorious and permanent (II Cor. 3:11) ministry of life and justification. The Gospel and sacraments themselves—not organizational chains of command—are the content, nature, task, and

5. "For we must believe and be sure of this, that baptism does not belong to us but to Christ, that the gospel does not belong to us but to Christ, that the office of preaching does not belong to us but to Christ, that the sacrament [of the Lord's Supper] does not belong to us but to Christ, that the keys or forgiveness and retention of sins, do not belong to us but to Christ" (*On the Private Mass and Consecration of Priests* [1533], *LW* 38:200; *WA* 38:240.24–28).

6. ". . . there is one office, not a charismatic one, which the Holy Scriptures indicate the Church must have. It is the office of elder," (W. F. Arndt, "The Doctrine of the Call into the Holy Ministry," 339–340). Arndt appeals to the apostolic direction in Tit.1:5. But an apostolic direction is not yet a divine institution.

7. "Finally, the title 'pastor' is itself a legacy of the Pietist contribution to the Lutheran theological tradition. Earlier developers of this tradition usually spoke of the congregation's minister as the *Prediger* or the *Pfarrer* or even as the *Priester*. But the title of 'pastor' as the designation of the congregation's minister came into general use during the 18th century as a result of the influence of Pietism" (J. Pragman, *Traditions of Ministry*, 126).

8. See also W. Elert's discussion of "jurisdiction" and discipline as it pertains to the Office of the Keys, *The Structure of Lutheranism*, 354–363.

power of the office. The "Old Lutherans" understood this very well: "As all ordinances of God in the New Testament are not laws but gracious institutions of God for the salvation of souls, so also the ordinance of the public office of preaching."[9]

Completely contrary to all this is the sectarian/activistic notion of the ministry as basically "trainers" of the laity.[10] As if Christ had said not, "Feed my sheep," but, "Organize my sheep into work-brigades, to do the 'real' ministry themselves"! If the task of the ministry is not the distribution of Gospel treasures but something else, then it is no longer an evangelical institution in the sense of AC V, but a legal and legalistic one. Furthermore, the evangelical ministry is not manipulative. It relies totally on God's own working through His holy means *"when and where he pleases"* (AC V.2)—not when and where human surveys, strategies, and "goal-settings" may predict or prescribe. The humble pastor of the famous prayer which adorns many Lutheran sacristies[11] is a far cry from the strutting modern religious entrepreneur, whose mastery of "scientific" technique guarantees him *x* per cent of statistical success for *y* per cent of "effective" effort.[12] What exactly is it then about the ministry that is divinely instituted? The whole argument is not about a so-called "ministry in the abstract," but about the concrete office of Word and sacrament, with which flesh-and-

---

9. LCMS Western District essay, cited in *Thesen für die Lehrverhandlungen der Missouri—Synode und der Synodalkonferenz biz zum Jahre 1893*, 13. This fascinating collection of doctrinal theses is a sort of Synodical Conference "Denzinger."

10. "The pastor is the called shepherd of the royal priesthood, but he is not there to do ministry for the sheep. Shepherds don't reproduce sheep, anyway. Sheep reproduce sheep! Mission and ministry belong to the people. The pastor is there to be the trainer, the equipper of the people. The pastor is like a playing coach. He does ministry himself, but his primary responsibility is to train Christians to do this ministry" (K. Hunter, *Foundations for Church Growth*, 65).

11. "Lord God, Thou hast appointed me in the church as bishop and pastor. Thou seest how unfit I am to attend to such a great and difficult office, and if it had not been for Thy help, I would long since have ruined everything. Therefore I call upon Thee. Of course, I want to put my mouth and heart to use. I shall teach the people, and I myself shall learn and shall meditate diligently on Thy Word. Use me as Thy instrument. Only do not forsake me; for if I am alone, I shall easily destroy everything" (*Genesis Commentary* [1542], *LW* 5:123, *WA* 43:513.9–15).

Luther adds: "The sects and the sectarians do the opposite, for they ascribe to themselves the wisdom and the ability to rule and to teach. Therefore they burst rashly into the church, do not pray, and do not believe that the administration either of the church or of the state is a gift of God; but they force themselves in as teachers and leaders. Therefore it eventually happens that they confuse and hinder what has been profitably built by others" (*Genesis Commentary* [1542], *LW* 5:123; *WA* 43:513.15–20).

12. The intrusion of such secular ideologies even into Lutheran circles is appalling. It is difficult to see, for instance, what the following organizational quantification has to do with "the New Testament understanding of the church as the body of Christ," which is allegedly the topic under discussion: "There are six classes or kinds of workers in the Christian

blood men here on earth are entrusted. "In the abstract," that is, considered simply as the *functions* of proclaiming the Gospel and administering the sacraments, even Höfling cheerfully granted the divine institution of the "ministry."[13] A "ministry in the abstract," however, is as fanciful as an abstract Gospel and abstract sacraments. These incarnationally concrete divine means of salvation [*media salutis*] are to be administered by an equally concrete divinely instituted public ministry, without the latter thereby becoming yet another "means of grace" itself.

It will be well to clear up some confusions on this score. Why does the Tappert edition of *The Book of Concord,* following the example of the Göttingen critical edition, consider the title of AC V ("The Office of the Ministry," *Vom Predigtamt*) "misleading" without the gloss that "the Reformers thought of 'the office of the ministry' in other than clerical terms" (p. 31n)? It is rather this anti-clerical gloss that is misleading. Of course if by "clerical" is meant the pomp and circumstance of social and political "establishment," as in state-churchism, then all this is rightly rejected. The New Testament office is a service (διακονία), diametrically opposed to all self-assertion and domination (Mt. 20:24–28). It is not indeed a legal office, nor are the sociological and juridical trappings with which it came to be invested in certain times and places, essential to it. Nonetheless the Gospel-ministry is an office, albeit an evangelical, or rather *the* evangelical office.

A related muddle arises over the question whether the ministry is to be understood "functionally" or not. Well, that all depends. If "functional" means that there is no divinely instituted office of Gospel-proclamation, but that divinely instituted functions are

church. . . Growing, healthy, active churches have a different percentage of workers in certain classes than churches that are inactive and declining. . . *Declining congregations have about 20 percent Class 1 workers, one percent Class 2 workers and 75 percent Class 6 workers. . . About 40 percent of the members of a healthy congregation are volunteers within the church* (Class 1). Class 2 workers, unpaid outreach workers, make up 20 percent. The growing, active church will have no more than about [!] 36 percent of its members as dead wood. With any more than that, it could not be healthy" (K. Hunter, "Church Growth paper continued," 12d–12e. Italics in original). Substantive questions about sound and faithful preaching and sacramental celebration enter such calculations not at all. The theological constants, it would no doubt be said, can be "taken for granted."

13. "It ever is and remains the office of the administration and use of these means of grace, divinely instituted simultaneously with the divine givenness of Word and sacrament,. . . an office, then, which derives its power and authority as well as its origin, not from men and their will, but from God" (Höfling, *Grundsätze,* 38, our translation). But this "ministry" belonged, for Höfling, to all Christians, and was exercised by particular, chosen ministers only for the sake of order, and this not a divine order, but only one "belonging to the human ecclesiastical and liturgical order," although this arrangement arose from an "inner necessity" (30, 37).

simply assigned to various people by human authority, then obviously the ministry is not "functional." But if "functional" means to say that the ministry is entirely bound up with its sacred task, that it is not a sinecure without stringent accountability, but the solemn and all-consuming[14] task of faithfully distributing Gospel-treasures, by which criterion the incumbents of the office must also be judged, and if necessary removed, then this is in principle admitted today also within Roman Catholic theology.[15]

Even W. Maurer's invaluable *Historical Commentary on the Augsburg Confession* is not a reliable guide at this point. Behind the inadequacy of the relevant section[16] lies Maurer's assumption that the public ministry or office of AC XIV is only a "special case" of the general functioning of the Gospel and sacraments of which alone AC V allegedly treats.[17] This interpretation is based on Maurer's fear that if the actual public office itself were meant in AC V ("To obtain such faith God instituted the office of the ministry"), then justification and salvation would wrongly depend on the office.[18] But this is pressing the language unduly. The same logic would lead to a non-sacramental "baptism in a wider sense" in AC IX ("Baptism is necessary for salvation"). Luther has no such inhibitions when he speaks of the concrete "office of preaching and the service of the word and sacraments and which imparts the Spirit and salvation, blessings that cannot be attained by any amount of pomp and pageantry."[19] AC XXVIII uses even stronger

14. See K. H. Rengstorf, *Apostolate and Ministry*, 97–113.

15. To illustrate what he regards as an "echo of Luther's concerns," W. Stein cites leading Roman Catholic theologians as representing the thesis that the "legitimacy" of concrete forms of the one office "must be measured by whether it fulfills 'its essential function over against the Gospel'"(*Das Kirchliche Amt bei Luther*, 214, 215).

16. W. Maurer, *Historical Commentary on the Augsburg Confession*, esp. pp. 347–360. The translation of this classic is unusually prone to inaccuracies, e.g. "a literal interpretation" (p. 348) for Maurer's "understanding of the Word"—with disastrous consequences for the whole sentence. Maurer's discussion must be seen in light of a certain critical reserve with which he approaches the Confession itself: "In the final version of CA 5, as indicated by its title, 'On the Preaching Office,' this allusion from Schwab. 7 gets far too much emphasis" (348–349).

17. W. Maurer, *Pfarrerrecht und Bekenntnis*, 70–73, 119.

18. Ibid., 72; *Historical Commentary*, 359.

19. *A Sermon on Keeping Children in School* (1530), *LW* 46:220; *WA* 30:II:528.25–27. C.F.W. Walther, who certainly had no wish to make a means of grace of the pastoral office, commented on AC XXVIII.8–9 ("These gifts can be obtained in no other way than by the ministry of preaching and the administration of the sacraments alone"): "But this is not because the eternal gifts of Christ's kingdom could in no wise be obtained without the administration of the means of grace by [public office-bearers], but because God desires ordinarily to impart these gifts to men only in this way" (*Church and Ministry*, 192). Walther adds this quote from Luther's *House Postil*: "Indeed, many blurt out and say: 'Why do we

language than AC V (see previous note), and clearly with reference to the pastoral/episcopal office.

Nor may various expressions of Luther be used to broaden the scope of AC V contrary to its own clear language and intent. After all, Luther's lovely comment on Mt. 6:26, about the finches and nightingales preaching the Gospel to us,[20] is surely not intended to include these chirping "doctors" and "preachers," as he calls them, in the office of AC V! A competent and detailed correction of Maurer's blind-spots here is provided by Lieberg.[21]

For the origin of the concrete ministry of the Gospel we must look in the first instance not to "presbyters" or "bishops" but to the divinely chosen and appointed *apostles*. The Treatise rightly points us in this direction by seeing in the equality of Peter and Paul in Gal. 2, the "certain doctrine that the ministry [*Predigtamt*] derives from the common call of the apostles" (Tr. 10, German). Schlink put it very well: "The public ministry of all times was instituted with the calling of the apostles, without disparagement of the unique church-founding position of the apostles."[22]

Even critical historical scholarship regards it as "probable" that the appointment of The Twelve "really does go back, as the tradition would have it, to Jesus himself."[23] It is as official witnesses to the resurrection that "not only Peter and the Twelve, but also James and 'all the apostles,' right through to Paul, the last apostle, are in fact part of the 'gospel.' "[24] Therefore: "As witnesses, messengers, and personal representatives of Christ the apostles are the principal and most eminent figures in the whole primitive Chris-

---

need more pastors and ministers, since we can read [the Bible] ourselves at home?' So they go their way in carnal security, and do not read it at home. Or even if they do read it at home, it is neither as fruitful nor as effective as the Word is efficacious when it is publicly proclaimed by the mouth of the pastor whom God has called and appointed to preach and teach it to you" (193).

Walther himself, however, may have over-interpreted L. Hartmann (*Church and Ministry*, 178), whose citation says not that there is an abstract office and then also a concrete office, but rather that *one and the same office* may be *considered* abstractly, in respect of the office and estate [*Stand, status*] itself (as in AC V), or concretely, in respect of the persons who function in this sacred office (as in AC XIV). There is only one divinely instituted office, which is ordinarily—and this is part of the divine institution—exercised by the divinely called incumbents of that office, but which may in emergencies be exercised to the extent necessary by anyone. See further discussion in a later section.

20. *Commentary on the Sermon on the Mount* (1532), *LW* 21:196–198; *WA* 32:462.26–27.

21. H. Lieberg, *Amt und Ordination bei Luther und Melanchthon*, 276–279.

22. E. Schlink, *The Theology of the Lutheran Confessions*, 241.

23. H. von Campenhausen, *Ecclesiastical Authority and Spiritual Power in the Church of the First Three Centuries*, 14.

24. Ibid.,23.

tian Church, and in Jerusalem and among the Gentile congregations alike theirs is the supreme authority."[25]

K. H. Rengstorf has shown that the New Testament use of "ἀπόστολος" (sent one, apostle) was shaped by the Jewish institution of the *"shaliach"* (sent one, fully authorized representative).[26] The *shaliach* was the plenipotentiary deputy, the legal equivalent of the one who had sent him, whose exercise of his power of attorney was therefore valid, binding and final. This purely legal, secular meaning of "ἀπόστολος" as *"shaliach"* is clearly intended in Jn. 13:16. From this it is also evident that simply being an "ἀπόστολος" means very little. The whole weight and value of the position rests with the person of the sender and with the object and scope of his commission. Everything depends on *whose* apostle one is, and to what purpose. St. Paul therefore can use the term ἀπόστολος also for men who are not "apostles" in the technical sense but simply congregational emissaries for practical purposes (II Cor. 8:23; Phil. 2:25). But in his own case Paul makes it very clear that he is "an apostle not from men nor by men but by Jesus Christ and God the Father, Who raised Him from the dead" (Gal.1:1).

Behind the sending of the apostles stands the sending of the Son Himself: "As You have sent [ἀπέστειλας] Me into the world, so also have I sent [ἀπέστειλα] them into the world" (Jn. 17:18). The Son Himself therefore, "in Whom all the treasures of wisdom and knowledge are hidden away" (Col. 2:3; cf. Mt. 13:44), is *the* unique Apostle (Heb. 3:1) behind the apostles whom He sent to publish and distribute His riches (Eph. 3:8)—just as it is the great Good Shepherd Himself (Jn. 10:11; Heb. 13:20) Who sends "pastors" (shepherds) to tend His flock in His name (Jn. 21:16; Acts 20:28; Eph. 4:11; I Pet. 5:2).

In keeping with the *"shaliach"* background, one must distinguish between preliminary and provisional missions (whether of the Twelve, Lk 9:1ff., or of the Seventy, Lk. 10:1ff.) on the one hand, and the permanent, universal mission (Mt. 28:16–20) on the other, which constitutes the apostolate in the proper sense. It is the resur-

25. Ibid.,22.

26. See "ἀποστέλλω," *TDNT*, I:389–447. In citing from this work below, we shall wherever precision demands it supply our own translation, attributing it to the *TWNT* without further ado.

rection that makes the decisive difference[27]—not of course in the sense of those who would substitute a nebulous communal "Easter experience" for the actually risen Jesus. As official witnesses to the resurrection the "ἀπόστολοι (I Cor. 12:28ff.) are not a congregational office, let alone 'the most eminent' such office, but the office of Jesus, which builds the church."[28] Yet one must not forget Paul's "all things are yours" (I Cor. 3:21)!

Although the apostolic title is not rigidly limited[29] to the Twelve—Paul being of course a special case—the apostolic office in the proper sense is identified with the Twelve in Acts 1:21–26. It is also treated there as a genuine office, not of course in some juridical, bureaucratic sense, but in a sense proper to the evangelical nature of the church. Only here and in three other places (Rom. 1:5; I Cor. 9:2; Gal. 2:8) does the New Testament use the term ἀποστολή, and "in all cases with clear reference to the exercised office of the ἀπόστολος of Jesus, in the technical sense."[30] This foundational (Eph. 2:20) apostolate is unique and unrepeatable: "The risen Lord does not now appoint His representatives merely for a limited span but for the whole period, of unknown duration, between Easter and His return. Yet He makes only the one appointment, and therefore it is only logical that the apostolate [remained] limited to the first generation and [did] not become an ecclesiastical office."[31]

---

27. "The Gospels and Acts leave us in no doubt that it was solely the act of the Risen One, when the scattered circle of disciples became a congregation joyously hopeful and willing to work. But the act of the Risen One was also the renewal of the commission for the disciples in their definitive appointment as ἀπόστολοί ... the apostolate is not taken over into the developing church from the time before Easter, but . . . Jesus after His resurrection, in the apostolate first makes the congregation at all possible as the congregation of the proclamation about Him. . . As Jesus is exalted above all and His aim is the all-embracing congregation, so also their office has now become universal" (*TWNT* I:431, 434).

28. *TWNT* I:423.

29. According to Gal. 1:19 (cf. I Cor. 9:5), also James, the Lord's brother, was an apostle, and in Acts 14:4.14 Barnabas shares this title with Paul. The case of Andronicus and Junias (Rom. 16:7)—the latter name "must because of what follows designate a man" (H. Lietzmann, *Handbuch zum Neuen Testament*, 125)—is not clear. "Distinguished among the apostles," describes them "either as being themselves, in a secondary sense, devoted '*apostles*,' Christ's missionary delegates, though not of the Apostolate proper, or as being honored above the common, for their toil and their character, by the Apostolic Brotherhood" (H. C. G. Moule, *The Epistle to the Romans*, 428).

Lietzmann took "all the apostles" of I Cor. 15:7 as referring to a "wider circle" than "the Twelve" of v. 5. He cited Holl as taking "all the apostles" to mean "the Twelve together with James," and von Harnack as identifying "all the apostles" with "the Twelve" (*Handbuch zum Neuen Testament*, 79–80).

30. *TWNT*, I:447.

31. *TDNT*, I:432.

The apostolate in its unique, original form then came to an end with the death of the last apostle. But its basic commission has not run out: "make disciples of all nations, baptizing. . ., teaching. . .; and behold, I am with you all the days until the completion of the age" (Mt. 28:19.20). Unless one assigns to the "αἰών" here some impossible meaning, like "age of the apostles," the "*you*" who are promised Christ's perpetual presence must envisage *successors* of the apostles. The fate of the Gospel is not left to the devices of some informal "ministry in the abstract": "But how are they to hear without someone preaching? But how are they to preach unless they are sent (ἀποσταλῶσιν)?" (Rom. 10:14.15). This "sending," or "apostling," as the Greek ear would have heard it, must continue, and with it the evangelical substance of the apostolic commission, the handing on of the (apostolic, Eph. 2:20!) Gospel and sacraments (Mt. 24:14; 26:13; I Cor. 1:18–23; 4:1; 11:23–26; 15:1ff.; II Cor.3:11; 5:19–21). Beneath the dramatic differences of outward form, the modern ministry in substance continues the once-and-for-all apostolate.[32] We have a hint of the kinship with apostolic origins in our term "missionary," which is simply Latin (*mitto*, send; *missio*, a sending or being sent) for the Greek "apostle," although in general usage the connection remains largely unnoticed.

This substantive—not formalistic or juridical—"apostolic succession" of the Gospel–office is expressly taught in II Tim. 2:2: "And the things you have heard me say in the presence of many witnesses, entrust to reliable men who will also be qualified to teach others" (NIV). It is not at all a question here of "discipling" gifted laymen, but of transmitting the public preaching office (I Tim. 3:1–7; 4:11–14; II Tim. 1:6; 2:24.25; 4:2–5). F. Pieper comments: "Timothy performed the work of a theological professor when he committed the things he had learned from the Apostle Paul 'to faithful men, who shall be able to teach others also' (2 Tim. 2:2)."[33] Luther captures the larger significance best of all:

> However, listen how simply St. Paul speaks about ordination in II Timothy 2 [:2]: "What you have heard from me before many witnesses entrust to faithful men who will be able to teach others also." Here there is neither chrism nor butter; it is solely the command to teach God's word. Whoever has received the command, him St. Paul regards as a pastor, bishop, and pope, for everything de-

32. This is the central thesis of K. H. Rengstorf, *Apostolate and Ministry*.

33. F. Pieper, *Christian Dogmatics*, I:43. This has ever been the understanding of the church and is taken for granted in M. Chemnitz, *Ministry, Word, and Sacraments: An Enchiridion*, 27, 28, 32, 33, 34.

pends on the word of God as the highest office, which Christ himself regarded as his own and as the highest office.[34]

Elsewhere Luther put it like this:

> Now, if the apostles, evangelists, and prophets are no longer living, others must have replaced them and will replace them until the end of the world, for the church shall last until the end of the world [Matt. 28:20]. Apostles, evangelists, and prophets must therefore remain, *no matter what their name*, to promote God's word and work.[35]

And further:

> Afterwards the apostles called their disciples, as Paul called Timothy, Titus, etc. These men called bishops, as in Titus 1:5ff.; and the bishops called their successors down to our own time, and so on to the end of the world. This is a mediated calling, since it is done by man. Nevertheless, it is divine.[36]

Luther's "no matter what their name" also alludes to the basic oneness of the apostolic Gospel-office, beneath the appearance of diversity. In the New Testament itself we face a bewildering set of "diversities of ministries" (I Cor. 12:5). It behooves modern readers to approach this topic with a fitting reticence, since even the experts are largely conjecturing about what exactly each office or function involved, and how that differed from the rest. Moreover, the matter was obscure already in the time of St. John Chrysostom.[37] Our chief source of information about the NT "diversities" is I Cor. 12 itself, which offers three somewhat divergent listings in vv. 8–10, 28, and 29–30. These are usually compared with the similar yet different lists of Rom. 12:6–8 and Eph. 4:11.

The first thing we note is that whenever they occur (three times), apostles and prophets are listed first and in that order—and alone in Eph. 2:20—with διδάσκαλοι (teachers) following either immediately (I Cor.12:28.29) or after "evangelists," but together with "pastors" (ποιμένας), in Eph. 4:11.

Secondly, some of the terms describe persons (apostles, pastors, etc.), while others name activities or functions (healings, miracle-powers, ruling, and so on). Indeed some terms occur in both forms (prophecy and prophets, teaching and teachers), with Eph. 4 at any rate listing only persons/offices.

Thirdly, these various phenomena divide roughly into two

34. *The Private Mass and the Consecration of Priests* (1533), *LW 38:212*; *WA* 38:253.25–31.

35. *On the Councils and the Church* (1539), *LW* 41:155; *WA* 50:634.10–15. Italics supplied.

36. *Galatians Commentary* (1535), *LW* 26:17; *WA* 40:I:59.20–23.

37. "This whole place [I Cor. 12:1ff.] is very obscure: but the obscurity is produced by our ignorance of the facts referred to and by their cessation, being such as then used to occur but now no longer take place" (*Homilies on I Corinthians NPNF* 1:XII:168; *MPG* 61:239).

classes, one embracing prophecy and the corresponding discernment, languages and their interpretation, miracles and healings, and the other, evangelists, pastors and teachers, and such activities as ruling and serving. The first kind are sometimes described as "charismatic," and the second as "non-charismatic." This, however, is misleading, and is based, in part at least, on the popular, non-biblical connotations of the word "charismatic" in English. The Greek χάρισμα means nothing particularly "charismatic". It means simply "gift," and is used quite "non-charismatically" for instance in Rom. 5:15.16; 6:23; 11:29; I Cor. 7:7; II Cor. 1:11. Moreover, "teachers" and "governings" are just as much among the "spiritual [persons or things]" (I Cor. 12:1) as all the rest, and the whole list of ministers of the Gospel in Eph. 4:11—apostles, prophets, evangelists, pastors and teachers—comprises "gifts" (δόματα) given (ἔδωκεν) by the triumphant Savior to His church (vv.7,11). Yet there is a difference between teachers and, say, prophets: "Whereas teachers expound Scripture, cherish the tradition about Jesus, and explain the fundamentals of the catechism, the prophets, not bound by Scripture or tradition, speak to the congregation on the basis of revelations"[38]—which is why prophets required the presence of someone with the gift of discernment (I Cor. 12:10) to adjudge the genuineness of the prophecy. This element of direct, immediate divine intervention, not to say ecstasy, characterizes prophecy, "languages" and "interpretations," healings, and miracles, but not teachers, pastors, or for that matter bishops. We may call the one type "extraordinary," and the other "ordinary," and think of them perhaps—in loose analogy to Mt. 9:17—as "bubbly" and "still" wines respectively. Clearly, the "bubbly" cannot be organized into continuing offices—the latter must hold "still." This is why the apostles, rather than the prophets who complement them, are succeeded by "bishops" and the like. Although the apostles were the most "effervescent" of all (Acts 8:17.18; II Cor. 12:12), their office was stable and did not depend on intermittent, situation-bound revelations. In fact the apostolate which Judas left behind, and which was then conferred on Matthias, is called ἐπισκοπή in Acts 1:20, that is, bishopric or bishop's office (I Tim. 3:1).

38. G. Friedrich; in *TDNT* VI:854.

The effervescence, to be sure, soon disappeared,[39] but we can never say with G. Friedrich that "the Spirit departed from the community"![40] The extraordinary aura of "special effects," as it were, characterized and authenticated the apostolic-prophetic *foundation* of the church (Eph. 2:20; Acts 5:12–16; 8:17.18; 19:11.12; II Cor. 12:12). There is no suggestion, however, that every Tom, Dick, and Mary should expect the same, either then or especially later. God of course remains perfectly free to do whatever He pleases at any time, and this may include special miraculous interventions.[41] These, however, even when genuine, cannot possibly be organized into a "movement" of "renewal." But the real power of Pentecost never did lie in the external manifestations as such. It lies in those three that continue to bear witness on earth, the life-giving Spirit of truth, the water, and the blood (I Jn. 5:6–8; cf. Jn. 6:63)—and these define precisely the glorious and ongoing apostolic ministry of the New Testament (I Cor. 4:1; II Cor. 3:6). To suggest that such "greater" (Jn. 14:12) things are less "spiritual" (II Cor. 3:7–9!) than alleged miracles and ecstatic speech, is to turn the whole New Testament upside down.

Human huffings and puffings can only pump up grotesque simulations, but cannot restore the vital and special but transitory effervescence of the church's founding. A related error, popularized by certain "Church Growth" writers, is to construct "inventories" of "*the* spiritual gifts"—which turn out to resemble nothing so much as the periodic table of chemical elements—and then challenge all and sundry to identify "at least one" of these standard items in themselves. Nothing more foreign to the New Testament could be imagined. All the "gifts" in Eph. 4, for instance, are incumbents of the one Gospel office, in its root and branch forms. These "gifts" are not personal aptitudes or inclinations, nor any sort of qualities of private individuals at all. Most of all, there is here no such thing as a "gift of evangelism," explanations of which inevitably suggest that God's converting power really attaches to that "gift," not to the means of grace. All schemes are self-condemned which present "the gifts" as if they were spiritual "en-

39. "The shortness of the list of *charismata* in Eph. IV. 11 as compared with the list here [I Cor. 12] is perhaps an indication that the regular exercise of extraordinary gifts in public worship was already dying out" (A. Exon, *A Critical and Exegetical Commentary on the First Epistle of St. Paul to the Corinthians*, 281).

40. *TDNT* VI:856.

41. See Ap. XXVII, 1–4 and 38, Tappert, 268–269, 275–276. Also F. Pieper, *Christian Dogmatics*, I:210–211, and note 22.

zymes" needed to activate the otherwise inert Word and sacraments! And it is simply absurd to take "ὁ προϊστάμενος" (Rom. 12:8) as a "gift of ruling," in the sense of an inclination and ability in search of fulfillment. Clearly what Paul has in mind is that he who has been assigned the responsibility of leading or presiding (possibly at the Eucharist), should do so with proper diligence—not that someone who enjoys ruling should diligently look for prospective followers and then press his services upon them! The "διακονία" of Rom. 12:7 (compare 16:1) is most likely to be taken "already in the technical sense of the office of deacon."[42] And "he who teaches" together with his "teaching" (διδασκαλία), in the same verse, can hardly be anything other than one of the official "teachers" (διδάσκαλοι) of Eph. 4:11.

We spare the reader any consideration of the wilder sorts of nonsense one sees, such as simple tips on how to discover in oneself the—apparently not uncommon—"gift of apostleship"! The whole inflated and overheated rhetoric about "spiritual gifts" must be regarded as pathological. What it really means to pray for the Holy Spirit and His gifts needs to be learnt anew from a saner, sounder devotion, and one biblically better nourished and therefore more nourishing.[43] A good beginning is the old *Veni Creator Spiritus*, with its "In giving gifts Thou art sevenfold,"[44] based on the Greek and Latin of Is. 11:2. The sevenfoldness here implies nothing quantitative, quantifiable, or marketable—via "spiritual gifts" industries.

---

42. H. Lietzmann, *An die Römer*, 109.

43. "We modern Christians seek the Holy Spirit where He is not to be found" (H. Sasse, "On the Doctrine of the Holy Spirit," *We Confess the Church*, 18). This profound essay appeared in 1960, just as the "Charismatic" or neo-Pentecostal movement was erupting on the American West Coast. That the "tongues experience" in neo-Pentecostalism functions in fact as a super-sacrament, rather than in the modest, subsidiary way of the NT "languages," is quite clear from the standard "testimonials" in, e.g. L. Christenson, *The Charismatic Renewal Among Lutherans*, 13–31, 79. This dynamic makes perfectly good sense where "religious assurance" has become an obsession, in the wake originally of Calvin's double-predestinationist denial of an objective, universal Gospel, and then also of Methodist second-blessing perfectionism, issuing in the excesses of the "Holiness" movement. But Pentecostalism and neo-Pentecostalism have no legitimate foothold at all in the church of the pure evangel and sacraments of Christ, the decisive exorcism of the *monstrum incertitudinis* (monster of uncertainty) having been the pastoral purpose of the Reformation. See also C. Lindberg, *The Third Reformation? Charismatic Movements and the Lutheran Tradition*.

44. *Come, God Creator Holy Ghost* (1524), *LW* 53:362; *WA* 35:446.14. Compare in *Lutheran Worship* hymns 156,3; 157,1; 158,1; 167,3. Note the rich content and balance of Luther's solemn Pentecost hymns (*Lutheran Worship*, hymns 154 and 155). For theological context and orientation in the Book of Concord see particularly the Third Article and Baptism (Tappert, 415–420; 436–446), Smalcald Articles, III/I/10 and III/VIII (pp. 303, 312–313), and Formula of Concord, S.D., II (519–539), as well as the illuminating interpretation of Is. 11:2 in FC SD VIII, 72–74 (pp. 605–606). One may of course distinguish between "sanctifying gifts" and

Returning now to the apostolate, we may say that this office is at once the most special and, in a sense, the least specialized! It overlaps all other offices. Although Paul does not call himself a prophet—he and Barnabas are so designated in Acts 13:1—he implies that he himself also exercised the "greater gift" of prophecy (I Cor. 12:31; 13:2.9; 14:6.39). Friedrich, on the basis of several concrete examples, describes Paul's epistles as "prophetic proclamation."[45] Beside speaking in "languages" (I Cor. 14:18), Paul was also granted "visions and revelations" (II Cor. 12:1), and had "the marks of an apostle—signs, wonders, and miracles" (II Cor. 12:12). Again, although Paul does not call himself an "evangelist"—perhaps a transitional office between apostle and bishop (II Tim. 4:5)—he was appointed to "evangelize" the Gentiles (Eph. 3:8). Nearly every occurrence of "evangelizing" (preaching the Gospel) in his letters is self-referential. Paul is also "herald (κῆρυξ) and apostle" and "teacher (διδάσκαλος) of the Gentiles" (I Tim. 2:7) or "herald and apostle and teacher" (II Tim. 1:11).

Peter, in turn, calls himself a "fellow-presbyter" (I Pet 5:1; cf. II Jn 1, III Jn 1), and had been appointed by the Lord Himself to "shepherd" (ποίμαινε, Jn. 21:16) His sheep, in other words to be a pastor (ποιμήν, cf. Eph. 4:11). The connection between "apostolate" and "bishopric" in Acts 1:20–25 has already been noted. The apostles then were truly "men for all seasons." They integrated in their one office all the various ministrations of the Gospel, and even called into being an auxiliary office for bodily support (Acts 6:1–6). It was this "generic" Gospel-office—minus their unique, constitutive standing as infallible teachers and resurrection witnesses, to be sure (Jn.14:26; Acts 1:21.22; Rom. 16:17; Gal. 1:8.9; Eph. 2:20; I Jn. 1:1–4), and minus the corresponding miraculous "effervescence"—which the apostles transmitted to future generations of ministers, for instance through Timothy (II Tim. 2:2). I Cor. 4:1 clearly embraces also Apollos (3:5–8) and therefore all other Gospel "ministers" (3:5) as well who were and are not apostles in the strict sense: "One ought to consider us as subordinates (under-

---

"office gifts" (for the latter, see I Tim. 4:14; II Tim. 1:6; cf. SA II/IV/9, Tappert, 300. The "equal in office [however they may differ in gifts]" clearly echoes I Cor. 12). But a rigid pedantry which would have "gifts of the Spirit" be one thing and "fruit of the Spirit" (Gal. 5:22) quite another, warps the whole perspective by assuming for the NT's "χάρισμα" a technical, "charismatic" sense, which as we have seen, it does not have. The precious fruit of Gal. 5:22 are *the* spiritual gifts *par excellence*, that is, literally, of the "more excellent way" of I Cor. 12:31 ff.

45. *TDNT*, VI:850.

lings) of Christ, and householders over the mysteries of God."[46] Apology XXIV.80 adds this illuminating interpretation:

> [The term "liturgy"] squares with our position that a minister who consecrates [offers] the body and blood of the Lord to the people, just as a minister who preaches [offers] the gospel to the people, as Paul says (I Cor. 4:1), "This is how one should regard us, as ministers of Christ and dispensers of the sacraments of God," that is, of the Word and sacraments.[47]

We sum up in language closely patterned after that of the great Wisconsin Synod dogmatician, A. Hoenecke: The public ministry of Word and sacraments is the divinely willed ordinary form and continuation of the one Gospel-ministry instituted by God in the extraordinary form of the apostolate.[48]

The oneness of the ministry and the essential equality of all Gospel-ministers derive from the corresponding attributes of the apostolate. There is no doubt that Peter held a special prominence among the Twelve. He was not, however, their superior. Neither Peter nor any other apostle had "jurisdiction" over his colleagues (Mt. 20:24–28; 23:8–12). Although it is customary to speak of the giving of the Keys to Peter in Mt. 16:19, a closer look shows the Lord's statement there to have been promissory for the future ("δώσω," I *will* give). The fulfillment of this promise Peter received together with the other apostles in Jn. 20:21–23, which solemn words, cited in the Catechism, are rightly treated therefore as "words of institution" of the office of the ministry.[49]

Peter is indeed "first among equals" of the Twelve (Lk. 22:32). Yet Peter and Paul are completely on a par; indeed, the apostolate of the one Paul, sent to the Gentiles, is in a sense equivalent to that of the Twelve put together (Gal. 2:6–9), whose particular (though

---

46. "The ἡμᾶς certainly refers to all who are charged with the ministry of the New Testament or Covenant (2 Cor. iii. 6)" (*International Critical Commentary, First Corinthians*, 74).

47. Tappert, 264. The Apology here cites the Latin Bible, which translates "μυστήρια" (mysteries) with "*sacramenta*" (sacraments), and then adds the necessary explanation, "that is, of the Word and sacraments." C.F.H. Henry, however, is wrong to deny and disparage "the medieval connection of mystery with ecclesiastical sacraments" (*God, Revelation, and Authority*, 11). Henry himself defines a mystery as "a truth or a fact which the human understanding cannot of itself discover, but which it apprehends as soon as God gives the revelation of it" (p. 13). To be sure, Baptism and the Holy Supper are not the only such truths in the New Testament, but they are certainly among them, and even prominently so. They are therefore fully entitled to the biblical designation, "mystery."

48. "The ordinary ministry [*Predigtamt*, preaching office] is the *continuation, willed by God Himself*, of the extraordinary apostolic office, and is in and with the *apostolic office* of divine institution" (A. Hoenecke, *Evangelisch-Lutherische Dogmatik*, IV:180).

49. N. Nagel, "The Office of the Holy Ministry in the Confessions," 288. This splendid issue of the *Concordia Journal* (July, 1988) is devoted entirely to the ministry, the other contributors being K. L. Barth, P. L. Schrieber, H. A. Moellering, Q. F. Wesselschmidt, and D. P. Daniel.

obviously not exclusive) commission was to Israel—hence twelve apostles for the twelve tribes. The original equality of Peter and Paul is documented even in the historic Roman rite itself, first of all by the very fact that both great apostles are commemorated jointly on June 29, but then also in the text of the hymn *Decora lux*. Paul and Peter, in that order, are described as "teacher of the world and heaven's doorman (*janitor*)," and as the true "parents of Rome." It is they who are the real glory of the imperial city:

> O blissful Rome, whose pavement bears the crimson stain
> Of priceless blood of those heroic captains twain.

Such an undifferentiating treatment of the "captains twain" (*duorum principum*) could hardly have arisen in the West after the exclusive claims about the Petrine primacy and jurisdiction had driven a huge wedge between Peter and Paul.

In the interpretation of Mt. 16:18 one must deal not with imagined Aramaic prototypes but with the actual Greek canonical text that we do have. That text clearly distinguishes between Πέτρος (Peter, the rock-man), and πέτρα (the rock-foundation), and that distinction may not be trivialized. St. Augustine's comment gets to the heart of the matter: "Therefore Peter is so called from the rock; not the rock from Peter; as Christ is not called Christ from the Christian, but the Christian from Christ. . . . that is upon Myself, the Son of the living God, 'will I build My Church.' I will build thee upon Myself, not Myself upon thee."[50]

In the New Testament it is axiomatic that the one ultimate foundation (θεμέλιος), to which no one can add another, is Jesus Christ Himself (I Cor. 3:11). The apostles and prophets are— together and collegially, with no special mention of Peter—the church's foundation ministerially, that is, as chosen agents and representatives of the Cornerstone, Jesus (Eph. 2:20). To build the church on persons rather than on their ministry is to confuse the vessels with the treasure (II Cor. 4:7; cf. I Cor. 3:4–8). It is certain, we confess in the Treatise, "that the church is not built on the authority of a man but on the ministry of the confession which Peter made when he de-

50. *Sermons on New Testament Lessons*, XXVI.1. *NPNF* 1:VI:340; *Sermons on the Gospel of John* CXXIV, *NPNF* 1:VII:450; *MPL* III:I:11376–1379. See also patristic references given in Tr. 12–29 (Tappert, 321–325). For a contemporary Eastern Orthodox perspective see J. Meyendorff, A. Schmemann, N. Afanassieff, N. Koulomzine, *The Primacy of Peter*. The Eastern theologians, while recognizing a Petrine primacy, regard all bishops, and not merely the bishop of Rome, as successors of Peter and the other apostles. Even "in the medieval Byzantine authors, Peter was always seen as the prototype of the bishop in each local church" (J. Meyendorff, "Church and Ministry—for an Orthodox-Lutheran Dialogue," 116).

clared Jesus to be the Christ, the Son of God. Therefore Christ addresses Peter as a minister and says, 'On this rock,' that is, on this ministry" (Tr. 25).

To the unity and equality of the apostolate there corresponds the unity and equality of the ordinary ministry of subsequent ages. In defining "the power of keys or of bishops" simply in terms of Word-and-sacraments ministry, the Augsburg Confession (XXVIII.5–10; 20–22) already implies that "the distinction between bishop and pastor is not by divine right" (Tr. 65). It "is evident rather that this power belongs by divine right to all who preside over the churches, whether they are called pastors, presbyters, or bishops" (Tr. 61). The realization of the theological untenability of any other view is becoming an ecumenical commonplace.[51] Although J. Meyendorff speaks of the episcopate as growing directly out of the New Testament itself,[52] the reference here is to the presidency of the local church, that is, of the Eucharistic community. Meyendorff specifically notes: "The terms ἐπίσκοπος and πρεσβύτερος in particular are used interchangeably and apply to the entire body of elders which, in the churches founded by Paul, exercised functions of leadership in each local church." Elert, following Sohm, holds that presbyters represented not an office but an order (like the widows) in the NT church, and that bishops were office-holding presbyters.[53] Such at any rate would have been those "who labored in Word and doctrine" (I Tim. 5:17). Even the Church of England's response to the Lima text "welcomes" the "estimate of the threefold order as not prescribed by Holy Scripture and yet desirable for unity."[54]

51. Regarding "the original oneness of the office" among leading Roman Catholic theologians, see W. Stein, *Das Kirchliche Amt bei Luther*, 215. The tensions beneath the surface of the official dogma may be surmised from K. Rahner, A. Grillmeier, H. Vorgrimler, "The Hierarchical Structure of the Church, with Special Reference to the Episcopate," 186–230. Rahner himself dilutes the notion of *"jus divinum"* (divine right) with a generous admixture of historical contingency, till it looks remarkably like Höfling's nebulous "divine institution" by inner historical necessity (K. Rahner, *Theological Investigations*, XIV:185–201; XIX:33–38). Says Rahner: "The relationship between the bishop and the kind of priest, generally called a parish priest, who presides over a genuine, living, and fraternal community of the faith in fact remains theologically and historically speaking unexplained right down to the present day. This much can be confidently asserted: in the old days the leader of such a community would have been called a bishop. . . For behind [the customary, restricted] terminology a crucial fact might under certain circumstances lie concealed, the fact, namely, that by our use of this term 'bishop' we have deprived the leader of the concrete community, who, for the theology of the early Church is a bishop, of those tasks, powers and liberties which should really belong to him" (*Theological Investigations* XIV:199–200).

52. "Church and Ministry," 116.

53. W. Elert, *Der Christliche Glaube*, 421.

54. M. Thurian, *Churches Respond to BEM*, III:53.

There is then "by divine right" no superiority of some ministers of the Gospel over others, or of some churches over others, since each local church is, by virtue of its connection to the Head, the body of Christ in that place.

Yet there is much conjuring in modern "ecumenical" discussion with the notion of "ἐπισκοπή" as a warrant for administrative structures beyond the local level.[55] The word tends to trade, like "charismatic," on its biblical overtones, which turn out to be largely pseudo-biblical, however. In its only two relevant occurrences (of a total of four) in the New Testament, "ἐπισκοπή" refers to the apostolic office in Acts 1:20 and to the bishop's office in I Tim.3:1. The verb "ἐπισκέπτομαι" means "visit" in Acts 15:36 (hence our ecclesiastical term, "visitor"), and "ἐπισκοπέω" means "oversee, care for" (I Pet. 5:2). Unlike the universal apostles, however, presbyters/bishops were appointed to and for particular churches and places (Acts 14:23; 20:17.28; Tit. 1:5; I Pet. 5:3; cf. "ἀλλοτριεπίσκοπος," "meddler in another's office," I Pet. 4:15).

Whatever of "ἐπισκοπή" then attaches to the one ministry of the Gospel, belongs equally to all incumbents of that office. Any administrative supervision by some ministers of others is strictly by human right, however desirable it may be for the sake of good order. Our Confessions, therefore, on the one hand regard the actual equality of ministers as ideal (SA II.IV.9), but given the shape of historical developments, express "the deep desire to maintain the church polity and various ranks of the ecclesiastical hierarchy, although they were created by human authority" (Ap. XIV,1). One thing, however, is clear: by divine right pastors and bishops have exactly the same office, that of preaching the Gospel and administering the sacraments. Any administrative distinctions between them exist solely by human right, for the sake of good order. And the purpose of the order, and so of "the humanly devised office of oversight (ἐπισκοπή) over pastors and congregations,"[56] is always that the Gospel might have free course. A bishop is there to assert the Gospel's right of way. Ecclesiastical office-managers do not become bishops simply by being called that, but only by doing the great evangelical work appropriate to bishops. One of the most urgent tasks of bishops is defending the flock against wolves—rather than making common cause with

55. See J. Reumann, *Ministries Examined*, 160–164.
56. H. Sasse, *We Confess the Church*, 57.

them.[57] Nor is there much point in devising organizational "signs of unity" (perhaps even a "Petrine function" supplied by Rome), when the "true unity of the church" is so dramatically absent that the very "ministries" supposed to signify unity, in fact either stand for theological vacuity, or else even actively collaborate with those who trample underfoot the apostolic Gospel.[58]

It follows from what has been said that distinctions like those between "pastor" and "assistant pastor" (or better, between the German *"Pfarrer"* [rector] and *"Prediger"* [preacher]) exist by human right and order alone. This needs to be said expressly, lest the ministry be defined in terms other than those of Word-and-sacraments stewardship (I Cor. 4:1). The full authority inherent in this Gospel ministry belongs to all ministers and can in principle be exercised collegially, as was apparently the case in the beginning, before the rise of the "monarchical episcopate." The differential exercise of ministerial authority according to humanly devised rankings, however, normally comports with the demands of good order, which is "very becoming" and "therefore necessary" (Ap. XV.22). As an expression of the supreme requirement of love, such order and tranquility in the church may never be lightly cast aside. But in an emergency—that is, when the Gospel is at stake—every public minister of that Gospel must act with full divine authority, and may not let himself be muzzled by human rankings into a "dumb dog" posture (Is. 56:10).

When it comes to auxiliary offices, the classic example is of course that of the Seven in Acts 6:1–6. Although the noun "διάκονος" (deacon) is not used in this account, "διακονία" and the verb "διακονέω" (serve, esp. in connection with food, Lk. 10:40) are used (vv.1,2). The office being created here is neither a new divinely instituted office, nor a specialization within the one

57. "According to divine right, therefore, it is the office of the bishop to preach the Gospel, forgive sins, *judge doctrine and condemn doctrine that is contrary to the Gospel. . .*" AC XXVIII, 21; Tappert, 84.

58. It is a shallow judgment that the Reformation, "whatever its positive results [!], shattered the unity of the Church in the West and introduced the contrast between the traditional structure of the ministry and the structures which developed from the Reformation, which are among the principal ecumenical problems of today" (*Churches Respond to BEM*, III:52–53). The one obvious ecumenical problem is the massive apostasy from apostolic substance and authority represented by the historical-critical outlook on Holy Scripture. If there were a genuine "convergence" toward substantive agreement in the purely preached Gospel and the rightly administered sacraments, there would then be plenty of time to discuss mutual accommodation in the niceties of structure. Until then the endless fuss about organizational formalities is not simply a harmless waste of time, but a stubborn evasion, bordering on the delusional, of the catastrophic dimensions of the dogmatic collapse in Christendom.

office of the Gospel and sacraments. It is rather an auxiliary service established by the church in Christian liberty precisely to enable the one apostolic office of the Gospel (διακονία τοῦ λόγου, ministry of the Word—note its intimate connection with προσευχῇ, prayer, v.4)[59] to devote itself to its proper work. This is the origin of the diaconate, whose special responsibility is the care of the needy.[60] In this technical sense we find "διάκονοι" (deacons) contrasted with bishops (Phil. 1:1; I Tim. 3:8). Phoebe was no doubt such a διάκονος (deaconess) of the church of Cenchrea (Rom. 16:1).

Needless to say, our modern world with its massive miseries offers ample opportunity for the exercise of love's healing διακονία. The relief of human wretchedness today calls for an inventive resourcefulness. But congregations, acting singly or together with others, need to take care that their diaconic labors truly proceed from the altar and lead to the altar, so that they are not perceived either within or without simply as ecclesiastical extensions of the welfare bureaucracy. The churchly institutions of W. Löhe can be our shining examples here.

The diaconate of love is not, however, the whole story of the Seven. It turns out that Stephen and Philip in particular preached, and this not simply in the capacity of private Christians in non-Christian surroundings, at least in Philip's case, for we are expressly told that he was an "evangelist" (Acts 21:8). The information is too fragmentary to permit any certain conclusion. Chemnitz held that the Seven were not originally ministers of the Word, but that "the apostles afterwards accepted into the ministry of teaching those from among the deacons who were approved, as Stephen and Philip."[61] Gerhard, on the other hand, believed that the Seven were "not simply excluded" from the work of teaching, but were "principally put in charge of tables." *Such* deacons, "con-

59. See Luther's strong admonition to pastors regarding their devotional life and discipline, in the Preface to the Large Catechism (Tappert, 358). Luther's own rugged spirituality was rooted in the Psalms, which so largely shape the traditional daily office. Moreover, as H. Sasse has said, our Confessions can and should be prayed, i.e. read devotionally.

60. ἀντιλήμψεις ("helpings," I Cor. 12:28): "These 'helpings' therefore probably refer to the succoring of those in need, whether poor, sick, widows, orphans, strangers, travellers, or what not; the work of the diaconate, both male and female" (*International Critical Commentary, First Corinthians*, 281).

Luther: "And the diaconate is the ministry, not of reading the Gospel or the Epistle, as is the present practice, but of distributing the church's aid to the poor. . ." (*The Babylonian Captivity of the Church* [1520], *LW* 36:116; *WA* 6:566.34–35). Chemnitz traces the deterioration of the diaconate from the service of the poor to ceremonial duties (*Examination*, II:687 ff.).

61. Ibid., 683.

joined with presbyters, preached the Word together with them, administered the sacraments, visited the sick, etc.," and so "were made teachers of a lower order in the church. . . Phil. 1:1. . . I Tim. 3:8."[62]

Be that as it may, what is clear is that the church's diaconic sharing at "tables" is not as such the διακονία τοῦ λόγου [ministry of the Word], from which it is expressly distinguished (Acts 6:2.4). The church therefore may ask one of its public ministers of the Word to attend also to "tables," but a person commissioned only for table-diakonia does not thereby become a public minister of the Gospel.[63] In principle this applies to all auxiliary offices, but in practice some of these offices presuppose that the incumbent is already in the public ministry, while others do not. Sasse put it like this:

> The apostles came to recognize that it would be helpful for their ministry if they were relieved of the work of caring for the poor and attending to money matters. So the office of the deacons was created as an auxiliary office. But the church was the church already before this office was created. So the church can at any time create auxiliary offices to meet the needs of the time. Examples of this in the history of the church are the office of an episcopate, or superintendency, or any other offices, whatever they may be called. But all these offices have their right of existence only insofar as they serve the one great office of the preaching of the Gospel and the administering of the sacraments. A bishop may be entrusted with the task of seeing to the running of a great diocese. But the meaning of such an assignment can only consist in this, that he thereby gives room and support to the church's ministry. His actual office is the office of pastor, also when he is a pastor for pastors. By human arrangement he may have the work of superintendency. By divine mandate he has solely the office of preaching the forgiveness and justification of sinners for Christ's sake.[64]

Such an understanding in principle untangles the confusion which has lately attended the question of the school-teacher's office in American Lutheranism.[65] While an office of catechist could be imagined which would be well within the one Gospel-teaching

62. J. Gerhard, *Loci Theologici*, XII.XXIV.29.

63. The mere word "deacon" by itself settles nothing. One needs to know whether in a given case "deacon" is meant strictly in the sense of the charitable diaconate ("tables") or in the later liturgical sense of assistant minister, entrusted also with preaching. The very first ordination carried out by Luther was that of George Rörer, in 1525. Rörer was ordained as deacon of the parish church in Wittenberg, and was thereby understood to have been "added, with equal rights, to the ranks of the other clergy of Wittenberg (who had already been consecrated under the papacy)" (H. Lieberg, *Amt und Ordination*, 182n).

64. H. Sasse, *We Confess the Church*, 71–72.

65. J. Pragman, *Traditions of Ministry*, 171 ff.; J. Reumann, *Ministries Examined*, 200 ff.

office of the church (Gal. 6:6), it is otherwise with the school-teacher's office as such. Neither Holy Scripture (I Cor. 12:28; Eph. 4:11; I Tim. 2:7; Ja. 3:1)[66] nor the Lutheran Confessions use the term "teacher" in the modern sense of "school-teacher." "Preaching" and "teaching" are in the Book of Concord often simply German and Latin equivalents, respectively. "Our teachers" in contexts like AC XX.1 means "our theologians." In an eminent sense the Apology speaks of "the apostle Paul, Athanasius, Augustine, and other teachers of the church" (IV.190). Luther too, himself a "doctor [teacher] and preacher," warns especially rectors and preachers against wanting to be "doctors [teachers] prematurely" (LC Preface. 7, 19). In principle then "teachers" are the public ministers of the "teaching" (*doctrina*) of God's Word (FC Ep. RN.1). By false or "ungodly teachers" (Tr. 41) are meant not wayward schoolmasters but heretical pastors/theologians. "Our churches and schools" in the Preface of the Formula of Concord refers to the higher theological schools or academies. It is interesting to note in this connection, that the members of the theological faculty in Wittenberg in Luther's time were considered to be "ministers of the Gospel of the church in Wittenberg."[67]

School-teachers in our modern sense appear in the Latin of the Small Catechism as the "paedagogues," who are to "teach their boys" the chief parts. The German speaks instead of house-fathers teaching their households. Although Luther can occasionally list schoolmasters, with sacristans, among the persons comprising the ecclesiastical order,[68] the Large Catechism derives the schoolmaster's office from that of the father, not from the ministry of the Word (Fourth Commandment, 141).

The church has no "cultural mandate" to teach reading, writing, and arithmetic. To speak with Walther's much enlarged edition of Baier's theological *Compendium*, it belongs rather to the "offices of

---

66. An earlier (1942) essay by Sasse, still well worth careful study, sees the NT teachers together with the apostles and prophets as the third source of today's ordinary ministry (H. Sasse, *In Statu Confessionis* 2:93–103). See also von Campenhausen's valuable chapter, "Prophets and Teachers in the Second Century," *Ecclesiastical Authority and Spiritual Power*, 178–212.

67. Since 1535 the Wittenberg theological faculty had the duty to perform ordinations for all of Saxony. See the ordination certificate for Nicolaus Gallus which bears the signature "*Pastor et ministri evangelii Ecclesiae Wittebergensis* [Pastor and ministers of the Gospel of the church of Wittenberg]" (*Ordinationszeugnis für Nicolus Gallus, 17 April 1543, WABr* 10:29.36–39). See H. Lieberg, *Amt und Ordination*, 219n for more examples.

68. Cf. e.g., *A Sermon on Keeping Children in School* (1530), *LW* 46:220; *WA* 30:II:528.29–30., but see comments in H. Lieberg, *op. cit.* 219n.

parents" to see to it that their children "are educated in all piety, sciences, and arts."[69] Bringing up their children in the nurture and admonition of the Lord is also the parents' obligation (Eph. 6:4), not that of pastors. Moreover, the schoolmasters' right to apply physical discipline can only be derived from parents, not from pastors, who have no such powers. Walther therefore quite naturally regarded the provision of schools as a parental and civil function. "Here in America," however, he argued, "the congregation takes the place of the government in this matter."[70]

How then did Walther relate the school-office to the one Gospel office? Walther held that in the apostolate Christ had "instituted only one office in the church, which embraces all others and by which the church of God should be provided for in every respect."[71] His 8th Thesis states therefore: "The preaching office [*Predigtamt*] is the highest office in the church, out of which office all other ecclesiastical offices [*Kirchenämter*] flow."[72] Accordingly, "every other public office in the church is a part of [the preaching office, *Predigtamt*] or an auxiliary office that supports the *Predigtamt*, whether it be the office of those elders who do not labor in the Word and doctrine (I Tim. 5:17) or the ruling office (Rom. 12:8) or the diaconate (office of service in the narrow sense), or whatever offices. . ." In this context also belongs the office of schoolmaster:

> Therefore the offices of Christian day school teachers [translation omits: who must teach God's Word in their schools], almoners, sextons, precentors at public worship, and others are all to be regarded as [ecclesiastical holy offices, which bear a part of the one ecclesiastical office and assist the ministry of the Word (*Predigtamt*)][73]

A certain tension arises from Walther's treatment of the *Predigtamt* (1) as the *one* office from which all others flow, and (2) as the *highest* office, distinct from the others, but assisted by them.

69. C.F.W. Walther, ed., *Baieri Compendium*, III:782.

70. C.F.W. Walther, *The Form of a Christian Congregation*, 89.

71. C.F.W. Walther, *Church and Ministry*, 289.

72. J.T. Mueller renders this: "The pastoral ministry [*Predigtamt*] is the highest office in the church, and from it stem all other offices in the church" (*Church and Ministry*, 289). The original has: *"Das Predigtamt is das höchste Amt in der Kirche, aus welchem alle anderen Kirchenämter fliessen."*

73. We have followed Mueller's translation, except for the bracketed words, which render more precisely Walther's sense: *"kirchliche heilige Ämter. . ., welche einen Theil des Einen Kirchenamtes tragen und dem Predigtamte zur Seite stehen."* Mueller: "ecclesiastical and sacred, for they take over a part of the one ministry of the Word and support the pastoral office." This is misleading in that the original (1) does not distinguish between "ministry of the Word" and "pastoral office;" (2) speaks of "the one office of the church," not "the one ministry of the Word."

What is quite clear is that also in Walther's view schoolmasters hold not the one *Predigtamt*, Gospel-ministry, but an important office auxiliary to it, like the diaconate, and the lay-eldership. Such teachers are therefore to be placed "under the supervision of the public ministry [*Predigtamt*]."[74] Much needless confusion on this score arises from a linguistic laxity, which ambles along amid "office" (*Amt*), "ministry," and "*the* ministry" (*Predigtamt*), without noticing the differences.

The church has the evangelical freedom to create new auxiliary offices and to change old ones, to recognize and provide for specializations and concentrations within the one Gospel-ministry, to attach auxiliary functions to Gospel-ministers, or to detach them, and to ordain incumbents of auxiliary offices into the one Gospel-office, when they are qualified. Only one thing the church may not do. She may not forget the difference between what God Himself has established in the church as His institution, and what men establish from time to time as fruits of faith and love.

Very illuminating and significant is the treatment in Pastor E.W. Kaehler's 1874 theses, adopted by the combined [Synodical Conference] pastors' conference of Columbus, and reprinted in *Lehre und Wehre*. The theses distinguish between "essential" and "derived" functions of the ministry (*Predigtamt*), and therefore between the ministry strictly speaking, and the ministry in a wider sense, the latter including non-teaching deacons, lay elders, and school-teachers. Relevant extracts follow:

"The rights conveyed with the office of the Word (in the narrow sense) are: the authority to preach the Gospel and to distribute the sacraments, and the authority of spiritual judgment. . .When the congregation confers an essential part of the ministry [*Predigtamt*], then it *virtualiter* [virtually, in effect] confers the whole of it, only with the provision to attend to the designated part alone. . .There are, however, services which are indeed necessary in the church for her governance and therefore belong to the ministry [*Predigtamt*] in the wider sense, which however do not necessarily involve the bearing of the office in the narrow sense; therefore such auxiliary services may be rendered also by such as do not thereby become entitled also to exercise the office of the Word and the sacraments. . .We know now that someone who has to attend to an essential part of the office of the Word can do that only because the whole office of the Word has been conferred upon him; he thus really occupies the ministry [*Predigtamt*]. . .The offices of councillors [*Vorsteher*], elders, almoners, school-teachers, sextons, and cantors in our congregations are therefore all to be regarded as holy, churchly offices. . . But they by no means involve the bearing of the ministry [*Predigtamt*] in the narrow sense" (*"Hat die Gemeinde das Recht, ordentlicher Weise einen wesentlichen Theil des heiligen Predigtamtes irgend einem Laien temporär zu übertragen?" Lehre und Wehre*, 20, 9,11,12 [Sept., Nov., Dec. 1874], 261, 331, 334, 336). For this and some other valuable references I am indebted to Mr. Mark Nispel.

74. C.F.W. Walther, *The Form of a Christian Congregation*, 89, cf. 91. The constitution of the Missouri Synod preserves Walther's understanding with crystal clarity when it distinguishes between "ministers of the Gospel, and teachers of the Evangelical Lutheran Church" (V, Membership). Again, when Art. X, Officers, provides that the "President, the Vice-Presidents, and the Secretary must be ministers of the church," this clearly refers to the one ministry of Word and sacraments, not to the school-teacher's office, or to the assorted "ministries" mentioned in the much later By-laws.

11

CALL AND ORDINATION

The "but how are they to preach if they are not sent?" of Rom. 10:15 is not some pragmatic lament over a "shortage of manpower." It echoes rather the solemn disavowal of unsent preachers in Jer. 23:21 (cf. Is. 6:8). AC XIV therefore deals with something much more than mere human orderliness: "Of ecclesiastical order [our churches] teach [!] that no one ought to teach publicly in the church or administer the sacraments unless he is rightly called [*rite vocatus*]." The German version, entitled, "*Vom Kirchenregiment* [of church government]," says that no one is to "teach or preach publicly,etc." without a regular call.[1] In what then does a proper or regular call or vocation consist? When is a minister "*rite vocatus*," rightly called? Both church and ministry belong to Christ, and therefore a proper call into the ministry must come from Christ Himself. While the Lord called His Twelve Apostles and St. Paul directly and immediately, He now calls and appoints their successors mediately, that is, through His church and her public ministry (II Tim. 2:2; Tit. 1:5). In respect of the divinity of their calls, Holy Scripture makes no distinction between the immediately called apostles and prophets, and the mediately called pastors and teachers: all are equally gifted to His church by Christ Himself (Eph. 4:8.11; see also Acts 20:28).

It is characteristic of Lutheran theology to define the *rite vocatus* in terms of theological realities, not legal or ritual/ceremonial formalities.[2] Chemnitz's exemplary treatment of the rich biblical and patristic material sums up the whole essence of the matter like this: "Always, however, in a legitimate call at the time of the apos-

1. The usual English "should" here is far too weak as a rendering of either "*soll*" or "*debeat*." The utter inadequacy of "should" is at once apparent if we substitute it for the same "*sollen*" in the Commandments: "You *should* not murder, you *should* not commit adultery, you *should* not steal,etc."! As Maurer rightly says: "If there is no divine call, preaching is a fiendish temptation for those who preach and for those who hear" (*Historical Commentary*, 192).

2. See representative citations in H. Schmid, *The Doctrinal Theology of the Evangelical Lutheran Church*, 607–611.

tles the consent of the church and the judgment and approval of the presbytery was present and required."[3] The "presbytery," or more particularly, the ministry, is not of course an entity beyond or in addition to the church, but is an office *within* the church, an office which therefore plays its proper part in the appointment of ministers by the church. Two examples are always cited to show the necessity of the church's consent in the appointment of her ministers. One is the nomination of Joseph and Matthias to Judas' vacant apostolate, in which the hundred and twenty appear to have collaborated (Acts 1, 15–26). The other is the election of the Seven (Acts 6:1–6). The argument in the first instance is from the greater to the lesser: if even the apostolic vacancy was not filled without the consent of the church, then how much more necessary is that consent for the appointment of ordinary ministers. The second case argues from the lesser to the greater: if the apostles did not impose even the auxiliary diaconate without the consent of the church, then how much less would they have done so when it came to appointing regular ministers of the Word.

While the word χειροτονέω can mean electing by a show of hands (so probably in II Cor. 8:19), it hardly means that in Acts 14:23 ("having appointed presbyters in every church"), as our older theologians assumed. Still less of course does the word as such mean "ordain with the laying on of hands." It often means simply appoint, designate, set in place. On the other hand, it would be absurd to assume that either Paul and Barnabas (Acts 14:23) or Titus (Tit. 1:5) were able or willing autocratically to impose unacceptable ministers on unwilling churches. Fraternal mutual consultation, accommodation, and cooperation are simply the self-evident rule of life in the New Testament church (Rom.14:1–3; I Cor. 9:19–22; Phil. 2:1–11; I Pet. 5:3).

The "consent of the church" always implies the involvement "of the whole church, so that in their choosing and calling both presbyters and people are partners."[4] Walther, too, insisted that the

---

3. M. Chemnitz, *Examination*, II:708.

4. M. Chemnitz, *Examination*, II:709. See also M. Chemnitz, *Ministry, Word, and Sacraments*, 34: "But do Anabaptists do right, who entrust the whole right of calling to the common multitude (which they take the word ἐκκλησία to mean), with the ministry and pious magistrate excluded? By no means. For the church in each place is called, and is, the whole body embracing, under Christ, the Head, all the members of that place. Eph. 4:15–16; I Cor. 12:12–14, 27. Therefore as the call belongs not only to the ministry nor only to the magistrate, so also is it not to be made subject to the mere will [and] whim of the common multitude, for no part, with either one or both [of the others] excluded, is the church. But the call should be and remain in the power of the whole church, but with due order observed."

church or congregation, "when properly [ordered] consists of both preachers and hearers."[5]

The basic principle is simple and remains the same. But the applications allow of considerable variety in practice, depending on circumstances. Some classic examples will illustrate the point. If a group of captive Christian laymen, isolated in a desert, were to elect one of themselves to baptize, preach, and administer the Holy Supper, that man would be their pastor "as though he had been ordained by all the bishops and popes in the world" (Luther).[6] The normal situation, however, is that there already are ministers of the Word either in the calling congregation itself, or, certainly, in neighboring congregations with which unity of doctrine and sacraments exists. This is the essentially "normal" situation envisaged in Tr. 72, despite the peripheral "abnormality" of a heretical episcopate: "Wherefore, when the bishops are heretics or refuse to administer ordination, the churches are by divine right compelled [with the cooperation of their pastors] to ordain pastors and ministers for themselves."[7] The reason is clear: "For wherever the church exists, the right to administer the Gospel also exists. Wherefore it is necessary for the church to retain the right of calling, electing, and ordaining ministers" (Tr. 67).

For the confessional Lutherans who came to America in the last century, the accustomed state church status was an Egyptian fleshpot for a return to which they did *not* pine: ". . . the church's independence of the state is not a defect or an abnormal condition, but the right and natural relation which ought always to obtain

---

The problem evident here is the status of the "pious magistrate." Despite Luther's original insistence that the magistrate as such had no right to rule in the church, the three estates (ecclesiastical order, economic order, political order) came increasingly to be seen as standing *within* the church. This fateful limitation of the orthodox dogmaticians was imposed on them by the heavy pall of the Constantinian Establishment, which could be effectively shaken off only in the New World.

5. C.F.W. Walther, *Church and Ministry*, 220.

6. *To the Christian Nobility of the German Nation* (1520), *LW* 44:128; *WA* 6:407.39–408.1. Sasse's comment is worth noting: "The question whether such isolated Christians as pictured by Luther and by More can, as a Christian congregation, rightfully put a man into the office of the holy ministry reveals whether a person thinks evangelically or not. There has never been an evangelical theologian who basically disagreed with Luther in such a case, not even A. Vilmar, the most 'high church' among the Lutherans of the last century, and certainly not Löhe" (*We Confess the Church*, 77).

7. The bracketed words are omitted by Tappert, *The Book of Concord*, 332, but are part of the authoritative Latin text: *"adhibitis suis pastoribus"* (*BKS*, 492). The *Concordia Triglotta* also omits these words from its Latin text.

between church and state."[8] It is natural and wholly commendable therefore that having lost "the magistrate" as a basic organizing principle, the immigrant Lutherans relied on the fullest possible lay participation, activity, and responsibility. This stress on the priestly dignity of the People of God had nothing to do with populist democratism. A priest is to tend to his priestly service, as prescribed by God, and is not free to "do as he likes." A "majority decision" here is not necessarily right or even valid. C.F.W. Walther, who is sometimes blamed—wrongly, as we shall see—for subjecting church and ministry to a secular, democratic "majority rule," held nothing of the kind. Walther taught, for example, that if a congregation were to exclude the existing ministers of the Word in its midst from their rightful part in calling other ministers, such "calls" would be invalid.[9]

As an evangelical theologian Walther insisted of course that the consent of the church was necessary for a valid call. He was not doctrinaire, however, about what procedural form that consent must take. Normally a free Christian congregation would of course involve its entire membership in the calling of ministers of the Gospel, which so vitally affects all members. Consent could, however, be tacit, so long as no oppression or tyranny was involved.[10] In an extreme case Walther even envisaged, with Luther, an abbess validly transmitting the church's call and appointment

---

8. C.F.W. Walther, *The Form of a Christian Congregation*, 6. The full title of Walther's classic is *"The Right Form of An Evangelical Lutheran Local Congregation Independent of the State,"* and this independence from the state shapes the entire volume.

9. "If there belong to the calling congregation also church-servants who are already administering the office, then they, and indeed according to the office which they already bear in the church they above all, belong naturally also to those calling, so that if the collaboration befitting their office is denied them here, then the call of the 'multitude' in such a case has no validity; because [that call] has then issued not from the congregation, but from individuals in the congregation, which, when properly ordered, consists of preachers and hearers" (*Kirche und Amt*, Thesis VI on the Ministry, our translation). The translation by J.T. Mueller in *Church and Ministry*, 220, "there is no longer any call of the 'multitude'" does not correctly render Walther's *"der Beruf der 'Menge' in solchem Falle keine Giltigkeit hat."* Walther says not that the "multitude" has not acted, but that it has acted, and that its action is invalid.

10. "This order is observed most properly if the matter of choosing and calling of ministers is handled by certain prominent members of the church in the name and with the consent of the whole congregation" (J. Gerhard, quoted in Walther's *Church and Ministry*, Thesis VI, 233). This quotation reflects of course state church conditions, and certainly does not represent Walther's ideal. Yet Walther takes the broad, Lutheran view that details of procedure cannot be prescribed as of divine obligation, but must accommodate themselves to changing circumstances. See also the next footnote.

to the ministry.[11] Similarly the Apology charitably surmised that "it is likely that here and there in the monasteries there are still some good men serving the ministry of the Word. . ." (Ap. XXVII.22). In other words, the Gospel ministry and its transmission are and remain valid even if the supporting church takes on quite eccentric outward shapes. Nor need conscientious ministers worry that some maneuverings behind the scenes might thwart the will of God for them. He who graciously overruled the evil intent of Joseph's jealous brothers (Gen. 45:5–8; 50:20), is well able to outwit cantankerous committees and scheming prelates, in order to work His will upon His church and ministry, whether in judgment or in grace—but the former always for the sake of the latter!

These considerations have already touched on the question of the ministry's proper contribution to the calling of ministers. We shall not go far wrong if we always remember the underlying relationships: the church is Christ's, and the ministry is His gift to her, and so part of her. Since the ministry is the church's "public service," public actions of the church are normally and naturally performed through that public ministry. It is pointless to ask therefore: "Is it the church or the ministry doing this?"—as though two separate entities were acting. It is rather Christ's church which baptizes, confesses, teaches, consecrates, prays, serves, and does everything else, including the appointment of ministers—and in so far as she acts publicly and officially, she does all this with and through her (and Christ's!) public, official ministry, without any competition between them.

Three main focal points may be distinguished in the calling or vocation of ministers: (1) the examination and determination of the candidates' fitness or qualifications; (2) the election of a particular person or persons; (3) the public and solemn inauguration and installation of those properly qualified into the public ministry, in the public worship of the church. Of these elements it is clear that the second pertains mainly to the hearers, while the first and third belong primarily to the public teachers, but never to the exclusion of the rest of the church. So, for instance, "[i]t goes

11. "For the pastors or ministers always remained outside and above the chrism through princes, lords, and cities, as well as through bishops and even through abbots and abbesses and other [e]states, and by their appointment the call and true consecration to the ministry or the pastoral office continued" (*The Private Mass and the Consecration of Priests* [1533], cited in Walther, *Church and Ministry*, 251. A more accurate English translation is found in *LW* 38:194–195; [*WA* 38:236.10–13]: "For the parishes or preaching offices have at all times been bestowed outside of, etc.").

without saying that those who are in the ministry and profess the pure doctrine can best judge the qualities of such as are to be called into the ministry."[12] On the other hand,

> Whoever has the duty to discern between teachers and seducers, to examine sound doctrine, to distinguish between the voice of Christ, the Chief Shepherd, and that of false shepherds, not to follow a stranger, but to flee from him, to anathematize those who preach another gospel than that proclaimed by the apostles, to him also belongs the duty to call ministers according to his status and order. But all this is the duty of the flock of Christ or the hearers (Matt. 7:15; John 5:39; 10:27; Gal. 1:9; I Thess. 5:19–21; I John 4:1; 2 John 10–11). Therefore, this cannot be refused and denied them.[13]

The hearers would be remiss indeed were they to fail to consult responsible and competent teachers, when such are available, about the doctrinal soundness of candidates for the public ministry. On the other hand such hearers would be equally irresponsible were they to bind their consciences uncritically to the judgments of officials and theologians. As G. K. Chesterton said in another connection: The experts must appear and practice before a jury of ordinary men and women. If the experts cannot convince the jury, they lose, and deservedly so. If ordinary matters of life and death—of which Chesterton spoke—cannot simply be left to the experts, how much less that holy truth on which eternal life itself depends? Christian conscience cannot be delegated (Mt. 7:15; 25:1–13; Rom. 14:23). But the "jury" must of course decide according to the "law," that is, the revealed Word of God, and not according to personal whim.

Just as the basic qualifications of an apostle were clearly spelt out before the election of Matthias (Acts 1:21 ff.), so also quite definite personal prerequisites are stated for those who would succeed the apostles in the ministry of the Word and sacraments (I Tim. 3:1 ff.; Tit. 1:5 ff.). A crucial requirement is that a pastor or bishop be "able to teach" (I Tim. 3:2; II Tim. 2:24). This includes the ability to "refute the opponents" of sound doctrine (Tit. 1:9; 3:10), and to do so with a gentle, evangelical dignity and self-restraint, without being quarrelsome (II Tim. 2:24; Tit. 1:7–8). Nor may the minister of the Gospel destroy with his behavior what he builds with his preaching. His life rather is to be such an "example" (I Tim. 4:12) and "pattern of good works" (Tit. 2:7), that he may say with St. Paul: "Become imitators of me, as I am of Christ" (I Cor.

12. J. Gerhard, quoted in Walther's, *Church and Ministry*, 232.
13. Ibid., 235–236.

11:1). Nothing could be further from the apostle's mind here than a showy, gloomy asceticism. What is meant, rather, is a cheerful Christ-likeness—embodied, to be sure, "in weakness" (II Cor. 12:9) and modesty by the ministrants of salvation, themselves ever penitently mindful of their own sin, yet dauntless in grace (Rom. 7). All Christians are called to follow the blessed example of Christ (I Pet. 2:21) by His strength, as St. Peter is at pains to show throughout his First Epistle, and in this regard the "elders" or ministers of the Gospel are to be "examples to the flock" (5:3).

In the church it is self-evident that God's First Article gifts, received with thanksgivings, are "consecrated by the Word of God and prayer" (I Tim. 4:5). This befits also the greater gifts of the Second and Third Articles, and therefore also the public ministry (Eph. 4:11)! Whatever of examination, negotiation, discussion, parliamentary "business," and even legal contract-writing may have gone before in the calling of a pastor, it all comes to a head in the public worship of the church, with the Word of God and prayer. Here the man is publicly and solemnly inaugurated into his sacred responsibilities, and commended to the church by God—and to God by the church.

What then is ordination? The word "ordination" comes from the Latin *ordo* (order), and is a close relative of "ordinance." It is in this general, substantive sense of "ordering, arranging, appointing"—as distinct from any ritual, ceremonial meaning—that the English Bible uses "ordain," for instance in Acts 10:42 (ὡρισμένος), Acts 13:48 (τεταγμένοι), Acts 14:23 (χειροτονήσαντες), Acts 17:31 (ὥρισεν), Rom. 13:1 (τεταγμέναι, cf. v.2, "ordinance," διαταγῇ), Tit. 1:5 (καταστήσῃς) and Heb. 8:3 (καθίσταται), cf. 7:28). The old hymn reflects this meaning exactly: "What God ordains is always good." The Book of Concord likewise uses *"ordinare/ ordinatio"* mainly in the sense of "order, institute/ ordinance, institution"—as applied for instance to marriage, civil arrangements, and sacraments.[14] Applied to the ministry, *"ordinare"* (ordain)/*"ordinatio"* (ordination) means basically nothing else than "ordering" or placing someone into the "order" (better: office) of the public ministry. What specific ceremonies or rituals (e.g. laying on of hands) are to be used in this connection, is another, secondary question, which should not be mixed into the primary, substantive, and root meaning of "ordination" as placement into the public ministry.

14. See for example AC and Ap. XVI; AC XXVII.18; Ap. VII/VIII.50; XV.43; XXII.2, 5; XXIII.7–9, 12; XXVII.46; XXVIII.2; LC Baptism.19, 22, 39, 60.

One must distinguish, therefore, between the theological "what" or substance of ordination, and its ritual form or "how." The former is a divine institution, in the sense that the bestowal or communication (*"Übertragung"*!) of the divine institution of the ministry through God's mediate call is itself part and parcel of the divine institution. "Vocation" or "call" and "ordination" in this *substantive* sense cover exactly the same ground. Luther: "For ordaining should consist of, and be understood as, calling to and entrusting with the office of the ministry. . . Our consecration shall be called ordination, or a call to the office."[15] In the narrow sense of the liturgical *form* or ceremony of the laying on of hands, however, ordination is not a divine institution, or something on which the validity of the ministry depends, but a good, apostolic and churchly custom (Acts 6:6; 13:3; I Tim. 4:14; 5:22; II Tim. 1:6), to be observed for that reason, but without superstition.

Mere apostolic custom and example cannot constitute a sacrament. The Lord Himself never "ordained" the apostles with the laying on of hands. He did in fact breathe His Spirit upon them (Jn. 20:22). This action, in the absence of an express Dominical mandate, instituted ordination-by-spiration no more than Mk. 10:16 establishes child-blessing ceremonies apart from Baptism.[16] Even the Roman Catholic K. Rahner, having described Pius XII's insistence on the laying on of hands in ordination as "a positive ecclesiastical directive," says: "This mode of the transmission of a ministry through the laying on of hands is certainly not divine

15. *On the Private Mass and the Consecration of Priests* (1533), *LW* 38:197; *WA* 38:238.7–8 and *LW* 38:214; *WA* 38:256.3–4. Also: "For basically consecration should not and cannot be anything other (if it is carried out rightly) than a call or a conferring of the office of the ministry or of the office of preaching. The apostles without chrism merely laid their hands on the heads and prayed over those whom they called to the office or sent out, as happened to St. Paul and Barnabas, Acts 19 [13:3] and as St. Paul instructs Timothy not to be hasty in laying hands upon someone [I Tim. 5:22]" (*LW* 38:186; *WA* 228.27–33) and "However, listen how simply Paul speaks about ordination in II Timothy 2 [:2]: 'What you have heard from me before many witnesses entrust to faithful men who will be able to teach others also.' Here there is neither chrism nor butter; it is solely the command to teach God's word. Whoever has received the command, him St. Paul regards as a pastor, bishop, and pope, for everything depends on the word of God as the highest office, which Christ himself regarded as his own and as the highest office" (*LW* 38:212; *WA* 38:253.25–31).

16. Chemnitz: "[Contrary to apostolic practice] with the papalists the suffragan of the bishop arrogates this to himself without shame. For as he breathes upon the ordinand he says: 'Receive the Holy Spirit.' But where is the command? Where the promise? It is blasphemy to pretend that the Holy Spirit is enclosed in the foul exhalation of the suffragan . . ." *Examination*, II:696.

Law. Really such a transmission of ministry can be thought of as taking place in any way, provided it is evident and clear."[17]

Biblically, the question about the laying on of hands comes to a head when we compare I Tim. 4:14, "the gift which was given you through (διά) prophecy with (μετά) imposition of the presbyterium's hands," with II Tim. 1:6, "the gift of God which is in you through (διά) the imposition of my hands." Assuming that both texts describe the same event, the simple διά of the shorter, more telescoped version must be resolved into the instrumental διά plus the merely associative μετά of the more detailed account. Strictly speaking then, the "gift" came *through* prophecy, *to the accompaniment* of the laying on of the hands of the college of presbyters, Paul's among them. If, on the other hand, a contrast is intended between the mere μετά in respect of the presbyters (who likely included both teaching and "lay" elders, I Tim. 5:17) and a fully instrumental διά in Paul's own case, then we are face to face here with Paul's distinctively apostolic prerogatives (Acts 8:18; 28:8; II Cor. 12:12; etc.), from which no conclusions may therefore be drawn for the efficacy of the imposition of non-apostolic hands, including Timothy's.[18]

Hands were laid on in various connections in both Old and New Testaments. We accept with Kelly that "ordination or appointment to office in the apostolic Church was modeled on the contemporary Jewish rite for the ordination of rabbis," and that this "in turn found its inspiration in Joshua's ordination as described in Num. xxvii. 18–23 and Deut. xxxiv. 9. . ."[19] The laying on of hands has always been understood in Reformation theology basically as pointed or focused prayer. That is the meaning of the standard rubric that the pastor is to place his hands on the baby's

17. K. Rahner, *Theological Investigations*, XVII:164n. On the same page Rahner also states: "One could finally point to the fact that, at least in fact, the Church does not recognize as a sacramental event (i.e. that total involvement on the Church's part which makes its word *opus operatum*) any transmission of ministry is [sic] not associated with, and illustrated by, the laying on of hands."

18. J.N.D. Kelly makes rather too much of what he calls the "contradiction" between the several presbyters of I Tim. 4:14 and the one Paul in II Tim. 1:6. By way of a solution he adopts D.Daube's "brilliant suggestion" that the phrase in I Tim. 4:14 really renders the technical Hebrew term *semikhath zeqenim*, which means "the leaning, or pressing, of hands upon someone with the object of making him an elder or rabbi." Kelly translates therefore: "along with the laying on of hands for ordination as an elder" (J.N.D. Kelly, *The Pastoral Epistles*, in *Harper's New Testament Commentaries*, 107–108). The suggestion, though no doubt ingenious, seems to lack linguistic plausibility (see Bornkamm's comments in *TDNT*, VI:666, n. 92). Kelly's rendition of "διὰ προφητείας" as "to the accompaniment of prophecy" is too weak, in that it translates the διά as if it were a μετά.

19. *Pastoral Epistles*, 106.

head while praying the Our Father at Baptism. Similarly, the rubric about touching the bread and the cup at the words of consecration reflects the ancient practice of the laying on of hands on the elements, and signals that it is *this* bread and *this* cup, and not all the bread and wine in the city or in the building, to which, by the mandate and promise of Christ, His Word is being added, to make them a sacrament (St. Augustine). No Lutheran theologian has ever imagined, however, that the pastor's hands add any "second blessing" to Baptism, or that the celebrant's touching—or not touching—the elements in any way affects the consecratory power of Christ's words. Just so in ordination the imposition of hands concretely invites the prayers of God's people for, and invokes His blessings upon *that* particular man being ordained. "And this earnest prayer at the ordination of ministers is not without effect," says Chemnitz, "because it rests upon a divine command and promise."[20]

When the Apology states, by way of concession, that "we shall not object either to calling the laying on of hands a sacrament" (Ap. XIII.12), this is clearly meant as synechdoche—letting a part stand for the whole. The argument is that the public ministry of Word and sacrament—as distinct from a neo-Levitical caste of mass-sacrificers—is divinely instituted. Therefore, if ordination [Latin: *ordo*] means putting someone into this divinely instituted office, the action may be called sacramental in that sense. And if all this—the whole mediate call by God through the church—is thought of as culminating concretely in the prayer-gesture of the laying on of hands, then even that action may for that reason and in that sense be called "sacrament."[21] The whole point is not that the laying on of hands is divinely instituted or has any intrinsic sacramental power, but that it shines in the *reflected* light of the real divine institution, the Gospel ministry: "For the ministry of the

20. M. Chemnitz, *Examination* II:694. C.F.W. Walther summed it up well: "Scripture does not tell us of any divine institution of ordination; it merely attests that it was used by the apostles and that at that time the communication of precious gifts was connected with the laying on of hands. According to God's Word there is, of course, no doubt that even today ordination is not a meaningless ceremony if it is connected with the ardent prayer of the church, based on the glorious promises given in particular to the office of the ministry; it is accompanied with the outpouring of heavenly gifts on the person ordained" (*Church and Ministry*, 248).

21. Chemnitz: "And there the words are added, 'We shall not object either to calling the laying on of hands a sacrament.' For that the term sacrament covers a wide range of meanings we have shown above. Thus Augustine says, Bk. 2, *Contra Parmenianum*, that ordination is a sacrament because it is conferred upon a man by some kind of consecration" (*Examination*, II, 694).

Word has the mandate of God and has magnificent promises. . . For the church has the mandate to appoint ministers" (Ap. XIII. 11, 12). The theological *that*, not a ceremonial *how*, is divinely instituted, and the *how* is—synechdochically—spoken of as sacramental only for the sake of, and by virtue of its connection to, the *that*. Any other interpretation would fly in the face of everything that is known about Luther's and Melanchthon's understanding of this matter. The Apology and the Treatise were written by the same author, and cannot reasonably be construed to contradict each other. And the Treatise gives the standard Lutheran view, which at least on this point quite remarkably anticipates what seems to be evolving into a modern ecumenical commonplace:[22] "there was a time when the people elected pastors and bishops. Afterwards a bishop, either of that church or of a neighboring church, was brought in to confirm the election with the laying on of hands; nor was ordination anything more than such confirmation [*comprobatio*, co-approval, attestation]" (Tr. 70). One can only agree with Fagerberg therefore in rejecting various "attempts to attribute a sacramental significance to [the laying on of hands] on the basis of [Ap.] XIII.12."[23]

22. J. Meyendorff, for instance, cites the *BEM* (Lima Statement) definition, that "ordination is an acknowledgement by the Church of the gifts of the Spirit in the one ordained, and a commitment by both the Church and the ordinand to the new relationship," and comments on "this *ecclesial* character of ordination—an act of the whole church and not simply the passing on of some powers from one individual to another. . ." ("Church and Ministry," 118). W. Stein says of Roman Catholicism: "The *ordo* is no longer understood unconditionally as sacrament in the sense in which Luther rejected it as a sacrament," and cites Dupuy, via Rahner: "Jesus established the office in the church. But He has spoken to us no recorded [*überliefertes*, handed down] word about its sacramentality" (*Das Kirchliche Amt bei Luther*, 216). The Council of Trent, however, made no bones about what it condemned: "If anyone says that order or sacred ordination is not truly and properly a sacrament instituted by Christ the Lord. . ., or that it is only a certain rite for selecting ministers of the word of God and of the sacraments: let him be anathema" (Denzinger, *The Sources of Catholic Dogma*, 295, # 963).

23. "Call, election, and ordination normally belonged together, and of these three the call was no doubt looked upon as most essential. Ordination was thought of as a confirmation of the call in the presence of the worshiping congregation, but the form it took was a matter of indifference. The laying on of hands was recommended by both reformers, but it was not held to be expressly commanded in Scripture and therefore did not have the character of a *ius divinum*. Attempts to attribute a sacramental significance to it on the basis of XIII 12 are not correct. What Melanchthon says there must be seen as a benign attempt to be courteous to his opponents, but it lacks fundamental significance" (H. Fagerberg, *A New Look*, 249). It is not correct to suggest, as some do, that Tr. 65, "ordination administered by a pastor in his own church is valid by divine right," implies a divine institution for the laying on of hands. Given the whole context, it does nothing of the sort. The sole point is to deny the Roman claim that only bishops can validly ordain—nothing more. By way of analogy, one may refer to AC XXVIII.22, according to which the churches (and their pastors, according to the German) are "by divine right" bound to obey the bishops when they exercise their office correctly. Yet "the distinction between bishop and pastor is not by divine right" (Tr. 65).

That said, however, one must likewise agree with Fagerberg that "according to Ap. XIV the call also includes a form of ordination."[24] Dogmatically this means that the whole church or congregation, that is, both hearers and preachers, must be allowed their rightful roles in the process of placing a man into the ministry. Good, churchly, apostolic order further requires—by human right—that the candidate be ordained with the laying on of hands by those already in office. The validity of ordination does not, as we have seen, depend on the laying on of hands as such. That is why in exceptional situations of utter isolation the ceremony may be omitted, or administered by the congregation's lay-leaders.[25] Yet on no account is ordination with the laying on of hands to be omitted in normal circumstances. To despise this apostolic custom and order of the church is to be "an obstinate ass" (Dannhauer).[26] Typical of the Old Lutheran attitude is the 1564 reply by the Rostock theological faculty to the question: "Whether a *doctor theologiae* who himself has not been ordained may administer *sacramenta* and ordain others?" The long and the short of it is that while the necessity for such ordination is not absolute, practically "the public ceremony of the ordination with the imposition of hands is for highly important reasons customary in all churches of these lands, which also the Apostles have observed, Acts 6:13, 18, 19, I Tim. 4:5; 2 Tim. 1; Heb. 6, etc." Therefore "it is useful for the maintenance of Christian order, for the unity of the church, and for the dignity of the holy ministry, that the ordination be maintained uniformly with all persons who are in the ecclesiastical office."[27]

24. Ibid., 248.

25. See note 6 above.

26. Cited in C.F.W. Walther, *Church and Ministry*, 266. See pp. 249–267 for a cross-section of standard Lutheran conviction on the subject. That the laying on of hands is in and of itself an adiaphoron was of course axiomatic in the early Missouri Synod. By no means did this imply loose, unchurchly practice, however: "Nonetheless we, in accord with the church of God, regard [ordination] as *relatively* necessary. For ordination is an ecclesiastical ordinance sanctioned by hoary apostolic practice . . . He who without necessity omits ordination is a schismatic, he separates himself from the orthodox church of all times" (*Lehre und Wehre*, 20, 12 [Dec. 1874], 364). The thesis under which these statements occur had originally been framed to read: "Whoever is to administer an essential part of the office of the Word should [*sollte*] be ordained or at any rate set apart for the ministry [*Predigtamt*]." The conference which adopted the essay, however, changed the wording as follows: "Whoever is to administer an essential part of the office of the Word *must* [*muss*] be properly called, thus set apart, but also be ordained according to churchly order" (p. 363).

27. Dedeken's *Thesaurus*, I, B, 490. There follows a warning reference to the deplorable case of Superintendent John Freder, who had ordained others without himself having been ordained, and who was in the end obliged to leave Pomerania on account of the furor which his stubbornness had provoked. The Freder case is described in detail in Lieberg, *Amt und*

The doctrine of the divinity of the mediate call into the ministry through the church has as its necessary corollary or twin the further truth that only God may dismiss His ministers from office. He does this either directly—by calling His servants away from the church militant into the church triumphant—or else mediately, through the church. The church may transfer a minister to another post by means of another legitimate call, or else depose him from office, the latter if and only if God Himself has made plain the man's unfitness to serve any longer on the terms set out in God's written Word.[28] In principle this means removal from office for one of three reasons—and these to be properly established, not simply assumed without proof (I Tim. 5:19): ungodly doctrine or life (Hos. 4:6; Rom. 16:17; Tit 1:5 ff., etc.), or incompetence (for example, not being "apt to teach," I Tim. 3:2; II Tim. 2:24). A divine call, be it noted, binds both ministers and congregations. The former may no more "resign" arbitrarily from their charges, than the latter may arbitrarily dismiss them. To presume, without valid cause, to drive called ministers out of their divinely assigned tasks and responsibilities, is to interfere sacrilegiously with God's government of His church. It is to mistreat God's servants as if they were the servants and hirelings of men (Ps. 105:15; Is. 55:8–11; Mt. 9:38; Lk. 10:16; I Cor. 4:1; Eph. 4:11; Heb. 13:17). Such lawless (II Thess. 2:3.4!) usurpation of divine prerogatives amounts to "temple-robbery" (see Acts 19:37 and Rom. 2:22).[29]

Ordination, 360–373. Especially in his treatment of Luther, however, Lieberg tends to over-interpret the laying on of hands in the sense of a divine institution and necessity (229–232). Both Luther (precisely the "old" Luther of 1542 and 1544 [*An Example of How to Consecrate a True Christian Bishop, WA* 53:257.1–11; *Genesis Commentary, LW* 7:146–147; *WA* 44:407.34–40]) and Melanchthon (Lieberg, *Amt und Ordination*, 373n) cited the wedding service as an analogue to ordination. Such an analogy would have been quite misleading, had anything more than a practical necessity for the sake of good churchly order been intended. Walther: ". . . just as the ecclesiastical wedding does not make the marriage, but only ecclesiastically confirms the marriage already entered into" (*Pastoraltheologie*, 65).

28. "In such a case the *congregation* does not actually dismiss its minister, but only *acts for God* in so doing" (J. H. C. Fritz, *Pastoral Theology*, 45).

29. Luther wrote a letter concerning this problem. See *That a Pastor Should Not be Silent at the Unjust Deposition of a Minister* (1531), *WABr* 6:77.8–79.99. Walther translates most of this letter and also provides quotations from Clement of Rome, and Cyprian, in *Church and Ministry*, 225–229, 243–245. Chemnitz, whom his translator, J.A.O. Preus, rightly calls "the father of normative Lutheran theology and . . . the forerunner of the period of Lutheran orthodoxy" (M. Chemnitz, *Loci Theologici* I:14), put it like this: "Therefore, as long as God endures in the ministry His minister who teaches correctly and lives blamelessly, the church does not have authority to remove someone else's servant. But when he no longer edifies the church by doctrine or life, but destroys [it], then God Himself removes him. Hos. 4:6; 1 Sam. 2:30. Therefore there are two reasons for which God removes unfaithful ministers from

It is in this context that the so-called "temporary call" must be seen for what it is: a "call" with built-in dismissal on unbiblical grounds. No one can without self-contradiction say to a minister: "God wishes you here for now, but wants you gone by Jan. 1 three years hence, unless we are pleased to keep you another three years." It is another matter, of course, if the position or task is itself by its very nature temporary, e.g. chaplain to an expedition, helping out in cases of illness, etc.[30] What is objectionable is the limitation of the "call" without intrinsic need, simply to allow the "calling" persons to dismiss the minister at their pleasure, without having to bother about proving ungodly doctrine or life, or incompetence. So strong was the early Missouri Synod's conviction on this point, that the original constitution expressly ruled out "temporary calls" as contrary to AC XIV.[31] Equally abhorrent to Missouri's founders was the system, then popular in other synods,

---

their office: (1) because of doctrine, when they teach error... (2) Because of life.... For just as God calls, so also does He remove through means. But just as a call in keeping with the instruction of the Lord of the harvest, so also, when someone must be removed from the ministry, it is necessary that the church can show with certainty that this is the judgment and this is the will of God. And just as the call, so also does the deposition pertain to the whole church in a certain orderly way. Hence the ancient church with diligent inquiry and accurate judgment in its councils dealt with the reasons for deposition" (*Loci Theologici*, II, 703). Mörlin, Chemnitz's contemporary, who had himself been unjustly driven out of office, wrote: "In sum, the world nowadays plays with the preaching office like hooligans with blind dice at their bench: whoever tells them a little something that doesn't please them, must be gone, and another be put in his place, who will do according to what we can endure and tolerate." Again: "[They imagine:] The preacher has his office from them, since they pay him. Therefore he must do as they wish, or else they have every right and power to dismiss him, as every master has in respect of his servant. So also the dear N. regards the ministry [preaching office] and the call of a preacher as nothing other than a contract of the sort one makes with a cowherd or sowherd... But I ask, For God's sake, tell me whoever can: By whom was the preacher called and placed into his office through orderly means?" (Dedeken's *Thesaurus*, I/2, 908, 913–914). For references to early Missouri Synod and Synodical Conference discussions of this matter, see "*Amtsentsetzung*" under "*Beruf*" in E. Eckhardt, *Homiletisches Reallexikon*, 371–375.

30. F. Pieper: "The essence of the temporary call does not consist in this that a call is limited as to time, but in this that human beings arbitrarily limit a call as to time, that is, that they want to determine how long a pastor is to be active at a certain place... If a congregation issues a so-called temporary call, that is, if it in advance and arbitrarily decides that the man to be called is to leave his place after one, two, three, or four years, it becomes guilty of encroaching upon God's office and work. Dr. Walther says: 'Neither is a congregation authorized to issue such a call, nor has a pastor the right to accept it.' Such a call is contrary to the divinity of a proper call to a pastorate in the Church as it is plainly taught in the Bible" (translated from *Lehre und Wehre*, 1898, 339–341, in P. F. Koehneke, "The Call into the Holy Ministry," 381–382).

31. "Proper (not temporary) calling of the pastors. . ." Constitution, II, conditions of membership, 5 (*Concordia Historical Institute Quarterly*, XIX, 3 [Oct. 1946], 3). The German has "*Ordentlicher. . . Beruf*," which is exactly the term used in AC XIV. See also the voluminous bibliography in Eckhardt's *Reallexikon*, "*Beruf des Pastors*," 358–360, and the representative discussion in Fritz, *Pastoral Theology*, 45–47.

of granting provisional, temporary "licenses" to preachers to see how they would turn out.[32]

Transfer to another field of service, through another proper call, is of course possible, and often desirable for the church, on account of the "diversities of gifts" (I Cor. 12:4) among her ministers. Long and faithful pastorates, however, make for stability in the church.[33] Frequent changes of ministers should be discouraged for this reason, and pastors themselves must scrupulously avoid even the impression of frivolity in such matters, and especially of all professionalist careerism, fired by greed and ambition. (On the other hand, of course, the church owes her ministers and their families adequate support, I Cor. 9:14; Gal. 6:6; I Tim. 5:17). To serve faithfully at his post, at the pleasure of the church's Lord, is a minister's greatest honor.

This distinction between the ministry as a life-long calling on the one hand, and the possible changes of fields of service on the other, is reflected in the difference between ordination and installation (or "investiture," to use an older term, and one unspoilt by images of soulless appliances). It is not strictly speaking the case, therefore, that, as is sometimes said, there is "no essential difference between the installation and the ordination."[34] Ordination signals a man's entry, life-long, into the sacred ministry of Christ's Gospel and church, while installation places him into a particular charge. So, for example, I Tim. 4:14 seems to refer to Timothy's ordination, while Acts 13:3 was clearly something more like an "installation" or commissioning for a particular task (cf. Acts

32. "From this [discussion of biblical qualifications for office] it may be seen what an unbiblical, unconscionable, and soul-destroying thing the so-called licensing system is, which is still practiced here in some synods, and according to which those whom one dares not ordain into the office because they are untried or because of their defective competence for office, are given only a so-called license, on the strength of which they are to work in a congregation on a trial basis" (C.F.W. Walther, *Pastoraltheologie*, 64). Synod's original constitution stipulated: "The so-called licenses which are in use in this country are not given by the Synod, because they are against Scripture and proper church practice" (*Concordia Historical Institute Quarterly*, XIX, 3 [Oct. 1946], 10).

33. The ancient church took a dim view of "translations" of clergy to other churches, the First Nicene Council even, in its Canon XV, seeming to prohibit the practice altogether. No such absolute prohibition was apparently intended, however. The great Gregory of Nazianzus was in fact "translated" from Sasima to Constantinople, yet resigned the presidency of the First Council of Constantinople largely on that account. See *NPNF*, 2:XIV:33; Mansi 2:690–691.

34. Fritz, *Pastoral Theology*, 69.

14:26). Ordination, then, is not repeated,[35] while installation is repeated as often as a minister is placed into a new field of service. To be sure, ordination may never be absolute, that is, without reference to a particular call to a particular field of service.[36] But by becoming a minister of one local church, one thereby becomes a minister in the church universal, and thus a recognized colleague of all other orthodox pastors, to be treated accordingly, for instance by being asked to take part officially in the liturgy when visiting.[37] This is the "plus" of ordination over installation.[38]

In light of all the above, it should be perfectly clear that being "properly called" (*rite vocatus*) means much more than simply being asked, or invited, or "authorized" to "conduct services" on one or more Sundays. To be *properly called* in the sense of AC XIV is to have been found personally and theologically qualified, and to have been solemnly entrusted by the church—and life-long, not "till further notice"—with the divinely established Gospel ministry, and this in some particular field of service for as long as it shall please God. Unless insurmountable isolation from the rest of the

35. In the Smalcald Articles Luther wishes to follow "the examples of the ancient churches and Fathers" in the matter of ordination, and appeals to the papal party's own laws, which hold "that those who are ordained by heretics shall also be regarded as ordained and remain so" (SA III.X.3). That this is not simply a tactical appeal to the opponents' own principles is clear from Luther's great treatise on *The Private Mass and the Consecration of Priests*, penned just four years earlier: "Even the pope himself has ordered in his spiritual statutes (though they were taken from the ancient fathers), that one should regard the consecration or ordination performed by heretics as a true consecration and not reconsecrate those who had been consecrated by heretics" (*On the Private Mass and the Consecration of Priests* [1533], *LW* 38:196; *WA* 237.4–7).

36. "Neither presbyter, deacon, nor any of the ecclesiastical order shall be ordained at large, nor unless the person ordained is particularly appointed to a church in a city or village, or to a martyr, or to a monastery. And if any have been ordained without a charge, the holy Synod decrees, to the reproach of the ordainer, that such an ordination shall be inoperative, and that such shall nowhere be suffered to officiate" (Canon VI, Council of Chalcedon, [451], *NPNF*, 2:XIV:271; Mansi 6:1226). This canon is cited with approval in Walther, *Church and Ministry*, 267.

37. W. Elert, *Eucharist and Church Fellowship*, 161–163.

38. The early Missouri Synod treasured such churchly traditions. The Synod's official organ, *Der Lutheraner*, for 28 Nov. 1848 (vol. 5, no. 7), printed the minutes of the St. Louis area pastors' conference, which included the following: "He who has been properly called by a congregation, has thereby been called by the whole church generally into the (preaching-office) ministry of the church for the duration of his whole life, for through such a proper call it becomes evident that he is called by God Himself to the ministry of the church . . . According to Gerhard ordination happens only once. For he says: 'In this investiture differs from ordination, in that ordination happens only once, but investiture is repeated as often as someone who was already ordained into the ministry of the church before, is called to another congregation or to another grade of the office in the same congregation. . .Ordination happens only once, because the church recognizes from the first call of a Christian into the ministry [*Predigtamt*] that he is chosen by God Himself for the service of the church, and it suffices that she publicly and solemnly attest this on that occasion' " (our translation).

orthodox church prevents it, such conferral of the public ministry of the Gospel includes, as a matter of good, apostolic, churchly order, also a rite of ordination with the laying on of hands. Without being "properly called" in this sense, no one is "publicly to teach or preach or administer the sacraments in the church." That is verbatim the teaching ("our churches *teach*") of AC XIV. This aspect calls for a few concluding comments. First of all it is necessary to understand that it is not here a question of "cannot"—in a sacerdotalist sense—but of "may not," in the sense of the divinely established evangelical order in the church. It is an evangelical axiom that the ministry derives its validity from the Gospel, and not vice versa (Phil 1:15–18). The minister therefore does not "make" a sacrament by some occult powers inhering in his person or office, as distinct from the rest of the people of God. Rather, as his title, "minister," indicates, he merely serves Christ and His people by "administering" the sacraments Christ Himself makes through the continuing efficacy of His words of institution.[39] The minister's function is strictly instrumental: "The person adds nothing to this Word and office commanded by Christ" (Tr. 26, German). Or, in Luther's famous remark of 1533:

> For our faith and the sacrament must not be based on the person, whether he is godly or evil, *consecrated or unconsecrated*, called or an impostor, whether he is the devil or his mother, but upon Christ, upon his word, upon his office, upon his command and ordinance.[40]

So long as Christ's words of institution are allowed to stand unperverted (see FC SD VII, 32), the means of grace retain their own inherent validity and efficacy.[41] Thus even where, as in the case of women (see excursus: "The Ordination of Women"), purported ordinations are null and void, because they are contrary to God's Word, sacraments celebrated by such persons are not to be

39. "We join the water to the word, as he commands us to do; however, not this action of ours, but Christ's command and ordinance make it a baptism. According to his command we join bread and wine to the word of Christ; however, not this action of ours, but Christ's word and ordinance effect the change ...; for Christ ... baptizes persons and gives them his body and blood, no matter whose hand it is or what kind of a hand it is by which he does it." (*On the Private Mass and the Consecration of Priests* [1533], *LW* 38:202–203; *WA* 38:242.22–26, 28–30).

40. Ibid., *LW* 38:200; *WA* 38:241.6–9.

41. "Offices and sacraments always remain in the church; persons are daily subject to change. As long as we call and induct into the offices persons who can administer them, then the offices will surely continue to be exercised. The horse has been bridled and saddled; if you place on it even a naked lad who can ride, the horse will proceed as well as if the emperor or the pope were riding it" (*The Private Mass and the Consecration of Priests* [1533], *LW* 38:201; *WA* 38:241.19–23).

regarded as invalid per se, but as disorderly and schismatic, that is, as having been done by private, uncalled persons.[42]

Secondly, the word "publicly" in AC XIV means not simply "in public" but "officially," in the name and on behalf of Christ's church. Christians in their various callings not only may but ought to proclaim the divine truth in the public realm (Acts 8:4). Christian university lecturers, for instance, do not in the least offend against the ordered ministry when they publicly bear witness to the truth of their holy faith, particularly in opposition to some of their colleagues, who might be ardent propagandists for Marxism, libertinism, nihilism, or what have you. In the public, official services of the church, however—as distinct from the "private" domestic, or the "public" political domain—no individual may take it upon himself to administer the communal treasures without proper authority, i.e. the divine call (*rite vocatus*). "Lay-preaching" on the basis of the priesthood of all believers, is a distinctively Methodist notion, and can claim no support in Luther's evangelical Reformation.[43]

Thirdly, AC XIV treats of the divine arrangements to which the church is ordinarily, normally, and normatively bound. In emergencies, when the normal order collapses or is inaccessible, love must serve the neighbor as best it can.[44] The Treatise therefore,

---

42. "Nothing less will do than taking the stand that all such ordinations are contrary to God's Word and invalid, and that all official acts done by these ladies are done by lay persons. Baptisms done by them stand as those done by a midwife" (H. Sasse, *We Confess the Church*, 60). It is an altogether different question whether baptisms in the name of some feminist goddess are valid, which of course they are not. This catastrophic sacramental devastation looming behind the issue of women's ordination, has been addressed by my colleague, D. P. Scaer, in "The Validity of the Churchly Acts of Ordained Women." Where such purported baptisms must be regarded as invalid, however, the reason can never be some defect in, or even the total absence of, ordination, but can only be the public perversion of Christ's words of institution, whether by Unitarians or by feminist goddess cultists who reject God's self-revelation as Father, Son, and Holy Spirit. See also A. F. Kimel, Jr., "The Holy Trinity Meets Ashtoreth: A Critique of the Episcopal 'Inclusive' Liturgies."

43. The priesthood of all believers "has been used to support a bewildering variety of practices, such as congregational polity, the Quaker meeting, pietistic *ecclesiolae*, and the Methodist commissioning of lay preachers" (B. A. Gerrish, *The Old Protestantism and the New*, 90). See also *Infiltrating and Clandestine Preachers*, (1532), *LW* 40:379–394; *WA* 30:III:518–527.

44. "Of course everyone who thus departs from the order must also know why he does this. The basis for this however is none other than the one which God's Word itself cites, namely that love is the fulfilling of the law. He who does not know this basis, and does it nonetheless, by the seat of his pants [*auf's Geradewohl hin*], sins against conscience and misuses his Christian liberty. Besides, one must also carefully consider that one may depart from God's order in an emergency only so long and so far as the emergency persists. Continuing to break the order without necessity, while appealing to love, would be mere self-will and contempt of the divine order and majesty, which has established such order" (*Lehre und Wehre* 20, 9 [Sept. 1874], 264).

citing Augustine's famous example of the two laymen in a ship, states: "So in an emergency even a layman absolves and becomes the minister and pastor of another" (Tr. 67). This shows that (1) the means of grace do not depend for their "validity" on anyone's ordination,[45] and (2) the Gospel-ministry belongs by Christ's gift to the spiritual priesthood, the church, and its exercise therefore reverts to that priesthood directly in emergencies.[46]

A special case, however, is the Sacrament of the Altar, and this not because it is somehow "above" the ministry of the Word. Walther sums it up well:

> The great majority of our theologians, Luther at the head, hold that the Holy Supper should never be administered privately by someone not occupying the public ministry, or a so-called layman; partly because in respect of the Holy Supper there cannot arise, as with baptism and absolution, an emergency such as would justify the departure from God's order (I Cor. 4:1; Rom. 10:15; Heb. 5:4), partly because the Holy Supper "is a public confession and therefore must have public servants," partly because through such secret communion schisms could easily be occasioned... That the administration of the Holy Supper by a layman is never *recta* [right] and *legitima* [legitimate] and never happens *de jure*, most [orthodox theologians] declare; but that it is *rata* [valid] and can happen *de facto*, none denies.[47]

"Emergency" in this context, moreover, means not mere inconvenience, but imminent danger of death or severe spiritual anguish and affliction, combined with the actual inaccessibility of any orthodox ministers.[48] Where such conditions obtain, Chris-

---

45. W. Stein has drawn attention to the fact that several pre-Reformation theologians, including Albert the Great, the teacher of Thomas Aquinas, maintained the sacramentality of lay-absolution in emergencies (*Das kirchliche Amt bei Luther*, 51–52).

46. "So when women baptize [in cases of necessity], they exercise the function of priesthood legitimately, and do it not as a private act, but as a part of the public ministry of the church which belongs only to the priesthood" (*Concerning the Ministry* [1523], *LW* 40:23; *WA* 12:181.30–32).

47. C.F.W. Walther, *Pastoraltheologie*, 175–176. Appealing to the same Luther-quote (*WABr* 7:338–339), B. Gerrish states: "It seems that the only priestly function the unordained may not perform, either regularly or occasionally, is the administration of the Lord's Supper. Luther offers three reasons for this firm refusal: the Lord's Supper is by its very nature a public act of the church; it is not (as is the Word or gospel) absolutely necessary for salvation; and to administer the Supper outside of public worship would be schismatic" (*The Old Protestantism and the New*, 102). The last point, however, is not stated precisely enough, since Luther does not dream of forbidding "private" communion of the sick, provided this is done by the public ministers of the church.

48. The older divines cited by Walther use such expressions as "the highest and most extreme emergency," "highest mortal danger," "the most extreme emergency and in danger of death," "one in affliction who burns to the utmost with desire for the reception of the sacrament" (*Pastoraltheologie*, 178–180). "Thesis 22. *No emergency exists where by keeping the divine order, souls are obliged to take upon themselves only a temporal and bodily inconvenience.*

tians must act as charity directs and conscience allows, and they should also take a charitable view of any differences in judgment that might arise. Certainly, however, genuine emergency-communions by laymen cannot in the nature of the case be organized into a permanent, ordered practice. The latter therefore amounts to regularized irregularity, or disorder disguised as order, and thus to a legitimation of disregard for what God Himself has instituted in His church. Whatever love may have to do strictly occasionally and temporarily in *extraordinary*, emergency cases, the *ordinary*, regulated, continuing practice can only be public preaching, teaching, and administration of the sacraments by properly qualified and called ministers of the Gospel.[49]

People who live at some distance from established congregations often, in order to violate the divine order, make an emergency of something which is not actually an emergency. If they must perchance travel 10 to 20 miles in order to get to neighboring Lutheran preachers, then they call that an emergency in respect of the reception of the Word and sacraments, because it is inconvenient, too far or too costly to make their way there, and on that account they request a travelling preacher [*Reiseprediger*]; while they should be glad, if this is possible for them, to travel hundreds of miles in order to receive Baptism for an as yet unbaptized baby from a regularly called preacher, rather than break the order. That sort of thing is after all not a spiritual but a bodily emergency, for the sake of which the divine order may not be broken. A spiritual emergency exists only where by observing the divine order the soul would come into the danger of being lost" (LCMS Western District Convention Essay, 1865, *Proceedings*, 67, our translation).

49. The old divines could envisage the boundary-case of a man called by the congregation provisionally and only for the duration of the emergency (e.g. "at a time of the plague, when all regular servants have been taken away by death, likewise in times of public collapse, when the order of the church is dissolved . . .," and then only to teach the Word "only by reading," and to give the Holy Supper to those who desire it, "until they are again provided with a regular servant. But in this way the layman administers not as layman, but as a truly and for a time called servant" (cited in Walther, *Pastoraltheologie*, 180–181). The 1874 *Lehre und Wehre* theses cited earlier, refer to this place in Walther's book and add: "yet we must stoutly emphasize that only the most pressing emergency permits this" (Dec., p. 364). These theses address the question: "Has the congregation the right in the regular way [*ordentlicher Weise:* 'ordinarily' now means simply 'usually,' and is therefore too weak; divine order or ordinance is at stake here] to confer an essential part of the holy ministry [*Predigtamt*] temporarily upon some layman?" A clear "No!" is the answer given in the concluding thesis: "The congregation may therefore in the regular way [*ordentlicher Weise*] confer an essential part of the holy ministry only on him whom she has regularly [ordentlich: same as in the 'ordentlichen Beruf' {regular call} of AC XIV] called and set apart for the office of the Word, namely for as long as it shall please God, the Founder of the office" (p. 369).

Another essay articulates the maxim: *"No arrangements may be made by which the departure from the divine order of the public minstry is made into a standing order"* (LC-MS Western District Convention Essay, 1865, *Proceedings*, p. 68. Italics in the original). Given the state of transportation and communication in modern North America, emergencies owing to the inaccessibility of orthodox pastors are virtually unimaginable.

Purely assisting functions, such as reading printed sermons in the pastor's absence, or helping him with the distribution of the Sacrament (as distinct from consecrating or deciding who may be admitted to the Lord's Table), may of course be delegated to suitable laymen.[50]

50. "Vicars," in the North American Lutheran sense, do not strictly speaking "preach," but deliver sermons for which the properly called pastors take responsibility. P. Brunner rightly says that assistance in the distribution of the sacrament was "an important liturgical function of the ancient deacon" (*The Ministry and the Ministry of Women*, 36). It does not follow, however, that women or deaconesses may be allowed to do this. On the contrary, while deaconesses in some parts of the ancient church carried the Sacrament to sick women at home, the exercise by women of the full liturgical diaconate in the public worship of the church (including the dispensing of the Cup) was always a hallmark of heretical deviation, and was not the practice of the orthodox church (see "Excursus on the Service of Women in the Early Church," *Women in the Church*, CTCR Report, 1985, pp. 12–17). Such public service at the altar is not in keeping with the feminine dignity and modesty (I Cor. 14:33–36) implicit in the κεφαλή-structure which shapes the church (see "Excursus: The Ordination of Women" which follows).

EXCURSUS

THE ORDINATION OF WOMEN

According to the revealed will of God, women cannot occupy the office of the Gospel ministry. Whatever else may and must be said on the subject—and that is a great deal—the inspired apostolic prohibitions in I Cor. 14:34 and I Tim. 2:12 make it impossible to recognize female pastors anywhere within the one, holy, catholic, and *apostolic* church. A church which ordains women into the public ministry of Word and Sacraments, thereby certifies itself to be un-apostolic and anti-apostolic. Behind the apostle stands of course the Lord Himself. Despite the prominence, exemplary devotion, and courage of women in His cause and service (Mt. 27:55.56), and despite the temporal priority of women as witnesses to His Resurrection (Mk. 16:1–8; Jn. 20:1 ff.), Christ appointed not a single woman as His apostle. If the reason for this be sought in the Jewish legal system, in which a woman could not be a *shaliach* for instance, then such considerations do not apply in the case of the "apostle to the Gentiles," since priestesses of all kinds were well entrenched, culturally, in the Greco-Roman world. The facts remain that in Jesus, God became a man, not a woman; that His chosen apostolate, in, with, and under which our public ministry was divinely instituted, included no women, not even those very near and dear to Him; and that by express apostolic command the public ministers of the Gospel, that is, those who in this special way "do not represent their own persons but the person of Christ. . . . in Christ's place and stead" (Ap. VII/VIII.28), must be qualified men, not women.

The apostolic prohibitions on this score must not be put on a par with transitory, culture-dependent directives like those about Mosaic proprieties (Acts 15:29) and head-coverings (I Cor. 11).[1] The first case is clearly one of missionary accommodation (Acts 15:21), and in the second Paul appeals ultimately to the church's "custom" (συνήθεια, I Cor. 11:16). The immutable principle behind

1. Compare AC XXVIII, 54–66.

changing customs like those to do with head-coverings, is that of "headship," or the "κεφαλή-structure" (I Cor. 11:3, cf. Eph. 5:23), built into the creation itself.[2]

As a divine institution the public ministry is by definition culture-invariant in its essence. The headship principle either applies here, in this clear-cut case, or else it cannot be applied at all. "The main application of [I Cor. 14:33b–35 and I Tim. 2:11–15] in the contemporary church is that women are not to exercise those functions in the local congregation which would involve them in the exercise of authority inherent in the authoritative public teaching office (i.e. the office of pastor)."[3] This implies that there could, no doubt even should, be other applications of the basic headship/subordination principle. It is after all in the nature of Christian faith and love to seek to please God as much, and not as little, as possible. Only, in most other cases we are not dealing with the unambiguous theological category of a divine institution—there is a doctrine of the ministry, but there is no such thing as a "doctrine of head-coverings," for example!—and to that extent further applications will be less conclusive, and more subject to individual judgment, in the spirit of Rom. 14:19–23.

Although the ordination of women was not an issue in Luther's day, he grasped the theological import of the question more keenly than did some of the later theologians.[4] Luther was well aware of the prominent leadership positions occupied by certain women in the Old Testament, and he taunted the anti-clerical fanatics for having overlooked these examples seemingly favorable to their cause. "But in the New Testament," he wrote, "the Holy Spirit, speaking through St. Paul, ordained that women should be silent in the churches and assemblies [I Cor. 14:34], and said that this is

2. P. Brunner, *The Ministry and the Ministry of Women*, esp. 23–35. See also *Women in the Church: Scriptural Principles and Ecclesial Practice*, esp. 27–41.

3. *Women in the Church*, 38.

4. See the brief discussion in P. Brunner, op.cit., 11–12. For an accurate report of Luther's actual position, citing in full ten of his references to the matter, see H. Kirsten, "Luther und die Frauenordination," 139–148. Rather incredible, in view of the evidence is W. Maurer's remark that Luther meant to exclude only married women from the public ministry (*Historical Commentary*, 359, n.440). The reference is to Luther's Timothy-commentary of 1528, as reconstructed from Rörer's often fragmentary notes (*LW* 28:276–277). The sentence occurs there: "Here we properly take 'woman' to mean wife, as he reveals from his correlative phrase (v. 12) 'to have authority over man,' that is, over her husband." However, other statements in that very context show that Luther did not understand St. Paul's prohibition to apply only to *married* women: "Where men and women have been joined together, there the men, not the women, ought to have authority . . . Where there is a man, there no woman should teach or have authority . . . Where there are men, she should neither teach nor rule . . . Then comes the teaching, and Paul does not entrust the ministry of the Word to her . . . You must always understand this with the condition that men are present."

the Lord's commandment." On the underlying headship/subordination principle Luther wrote: "The gospel, however, does not abrogate this natural law, but confirms it as the ordinance and creation of God."[5]

In opposing the ordination of women, modern Lutherans should take care not to align themselves with the misogynist ethos of the celibacy-oriented Roman Catholic hierarchy, and of its imitators among "Anglo-Catholics": "Daniel says that it is characteristic of Antichrist's kingdom to despise women (11:37)" (Ap. XXIII. 25). G. Stoeckhardt was on the right track when he spoke of womanly "reserve" and "decorousness"—thereby suggesting that what was at stake in I Cor. 14 was not an ontological inferiority of women, but their distinctively feminine modesty and dignity.[6] On the other hand, it is patent nonsense to argue that modern church-life is too male-oriented and needs to be made more appealing to women. On the contrary, religion in modern Western society is already a predominantly female affair, and is becoming more so.[7] It is important to understand that the real push for female pastors comes not from any sort of biblical considerations at all, but from a militant, and essentially secular, feminism.

To talk of the New Testament as "an intrinsically oppressive text," even renaming it "the Second Testament"[8]—clearly in order to deny it finality—is to abandon all pretence of Christian exegesis or interpretation. The glib deployment of Gal. 3:28 ("there is neither male nor female") against the express apostolic prohibition of female pastors, points in the same direction, for it logically entails also a total interchangeability of the sexes in marriage—in other words, same sex "marriages"! Some do not hesitate to go to such

5. *Infiltrating and Clandestine Preachers* (1532), *LW* 40:390–391; *WA* 30:III:518–527 and *On the Councils and the Church* (1539), *LW* 41:155; *WA* 50:633.23–24. Note also E. Stauffer's comment in *TDNT* II:440–441: "Men and women are both members of this organism, but in their own way. It is precisely in the Church that the distinction of sexes acquires its final seriousness from the biological and practical standpoint. Woman is to be silent in the Church, not because she has no gifts or is perhaps too eloquent, but simply because she is a woman (I Cor. 14:34f.). The 'subjection' of woman to man is established rather than overthrown in the Church."

6. G. Stoeckhardt, *"Von dem Beruf der Lehrerinnen an christlichen Gemeindeschulen,"* 768.

7. Ann Douglas, *The Feminization of American Culture*. H. Mol, *Religion in Australia*, 27 ff. dramatizes "the over-representation of women at Protestant church services" with a hymn-parody:

In the world's great field of battle,
In the bivouac of life
You will find the Christian soldier
Represented by his wife.

8. So Sandra M. Schneiders, "Feminist Ideology Criticism and Biblical Hermeneutics," 3.

lengths, and patronizingly dismiss St. Paul's condemnations of sodomy as the culture-bound judgment of "a faithful apostle and a profound interpreter of the central message of the gospel, yet one who was also a fallible and historically-conditioned human being."[9] To discard at will so crystal-clear a piece of consistent prophetic-apostolic teaching is to throw the whole Bible to the winds.

By far the greatest effort of J. Reumann's *Ministries Examined* is devoted to the defense of the indefensible ordination of women into the public ministry of the Gospel. His chapter, made up mostly of earlier presentations on the subject, lays claim to having significantly shaped "the present configuration" of U.S. Lutheranism by making women pastors theologically acceptable within what is now the ELCA.[10] The chief merits of Reumann's treatment lie in his prodigious documentation, his insider's account of recent U.S. Lutheran discussion on the subject, and above all his recognition of the decisive role of "the Scripture issue"[11]—something not always admitted in this connection. The "real problem," Reumann rightly notes, "is hermeneutical."[12] Reumann's own conclusions in favor of women pastors are inseparable from his historical-critical premises. Thus he can wonder, for instance, about "the extent to which the 12 apostles are a Lucan creation."[13] The two most explicit texts against the ordination of women, I Cor. 14:34 and I Tim. 2:12, are got rid of as "a later gloss" and as part of the Pastoral letters, none of which were written by Paul, respectively.[14]

9. J. B. Nelson, *Embodiment*, 188, cf. 208; cf. 51 and 103 for the antinomian exploitation of Gal. 3:28. The book promoting the nihilistic drivel cited bears rhapsodic endorsements from prominent "theologians.".

10. "My essay, as part of the Division of Theological Studies process, had effects first within the Lutheran Council in the U.S.A. . . It helped show there are no conclusive grounds in Scripture against ordaining women. . . The view that women could be ordained prevailed. . . The DTS position held up within the Council, indeed was received with enthusiasm, at its annual meeting. . . The essay, secondly, played some role, as part of the LCUSA study, in gaining convention approval in the LCA and ALC and a smooth transition in those bodies to having *persons* in the ordained ministry and not just men. . ." (J. Reumann, *Ministries Examined*, 131, cf. 16–19). "It is not too much to say that the work on ordaining women in 1968–1970 contributed to the present configuration of Lutherans in the United States. . ." (p. 18).

11. J. Reumann, *Ministries Examined*, 224, cf. 18. and note 3.

12. Ibid., 99.

13. Ibid., 252, n. 111.

14. Ibid., 111–112 ("we must distinguish Paul's own writings from those of his followers in his name, i.e., the deutero-Paulines and the Pastorals"). Reumann's historical-critical approach is more subdued in the earlier "stratum" of his chapter and more open later. This no doubt reflects the differing church-political realities before and after general acceptance of women pastors was assured in the former ALC and LCA. Earlier, Reumann had signalled rejection of "[a]ttempts. . . to brush [I Cor. 14:34] aside as mere cultural accommodations to

Reumann's repeated appeals to Gal. 3:28 stand clearly within the framework of his gnosticizing understanding of eschatology.[15] The idea is that the unfolding of "God's plan"—which embodies, apparently, large chunks of democratic ideology—progressively abandons things like "the ancient patterns of subordination to the state (cf. Romans 13);" that now, "in this decade [1970's], the social, cultural milieu, at least in the United States and Europe, has brought the question of the place of women in society and church to our agenda as never before;" and that in this way we are "challenged to implement more of the impact of our own gospel, that in Christ God's original will is being restored for humankind."[16] It is well worth quoting the late H. P. Hamann's trenchant response to Reumann's eschatology:

> We are not to see the new order in Christ as gradually transforming the old orders of creation, until the new order of things has completely dispossessed the old. A true understanding of the New Testament rather sees . . . the old order of creation, as ruined by sin, continuing till the end when Christ returns, while the new order of things in Christ ("the old has passed away, behold, the new has come," 2 Cor. 5:17) runs parallel with the old—there is an overlapping of the two aeons—till that same return of Christ. But the new is there in faith, not sight. Nothing of the new is visible, demonstrable: not Christ, not the Spirit, not the *Una Sancta*, not the new birth in Baptism, not the body and blood of the Sacrament, not the forgiveness of sins—nothing. All these are realities, and faith is sure of them,

---

the day, no more valid for us than Paul's opinions on clothes or hairstyles" (p. 89). Later something very similar becomes part of Reumann's argument: "that Jesus was male; that his message was spread publicly primarily by men, including 12 he chose during his lifetime—all these and many other details are part of the economy in the sense of God's condescending and accomodating the divine self to the modes of the time. *They are no more determinative for future structures in Ministry than the use of Hebrew and Aramaic or the wearing of sandals and beards*" (p. 130, our emphases). "In the later New Testament, and the patristic church, the dominant, patriarchal line comes to control," Reumann admits (p. 115). His "thesis," however, in light of the alleged "situation in the New Testament," is "that a church today may, and, indeed, has the task and the right to recognize ministries, or, if it chooses to use the term, to 'validate' them, on the basis of whatever New Testament standards, developed traditions, sense of order and implications of reason, or current needs, it chooses" (p. 116). By contrast, the Missouri Synod's *A Statement of Scriptural and Confessional Principles* (officially adopted in 1973) expressly rejects "the claim that Paul's statements on the role of women in the church are not binding today because they are the culturally conditioned result of the apostle's sharing the views of contemporary Judaism as a child of his time" (IV, F, 4). This section was specifically invoked against the ordination of women by the 1972 *Report of the Synodical President* ("The Blue Book"), p. 118.

15. *Ministries Examined*, 120 and passim. "The 'eschatological question' continues to seem to me the most significant and the most neglected" (p. 259, n. 187). Following R. Scroggs, Reumann alleges a "tension" between Paul's "Hellenistic Judaism and his basic Christian theological stance" (p. 254, n. 139).

16. Ibid., 130–131.

> because of the Word of God, but they are all hidden in this world, where what is visible is exactly what has been there from the beginning. There is a realism about this proper view of eschatology which stands in marked contrast to the wishful thinking and enthusiasm of all eschatologies which look for a change in the present world's basic structure.[17]

In light of all the foregoing one can only agree with Reumann that "admission of women to ordination cannot help but reshape the ministry itself and ultimately theology."[18]

17. H. P. Hamann, "The New Testament and the Ordination of Women," 107. The comments cited were in response to statements in J. Reumann, "What in Scripture Speaks to the Ordination of Women?" 5–30, which comprises the first part of Reumann's "Ordination of Women" chapter in *Ministries Examined.*

18. *Ministries Examined,* 124.

CHURCH GOVERNANCE

Inasmuch as the power of the church or of bishops bestows eternal gifts and is used and exercised only through the office of preaching, it does not interfere at all with government or temporal authority.

Augsburg Confession XXVIII, 10

12

THE TWO KINGDOMS OR GOVERNMENTS

Neither the church nor her ministry can be properly understood without the crucial distinction between God's two kingdoms, realms, or governments. On the one hand God (and so Christ) rules the whole universe by His almighty power (Ps. 46; 50:9–12; 102:25–27; Is. 44–47; Mt. 28:18; Jn. 1:1–3; Eph. 4:10; Col. 1:15–17). This is the so-called "Left Hand" kingdom of God.[1] On the other hand the kingdom which has come "near" in Christ (Mk. 1:15) is something totally different. This "Right Hand" kingdom, though it presupposes the "Left Hand" and the defeat of the "powers" of darkness (Ps. 110; Col. 1:13; 2:15; cf. Jn. 16:33), is *for mankind* one of grace and mercy (Jn. 1:14.17), not of condemnation (Lk. 9:55; Jn. 3:17). This kingdom or reign is "not of this world" (Jn. 18:36), yet it lives and flourishes already in this world (Lk. 17:20.21)—but in a humble (Mt. 21:5), hidden (Mt. 13), and embattled (Mt. 10:34–11:19) way during this present age. In the age to come, at the Savior's return (Mt. 24–25), the kingdom of His full and unveiled glory will encompass the new heavens and the new earth (II Pet. 3:13; Rev. 21:1), "and He shall reign forever and ever" (Rev. 11:15), together with the Father and the Holy Spirit (I Cor. 15:24–28; Rev. 22:1.3.17).[2] It is customary therefore to speak of Christ's threefold kingdom: that of power, grace, and glory.

The phrase "two kingdoms" can bear still another sense. It may be used to contrast God's kingdom or rule with the kingdom[s] of the world (Mt. 4:8) or of Satan (Mt. 12:26; cp. Jn. 12:31; 14:30; II Cor.

1. "Secondly, by the right hand of God is understood the fact that the Lord Christ's Kingdom is a spiritual, hidden kingdom, while the visible and bodily kingdoms or goods are called the left hand of God, although they are all subject to Christ" (Luther on Psalm 110:1, *WA* 1:692.8–12).

2. This twofoldness of the "already" and the "not yet" in the New Testament, leads to the traditional threefold distinction of the kingdoms of power, grace, and glory. The main distinction for the church in the present age, however, is that between God's general reign of power, and His special reign of grace in His Son.

4:4; Eph. 2:2; I Jn. 5:19). This is the basic division in St. Augustine's monumental *City of God*. As a Christian theologian, however, Augustine was well aware that the "city of man" is not some autonomous zone of uncontrollable evil. God's providence rules and over-rules there as everywhere.[3] Unguarded talk about "two kingdoms" could suggest that God is in charge of only one of them—and that by far the smaller of the two. God, of course, is Lord and King of the entire universe, not of a small "churchy" ghetto. He and the devil are as unequal as Creator and creature must be. To ward off dualistic semblances, therefore—as though two well-matched rivals were locked in eternal combat—one may, with Luther and the Augsburg Confession, speak more specifically of "two governments" (German: *Regimente*; Latin: *potestates*, powers), the civil and the spiritual.[4] This way of speaking at once suggests that it is one and the same divine King Who rules through both governments. Both are equally His instruments in dealing with His fallen creation, although their ways, means, and ends differ greatly. In this chapter, when the two kingdoms, or realms, or governments, or powers, or spheres are named, it is exactly the same distinction that is meant. We are speaking here about the two kinds of rule of the one genuine King, not about the cleavage between that King and the doomed usurper or pseudo-king, Satan.

For the preservation and protection of man's temporal life and society, God has established rulers or governments, whose duty it

3. On the one hand: "By two cities I mean two societies of human beings, one of which is predestined to reign with God for all eternity, the other doomed to undergo eternal punishment with the Devil." On the other hand: "Nor did God remove man from his power, even when he made him subject to the Devil by way of punishment; for God has not put even the Devil outside his dominion" (Augustine, *City of God*, 595, 1070).

4. "Therefore, the two authorities [*Regimente*, governments], the spiritual and the temporal, are not to be mingled or confused, for the spiritual power has its commission to preach the Gospel and administer the sacraments. Hence it should not invade the function of the other, . . . should not make or prescribe to the temporal power laws concerning worldly matters. Christ himself said, 'My kingship is not of this world,' and again, 'Who made me a judge or divider over you?' Paul also wrote in Phil. 3:20, 'Our commonwealth is in heaven,' and in II Cor. 10:4,5, 'The weapons of our warfare are not worldly but have divine power to destroy strongholds and every proud obstacle to the knowledge of God.' Thus our teachers distinguish the two authorities [governments] and the functions of the two powers, directing that both be held in honor as the highest gifts of God on earth" (AC XXVIII, 12–18, Tappert, 83).

is to defend and commend those who do what is right, and to punish criminals (Rom. 13:1–7;[5] I Tim. 2:2; I Pet. 2:13.14). Law, reason, compulsion, rewards and punishments, even capital punishment and war ("the sword," Rom. 13:4), are among the proper means by which civil society and the state attain their proper ends in God's Left Hand kingdom. All these matters are subject to reason and common sense. Only "reason" must not be misunderstood here, in the modern, reductionist manner, as though it meant something purely instrumental and content-free, namely logic, "I.Q.," or the computing function. "Reason" in this context means rather a power of judgment deeply embedded in man's irreducibly *moral* nature (Rom. 1:20; 2:14.15).

All this, however, is secondary, provisional, ancillary, penultimate. The whole "Left Hand" kingdom is but a vast scaffolding for God's ultimate purpose: the eternal salvation of His church (Rom. 8:22–39; I Cor. 4:9; Eph. 3:2–12; Phil. 2:5–11; Col. 1:15–2:19). Everything else must ultimately subserve this saving purpose of God (Rom. 8:28.38.39). Here we have God's "Right Hand" kingdom, or "the kingdom of His beloved Son" (Col. 1:13). In this kingdom He does not rule by means of natural reason, law, and coercion. Rather, He gently (and therefore resistibly, Mt. 23:37!) "draws" (Jn. 6:44.65) and invites (Mt. 11:28) sinners into His king-

5. O.Cullmann (*The State in the New Testament*) has argued that the ἐξουσίαι (powers) in Rom. 13:1 ff. are to be understood as referring not only to the earthly governments, but also to the angelic powers that loom behind and manipulate them. These powers are supposed to be defeated demons, vanquished by the Cross of Christ, and now made to serve Him! This scheme is supposed to provide a genuinely Christological foundation for even the pagan state, by accounting for the latter's right intuitions about good and evil without recourse to *natural law*—for which it is allegedly "difficult to find evidence in Paul" (pp. 113–114). This latter point flies in the face of Rom. 2:14.15, about which Cullmann is oddly silent. That demonic forces lurk in the background, and seek to exploit and twist also legitimate institutions of God, is of course true enough. Cullmann himself concedes to his critics, however, "that we have no text in the New Testament where it is explicitly said that the defeated powers are subjected in service." It seems grotesque to suppose that Paul could have exhorted Christians to render conscientious (Rom. 13:5!) obedience to defeated demons, whose captivity and enforced subservience to God are so tenuous, moreover, that Christians must constantly guard against these state-demons "once again breaking loose and becoming satanic," as in totalitarian regimes (p. 90)! Finally, the ἐξουσίαι of Rom. 13 are indisputably identical with the ἄρχοντες (rulers) of v. 3. Yet if the latter are conquered demons, capable of "breaking loose," whence the assurance that they are "not a terror (φόβος) to good works, but to the evil"? Genuinely demonic rulers (e.g., the ἄρχων "τῆς ἐξουσίας τοῦ ἀέρος") remain evil and seduce to evil (Eph. 2:2.3), as the devil prowls about like a roaring lion, seeking whom he may devour (I Pet. 5:8). Or are there conquered and unconquered demons? Despite brilliant insights and ingenious details, the scheme as a whole is incongruous. For a handy 1970 summary and analysis of the state of German scholarship in respect of Rom. 13, see U. Duchrow's treatment, which in turn follows E. Käsemann's report in *Zeitschrift für Theologie und Kirche* [1959] (U. Duchrow, *Christenheit und Weltverantwortung*, 137–180).

dom, gathering and sustaining them there with forgiveness, life, and salvation through His holy Gospel and sacraments (Mt. 13; 22:1–14; Jn. 3; 6; 10; 15; 20).

This "kingdom of His beloved Son" (Col. 1:13) is precisely co-extensive with Christ's one holy church (Rom. 8:9; Gal. 3:27; Eph. 4:4–6). This identification is axiomatic in the Church of the Augsburg Confession: "The church, which is truly the kingdom of Christ, is, precisely speaking, the congregation of the saints" (Ap. VII/VIII.16). Pieper: "The Kingdom of Grace is synonymous with the Church of God on earth (*ecclesia militans*)."[6]

Traditional Roman Catholicism errs here not by identifying the kingdom of grace with the church,[7] but by equating this church with the papal dominion. The Roman Catholic modernist A. Loisy's oft-cited *bon mot*: "Christ promised the kingdom, and what came was the church" was not originally meant as a barb, but easily takes on that meaning. The church simply is not an outward power-structure. She is rather the mystery of Christ's holy people and kingdom, "hidden under the cross" (Ap. VII/VIII.18) for now.

Reformed theology takes a different view. Calvin indeed said that "the church is Christ's Kingdom, and he reigns by his Word alone."[8] The modern Calvinist dogmatician L. Berkhof seems to break with Calvin when he hesitates to identify the kingdom of grace with the church.[9] Berkhof sees "Christian labor unions, and Christian political organizations" also as "manifestations of the Kingdom of God, in which groups of Christians seek to apply the principles of the Kingdom to every domain of life." He continues:

> The visible church and the Kingdom, too, may be identified to a certain extent. The visible Church may certainly be said to belong to the Kingdom, to be a part of the Kingdom, and even to be the most important visible embodiment of the forces of the Kingdom. . . . The Kingdom may be said to be a broader concept than the Church, because it aims at nothing less than the complete control of all the manifestations of life. It represents the dominion of God in every sphere of human endeavor.[10]

The difference with Calvin here is more one of words than of

6. F. Pieper, *Christian Dogmatics* II:385.

7. ". . . the kingdom of Christ, that is, his Church. . ." (*The Roman Catechism*, 514).

8. J. Calvin, *Institutes*, IV.II.4. On one occasion it was Calvin's "desire that the Genevan citizens should be herded into the Cathedral of St. Pierre, lined up by the police, and obligated to confess under oath that this [*Genevan Catechism*] was their faith (July 1537)" (Gerrish, *The Old Protestantism and the New*, 123).

9. L. Berkhof, *Systematic Theology*, 409. 569.

10. Ibid., 569–570.

substance. In Calvin as in Berkhof what matters ultimately is the keeping of the Law, not the preaching of the Gospel.[11] K. Rieker framed this point well in his 1899 treatment of the differences in character between the Lutheran and the Reformed churches: "The Calvinist thinks here first of all of the Law of God; where and only where it holds sway, there is the Kingdom of Christ on earth."[12]

In actual fact, however, Christ's church and ministry are Gospel-wrought through and through. They are gracious, evangelical, salvatory gifts and institutions of God, not legal ones, nor Law/Gospel hybrids: "Therefore everything in the Christian church is so ordered that we may daily obtain full forgiveness of sins through the Word and through signs appointed to comfort and revive our consciences. . ." (LC Creed. 55). This means of course not that the Law need not be preached in the church, but rather that this "alien" work of God is done for the sake of His own, "proper" work (Ap. XII.51–53).[13] The Calvinist understanding is totally different—as indeed it must be if, owing to double predestination, grace is not universal, and so there really cannot be objective means of grace: "For the Reformed, the visible church is

11. Calvin can and does speak also of the Kingdom as meaning "the forgiveness of sins, salvation, life. . ." (*Institutes*, 1:613). The real accent, however, lies elsewhere: "But even though the definition of this Kingdom was put before us previously, I now briefly repeat it: God reigns where men, both by denial of themselves and by contempt of the world and of earthly life, pledge themselves to his righteousness in order to aspire to a heavenly life. Thus there are two parts to this Kingdom: first, that God by the power of his Spirit correct all the desires of the flesh which by squadrons war against him; second, that he shape all our thoughts in obedience to his rule" (*Institutes*, 2:905). "And as the magistrate ought by punishment and physical restraint to cleanse the church of offenses, so the minister of the Word in turn ought to help the magistrate in order that not so many may sin" (*Institutes*, 2:1215-1216). The "true religion" is the one which "is contained in God's law" (*Institutes*, 2:1488). "As if God appointed rulers in his name to decide earthly controversies but overlooked what was of far greater importance—that he himself should be purely worshiped according to the prescription of his law" (*Institutes*, 2:1495). See also the discussion in H. Sasse, *Here We Stand*, 110–180.

12. K. Rieker, *Grundsätze reformierter Kirchenverfassung*, 90, our translation. A more recent writer states: "In Calvin's thought the emphasis on order moves from order in the church to the task of the church bringing order to the world. Calvin believes that whenever order is brought to the world, the kingdom of God is expressed. And the work of the church is to fill the whole created order with the kingdom of God, the rule of Christ over all things" (R. E. Webber, *The Church in the World*, 131).

13. F. Pieper: "When we speak of 'the articles of Christian doctrine,' this is to be understood as the revelation and preaching of Christ. . . The Law does not come into consideration here. The foundation on which the Christian church is built is Christ, the Gospel. . . The Law does not create the church, neither does the Law unify the church. Only the Gospel does that. Therefore the Law does not belong into a definition of Christian unity or unity in the faith. . . . acceptance of the Law is nevertheless a necessary presupposition of unity in faith" ("Of Unity in the Faith," 6–13. Our translation).

not so much salvatory institution [*Heilsanstalt*] as sanctifying institution [*Heiligungsanstalt*]."[14]

Quite exotic is the "dispensationalist" scheme proposed by what is sometimes regarded as the most influential religious book in the United States, the *Scofield Reference Bible*. Biblical terms are gerrymandered there on a grand scale in the interests of an imaginary "kingdom, political, spiritual, Israelitish, universal, over which God's Son, David's heir, shall be King, and which shall be, for one thousand years, the manifestation of the righteousness of God in human affairs."[15] The church is demoted thereby to a sort of interim consolation prize, until the interrupted fulfillment of Lk 1:32 can be taken up again in the "political, spiritual, Israelitish" world dominion to be exercised by Christ from Jerusalem for a thousand years! Such surrogate "sacraments" are the fate of a moralistic pietism too lofty and "spiritual" to acknowledge the real sacraments.

What all of this adds up to is that the proper distinction between the two kingdoms or governments is part and parcel of the right distinction between Law and Gospel. The former distinction is necessarily entailed by, or is "nested" in, the latter. Therein lies its enormous significance. "The reason why the Lutheran Reformation knows no Christian state, of which all other confessions dream," wrote Sasse, "is this, that a Christian state would be a church." Spiritual and temporal power, Law and Gospel, would then be radically confused. "The Gospel would become a new Law—that it has become wherever people want to Christianize, churchify, or convert the state as such and the world—and that would be the end of the Gospel as Luther understood it."[16]

---

14. K. Rieker, *Grundsätze*, 64. He continues: "This is connected with the central position occupied in the Old Reformed world-view and view of life by the dogma of predestination. If God has from eternity by an absolute decree determined some men to salvation and others to damnation . . . then the church cannot properly have the task of being an institution for the proffering of the salvation obtained for mankind by Christ . . . The task of the church is rather the sanctification of her members . . . For the Reformed believer the visible church comprises the object and the scope of his Christian-ethical activity; through the good works which he does in her and for her, he becomes certain of his election; by working upon her he builds the state of God [*Gottesstaat*] on earth; the whole civil and societal life must from there be reformed in accordance with the Law of God" (64–65.68).

15. Comment on Rev. 14:6 in C.I. Scofield, *The Scofield Reference Bible*, 1343. That same page distinguishes between (1) a "Gospel of the kingdom" (with "two preachings," one past and one future), (2) a "Gospel of the grace of God," (3) "the everlasting Gospel," and (4) "That which Paul calls 'my Gospel.'" Comments on Mt. 3:2 and 6:33 urge impossible distinctions between "the kingdom of God" and "the kingdom of Heaven" (pp. 996, 1003).

16. H. Sasse, *In Statu Confessionis*, II:358. See also pp. 357–358: "*There is no such thing as a Christian state.* That is one of the foundational insights of Lutheranism, a view which distinguishes it fundamentally from all other confessions, from the [Roman] Catholic and

To be sure, the theological distinction between the two governments is not the same thing at all as the political "separation of church and state." Yet it is the proper relation between church and state, as the concrete domains of the Gospel and of the Law respectively, that is at issue here:

> Inasmuch as the power of the church bestows eternal things and is exercised only through the ministry of the Word, it interferes with civil government as little as the art of singing interferes with civil government. For civil government is concerned with other things than the Gospel. The state protects not souls but bodies and goods from manifest harm, and constrains men with the sword and physical penalties, while the Gospel protects souls from heresies, the devil, and eternal death. Therefore, ecclesiastical and civil power are not to be confused (AC XXVIII.10–12).[17]

Some have, partly under the spell of war hysteria, professed to find in this Lutheran distinction between the two kingdoms the ultimate explanation for the horrors of Hitlerism![18] The idea is that by freeing the state from the supervision of the church, Luther gave it a false autonomy and so let it grow into the lawless monster of modern totalitarianism. Karl Barth himself, however, whose immense personal prestige lent credibility to the anti-Lu-

---

the Reformed churches, and from those issuing from the fanatical movement [*Schwärmertum*] of Reformation times. No more disastrous falsification of our confessions' doctrine of the state has occurred than the introduction of the false doctrine of the Christian state."

17. "Constantly I must pound in and squeeze in and drive in and wedge in this difference between the two kingdoms. . . The devil never stops cooking and brewing these two kingdoms into each other. In the devil's name the secular leaders always want to be Christ's masters and teach Him how He should run His church and spiritual government. Similarly, the false clerics and schismatic spirits always want to be the masters, though not in God's name, and to teach people how to organize the secular government" (*On Psalm 101* [1534], *LW* 13:194; *WA* 51:239.22–29).

18. "[Luther's] teaching leaves the impression that in the secular realm the government is supreme, and that from it, and not from Christ, the Christian must take his duty. And it is this very fact which allowed Hitler to come to power and begat Belsen and Dachau. The Lutheran church did not stand out, for it was conditioned to accept the civil power. . .

It might not be too much to say that Luther's ethic of church and state was the greatest disaster in all the history of ethics, for it opened the way for a kind of Christianity which allowed the state to do terrible things, and in too many cases made no protest. It is impossible to divide life into spheres like that" (W. Barclay, *Ethics in a Permissive Society*, 187–188). Although Karl Barth seeks to implicate Luther in a fateful pedigree leading from Frederick the Great via Bismarck to Hitler (K. Barth, *Eine Schweizer Stimme 1938–1945*, 113, 395–396), Barth's explanations and qualifications (pp. 6, 115, 121–122, 341–344), and his obvious high regard for the Reformer, save his treatment from vulgarity. Barth objects to "the error of Martin Luther regarding the relationship between Law and Gospel, of temporal and spiritual order and power, through which his natural paganism was not so much bounded and limited as much rather ideologically transfigured, confirmed and strengthened" (113). Again: "Lutheranism has in some measure provided air for German paganism, and (with its

theran canard, complained of a certain "gap" in Calvin's and Zwingli's doctrines of the state as well![19]

At least three points ought to be urged in reply. Firstly, Luther in principle and practice never advocated the emancipation of rulers and governments from the moral law of God—accessible to non-Christian rulers as natural law and to Christian rulers also in special revelation. The Table of Duties was to be preached to all Christians, including rulers, and the Smalcald Articles take it for granted that church councils must reform "such fundamental matters of the ecclesiastical and secular estates as are contrary to God" and that "God's commands and precepts" are to be obeyed by Christians "in the spiritual and temporal estates" (SA Preface. 12, 13).

Secondly, the real "emancipation" of public life from transcendent moral controls and constraints came not in the wake of Luther but in that of Charles Darwin. The latter's "natural selectionism" claimed to account for the semblance of design in nature without any designer, and so made God intellectually redundant. This scientific and philosophical shift "eventually took God out of nature (if not out of reality) as effectively as atheism."[20] There ensued a massive cultural revolution which has not ceased to vent its spleen on the Christian truth-claims in particular and on the

separation of creation and the Law from the Gospel) assigned to it something like its own sacral space" (122).

Other things aside, it seems incongruous to cast Bismarck's Prussia in the role of transmitter of Luther's heritage. Far from embodying an authentically Lutheran dynamic, that power had, since 1817, stood for the rape of the Lutheran church by a union policy and politics of Calvinist orientation. It was this wily, violent, and persistent imposition of confessional indifference and surrender, and not the full-blooded Lutheranism of the Formula of Concord (Paul Gerhardt!), that accustomed Lutherans to bootlicking and extracted their spines.

For a competent exposition of Luther's actual stand, see J. Stephenson, "The Two Governments and the Two Kingdoms in Luther's Thought," 34:321–337.

19. In a 1938 essay in his *Schweizer Stimme* (14–17) Barth blames Luther, Calvin, Zwingli, and the Lutheran and Reformed symbolical books equally for the "gap" between their doctrines of justification and their views of political "right" or justice.

20. N. C. Gillespie, *Charles Darwin and the Problem of Creation*, 153. M. Ruse, *The Darwinian Revolution*, ix, notes that Darwin's theory was at once "seen to have implications far beyond biology." Julian Huxley, grandson of "Darwin's bulldog," Thomas Huxley, crowed at the Darwin Centenary in Chicago that "Darwinism removed the whole idea of God as the creator of organisms from the sphere of rational discussion" (S. Tax and C. Callender, eds., *Evolution After Darwin*, III:45). The distinguished Canadian entomologist, W. R. Thompson, F.R.S., on the other hand, in his splendid introduction to the Everyman's Library centenary edition of the *Origin*, wrote that he was "not satisfied that Darwin proved his point or that his influence in scientific and public thinking has been beneficial." Apart from its scientific shortcomings Thompson noted Darwinism's "strong anti-religious flavour. . . For the majority of its readers, therefore, the *Origin* effectively dissipated the evidence of providential control" (C.Darwin, *The Origin of Species*, vii, xxiii).

moral values of Western Civilization in general. The Victorians already suspected that having jettisoned Christian dogma they were living, ethically, on the "perfume of an empty vase."[21] The effect in our own time has been more that of a broken sewer inundating our public culture with all that is ugly and vile, its crowning shame the frightful mass-exterminations of the unborn.

Thirdly, the Lutheran two-governments approach is in fact the only possible one in to-day's pluralistic culture. To dream now of imposing and enforcing "Christian" or "biblical" standards on society in general[22] is to play into the hands of those who cry "Inquisition!" or "First Amendment!" whenever their trade in human blood and souls is challenged. Arguments about public policy must rest on reasonable grounds accessible to all, not on special revelation acknowledged as such only by faith. The state accordingly must punish crimes against humanity, not sins against God. Here lies the "contrast between a Lutheran theology of two kingdoms and a Calvinist theology of one kingdom. A Lutheran works to 'humanize' the secular realm; a Calvinist has to 'Christianize' it" (W. Lazareth). [23]

Ideally, of course, appeals to natural law (Rom. 2:14.15) can take natural theology (Rom. 1:20) for granted, and that whole field belongs to philosophers and jurists rather than theologians. The present climate of opinion is sub-rational, in that reason is not allowed to pursue normal probability arguments for the existence of an intelligent Creator, but is forced instead to befuddle itself with the dominant cultural myth of the origin of everything from nothing by itself.[24] Although that malignant cosmogony appears to be self-destructing,[25] Christian citizens cannot simply await its demise, especially since another, worse lunacy—the murky

21. The phrase is Renan's. Sir Arnold Lunn and G. Lean, *Christian Counter-Attack*, 18.

22. Calvinism itself is deeply divided over this matter, and the problems seem insoluble. See G. S. Smith, ed., *God and Politics: Four Views on the Reformation of Civil Government: Theonomy, Principled Pluralism, Christian America, National Confessionalism*.

23. Cited in K. H. Hertz, ed., *Two Kingdoms and One World: A Sourcebook in Christian Social Ethics*, 324. It is a pity that Lazareth later endorsed the notion of an "inclusive mission" for the church, embracing both salvation and political-economic "liberation" (C.E. Braaten, ed., *The New Church Debate*, 15–38). This "liberationist" social gospel was built into the outlook and structure of the Evangelical Lutheran Church in America at its formation, and has been effectively criticized ever since in *Forum Letter*.

24. See the special pleading against the *prima facie* evidence of an incredibly ordered cosmos in J. D. Barrow and F. J. Tipler, *The Anthropic Cosmological Principle*. Cf. W. L. Craig's effective critique in the *British Journal for the Philosophy of Science*, 389–395.

25. The extent to which the Darwinian sacred cow has lost status may be gauged from the fact that the scientific merits of anti-evolutionary, "abrupt origins" theories were actually debated before the U.S. Supreme Court in 1987, something previously unthinkable. The

mumbo-jumbo of occultistry—is already waiting in the wings.[26] In seeking their neighbors' welfare, Christian citizens can, in their various callings, press for basic human decencies and for values which most people will intuitively recognize as sound and sensible, even apart from an explicit natural theology. (However, while natural theology in some form is being rehabilitated, the monopolistic pretensions of Secular Humanism under the First Amendment must be firmly resisted[27]).

Unlike one-eyed utopians intent on chopping and stretching long-suffering mankind to fit their Procrustean ideologies, Christian citizens are free to cultivate a compassionate realism, in-

---

Court, remarkably, took for granted that public school teachers were already free "to supplant [supplement?] the present science curriculum with the presentation of theories, besides evolution, about the origin of life." W. R. Bird, who argued the case before the Court, has published the massive documentation in the two volumes of *The Origin of Species Revisited*.

26. See E. Miller, *A Crash Course on the New Age Movement*.

27. Leo Pfeffer, a mentor to the U.S. Supreme Court on church-state issues, boasted that in all confrontations over social questions in the United States between traditional Christianity and secular humanism, the latter has won out, and that the one remaining issue, abortion, will be settled in secular humanism's favor as well (*"Issues That Divide: The Triumph of Secular Humanism,"* 203-216). The jaundiced perspective of a total "wall of separation" between church and state has, while zealously seeking to hound all explicitly Christian manifestations out of the vast realm of tax-funded activities, in effect established secular humanism as the state religion. Defenseless school-children are indoctrinated with it by the millions, at tax-payers' expense (e.g., the moral squalor of a "sex education" amounting to "propaganda for promiscuity" [Sir John Peel on the British version], or the all-pervasive evolutionism and relativism, the effects of which are such that by the time the students reach university, almost all of them can be counted on to be convinced "that truth is relative" [A. Bloom, *The Closing of the American Mind*, 25]). Political and legal theory must learn again to cope with the natural (that is, philosophical) theology of the Declaration of Independence, which appeals repeatedly to "the laws of Nature and of Nature's God." The new Canadian constitution likewise anchors its Charter of Rights and Freedoms in the declaration that "Canada is founded upon principles that recognize the supremacy of God and the rule of law." The current U.S. approach naively identifies the word "God" with "religion," and then panics about the "establishment of religion." This implies the absurdity that the Fourth of July might be "unconstitutional," because of the Declaration's appeal to God! But as Mortimer Adler showed, even before himself becoming a Christian, it is perfectly possible "to engage in thinking about God that is not only philosophical but also pagan" (*How To Think About God*, 9). Beyond that, even the positive "religion" of the churches was never meant to be quarantined and banished from public life by the "establishment" clause (R. L. Cord, *Separation of Church and State: Historical Fact and Current Fiction*. For a vivid account of the non-rational factors that shaped certain landmark cases, see W. J. Murray, *My Life Without God*. Murray is the son of the vociferous atheist Madalyn Murray O'Hair).

formed by the accumulated wisdom of the ages.[28] There is no distinctively Christian brand of politics.[29] What distinguishes

28. "Therefore whoever wants to learn and become wise in secular government, let him read the heathen books and writings. They have truly painted it and portrayed it quite beautifully and generously, with both verses and pictures, with teachings and examples; and they became the source for the ancient imperial laws. I am convinced that God gave and preserved such heathen books as those of the poets and the histories like Homer, Vergil, Demosthenes, Cicero, Livy, and afterwards the fine old jurists—as He has also given and preserves other temporal goods among the heathen and godless at all times—that the heathen and godless, too, might have their prophets, apostles, and theologians or preachers for the secular government" (On *Psalm 101* [1534], *LW* 13:199, *WA* 51:242.36–243.3). The ancient heathen are actually better in this respect than those of their modern successors who, "disowning the past" (T.S. Eliot), profess to love humanity in the abstract while imposing on concrete human beings a terrible yoke of rigid, bloodless idealisms. For a perceptive diagnosis of this pathology see P. Johnson, *Intellectuals*; and for historical perspective, R. Nisbet, *History of the Idea of Progress*; C.S. Lewis, *The Abolition of Man*; R. Kirk, *The Conservative Mind*. Sir Karl Popper has repeatedly warned against recipes for large-scale social reconstruction, which always turn out to have unforeseen and even disastrous consequences. See K. Popper, *Conjectures and Refutations*, 124–125; and *The Poverty of Historicism*, 69. Chilling empirical confirmation is provided, for example, by the American Liberal, N. Glazer, who writes that "our efforts to deal with distress themselves increase distress," and notes that "America has gone further in the destruction of tradition than other countries. In doing so, America comes face to face, more sharply than any other country yet has, with the limits of social policy" (J. M. Mileur, ed., *The Liberal Tradition in Crisis*, 81–98). For a major critique of the "liberal modernist" notion of the state see S.R.L. Clark's three-volume *Limits and Renewals*, of which the first volume, *Civil Peace and Sacred Order* has just appeared.

29. Barth himself came to moderate his "Christian crusade" rhetoric. In his famous 1938 letter to Hromadka, Barth had projected a holy war against Hitler: "Every Czech soldier who then fights and suffers, will do it also for us—and, I say it to-day without reservation: he will do it also for the church of Jesus Christ, which can, in the fumes [*Dunstkreis*] of the Hitlers and Mussolinis, only fall prey either to becoming a laughing-stock or to extermination." (In that same letter Barth, who is sometimes accused of having been pro-communist, referred to Soviet help as "driving out the devil by means of Beelzebub"). Defending that sentence a month later, Barth argued that the church was "indirectly" involved, and that when a lawful state is attacked by a brutal tyranny, the church must "take her stand beside it in solidarity." The statement about the Czech soldier, he said, was but a "concrete application" of what I Tim. 2:1–3 gives as the basis for Christian intercession for the government (*Schweitzer Stimme*, 58–59, 67–68). For British and American Christian circles Barth stressed in 1941–1942 that it was not a question of defeating the enemies of God, since that battle had already been fought and won on Calvary; hence "we will see in this war neither a crusade nor a religious war" (p. 193); that the war was rather "a police-measure in grand style" (p. 194); that the church must learn to become church again (p. 281), and that the "earnest police-action against the Hitlerite nihilism" must be seen as "a necessary task of a lawful state" (p. 282). "What are [the churches] to preach? The Word about the reconciliation of the world with God through Jesus Christ (2 Cor. 5: 17–21) and nothing else" (p. 283). Again: "Identification of the church with a political cause? No, under no circumstances and not even within the most modest limits!" To identify herself in the slightest measure with any political cause, such as that of the Allies, would be to misconceive her task as being that of supplying the "accompanying music" to the frightful noises of the world (p. 285). Yet Barth criticizes British Christian talk about defending "Western civilization," "freedom," and the like, in the name of natural law, and insists that the issue is, "Jesus Christ or natural law?" (p. 190–192). That seems rather inconsistent. If one is fighting for Jesus Christ, one is presumably engaging in a holy war. But if it is a mere "police action" on the part of lawful states, is not natural law precisely the right category?

Christians from other persons of good will in the public arena is their supernatural motivation of love for God and their fellow human beings, and of that only God can be the Judge (Col. 3:3). The New Testament offers no blueprint for the reconstruction of society as such. Political or economic schemes may therefore be competent or incompetent, humane or barbarous, but they can be "Christian" no more than chemistry can be "evangelical" or botany "Lutheran."

Returning now to AC XXVIII, we can appreciate anew its much-neglected Reformation *"tantum"* (only), which might have gained more notice had it been a *"sola"* (alone): The power of the church or of bishops is spiritual and is exercised *ONLY* by preaching and administering the sacraments (XXVIII.8, 10), and by everything which this entails, such as judging and rejecting all doctrine that runs counter to the apostolic Gospel (XXVIII.21).

We are face to face here with the so-called "mission of the church."[30] The church has only one divinely-assigned task: to build herself up in faith and love, embracing more and more of fallen humanity, to the praise and glory of God, by and for the transmission of forgiveness, life, and salvation through the holy Gospel and sacraments of Christ (Mt. 28:19.20; Jn. 15:1–17; Eph. 2:19–22; 4:1–16; I Pet. 2:1–12; I Jn. 1:1–4; 5:1–13). The church does not have the additional tasks of supervising society and governments as such, devising recipes for peace and social justice, or asserting some special dominion or protectorate over the "earth's resources." Not that such tasks are unimportant—far from it! They belong, however, to God's other, "left-hand" government. Christians live and serve of course in and under both governments—as church in the one, and as citizens, workers, etc., in the other. But these roles are quite distinct and must not be confused. Although the faithful and competent service of Christians in their various callings honors God and benefits humanity with genuine good works, these cannot simply be attributed to the church as such. That would amount to absurd category-mistakes like: "The church

30. It has become popular in the wake of the Church Growth movement, to compose "mission statements" for congregations and church-bodies. This can be a good exercise if it digs down to first principles. The danger lies in soaking up uncritically the torrents of "biblical" sounding verbiage pouring forth from sectarian circles and saturated with an alien, non-sacramental and therefore unevangelical theology. Lutheran congregations and synods must learn again to treasure the Book of Concord as their best and most authentic "mission statement," and to implement its doctrinal and sacramental substance full-strength in the actual shaping of their church-life.

drives tractors, buses, and trains; generates electricity; arrests, tries, and punishes criminals; builds and uses tanks, machine-guns, and bombers." The church is not a sector of earthly society, or one of the "resources of the community," along with the public library, the Kiwanis, and the Red Cross. She is rather the beach-head of heaven on earth, conquering darkness with the life-giving weapons of light, distributing and celebrating the supernatural, saving riches of God. This is not merely her "primary task"—as though the Lord had said: "My Kingdom is not *primarily* of this world"!—but her only task, her singular and single mission, the sole reason for her existence.[31]

Given that the church is the realm of the Gospel, she can and must be governed by the same power by which she is created, extended, and preserved: the Gospel. This of course necessarily involves also the preaching of the Law, as God's "alien" work. But the Christian as new creation, and so the church as church, is ruled, that is fed and tended, by Christ through His Gospel Word and sacraments.[32] Here lies an essential difference between the Lutheran and the Calvinist understandings of *"sola Scriptura"* or the sole authority of God's Word, as opposed to human traditions. The Lutheran Church confesses the Bible to be essentially God's gracious Book about His Son, Jesus Christ, whilst Calvinism knows no radical Law/Gospel distinction, and therefore tends to read the Bible largely as rules for behavior, including a divinely-

---

31. ". . . the church has only one aim and world development is not part of it. . . . In any case, it is clear what the Lutheran Church ought to be doing. It ought everywhere to be resisting the present current of thought. It ought to be insisting everywhere: the one function of the church is the pure preaching of the Gospel and the right administration of the sacraments. This is not merely the main function of the church, its primary task, it is its *only* function, its *whole* mission" (H. P. Hamann, "The Church's Responsibility for the World: A Study in Law and Gospel," 72, 80). "According to our Confessions the church's ministry (mission) is confined to the proclamation of the Word of God. . . It is clear from the foregoing, in the light of the sharp distinction in our Confessions between the secular and the spiritual realms. . . that the ministry of the church and pastor is definitely limited. It is a spiritual function and ministry which the church has, the ministry of preaching the Word and administering the sacraments. It is the power of the keys, no more and no less" (R. D. Preus, "The Confessions and the Mission of the Church," 23, 24).

32. See Luther's magisterial treatment of Paul's parable about Hagar and Sarah in Gal.4:22 ff.: "Therefore the Jerusalem that is above, that is, the church, is not subject to the Law and works; but she is free and is a mother without Law, sin, or death. . . Therefore this allegory teaches in a beautiful way that the church should not do anything but preach the Gospel correctly and purely and thus give birth to children" (*Commentary on Galatians* [1535], *LW* 26:441, *WA* 40:I:664.23–25, 27–38). And this "heavenly Jerusalem above" is precisely not the church triumphant in heaven, but the church militant on earth, scattered throughout the world, but having the same Gospel, faith, Holy Spirit, and sacraments (p. 439).

prescribed form of church organization.[33] The place of ceremonies, customs, and regulations in the outward ordering of the church will be taken up in the section on polity.

It remains to consider two border regions where the boundary-line between the two kingdoms has become particularly fuzzy in our time. One is the first use of the Law, and the other goes by the name of "social ministry."

The so-called "first use" of the Law is the civic or political one. That at once alerts us to the fact that this use belongs fundamentally not in the church but in the state and in society.[34] This political use of the Law involves coercion and serves as a deterrent to unbelievers, but also to the flesh of Christians, and so keeps order in the world (SA III.II.1, 2 and FC Ep VI.1, Latin). The church,

---

33. See H. Sasse, *Here We Stand*, 110–136. Note the definitions found in the classic Calvinist "Princeton theology" of Charles and Alexander Hodge: The "external call" preached by the church is said to include: "1. A declaration of the plan of salvation. 2. A declaration of duty on the part of the sinner to repent and believe. 3. A declaration of the motives which ought to influence the sinner's mind, such as fear or hope, remorse or gratitude. 4. A promise of acceptance in the case of all those who comply with the conditions." Or: "Being a proclamation of the terms on which God is willing to save sinners, and an exhibition of the duty of fallen men in relation to that plan, [the universal call] of necessity binds all those who are in the condition which the plan contemplates. In this respect it is analogous to the moral law" (cited in F. Pieper, *Christian Dogmatics* III: 248). Despite much that is valid and valuable in his discussion of Christ's kingship, O. Cullmann too waxes strangely pallid in describing the real difference between the church and the rest of the universe, all of which is equally Christ's kingdom: "That the members of the church know all this; that they know that Christ reigns; that they are therefore *knowingly* [*mit Wissen*] members of the kingdom of Christ: therein above all do they differ as church from all the remaining members of the *regnum Christi* [kingdom or reign of Christ], who can stand in the service of this reign without knowing it" (*Königsherrschaft Christi und Kirche im Neuen Testament*, 35. Our translation). Is extra knowledge then the decisive difference between the church and the world? The failure to distinguish the church as Christ's *kingdom of grace* from the rest of creation as the kingdom of power, the failure, in other words, to appreciate the radical otherness of Law and Gospel, leads here to an impotent *intellectualism* akin to that of Karl Barth, of whom G. Wingren wrote: If "Barth is permitted to construct his whole system in peace, remove the objective existence of evil, the natural knowledge of God, the rule of law in the world, place the revelation of God through the incarnation in the center, define the gospel as a word about God's disclosure of himself; if he can do all this, then within this framework he can use the whole vocabulary of the New Testament. He can speak of our sin and guilt, our hostility to God, our demonic character. Everything is here, but it is within the frame of reference of our ignorance, and it is a reality only on the basis of our ontological mistake which makes the nonexistent evil into something that exists. Barth has the ability to a very large degree of being able to employ the language of scripture in a system that is totally foreign to the Bible" (*Theology in Conflict*, 125).

34. "Thus the first understanding and use of the Law is to restrain the wicked. . . This is why God has ordained magistrates, parents, teachers, laws, shackles, and all civic ordinances, so that, if they cannot do any more, they will at least bind the hands of the devil and keep him from raging at will. . . This civic restraint is extremely necessary and was instituted by God. . . Paul is not discussing that civic use here [Gal. 3:19]" (*Galatians Commentary* [1535], *LW* 26:308–309, *WA* 40:I:479–480). Later a "third use," for believers only, was distinguished from the "second," or theological use. While Luther may not have used the term

however, has no authority to coerce anyone,[35] and her preaching of the Law is shaped and bounded by the exclusively salvific intent of her divine commission (Mt. 28:19.20). Yet it may be preferable to speak in this connection of three "functions" of the Law, rather than "uses." That is because in practice it is not the preacher's conscious intent but God Who finally determines just how and in what proportions to apply a given Law-proclamation to a sinner's heart as sledge-hammer, scarecrow, scalpel, mirror, rule, and so on.

The important point is that in preaching the Law the church's purpose is to make sinners ready for the Gospel through contrition, and to instruct converted sinners about good works. She has no interest in or warrant for instructing unrepentant unbelievers in how to behave. To unbelievers she has nothing to say except: "Repent and believe the Gospel!" To Christian rulers and citizens alike the church must faithfully expound the Table of Duties. And she must of course intercede for lawful authorities (I Tim. 2:1–3). But to the state as state the church as church has nothing to say.[36]

To talk here about "prophetic witness"[37] in the sense of the Social Gospel is to forget that the Old Testament theocracy has been fulfilled, transcended, and abolished in Christ (Lk. 24:25–27; Jn. 1:17; 5:39; Acts 10:43; Col. 2; I Pet. 1:10–12). The church in her evangelical, sacramental fullness *is* the new, spiritual Israel—with no political or territorial remainders of any sort (Jn. 18:36; Rom.

"third use of the law," he certainly had the distinction in mind. In his Large Catechism Luther wrote: "Here, then, we have the Ten Commandments, a summary of divine teaching on what we are to do to make our whole life pleasing to God. They are the true foundation from which all good works must spring, the true channel through which all good works must flow. Apart from these Ten Commandments no deed, no conduct can be good or pleasing to God, no matter how great or precious it may be in the eyes of the world." (LC, Conclusion of the Ten Commandments; Tappert, 407).

35. ". . . the old Lutheran Orthodoxy had . . . justified the triple use of the law in the church by pointing, *i.a.*, to the unregenerate within the external Christian confessional fellowship" (J. Heckel, *Das blinde, undeutliche Wort 'Kirche'*, 720. Our translation). The confusion had arisen from the tendency of the later post-Reformation divines to see the three estates as standing *within* the church.

36. The Missouri Synod's leading dogmatician, F. Pieper, was adamant on this point: "The principles of Christ's rule over His Church are subverted" also by "those who would make of the State a spiritual kingdom by attempting to rule the State not by reason but by the Word of God, by 'Christian principles'" (*Christian Dogmatics* II:392–393). ". . . the State cannot and should not be ruled with the Word of God, but should be organized and ruled according to natural reason (common sense)" (III:418). See also I:103–104; II:387–388; III:178–182.

37. Such "prophecy" is often naively ideological. Thus Marxist revolutionary rhetoric is warmly embraced within the church, "where its repetition, drawn straight from the secular political groups who invent and promote it, is known as 'prophetic' discernment" (E. Norman, *Christianity and the World Order*, 19).

2:28.29; 9:6–9; I Cor. 10–11; II Cor. 1:18–5:21; Gal.4:22 ff.; Eph. 2:19–22; 3:14–4:16). Her "prophetic" ministry is to take the apostolic Gospel of and about Jesus to the uttermost parts of the earth—that and nothing else (Mt. 28:19–21; Jn. 14:15–27; 15:26–16:15; Acts 1:8; I Cor. 2; I Jn. 1:1–4; 5:6–12).

As for "social ministry," everything depends on how this ambiguous phrase is understood. If it means the church's care for her members suffering bodily distress, then this is a most sacred obligation of love (Mt. 25:31–46; Acts 24:17; I Cor. 16:1–4; Gal. 2:10; I Tim. 5:16; Jas.1:27; 2:14–17; I Jn. 3:17.18). It was for this very purpose, as we saw in an earlier section, that the church established that glorious auxiliary office, the diaconate (Acts 6:1–6; Rom. 12:7.8; 16:1.2; Phil. 1:1). And the church's diaconic love for her own has of course always "spilt over" to help also the needy outside her own ranks, to the best of her ability (Gal. 6:10). Yet the collection among the Gentile churches was for "the saints" in Jerusalem (I Cor. 16:1), not for the poor generally in the large population centers of the Roman Empire.

Usually, however, "social ministry" nowadays means something altogether different, also among Lutherans. A typical advocate of "the 'whole ministry' of the church to persons, society, and culture," which would exhibit "priestly-prophetic-political integrity," expressly calls for the abandonment of what he calls a "Private Christianity," in favor of "another tradition of Public Christianity that evolved from the Calvinist movement, and reads in the Bible a message of human solidarity and a promise of world transformation."[38]

This understanding of "social ministry," and it is the leading one by far, is simply an updated version of the old "Social Gos-

---

38. D. Hessel, *Social Ministry*, 13–14, 28. This "whole ministry," we are told, includes participation in "movements for arms control, life-styles of sufficiency, preservation of human rights, renewable and conserving energy systems, reform of public education and of the criminal justice system, empowering ministry with the aging, economic justice for minorities and women, action to reduce hunger and poverty and to develop more adequate human services. In so doing, we share and add to the grand tradition of Christian social ministry" (p. 33). Indistinguishable from this approach is *Social Ministry Affirmation: A Challenge to Lutherans Toward the Year 1990*, a document claiming to have "emerged from a process which involved many of the leaders of social ministry" in the antecedent bodies of the ELCA and in the LCMS, "who worked together through the Division of Mission and Ministry of the Lutheran Council in the USA." The task of "social ministry" is there defined as including: "*Analysis*, discovering what is happening in society. What's wrong and how can it be righted? What are the major needs of our neighborhood, nation, and world? *Education*, helping church members to understand human needs in light of the biblical vision for human community. . . *Service*, . . . How can all of us—oppressor and oppressed—be helped to live enriched lives? *Change*, helping to reform laws, systems,

pel." Cambridge historian E. Norman put it well when he spoke of "the politicization of Christianity as a symptom of its decay as an authentic religion."[39] Dean Norman rightly called attention to the decidedly, even ludicrously, leftist bent of the fashionable ecclesiastical politics.[40] The real problem, however, is not the particular brand of the politics pursued by churches—there are also "conservative" churches promoting "right-wing" politics—but the very fact that churches engage in political agitation at all. The fatal flaw lies in the view so readily taken for granted in the concluding sentence of the report on "The Church and the Disorder of Society" at the inaugural meeting of the World Council of Churches in 1948: "The responsible society of which we have spoken represents, however, the goal for which the churches in all lands must work, to the glory of the one God and Father of all, and looking for the day of God and a new earth, wherein dwelleth righteousness."

No! We read nothing in Mt. 28:19.20 about building "the responsible society." Still less do we read anything about "the participation of the *Church as Church* [sic] in the struggle of God for the

structures and institutions in an effort to create more justice. . . Social ministry includes both direct services and systemic change. . . We seek a social ministry which will give substantial resources to advocacy exerting pressure on centers of political and economic power to be socially responsible. We work for systemic change. . ." The document lists the pro-sodomy lobby, "Lutherans Concerned," as one of those "Lutheran groups with a particular social interest" which "exist independently of official church structures" and are "making significant contributions."

39. E. Norman, *Christianity and the World Order*. The BBC Reith Lectures, 1978, 13. Norman sees Christianity's "content [being] drained away into the great pool of secular idealism" (*Ibid.*). See also J. H. S. Kent, *The End of the Line?*, 63: "Indeed, the modern ecumenical movement partly originated in the anxiety of church leaders to replace the vanished social order in which the Churches had played an accepted part with a united ecclesiastical institution capable of holding its own as an independent structure with the increasingly independent and secular state." This shrewd assessment goes together with Kent's nihilistic thesis—unavoidable when the authority of Holy Scripture as God's Word is consistently thrown overboard—"that if Christianity is nearing the end of its main, public line, this is because it has exhausted ways of keeping its images alive" (p. ix). All that is left in the end is "faith in the underlying rationality of the universe" and "in the quality of life commended in what seems to have been the teaching of Jesus" (p. x).

40. "Officials of the World Council [of Churches] admit that the staff are 'nearly all socialists'" (*Christianity and the World Order*, 26). See also E. W. Lefever, *Amsterdam to Nairobi: The World Council of Churches and the Third World*, and *Nairobi to Vancouver: The World Council of Churches and the World, 1975–87*. In America there was the notorious case of Harry F. Ward, who as professor at Union Theological Seminary for several decades influenced thousands of future U.S. church leaders. He had written for the Federal Council of Churches *The Social Creed of the Churches* (Abingdon, 1914). It turned out later that he was an actual member of the Communist Party in the USA.

liberation of humanity."[41] These political passions breathe the spirit of the "liberationist" terrorist Barabbas, not of Jesus, the Deliverer from sin, death and hell. There is no necessary connection between spiritual and political freedom. Our Lord Himself has commanded us to give to Caesar the things that are Caesar's and to God the things that are God's (Mt. 22:21). Caesar—and pseudo-churches ruling with his help—also have clear limits: "We must obey God rather than men" (Acts 5:29). Those who want the church to dispense "social justice," must in the first place face up to the immense difficulties of making that abstraction concrete.[42] But above all they must ponder the Savior's remarkable reply to an aggrieved brother: "Man, who appointed Me a judge or an arbiter between you?" (Lk. 12:14). Can the church accept jurisdiction where the Judge of the living and the dead has refused it? And what does it mean that the Apostolic Council of Acts 15 totally ignored the pressing social problems of the Roman Empire, and dealt only with theological issues, that is, with questions which would have seemed "trivial" to a contemporary political reporter?

We repeat the biblically and confessionally sound thesis of H. P. Hamann: "The church has only one aim, and world development is not part of it."[43] This is the authentically evangelical understanding of the church as God's "worthy maid," who in the Gospel word and sacraments bears "a noble Son Whom all the world

41. U. Duchrow, *Conflict Over the Ecumenical Movement*, 27. This book, by a former Lutheran World Federation staff member, criticizes the LWF for dragging its feet about full "conciliar fellowship," WCC-style. The urgencies of the political-social agenda for the world, especially "peace," overshadow the historic confessional differences here. David Jenkins, now the controversial Bishop of Durham, is praised for his commendation of the "Marxist critique" (p. 35), while his surrender of Christian essentials like the bodily resurrection of Jesus matters not at all. Still, given Duchrow's historical-critical premises, his book is clear-headed and incisive, and certainly more honest than the hollow confessional pretences of the "Lutheran" World Federation.

42. See for example R. H. Nash, *Social Justice and the Christian Church* and the critiques of the first draft of the U.S. Roman Catholic bishops' pastoral letter on the U.S. economy, gathered in *Challenge and Response*.

43. H. P. Hamann, ed., *Theologia Crucis*, p. 72. The "development" issue was raised for the Lutheran World Federation by the 1972 statement of the Evangelical Church Mekane Yesus (Ethiopia) "On the Interrelation between Proclamation of the Gospel and Human Development." Contrary to fashionable expectations, the Ethiopian church's "increasing disquiet" was over "a disproportionate readiness on the part of European and American churches to provide financial assistance for development programs as compared to programs of evangelism" (p. 187)! The statement produced a flurry of discussion, culminating in a "global consultation" on "Proclamation and Human Development" in Nairobi in 1974.

must honor."[44] The dear Sarah of Christ's Gospel (Gal. 4:22 ff.) cannot exchange her glorious crown for the dreary uniform of a spiritual policewoman, a Hagar of the Law, patrolling the "public square."[45]

We may not fudge these clear alternatives by introducing here talk about "primary" and "secondary" tasks of the church. Such a distinction is perfectly valid if one is comparing the faith-creating ministry of Word and Sacrament with its precious fruit of diaconic love, expressed also in appropriate auxiliary offices of the church. The primary/secondary pairing is wrong, however, when the comparison is between Gospel proclamation and political crusading in the name of the Law (or even worse, of the Gospel). Politics as such is not the task of the church at all—although it is of course the duty of Christian citizens to pursue their neighbors' welfare also by proper political means. As Hamann rightly points out, "the most significant contribution of the church to the welfare of society and the world is by way of its members, as each in his own niche in life and in accordance with his own special capabilities works for and serves his fellow-men. . ."[46] Here we see again how the Two Kingdoms doctrine liberates Christian citizens to serve their fellow human beings according to their lights, and to do it all the better for not being "guided" politically by the dead hand of centralized ecclesiastical bureaucracies. The latter cannot possibly

44. Luther's hymn, "To Me She's Dear, the Worthy Maid," based on Rev. 12 (*LW* 53:294; *WA* 35:462–463). See also his comment on Hagar and Sarah in Gal. 4:22 ff.: "Therefore this allegory teaches in a beautiful way that the church should not do anything but preach the Gospel correctly and purely and thus give birth to children" (*LW* 26:441; *WA* 40:I:664.27–28).

45. Despite much that is sound and sensible in it—including a firm rejection of theocracy—an article by Carl F. H. Henry nevertheless tends to blur the images of Sarah and Hagar. On the one hand Henry speaks of the "church's unique mission . . . to announce to every nation the universal human need of redemption and the glad tidings of God's ready forgiveness. . ." On the other hand he says: "the church functions among mankind to exemplify and demonstrate moral and spiritual obedience to the crucified and risen Lord. . . Both by word and deed, the church is to publish to the world the standards by which the Coming King will judge all rulers and nations, and even now judges them. She is to mirror the righteousness and mercy of God in interpersonal relationships and to pursue social justice in the world of politico-economic affairs" (C.F.H. Henry, "Church and State: Why the Marriage Must Be Saved," 9). See Elert's comment on Calvin's development of Augustine's ecclesiology: "With him the church stands by no means only in the service of the Gospel. She has still quite other tasks" (W. Elert, Der Christliche Glaube, 397).

46. H.P. Hamann, *Theologia Crucis*, p. 86. See also W. M. Oesch, *Three Chapters*, p. 26: "The legitimate 'penetration of the world with the forces of the Gospel' for which the parable of the yeast (Mt. 13:33) is fondly adduced, does not happen in this way, that ecclesiastical organizations act directly as political realities and exert pressure, with which rulers or potentates in the public realm must reckon, . . . but consists rather in the yeast-like influence of Christians by virtue of their ΑΓΑΠΗ [love] flowing out of ΠΙΣΤΙΣ[faith], which influence irradiates the surrounding world."

possess the universal competence needed to redress all the world's ills. In the political field, church leaders "tend to amateurism" and, as Norman goes on to say, charitably, "are permanently liable to absorb seemingly any account of world conditions which exploits their generosity."[47]

It is the real aim of the Two Kingdoms distinction to safeguard the integrity and autonomy of the pure proclamation of the Gospel, in light particularly of the fundamental Law/Gospel dichotomy. The aim is not pedantically to prevent or dissolve all untidy entanglements of the two realms in practice. We catch a glimpse of this attitude in that typical "evangelical touch" with which AC XXVIII.77 would leave to the bishops their princely dominions, provided that they would allow the Gospel to be taught purely and would not force sinful practices on Christian consciences. If only the power of bishops as bishops is clearly distinguished from all other powers, which bishops hold not as bishops, by divine right, but merely by human right and tradition (XXVIII.19, 29), then all is well. If bishops claim and exercise as bishops no other authority than the spiritual, churchly power of preaching and the sacraments, then one can, in principle and within limits, put up with their playing other roles as well.

The same applies today. So long as churchly and civil functions and responsibilities are kept clearly distinct in principle, one must not insist on a "foolish consistency" in practice by which love would be injured. Principled distinction does not mean doctrinaire separation. If the members of a church intervene corporately (hence more effectively) with a government agency in behalf of some genuine victims of injustice (e.g., unborn babies, threatened with abortion), one should cheerfully explain: "We did this, strictly speaking, as citizens, not as church." The danger of course

47. E. Norman, *Christianity and the World Order,* 18–19. Well meaning but ill-informed political meddling can actually do great harm. J. Ellul complained that amid the calamities that finally led to World War II "the Christians, full of good intentions, were thinking only of peace and were loudly proclaiming pacifism! In matters of that kind, Christian good intentions are often disastrous" (J. Ellul, *False Presence of the Kingdom,* 188). K. Barth also denounced the unthinking pacifism which, for instance, celebrated the surrender of Czechoslovakia to Hitler at Munich in 1938 with the ringing of church-bells throughout Europe (*Schweizer Stimme,* 273–274). Marxism-Stalinism could later count on even more fervent support from the churches for one-sided "peace" and "disarmament" campaigns. See D. Martin and P. Mullen, eds., *Unholy Warfare: The Church and the Bomb,* and D. L. Davidson, *Nuclear Weapons and the American Churches: Ethical Positions on Modern Warfare.* Indeed, the chief Soviet government orchestrator of "peace" campaigns throughout the world formally "urged Communist parties to work more closely with religious organizations" in this regard (*The Times* [London], 8 Nov. 1981).

is ever-present that carelessness or inconsistency in practice will lead ultimately to a change or surrender of principle. On that score the rule is: *Principiis obsta* (resist the beginnings). Or in St. Paul's words: "A little yeast leavens the whole lump" (Gal. 5:9). When the great apostle himself appealed to Caesar (Acts 25:11), and insisted on due respect from lesser magistrates (Acts 16:37), he did this of course not as an apostle, but as a Roman citizen. Yet appeal and insist he did—for the sake of the Gospel (Acts 23:11).

13

LOCAL CHURCH, LARGER CHURCH, AND POLITY

It is a well-known fact that the term "ἐκκλησία" in the New Testament designates both the local church and the church universal. In Acts 9:31 the word also stands for the church of a particular region or regions ("the church in all of Judaea Galilee and Samaria"), which has its being of course in a number of local churches. Qualitatively the same reality is meant in each case.[1] Any distinction between "congregation" and "church" is purely verbal, without either linguistic or theological basis in Holy Writ. It is a distinction without a difference. The local/universal bi-polarity belongs to the nature of the church on earth. She is at once local and universal, and neither "pole" may be suppressed. Whatever details of outward structure are adopted in Christian liberty, it must be clear that in principle local churches are not administrative sub-divisions of a "higher" level of the church, and the universal church is not a creation or confederation of "autonomous" local churches. All such talk is in fact full of "category mistakes," as we shall see.

The key to this whole matter is the right understanding of the local church. From Mt. 20:26 ("Let it not be so among you") in particular, and from the evangelical nature of the church in general, we know that the church cannot be defined in legal or juridical terms. Nor therefore can she be defined in the organizational terms or "flow-charts" of modern bureaucratic business empires. This is not to say that the church cannot in Christian liberty make use also of such elements in her external arrangements. It is to say only that such juridical/bureaucratic features can never be deci-

1. It may of course be argued that Acts 9:31 occurs prior to the great missionary journeys, and that "the church in all of Judaea, Galilee, and Samaria" was therefore practically equivalent to the universal church. The fact remains, however, that we have a New Testament precedent here for speaking of the plurality of local churches in a particular region in the singular, as "the church" of that area. In any case, since the ἐκκλησία is qualitatively the same irrespective of the territory covered, nothing of importance hinges on Acts 9:31, one way or the other. See also II Cor. 1:1.

sive, definitive, constitutive, or essential. They must remain always peripheral, accidental, ancillary, changeable, and thoroughly subject to those realities by and in which the church really is constituted and lives.

The truly decisive and constitutive realities for the church are, as we have seen at length, the pure preaching of the Gospel and the right administration of the holy sacraments (AC VII). That at once entails the public ministry (AC V), as bearers and stewards of the mysteries of God (I Cor. 4:1), "that is, of the Word and sacraments" (Ap. XXIV.80). So intimate is this connection between the Gospel and the office which preaches it, that the German of Ap. VII/VIII.20 can simply identify them when naming the church's "outward signs: the preaching office [*Predigtamt*] or Gospel and the sacraments." Hence Luther can give this rule-of-thumb definition: "The church is the number or gathering of baptized and believing persons under one pastor [German: or bishop], whether it be of one city or of a whole province or of the whole world."[2]

The "one pastor" here of course must not be pressed, but taken in the sense of "at least one," since a church can be tended with the Gospel collegially by several ministers together. It is not the ranking of ministers that matters. What matters is that God's own provision for tending His flock through His ministry of Word and sacraments be faithfully observed (Jn. 20:19–23; 21:15–17. Cf. Tr. 10 [German], 25–31). A church then consists of both hearers and preachers, not of one part without the other.[3]

---

2. Thesis XV (German: XVI) of the "Propositions against the whole synagogue of Satan and all the gates of hell," which appeared in Augsburg in July 1530 (*WA* 30:II:421). The English version of Pieper's dogmatics renders this: "A church is a group or assembly of baptized and believers under one shepherd, whether of one city, or of an entire country, or of the whole world" (*Christian Dogmatics*, III:431).

3. C.F.W. Walther: ". . . the congregation, . . . when properly ordered, consists of preachers and hearers" (*Kirche und Amt*, 1875, Part II, Thesis VI, p. 245). Mueller's rendering of "*gehörig geordnet*" as "properly organized" in *Church and Ministry*, p. 220, is inadequate. Walther's "ordered" refers to the *divine* order in the church. "Organized," on the other hand, suggests parliamentary, etc., forms which, however inescapable in practice, are very much in the realm of *human* order, and so of *adiaphora*. Does a congregation then cease being a church when its pastor dies or accepts a call elsewhere? Of course not. It is then simply in an abnormal interim state, seeking to return to normal as soon as possible by filling the vacant office in its midst. If, however, it decided to scuttle the public ministry of Word and sacraments, and to rely instead on having its members lead worship and Bible-study by turns, it would no longer be a church—which has nothing to do with the question whether there are individual Christians in its membership. Walther: "The ministry [*Predigtamt*] is not an optional [*willkürlich*] office, but one which the church has been mandated to set up and to which the church is ordinarily bound till the end of time" (Thesis III. Mueller's "arbitrary" for "optional" [*Church and Ministry*, p. 191] misses the point. Also the English "ordinarily" does not convey the strength of the original "*ordentlicher Weise*," which again refers to the divine order).

To appreciate the real import of the ministrations of the Gospel as definitive and constitutive of the church, one must first unpack somewhat abstract phrases like "means of grace" or even "Word and sacraments," in order to display their concrete content. Unless this is done, it is too easy to think of "means of grace" or "marks of the church" or "sacraments" as standard, mechanically interchangeable functions, any one of which, either by itself or in any combination with the others, automatically defines a gathering as a church. Then a family gathering for an emergency Baptism, or a camp-fire Bible study group at a youth outing, could not in principle be distinguished from a congregation.

In fact, of course, the holy means of salvation [*media salutis*] are not isolated functions, to be mixed up at will. There is among them a certain τάξις or order: Baptism stands at the beginning, followed by Absolution, the Holy Supper stands at the end, and preaching happens in the middle—as well as before, after, and all around. It is not arbitrary or accidental that the multitude on Pentecost is invited first not to the Supper but to Baptism (Acts 2:38), and that the Corinthians are urged to keep coming together not to be baptized again, but to observe the Holy Supper properly, again and again (I Cor. 11:17–34). The movement is from Baptism to the Eucharist, from once-for-all entrance to frequent consummation, and this direction is irreversible. The salvific gift is of course essentially the same in all the forms of the Gospel—God gives no more and no less than "all things" in and with His Son (Rom. 8:32)—but the mode of this gifting varies according to the gracious institution of the infinitely resourceful Giver. The "one Baptism" (Eph. 4:5) is the initial washing of regeneration into Christ and His church, while the Supper is the oft-repeated feasting on those very riches which accomplished our redemption, the Lord's body and blood (I Cor. 10:16). This matchless presence and distribution of Christ's very body and blood are unique to the Sacrament of the Altar (cf. Heb. 13:10). It is no exaggeration therefore to call this mystery "nothing less than the Holy of Holies of the Christian Church, the Ark of the Covenant and the Mercy Seat of the New Testament [Covenant]. . . . the real crown of all the means of grace" (C.F.W. Walther).[4]

---

4. *Amerikanisch-Lutherische Evangelien Postille*, 147. C. P. Krauth put it like this: "The Sacramental Presence is the necessary sequel, the crowning glory of the Incarnation and Atonement. . . . The glory and mystery of the Incarnation combine there as they combine nowhere else. Communion with Christ is that by which we live, and the Supper is *'the* Communion' " (*The Conservative Reformation and Its Theology*, 650, 655).

Behind and in the sacraments, moreover, stands the evangelical majesty of God's bestowing Word: "Even if Christ were given for us and crucified a thousand times, it would all be in vain if the Word of God were absent and were not distributed and given to me with the bidding, this is for you, take what is yours."[5] Hence the evangelical (I Cor. 1:17) primacy of preaching: "the chief worship of God is the preaching of the Gospel" (Ap. XV.42).[6] "There is nothing that keeps the people with the church more than good preaching" (Ap. XXIV.50, German). If "the American clergyman" has indeed come to be perceived "as a pompous bore, a disagreeable zealot, or a genial incompetent," as Harvey Cox observed some years ago, then the solution is not the addition of yet a fourth kind of buffoon, Cox's "New Breed" of "the socially activist clergyman."[7] The only remedy rather is a penitent return to the ministry as *Predigtamt* (preaching office), that is to the sacred, central, and exacting work of serious preaching, from which alone all genuine renewal in the church flows (II Cor. 2:14ff.; I Tim. 4:11–16; II Tim. 4:1–5). True love and respect for the Gospel demands competent preachers. To "ordain rude asses" (Ap.XXVIII.3, German) is to pour contempt on the Gospel.

The life of the church, precisely of the local church, is shaped by the nature of Gospel preaching and Gospel sacraments, and by their inner connections. There is no rivalry whatever among these holy instruments of salvation, but only the closest possible integration. The One Baptism (Eph. 4:5) is into the One Lord and the One Faith which are the content of all Gospel proclamation. When Philip "evangelized" [εὐηγγελίσατο] Jesus to the Ethiopian eunuch (Acts 8:35), Baptism was an inseparable part of this "evangelism," which therefore led directly to the request for that sacrament (v. 37). The Sacrament of the Altar, too, is for the proclamation "of the Lord's death till He come" (I Cor. 11:26). With reference to "the proclamation of the Gospel, faith, prayer, and thanksgiving," the Apology confesses what was self-evident for the Reformation: "the ceremony [of the Mass or the Holy Supper] was

5. *Against the Heavenly Prophets* (1525), *LW* 40:213; *WA* 18:202.38–39. Cf. LC, Lord's Supper, 30: "Christ's body can never be an unfruitful, vain thing, impotent and useless. Yet, however great the treasure may be in itself, it must be comprehended in the Word and offered to us through the Word, otherwise we could never know of it or seek it."

6. The German has: "For the greatest of all, holiest, most necessary, highest worship of God [*Gottesdienst*], which God has required as the greatest in the First and Second Commandments, is to preach God's Word; for the preaching office [*Predigtamt*] is the highest office in the church."

7. *Daedalus* (Winter, 1967), 137.

instituted because of them and ought not be separated from them" (XXIV.35).[8] Word and sacraments are not diverse entities loosely strung together. They are indivisibly part and parcel of each other. The sacraments are embedded in the Word, and the living and life-giving Word (I Pet. 1:23), itself sacramental,[9] culminates in the sacraments. And so the three witness-bearers, the spirit, the water, and the blood, "come to one and the same thing" (οἱ τρεῖς εἰς τὸ ἕν εἰσιν, I Jn. 5:8).

Christian preaching aims at Baptism for those outside and at the Lord's Supper for the community of the baptized,[10] with Holy Absolution as the Gospel individualized (Jn. 20:22.23, cf. Mt. 9:8; 18:15–18). The corporate life of the baptized community is shaped specifically therefore by the interplay of preaching and the Supper of Christ, where the Savior has "in a wondrous Sacrament left us a memorial of [His] passion" (Maundy Thursday Collect). The "memorial" is of course a living and not a dead one, for it celebrates Him "Who by His death has destroyed death and by His rising to life again has restored to us everlasting life" (Easter Preface).[11] This lively remembrance the Lord Himself has planted in the midst of His church (I Cor. 11:23–26), and it is therefore the unifying (I Cor.

8. The German adds: "for [the ceremony of the Mass or Supper] was instituted for the sake of preaching." Luther: "For properly speaking, the mass consists in using the Gospel and communing at the table of the Lord" *An Order of Mass and Communion for the Church at Wittenberg* (1523), *LW* 53:25; *WA* 12:211.9–10.I. "For among Christians the whole service should center in the Word and Sacrament" (*LW* 53:90; *WA* 19:113.2–3). In *Concerning the Order of Public Worship* of 1523 Luther wrote, "The divine service [*Gottesdienst*] which now prevails everywhere has a Christian, fine pedigree, just as the ministry [*Predigtamt*] does too." *WA* 12:35.1–2; *LW* 53:11.

9. The Gospel pericopes, wrote Luther, are not mere histories, "but are sacraments (*sed sunt sacramenta*)" which actually work and convey what they express, (*A Sermon on Matthew 1:1* [1519], *WA* 9:440.9–10).

10. O. Cullmann has shown that unlike the Word-only worship of the synagogue, that of the church was from the beginning also sacramental: "it is not as though early Christianity had known three kinds of service, as we are in the habit of imagining, following the modern example: service of the Word and, alongside of it, Baptism and the Lord's Supper. *It is rather so: in the early Church there are only these two celebrations or services—the common meal, within the framework of which proclamation of the Word had always a place, and Baptism.* This is the reason for the close connection in early Christianity between Baptism and the Lord's Supper. This association of the *two* sacraments arises not in some later period, it is present already and quite clearly in Paul in I Cor. 10:1–5 (cloud and sea—meat and drink). . ." (*Early Christian Worship*, 31–32. Italics in original). As in the NT (Acts 2:42; 20:7; I Cor. 11:17 ff.) so in the Book of Concord (AC and Ap. XXIV) the Sacrament of the Altar is not an occasional extra, but a regular and central feature of congregational worship. See also J. Stephenson, "The Holy Eucharist: at the Center or Periphery of the Church's Life in Luther's Thinking?"

11. See Cullmann's illuminating discussion of the close connection between the Supper and the Resurrection, *op. cit.*, 14–20. Cf. Ap. X.4: "We are talking about the presence of the living Christ, knowing that 'death no longer has dominion over him.'" It is striking that in I Cor. St. Paul uses solemn transmission language only of the Holy Supper (παρέλαβον ... ὃ

10:17!) framework, setting, and context of congregational preaching, worship, and life.[12] "The sacrament and the sermon belong together," wrote Sasse, "and it is always a sign of the decay of the church if one is emphasized at the expense of the other."[13]

Using today's generally accepted terminology, we may therefore define a local church as the Eucharistic community in that place, with the understanding that this involves and includes (1) the whole evangelical-sacramental praxis (Mt. 28:19.20), which comes to a head,[14] as it were, in the Feast of the New Testament (I Cor. 11:26); (2) the divinely instituted ministry as public bearers and stewards (I Cor. 4:1) of the Word and sacraments in principle, even though a particular congregation may temporarily be without its own incumbents of that office; and (3) the truth that only the "saints" or believers belong to a local church in the proper sense (*proprie dicta*, Ap. VII/VIII.28). The (orthodox) local church then is simply "the congregation of saints, in which the Gospel is purely taught and the sacraments are rightly administered" (AC

καὶ παρέδωκα [I received what also I handed on], 11:23) and of the Resurrection (παρέδωκα) ...ὃ καὶ παρέλαβον [I handed on what also I received], 15:3). On 15:1 and 3 W. Pannenberg comments: "Paul explicitly emphasizes the traditional character of the following information, and the language of the subsequent formula or formulae is formalized into a creed" (T. L. Miethe, ed., *Did Jesus Rise From the Dead? Gary Habermas and Antony Flew: The Resurrection Debate*, 128). Both Eucharist and Resurrection were core constituents of the "Gospel" (I Cor. 4:15; 15:1) as preached by Paul.

12. The Old Lutherans took very seriously the implications of I Cor. 11. J. Gerhard gave as a "less principal" purpose of the Sacrament: "That we might preserve the public assemblies of the Christians, the strength and bond of which is the celebration of the Lord's Supper, I Cor. 11:20" (C.F.W. Walther, ed., *Baieri Compendium Theologiae*, III:529). Or: "Because therefore it has been accepted as a practice in the Christian church, that in the public assemblies of the church after the preaching and hearing of the Word, this Sacrament is celebrated, therefore this custom must not be departed from without urgent necessity. . . . it is . . . clear from Acts 20:7, I Cor. 11:20,33, that when the Christians did gather at one place, they were accustomed to celebrate the Eucharist"(J. Gerhard, *Harmonia*, II:1085). F. Lochner argued from Acts 2:42 and I Cor. 11 that a divine service is a "main service" (*Hauptgottesdienst*) if and only if it includes both the preached Gospel and the Sacrament of the Altar. "All other services. . . become minor services, no matter how rich their liturgical appointments" (*Der Hauptgottesdienst der evangelisch-lutherischen Kirche*, 6). C.F.W. Walther recognized as a subsidiary purpose of the holy sacraments their function as "distinguishing marks of confession and bonds of liturgical [*gottesdienstlicher*] fellowship" or "holy bonds and fences within which the Christians confront the world." There are repeated references to I Cor. 10 and 11. Then: "The sacraments are to gather the church and designate her members" (*Theses on Communion Fellowship with those Who Believe Differently*).

13. H. Sasse, *This Is My Body*, 2. On the same page: "Thus this sacrament was in every respect the life of the church. It was never to be separated from the Gospel. The church of the first centuries was the church of the Eucharist. A Sunday, a Lord's Day, was unthinkable without the Lord's Supper. But if ever the church was a preaching church, the church of the Apostles and the Church Fathers was. The same is true of all great periods of the church."

14. See J. Stephenson, "Admission to the Lutheran Altar: Reflections on Open Versus Close Communion."

VII.1) in a particular place. Here "the church is to be found, whole, local, and tangible. . . This is no mere organizational form or association of individuals, but the one church that will remain forever (*Una Sancta perpetuo mansura*) in the exercise of its God-given, spiritual functions (office of the keys)."[15]

We have seen that it is not possible to define the local church or congregation in juridical-organizational terms. The preceding also shows that one cannot get at the church by talking about "groups of Christians" loosely associated with the Gospel in some form. The Gospel "purely preached" and the sacraments "rightly administered" comprise highly concrete, specific unities and continuities (the durative present of the verbs in AC VII is not accidental) very unlike the casual, intermittent, private, voluntarist nature of Bible-study circles and similar "groups." Whether believers are present in such groups—how could they be detected with certainty?—is irrelevant. Organizations likely to include Christian believers do not thereby become churches—or else labor unions, shopping malls, and whole nations would be churches. And while it is true that only "two or three" *could* constitute a congregation (Mt. 18:20), not any two or three Christians actually *do* so. In Mt. 18:16–17 even the two or three jointly intent on the divinely mandated mission of trying to win a brother, are not yet the ἐκκλησία, but are expressly distinguished from her. Only the purely preached Gospel and the rightly administered sacraments suffice to document a church as church (as distinct not only from an amorphous "group," but also from a sectarian quasi-church[16] or a totally apostate non-church, depending on the relation to the church's marks).

Given this nature of the local church, it follows that each such church has all the necessary spiritual authority for its life and work. There is no divinely established administrative dependence of one local church or its ministry on another. That is because each

15. "Fellowship in Its Necessary Context of the Doctrine of the Church" (Statement of the Overseas Committee), 9–10. See also W. M. Oesch: "The only thing that can be said about the size of the local congregation is that it must be able to assemble and be served somehow from one place. . . . the pneumatically-bodily functioning local congregation does not merely represent the *una sancta,* as if she were only the fringe of her mistress's garment, but she is the One Bride of Christ at that place in the *traditio spiritus sancti* [transmission of the Holy Spirit] through means of grace and faith (Mt. 18:20; I Cor. 3:21–23, etc.)" (*Three Chapters,* 20.22).

16. Heterodox churches are hybrids: "Churches they are in so far as they still retain enough of the Gospel of Christ that men can come to faith in Christ and thus can become true children of God. Sects they are in so far as they have combined to further their deviations from the doctrine of Christ and thus cause divisions in the Church. . ." (F. Pieper, *Christian Dogmatics,* III:423).

church has, in the Gospel and sacraments, Christ Himself in His pneumatic-evangelical-sacramental fullness (Gal. 3:2–5; Eph. 1:3ff.; Col. 2:2–19). "According to the New Testament the smallest congregation is as truly the Spiritual Body of Christ as the Church Universal is. Matt. 18:20; I Cor. 12:27."[17] Bonds among the churches there are of course aplenty, but they are the bonds of faith and love. Such administrative superordination and subordination among churches and ministers as good order and the church's needs may indicate, exist only by human custom, right, and agreement, and must always subserve faith and love.

A word must be said here about local churches in relation to larger church-bodies, for instance at regional, national, and international levels. Geographical or political boundaries have of course in principle no significance for the church. The traditional Lutheran distinction is between "simple church" (*ecclesia simplex*) and "composite church" (*ecclesia composita*). The "simple" church is the local church, the gathering round a particular font, pulpit, and altar. The "composite" church is composed of several "simple" churches.[18] The local church is the minimal entity that can be unambiguously identified as a church. On the other hand, local churches do not cease to be churches when they act together as, say, "synods," in their common churchly confession and work. Such synods are clearly churches—"composite" churches—because they are made up of churches. A "synod" in the sense of a deliberative assembly[19] ("convention," nowadays) is "representative church" (*ecclesia repraesentativa*), and this not because large numbers of "Christians" are present and occupied somehow with God's Word, but because the churches are officially represented, first of all by their public teachers and then also by other competent delegates. All this was quite clear to the founders of the Missouri Synod, who placed "the example of the Apostolic Church (Acts 15:1–31)" at the head of their synodical constitution[20] and later, in founding the Synodical Conference, wrote into that body's constitution as its "aim and purpose" the "consolidation of all

17. *Theses of Agreement*, V, 11.

18. Contemporary analogies might suggest "atomic" and "molecular" churches, or "single-celled" and "many-celled" churches. But atoms are dead, and combine into qualitatively different molecules. Cells are better, because alive, but "single-celled" carries the stigma of "primitive." We stay therefore with the drab "simple" and "composite."

19. The Apostolic Council in Jerusalem (Acts 15) is the great model for all later "synods" or "councils." It is of this churchly institution that Tr. 56 states that "the judgments of synods [German: councils] are the judgments of the church, not of the pontiffs."

20. *First Synodical Constitution*, 2.

Lutheran synods of America into a single, faithful, devout American Lutheran Church."[21]

Those who urge that nothing beyond local congregations can really be a church, often do so without adequate theological reflection, simply in order to avoid the spiritual tyranny of a "superchurch"—whatever that is. This well-meaning argument is badly mistaken, however. It is precisely as *churches* that synods are controlled by faith and love, and therefore cannot tyrannize anybody. The more this churchly constitution and its constraints are forgotten, and replaced by political notions of majority rule and commercial chains of command, the more scope there is for worldly, carnal power and all its works. This goes to the heart of the question of the nature of church government.

The whole New Testament in its length and breadth, together of course with its Old Testament foundation (Is. 55:1ff.; 61:1ff.; Jer. 31:31–40; Ez. 36:24–37:14) is a liberating Magna Charta (Jn. 8:31.32; Acts 15; II Cor. 3:17; Gal. 2:4.5; 4:21–5:1), which bestows, guarantees, and celebrates the freedom and dignity of the church as Christ's holy and elect Bride. This apostolic-prophetic constitution of the church (Eph. 2:20) declares all Christians brothers and sisters in Christ, and Him their sole Master and Lord (Mt. 20:25.26; 23:8). He in turn rules His dear church not with the Law's relentless rod of iron (Ps. 2:9), but with the life-giving Gospel of His grace (Mt. 11:28–30; 21:1–9; Jn. 1:14–17; 5:45; 10:1–16). And if He Himself came "not to be served but to serve" (Mt. 20:28), how much more so His servants? Christ's ministers are not lords but servants in the Gospel to His flock (I Cor. 4:1; II Cor. 4:5), not domineering over, but tending and caring for His church in His name (Jn. 21:15–18; I Tim. 3:5.15; I Pet. 5:1–4). "The apostolic way is this," wrote St. Bernard of Clairvaux: "Domination is forbidden, bidden is ministration."[22]

The "governing" or "ruling" of the church therefore is done entirely with God's own Word and sacraments. "Church Government" (*Kirchenregiment*) in the Augsburg Confession (Art. XIV) does not mean "administration" in the modern sense, but the proper provision and ordering of the sacred ministry of the Gospel

21. R. C. Wolf, *Documents of Lutheran Unity in America*, 196. At the 1871 LCMS Western District convention, where the Synodical Conference constitution was presented and discussed, it was noted, however, presumably in Walther's presence, that the "final goal" of one single orthodox American Lutheran Church "will likely remain only a pious wish" (1871 Western District *Proceedings*, 62).

22. *"dominatio interdicitur, indicitur ministratio"* (*de consideratione,* cited in Walther, *Kirche und Amt*, 383).

(Art. V).[23] The "ministers of the Word," as the leaders (*Vorsteher*) of the community of God, or as those whom the Lord has "prefaced" (*praefecit*, placed before) to his church "to govern it" (*regendae*),[24] do so only by means of their divinely assigned pastoral work of preaching, absolving and retaining, and administering the sacraments.[25] To try to rule the church by human power and authority, that is, to bind consciences to man-made rules and regulations is presumption, usurpation, and sacrilege, for it seeks to enslave the free Bride of Christ (Mt. 15:9; Gal. 2:11ff. Cf. AC and Ap. XV; Ap. XXVIII.7–11; FC X).[26]

That same Holy Scripture which is able to make sinners wise unto salvation through faith which is in Christ Jesus (II Tim. 3:15) is also "profitable" for all those things with which the "man of God," the preacher of the Gospel, needs to be "outfitted" for "every good work" of his office (vv. 16.17). Steeped in the Spirit-taught (διδακτοῖς, I Cor. 2:13) words from the "mind of Christ" (v. 16), he becomes "apt to teach" (διδακτικόν, I Tim. 3:2) others, as a resourceful householder, ever drawing out of his treasury things new and old (Mt. 13:52).

This needs to be stressed today in the face of what often passes for theological education but actually unfits a man for the ministry in general and for preaching in particular—either by robbing him outright of any and every firm Word from God, or by sidelining serious preoccupation with revealed truth as "impractical". The historical-critical or pragmatic stones substituted for the Bread of Life cannot of course nourish or sustain their victims, let alone build the church or advance her mission. Where real theology is destroyed or despised,[27] heaps of "practical" courses are then

23. Although AC XVI (Latin) is entitled, "Of Civil Matters," the Apology's headings of Arts. XIV and XVI are completely parallel in both languages and so reflect the Two Governments: *Vom Kirchenregiment/De Ordine Ecclesiastico* (Of Church Government/Of the Ecclesiastical Order) on the one hand, and *Vom weltlichen Regiment/De Ordine Politico* (Of Worldly Government/Of the Political Order) on the other. If we add to these the Large Catechism's (4th Commandment, parr. 142–143) *Hausregiment* (the domestic government or order), we have all "three hierarchies." On the latter see W. Maurer, *Luthers Lehre von den drei Hierarchien und ihr mittelalterlicher Hintergrund.*

24. FC SD X.10.

25. Tr. 59–61. The Treatise here speaks of those who *"praesunt"* (Latin) or *"furstehn"* (German), that is, "preside" over the churches, and expressly refers back to what the AC and Apology have said about "ecclesiastical power," that is, in Art. XXVIII.

26. F. Pieper: "All government of the Church which does not bind the consciences of Christians to Christ's Word, but to the word of men, is pseudo-government" (*Christian Dogmatics*, II:394).

27. "The present ethos of the Protestant churches is such that a theologically oriented approach to the preparation of ministers is not only irrelevant but counterproductive. . . In fact, the 'theologically' oriented graduate may actually be punished by the ecclesiastical

piled up, designed to equip the future minister with the psychological and sociological "skills" necessary to manipulate people in the mass market of religion. No longer a man of God, shaped by wrestling with God (Gen. 32:24–31) in hallowed text and sacrament, by prayer, study, and trial (*oratio, meditatio, tentatio*)[28], the "minister" is then but a hollow functionary plying his trade for profit and success.

Faithful churches and ministers will recoil from the false glitter (Mt. 4:1–11!) of this travesty, pray the Lord of the harvest to send workers into His harvest (Mt. 9:38), and do all in their power to hand on the faith to faithful men who will in turn be able to teach others (II Tim. 2:2). A serious and solid theological preparation honors the primacy of God's Word and therefore of preaching in the church. The substance of the Gospel itself will then determine and integrate all exegetical, dogmatical, historical, and practical disciplines, without the fatal "theory/practice" schizophrenia of modern pragmatic church-marketeering.[29] "Not by might nor by power but by My Spirit, says the Lord Almighty" (Zech. 4:6). The man of God renounces the technician's contrivance and manipulation (II Cor. 2:17; 11:20; Gal. 4:17; Eph. 4:14), because he trusts the divine message he "stewards" but does not control (AC V)—and just so he unleashes in the Gospel not mere words but power (I Th. 1:5).

Since "Christians can be ruled by nothing except God's Word" (for they are ruled by faith, and faith "can come through no word of man, but only through the word of God, as Paul says in Rom. 10 [:17]"),[30] and since the New Testament church has no Levitical regulations prescribing the details of her outward life, there ex-

---

system which rewards un- and anti-theological approaches to ministry" (E. Farley, *Theologia: The Fragmentation and Unity of Theological Education*, 4, 15). Farley's incisive analysis, which laments "practical theology's loss of its theological component" (p. 20), proceeds by way of a splendid historical overview, but offers only illusory escapes from the admittedly "bitter" choice "between *theologia* and the critical principle" (p. 22). That is because Farley is committed to the view that "the house of authority," by which he means actual God-given doctrine, *doctrina divina* in any form, has irretrievably collapsed, so that continuing to employ basic elements of it, like the Scripture principle, produces "incoherence" (E. Farley, *Ecclesial Reflection: An Anatomy of Theological Method*, xiv, cf. 171 and *passim*).

28. *Preface to the Wittenberg Edition of Luther's German Writings* (1539), *WA* 50:659.4; *LW* 34:285.

29. Farley rightly denounces a "theory practice" dichotomy "which threatens to turn all theological education into pragmatics and technology" (*Theologia*, 23).

30. *On Temporal Authority To What Extent it should be Obeyed* (1523), *LW* 45:117; *WA* 11:271.16–20. See this and other trenchant quotations, in Walther, *Church and Ministry*, 316.

ists a large realm of Christian liberty, or of "*adiaphora*," things neither commanded nor forbidden in God's written Word. In this realm consciences may not be bound, as if the observance of such externals were in itself necessary (AC and Ap. XV). The Church of the Augsburg Confession solemnly testifies before all Christendom: "It is not necessary [for the true unity of the church] that human traditions or rites and ceremonies, instituted by men, should be alike everywhere" (AC VII.3). Among these "human traditions" are all the details of church organization beyond the divinely made provisions for the orderly ministrations of the holy means of grace.

What then governs this realm of external arrangements in the church? In a word: Love (Rom. 13:8–15:13; I Cor. 13). "Love is the empress over ceremonies, and ceremonies must yield to love, but not love to ceremonies."[31] Since God is not a God of disorder but of peace (I Cor. 14:33), love seeks order and decorum (v. 40) at all times. Such order is not optional but "very becoming in the church and is therefore necessary" (Ap. XV.22). It is achieved essentially by mutual submission and accommodation: "Among Christians there shall and can be no authority [government]; rather all are alike subject to one another" (Rom. 12:10; I Pet. 5:5; Lk. 14:10).[32] It is to serve this harmonious decorum in the church that "bishops or pastors may make regulations so that everything in the churches is done in good order" (AC XXVIII.53). Such regulations are to be observed "for the sake of love and peace. . . in such a way that one does not give offense to another and so that there may be no disorder or unbecoming conduct in the church" (XXVIII.55).

It goes without saying that such "making of regulations" cannot be a matter of high-handed dictation by the pastors, but involves the willing consent of the people. "This pastor or prelate has nothing to command (because he is not the church) except with the consent of his church."[33] The principle works both ways of course:

31. Thesis 66 [German] of Luther's 1535 polemic against the Council of Constance. (*WA* 39:I:22–23).

32. *On Temporal Authority, LW* 45:117; *WA* 11:270.32–34.

33. *Against the Whole Synagogue of Satan* (1530), *WA* 30:II:421.22–24. See also Thesis IX, "The church of God has power to ordain ceremonies about festivals, foods, fasts, prayers, vigils, etc., not for others, but solely for herself, nor has she ever done or ever will do otherwise;" and Thesis XVII, "The pastor may urge and persuade the church, that she might consent for certain urgent reasons to impose on herself for a time fasts, festivals, prayers or other ceremonies, and again, when she wishes, to change and omit them." Simultaneously with these theses Luther insisted to Melanchthon, in response to his anxious question whether the bishops could not claim the right to command in their capacity as princes: "It is

"Therefore, the office of the ministry does not give to those who bear it, arbitrary power over Christians, nor does it deliver the ministers of the Word up to the arbitrary directions and commands of men."[34] Indeed, ministers are expected to have sober and informed judgments about churchly customs, and as custodians of wholesome traditions to guide their people accordingly.[35]

The question of the nature of voting in the church is most conveniently addressed at this point. In the temporal sphere, given democratic arrangements, to vote is to take part in and to exercise the awesome powers of Rom. 13:1ff. Voting is an act of supreme sovereignty, which can, within constitutionally specified limits, enforce the majority will with the ultimate sanctions of the death penalty and war. Voting can mean nothing like this in the church at all (Mt. 20:24–28). The church is not a democracy but a Christocracy: Christ alone is Lord. Voting is but a way of expressing agreement or consensus. Two cases are possible: (1) If the matter is clearly

---

certain that these two governments are separate and different that is, the ecclesiastical one and the secular one; Satan, through the papacy, has fundamentally confused and mixed them. We have to be sharply alert here, neither to have them brought together so that the two governments may again be mixed, nor to give an inch to any one or consent that he may mix [them]. For this would mean to make common cause with thieves and robbers, because in this connection we have the divine Word, which says, 'But not so with you.' It is the authority, and it commands that the two governments be preserved separate and unmixed. . . . As bishop, a bishop has no authority to impose on his churches any statute or ceremony, except with the expressed or silent agreement of the church. For the church is free and is lord of all and the bishops ought not to dominate the faith of the congregations, nor burden or oppress the congregations against their will. The bishops are, after all, only servants and stewards, and not the lords of the church. If the congregations, as one body, have agreed with the bishop, however, then the bishop may impose upon the faithful whatever the bishop wishes. . . . As sovereign, a bishop may impose even less on the church, since this would mean fundamentally to mix these two jurisdictions. . . . As sovereign, a bishop may impose upon his subjects, as subjects, whatever seems appropriate to him, as long as it is godly and permissible; the subjects are required to obey, since they obey not as members of the church, but as citizens. For the church is a twofold person in one and the same man. . . . It is the same as if Pomer forces his servants to abide by his house rule, but does not force his Wittenberg parish [to abide by this house rule]. . . . It is the same as if the emperor universally ordered all people to fast; then the members of the church would obey him too, since according to the flesh the church is under the emperor, but the church does not obey as church. . . . We are unable, therefore, either on the basis of the ecclesiastical or the secular law, to grant to the bishops the power to impose anything on the church, even if it is permissible and godly, since one ought not to do evil so that good may result" (*Luther to Melanchthon* [July 1530], *LW* 49:383–387; *WABr* 5:492–493).

34. *Theses of Agreement* (Lutheran Church of Australia), VI, 5.

35. Gerhard, speaking of "the authority to establish in outward or indifferent things directions and rules or definite ceremonies for order and propriety," states: "But these powers pertain [*pertinent*] to the whole church, and are not peculiar to the spiritual estate [the ministry], although we readily admit that the first and chief parts of this power are the province of [*competere*] the ecclesiastical ministry" (cited in C.F.W. Walther, *Church and Ministry*, 318, although we have here retranslated the last sentence in the interests of accuracy).

settled in God's Word, then voting does not establish the truth of it, but merely expresses confession or denial of that Word. Such a vote should never be undertaken lightly, but only after thorough discussion and painstaking efforts to clear up misunderstandings, since division here is fraught with weighty consequences.[36] (2) If the question is not clearly settled in God's Word, then it must be decided in love on the basis of such facts and arguments as can be brought to bear on the matter. As a matter of common sense, the minority should readily accede to the wishes of the majority here, but the latter have no inherent right to impose anything on the others. And if consideration for weak consciences for instance demands it, the majority must forgo its wishes and yield to the minority in love.[37]

So little room is there in the church for a secular majority rule, that Walther writes: "Should it happen that something were decided or determined by the congregation contrary to God's Word, then such decision and determination is null and void, is also to be so declared, and to be revoked."[38] In the church, neither majorities nor minorities rule, but only faith and love. Faith is governed

---

36. C.F.W. Walther: "Matters of doctrine and conscience are to be resolved unanimously according to God's Word and the Confession of the church (Is. 8:20. . .). . . Hence a congregation which wants to be Christian, more particularly Evangelical Lutheran, cannot presume to determine by vote [whether] something that has already been decided by God's Word and the Confessions of the church should be regarded by it as valid or be rejected by it. As soon as a congregation refuses to acknowledge the decisive standard of the Symbolical Books of the Evangelical Lutheran Church, it ceases to be Lutheran; and when it no longer is willing to subject itself to the clear declarations of Holy Scripture as the Word of the eternal God, it becomes a synagog of Satan (Rev. 3:9)" (*The Form of a Christian Congregation*, 56–58). When a stand had to be taken, at the 1881 LCMS Convention, for or against the biblical, confessional doctrine of the Election of grace, as formulated in Walther's 13 Theses, it was carefully explained that a vote could never determine truth or falsehood. The vote, rather, was to make clear "who belongs to us and who not," and whether "there are only a small number of those who reject the doctrine taught in our publications, and who will then have to leave our house, or whether we, who confess the true doctrine of the Election, are in the minority and must therefore leave our present synodical home" (1881 LCMS *Proceedings*, 32).

37. F. Pieper: "In *adiaphora* a vote is taken to ascertain what the majority regards as the best. The natural order is that in *adiaphora* the minority yields to the majority and acquiesces, not because the majority has the right to rule, but for love's sake. Since, however, love is queen here, it may happen that the majority will yield to the minority." If the spirit of the meeting is "sinking below the Christian level," the discussion should be interrupted "and the Christian spirit and frame of mind be restored by instruction and admonition, e.g., on the basis of 1 Peter 5:5" (*Christian Dogmatics*, III:430). See similar comments in Walther's *Pastoraltheologie*, 372ff., to which Pieper expressly refers.

38. C.F.W. Walther, *The Form of a Christian Congregation*, tr. J. T. Mueller, renders it: "Should anything in the congregation be decided and established contrary to God's Word, such a decision and establishment is null and void and should be declared rescinded as such" (56–57).

solely by God's Word. Therefore faith does not yield to love, but love yields to faith.[39] Everything else yields to love.

The same principles of government by faith and love apply equally to local or "simple" churches, and to "composite" church-bodies. The basic difference is that the divine institution of the means of grace and of the Gospel-ministry defines the life of the local church, baptizing, confessing, and gathered together regularly by and around His instituting mandate: "This do in remembrance of Me." This is the ministry which is "not optional" (Walther's 3rd Thesis on the Ministry), but mandated by God, as we have seen. By divine command and institution, however, there is no ministry or church structure above the level of the local church and ministry (Tr.60 ff.). (Here lies the crux of the divergence between the so-called "Missouri" and "Wisconsin" understandings of church and ministry).[40] Among these local churches and ministries there is full equality.[41] They are one in faith and love in the mutuality of church fellowship (pulpit and altar fellowship, mutual acknowledgement [Gal. 2:9], and common obedience to the missionary mandate). This God-given oneness among the churches is no greater for being expressed through joint administrative structures and organs, and no less for the lack of such organizational elements. Ideally therefore "the church cannot be better governed and maintained than by having all of us live

39. "Therefore in mere ceremonies love is to be judge and mistress, but not in faith or in the promises of God. Rather faith shall be lord over love, and love shall yield to it, and faith not yield to love" (*Against the Council of Constance*, [1535], *WA* 39:I:23.7–14).

40. See the excursus on "Missouri," and "Wisconsin" on Church and Ministry, which follows this chapter.

41. Note this important historical and theological testimony from within Eastern Orthodoxy: "in the apostolic age, and throughout the second and third centuries, every local church was autonomous and independent; autonomous, for it contained in itself everything necessary to its life; and independent by not depending on any other local church or any bishop whatever outside itself. . . . the local church is autonomous and independent, because the Church of God in Christ indwells it in perfect fullness. It is independent, because any power, of any kind, exercised over it would be exercised over Christ and His Body" (N. Afanassieff in J. Meyendorff et al., *The Primacy of Peter*, 73, 75). See also K. Rahner's remarks: "We wish to authenticate the nature of the Church's official ministry, and especially of the priesthood as doctrinally defined, on the basis of scripture and the apostolic age. And precisely because of this we must first proceed from the single ministry found in the local Church in the concrete, for it is here that the Church as such achieves its manifestation. By comparison with this single official ministry we can regard as secondary the ways in which it is subdivided and articulated into several possible higher or lower offices. . ." (*Theological Investigations*, XIV:205–206). C.F.W. Walther wrote: "All the rights of an Evangelical Lutheran local congregation are embraced in the keys of the kingdom of heaven, which the Lord gave to His whole church originally and immediately and in such a way that they belong to every congregtion in equal measure, the smallest as well as the largest. . . . all church rights and powers are embraced in the keys of the kingdom of heaven" (*The Form of A Christian Congregation*, 13).

under one head, Christ, and by having all the bishops equal in office (however they may differ in gifts) and diligently joined together in unity of doctrine, faith, sacraments, prayer, works of love, etc. So St. Jerome writes that the priests of Alexandria governed the churches together and in common" (SA II.IV.9). Practical considerations of good order, however, motivate "our deep desire to maintain the church polity and various ranks of the ecclesiastical hierarchy, although they were created by human authority" (Ap. XIV.1).

Since "the distinction between bishop and pastor is not by divine right" (Tr. 65),[42] the bishop, superintendent, visitor, president, or whatever he may be called, is in principle "first among equals" (*primus inter pares*). As pastor in a local church and so by "divine right," he is "equal," and as bishop,etc. he is "first," and that by "human right" only. What the "bishop" has beyond the office of pastor is "the humanly devised office of oversight (ἐπισκοπή) over pastors and congregations."[43] When and in so far as the bishop teaches the Word of God, he must be obeyed, and this "by divine right" (see AC XXVIII.21-28). Bishops must lead with the Word of God, not with opinion polls and popularity contests. Their great work of securing right of way for the Gospel and Sacraments of Christ must be done in fraternal love and collegiality, with due regard for the divine dignity of the churches and their ministers. A bishop must not be an ἀλλοτριεπίσκοπος ("one who meddles in things that do not concern him, a busybody," cf. Bauer, p. 40). Here

---

42. Given the standard Roman Catholic view, K. Rahner's suggestions on the subject, offered with all due tentativeness and deference to the magisterium, must be regarded as remarkable vindications of the Reformation position: Rahner speaks of the church's ministry as "ultimately *one*" or the "ultimately *single* official ministry" (italics in original), and explains: "And we might add to this reply that the function of the Church is rightly to preach the gospel and to dispense the sacraments throughout the ages, that faith, hope, and charity may be present in as many individuals as possible and in the most radical forms possible, and that this may be manifested even at the social level and in the constitution of the Church herself" (*Theological Investigations*, XIV:196, 209). Further: "First according to the witness of history it seems that at one time the monarchic episcopate existed side by side with other community structures in the apostolic age, and that at the time these were not regarded either as illegitimate or as embryonic or provisional" (p. 189). "The relationship between the bishop and the kind of priest, generally called a parish priest, who presides over a genuine, living, and fraternal community of the faith in fact remains theologically and historically speaking unexplained right down to the present day. This much can confidently be asserted: in the old days the leader of such a community would have been called a bishop. . . We may for instance remember the many hundreds of Italian bishops who, by our standards, are after all simply parish priests of so many larger parishes" (199–200).

43. H. Sasse, *We Confess the Church*, 57. Also: "By human arrangement he may have the work of superintendency. By divine mandate he has solely the office of preaching the forgiveness and justification of sinners for Christ's sake" (72).

applies also what Luther says about why St. Paul in Rom. 12:8 puts "ruling" last rather than first:

> But we must know that nothing is higher than God's Word and that this ministry [*Amt*] is above all others. Ruling is its servant, which should incite and wake it up, just as a servant wakes his master from sleep or otherwise reminds him of his duty [*Amt*]. . .But all should let one office or gift be more precious than the others, yet in such a way that one should serve the other with his office or gift and be subject to him. Thus the office of ruling is the most inferior, and yet all others are subject to it, while it again services all others by caring and providing for them. So also prophecy is the highest and yet it follows him who rules.[44]

The Reformation in many places called upon the princes to act as "emergency bishops," but the powers once assumed were never given up by the temporal governments. This led to a progressive subservience of the church to the state. That of course was not the original intention. Moved by the pitiful conditions in the churches, the Reformers wanted "the true episcopal office and practice of visitation re-established because of the pressing need." There were, however, to be "no strict commands as if we were publishing a new form of papal decrees" (although "undisciplined heads who out of utter perversity are able to do nothing in common or in agreement" were to be removed). Rather, it was a matter of giving sound guidance and advice, for which Old and New Testament precedents (e.g. Paul and Barnabas, Acts 15:2) could be cited. "More than any, Christ has done this kind of work on behalf of all, and on this account possessed no place on earth where he could lay his head," beginning "even while he was in the womb, for he went with his mother over the hills to visit St. John [Luke 1:39]"![45]

In this spirit the early Lutheran "consistories" therefore were advisory bodies, composed of experienced and respected churchmen (laymen and ministers), giving good counsel for difficult cases. These consistories "were originally without any jurisdiction,"[46] or legal power to compel compliance. In time, however, given the nature of such things, the consistories grew more and more coercive, so that Luther became alarmed: "We must tear the consistories to pieces, for we do not by any means want to have

44. *Church Postil, Epistle Portion, On the Second Sunday after Epiphany* (1525), *WA* 17:II:43.3–6, 12–17. Translation cited from C.F.W. Walther, *Church and Ministry*, 294.

45. Luther's preface to the *Instruction for the Visitors of Parish Pastors in Electoral Saxony* (1528) *LW* 40:271; *WA* 26:197.15–16.

46. C.F.W. Walther, *The Form of a Christian Congregation*, 11.

the lawyers and the pope in them."[47] State-churchism, however, was to prevail with a vengeance.

The founders of the Missouri Synod were very conscious of the blessed opportunity of letting the church govern herself according to her own nature and norms in free America.[48] They abhorred the legalism and juridicalism[49] of state churches gone sour, and wanted a system that was in full accord with Christian liberty. Yet they did not approve of the doctrinaire congregationalism of "some separatists in England," who "greatly exaggerate the idea of liberty."[50] What was wanted, in short, was neither chaos nor tyranny, but a churchly governance with God's Word alone.

It was the boast of the Missouri Synod that unlike some other bodies, it wished to bind its members to nothing but the revealed truth of Holy Scripture, as confessed in detail in the Book of Concord. Synod was to rely only on the power of the Word, "for in this manner the church also among us preserves its true character, its character of a kingdom of heaven." To claim other powers would be "robbing the church of Christ of the liberty which He has purchased. . . with His divine blood." In that case, too, "[o]ur chief battle would soon center about the execution of manufactured, external human ordinances and institutions and would swallow up the true blessed battle for the real treasure of the church, for the purity and unity of doctrine" (Walther).[51]

---

47. *Idem.*

48. Walther's 1863 classic, *Form of a Christian Congregation,* really had a longer title, which began: *The Right Form of an Evangelical Lutheran Local Congregation Independent of the State.*

49. From within German state-churchism R. Sohm radically criticised the whole notion of "Kirchenrecht" ("church law" does not quite convey the sense of "*Recht*" as right or justice). Sohm saw such legislation as in principle incompatible with love and the New Testament governance by "charisma" (See W. Maurer, *Pfarrerrecht und Bekenntnis,* 27–42). There was even a Russian translation (Moscow, 1906) of Sohm's influential *Kirchenrecht.* Sohm's sharp contrast between Spirit and Law influenced the anti-juridicalism of N. Afanassieff, who, however, accorded "Sohm's charismaticism . . . the correction of sacramentalism" (J. Meyendorff, "Church and Ministry," 120, n. 3). See also Afanassieff's anti-juridical "eucharistic ecclesiology" and A. Schmemann's espousal of it in J. Meyendorff, N. Afanasieff, R. P. A. Schemann, and N. Koulomzine, *The Primacy of Peter in the Orthodox Church,* 57–110 and 30–56. Some of the same "sacramental" correction of "charismaticism" might have been derived also from J. Gerhard, who at one stage appears to have displaced Aquinas in Russian theological education (D. W. Treadgold, *The West in Russia and China* I:102). Peter the Great admired the control exercised by the Protestant states over their churches, and imposed on the Russian Church a scheme patterned after the German church orders.

50. Veit Ludwig von Seckendorf, cited in C.F.W. Walther, *Church and Ministry,* 240.

51. *Concordia Journal* (Sept. 1976), 203. In the same essay Walther said: "Also our Synodical body has the same prospects of salutary influence if it does not attempt to operate through any other means than through the power of the Word of God. Even then we must expect battles, but they will not be the mean, depressing battles for obedience to human laws, but the holy battles for God's Word, for God's honor and kingdom."

In particular, it was not the external Synodical constitution that was to be the bond of unity. "Our Lutheran Church has no special ecclesiastical constitution to hold it together," wrote F. Pieper in 1880.[52] Therefore the various Lutheran churches throughout the world have very different constitutions. "To the true unity of the church," he continued, "there belongs, as our Confession says, only the pure Word and the right administration of the sacraments. The fact that the sects put so much stock in external forms is due to the fact that they do not maintain the distinction between Law and Gospel." The whole point of the Synodical arrangements, Pieper wrote in his later essay on church government, is to implement, not to supplement the Word of God:

> Therefore also we elect as Visitors and Presidents not people who are perhaps clever with documents or are better versed than others in our "Synodical Handbook," but people who are well experienced in God's Word and are better able than others clearly to present and apply it with reference to existing circumstances. The supervising offices established by our Synodical order are not to supplement God's Word, but serve God's Word, so that it—God's Word— might hold sway.[53]

State-church juridicalism, however, is not the only force that can violate the church's evangelical constitution. The present cultural threat is embodied rather in the corporate model of the commercial world, with its bureaucratic controls and empire building.

---

52. "Theses on the Distinction of Law and Gospel," (1880 LCMS Iowa District Proceedings, 44). See also another district essay (the essayist's name is not indicated): "True church unity is not a constitutionistic one. . . . We too are constitutional—but not constitutionistic. Those are constitutionistic who put the constitution in the place of the Word, who assign, entirely or in part, to the former the significance of the latter. That happened and still happens in the General Synod. If we ask about the flag which united and still unites it, we find: that is its constitution. . . One cannot frighten these people by telling them: you teach and act contrary to Holy Scripture; for their constitution permits them to interpret Scripture as they see fit. . . . but tell them: you are acting contrary to your constitution, then they take fright, for then unity is threatened" (*On Church Unity*, 1888 LCMS Eastern District *Proceedings*, 28ff).

53. "Kirche und Kirchenregiment" (Church and Church Governance), 1896 LCMS Proceedings, 40–41. See also this ringing defense of Synod's genuinely evangelical constitution: "Men have derided synods which have only advisory power. They have thought that nothing but 'confusion' and 'disorder' would have to result. . . This fear is groundless, as can be seen from the history of those Lutheran synods in America which have left consciences entirely unfettered in regard to synodical resolutions. . . We can truthfully say that government of the Church solely by God's Word has stood the test of nearly a century among us. Of course, the flesh of Christians has sought to create disorder also among us. But God's Word has proved its ability to rule and control everything. So firmly has a 'free church' government, abstinence from all commanding that exceeded God's Word, united and held us together that outsiders have surmised that we must have a 'High Church' government and must be the 'High Church' party in the Lutheran Church" (F. Pieper, *Christian Dogmatics*, III:433).

Sasse's complaints of the "modern overorganization of the church" and "the church politics with which modern bishops kill their own time and that of others," though first uttered in the European context, apply wherever the temptation is to have a "central bureaucracy running things not by the Word but by force *(non verbo, sed vi)*."[54]

The trend in American churches has been "to think of the Church as a kind of business corporation chartered to do the Lord's work," which entails "the subordination of questions of truth" to "efficiency of operation," in the manner of pragmatism. In the interests of "maintaining outward unity and efficiently conducting large enterprises," there occurred a "a simultaneously increasing administrative centralization and decreasing theological centralization." This "pragmatic conception of the Church" substituted "broad church inclusion of opposing theological views for theological answers to them." Thus "the Church's theology has been living in a modest colonial house, more and more overshadowed by the skyscraper of the Church's active work."[55]

These are the directions in which churches will inevitably drift if left to the buffetings of current cultural winds of doctrine (Eph. 4:14). The solution is not a fearful abdication in the face of modern challenges, but a conscious and clear-headed subjection of everything to the paramountcy of the evangelical truth. A church that "cuts corners" with the truth for the sake of popularity and statistical expansion must in the end disintegrate. The militant church on earth is a confessing and a confessional church. "The proper form of the historical church therefore is the confessing church, which in singlemindedness and enduring faithfulness preserves and propagates the saving truth in the power of the Holy Spirit."[56]

Although the synodical structure and organization is as such an adiaphoron, "everything is permissible, but not everything is edi-

54. *We Confess the Church*, 82.

55. L. A. Loetscher, *The Broadening Church*, 8, 59, 93. The preface states the author's belief that the Presbyterian experience, described in this volume, "finds broad parallels in many another leading American Church. Its story is a kind of theological barometer of the times."

56. *Einigungssätze zwischen der Evangelisch-Lutherischen Kirche und der Evangelisch-Lutherischen Freikirche*, 1948. These are the agreed theses of Missouri's German sister church, the Independent Evangelical Lutheran Church in Germany. Immediately before our quotation the document states (2C): "Since Christ is the sole Head of His one Church, it must be insisted in the constituted Church that everything which exists and happens in her be subject to the sole rule of Christ in the Word. All expressions of the life of the visible Church must grow out of the Confession and must prove themselves as direct or indirect effects of Word and Sacrament." The Lutheran Church of Australia's Theses of Agreement state: "It is the constant task of the Church as the 'fellowship of outward ties and rites' to see to it that

fying" (I Cor.10:23). If the pure preaching of the Gospel (not just in books or constitutions but in ongoing public proclamation, also by missionaries at large at home and abroad) and the right administration of the sacraments (in living, missionary, confessionally responsible congregations) are truly to be served, then clear constraints must apply. A synod dare not dissipate its energies on a cafeteria of heterogeneous "objectives," as if all were of equal importance. That way lies the slide into the pragmatism of "conducting large enterprises."

Rather, an orthodox synod's "first chief duty is to be confessionally faithful in word and deed."[57] "To stand guard over the purity and unity of doctrine within the synodical circle, and to oppose false doctrine," was therefore the very first duty and responsibility of the Missouri Synod in its original constitution.[58] In any real or potential conflict of interests, the evangelical truth must have right of way. Whatever else a synod is able to do is fine and good, but this must have top and overriding priority, for "the church's whole life and being consists in the Word of God *(tota vita et substantia ecclesiae est in verbo Dei)*. . . Mt. 4:4."[59] The only thing more urgent than the preservation of the purity and unity of evangelical doctrine is its restoration where it has been lost.

This means in practice that the synodical structure and its officials must come to the aid and support of faithful pastors and/or congregations when they are threatened by false doctrine or are oppressed or persecuted for the sake of the truth.[60] Such protection of churches and ministers with the Word of God is the chief function of bishops. Today as in Luther's day it is widely thought "that the office of bishop implies dignity and that he is a bishop who wears a miter on his head." Not so. "It is not a position that implies dignity. No, it is an office requiring that the incumbent must take care of us, watch over us, and be our guardian."[61] Fur-

the pure Gospel and the Sacraments as instituted by Christ are preserved, in order that the 'fellowship of faith and the Holy Spirit in men's hearts,' the Church strictly speaking, the Una Sancta, may remain with us. This includes the most sacred duty to reject error and heresy" (V, 19).

57. C.F.W. Walther in his famous essay "About several chief duties which a synod has, if it wishes to have a right to bear the name of an Evangelical Lutheran synod" (1879 LCMS Iowa District *Proceedings*, 9). Elsewhere Walther had indicated his conviction that "the chief activity of the synod should be directed towards the preservation and promotion and guarding of the unity and purity of Lutheran doctrine" (*Walther's Briefe*, I:16).

58. *First Synodical Constitution*, 5.

59. *Luther against Ambrose Catharinus*, (1521), *WA* 7:721.

60. Walther's classic "Chief Duties" essay of 1879 has much of value to say on this score.

61. *Commentary on 1 Peter* (1523), *LW* 30:135–136; *WA* 12:389–390.

thermore: "Now today one finds many people who can let the Gospel be preached, provided that one does not cry out against the wolves and preach against the prelates." But it is not enough to feed the sheep, without fighting off the wolf. In fact, the "wolf can surely let the sheep have good pasturage. The fatter they are, the more he likes them." The one thing he cannot stand is "the hostile barking of the dogs."[62] Hence the name of the Missouri Synod's first theological journal: *Lehre und Wehre* (doctrine and defense. See also FC SD RN.14). Historically the episcopate has, as a body, often fallen behind the rank and file, both pastors and people, on this score.[63]

Modern churches, distracted with a thousand agenda-items clamoring for attention, need structures and organs specifically designed to consider, evaluate, clarify, and adjudicate adequately and decisively, in accord with Holy Scripture and the orthodox Confessions, the welter of theological issues that must constantly arise. To "wrest judgment from the church" is a mark of the Antichrist (Tr. 40, 49–51). For "when proper judicial process has been taken away, the churches are not able to remove impious teachings and impious forms of worship, and countless souls are lost generation after generation." All the external machinery of the church must further, and if necessary yield to, but never obstruct the divine truth. Hence Pieper stresses that also parliamentary procedure, necessary as it is to that good order which love actively seeks and to which it gladly submits, must nevertheless yield to truth and love. So much so, in fact, that "every Christian has the right to call a meeting of the congregation, synod, council, etc., if he is convinced that conditions demand a meeting and that the officials are lax in doing their duty."[64] By the same token, of course, others are free not to attend, if they are not so convinced!

Finally, if the real governance of the church means tending her faithfully with Christ's Gospel and sacraments, then the confessing and confessional church cannot be quite as indifferent to the outward forms in which this happens, as much glib modern talk

62. Idem.

63. "The episcopate, whose action was so prompt and concordant at Nicaea on the rise of Arianism, did not, as a class or order of men, play a good part in the troubles consequent upon the Council; and the laity did. The Catholic people, in the length and breadth of Christendom, were the obstinate champions of Catholic truth, and the bishops were not. Of course there were great and illustrious exceptions. . . Athanasius. . . Hilary. . . Basil. . . the two Gregories, and Ambrose." So wrote J. H. Newman, whose remarks were never forgiven him, even though he eventually became a cardinal. *The Arians of the Fourth Century*, 445.

64. *Christian Dogmatics*, III:433, cf. 434.

about "culture" would suggest. It goes without saying that there is a genuine area of adiaphora (FC X). In an age, however, in which even physical science generally thinks of its observations or data as "theory-laden," rather than as rigidly "raw" or objective, churches should not be surprised if at least some apparent adiaphora turn out on closer inspection to be "theology-laden." One need not adopt MacLuhan's jingle about the medium being the message to realize that *how* something is said is a not insignificant part of *what* in fact is said.

The founders of the Missouri Synod did not take this matter lightly. By constitutional provision they made it the "business of Synod," in part, "10. To strive after the greatest possible uniformity in ceremonies."[65] This was not meant in the sense that how things are done does not matter, so long as they are done uniformly. The stated theological intent rather was to "purify" American Lutheranism of "the emptiness and the poverty in the externals of the service" taken over from "the false spirit of the Reformed."[66]

Crucial here is Luther's sensible and thoroughly churchly principle that "a council should occupy itself only with matters of faith,"[67] and that ceremonies "ought to be completely disregarded by the councils and should be left at home in the parishes, indeed in the schools so that the schoolmaster, along with the pastor, would be 'master of ceremonies.' "[68] But how do the pastors and

---

65. *First LCMS Constitution*, 5.

66. Ibid., p. 12. Points 14 and 15 (pp. 11-13) reaffirm with AC VII that "uniformity in ceremonies is not essential," but hold that it is "wholesome and useful," partly to avoid offending the weak, and partly to "avoid the appearance of and desire for innovations." Echoing the "case of confession" of FC SD X.2–3, the section provides: "All pastors and congregations that wish to be recognized as orthodox by Synod are prohibited from adopting or retaining any ceremony which might weaken the confession of the truth or condone or strengthen a heresy, especially if heretics insist upon the continuation or the abolishing of such ceremonies." Next, private confession is to be retained where it is practiced and where it is not, the pastor "is to strive through teaching and instruction to introduce it." Further, "Synod as a whole is to supervise how each individual pastor cares for the souls in his charge," and "[e]specially is Synod to investigate whether its pastors have permitted themselves to be misled into applying the so-called 'New Measures' [of Methodist revivalism.K.M.] which have become prevalent here, or whether they care for their souls according to the sound Scriptural manner of the orthodox Church." See also Walther's thoroughly evangelical treatment of "confessional ceremonies" in his *Pastoraltheologie* (53–57).

67. Hence the uniform stress in the Missouri Synod literature on doctrinal theses and essays as central to the business of synods and conferences. And of course, ceremonies can and often do have doctrinal implications, and when these become controversial, councils/synods/conventions (Acts 15, FC X) must attend to them.

68. *On the Councils and the Church*, *LW* 41:136–137; *WA* 50:619.5–7. See also *Exhortation to All Clergy Assembled at Augsburg*, (1530) *LW* 34:9–61; *WA* 30:II:268–365.

schoolmasters know which ceremonies to foster as wholesome[69] and which to discourage? Obviously the formation of an informed and churchly judgment needs to be a part of their preparation and training, and cannot be left to chance and whim. Neither antinomian buffoonery nor pettifogging legalism will do, but only a mature sobriety.

What is of interest dogmatically here is not this or that detail, but whether the pivotal position of the means of grace in the church is upheld or frittered away in favor of other attractions. That is what is at stake in the modern cultural pressures for a crowd-pleasing (II Tim.4:3) marketable consumer religion—dubbed "MacChurch" by a witty observer.[70] The demand for what is meant today by "experiential religion"[71] is ultimately incompatible with Gospel-teaching and sacraments as divinely given and exclusive channels of forgiveness, life, and salvation.

The argument is not of course about whether there is or ought to be religious experience (the intensity of Luther's is well known), but about its proper sources, meaning, functions, and limits. The choice, ultimately, is between Christ's means of grace, which "work spiritually and invisibly and for the future so that his church and bishops can only be smelled, as it were, faintly and from afar," and the alluring assortments of "God's ape Satan's" pseudo-sacraments, which "work promptly and help now and in this life, visibly and tangibly. . ."[72]

As the church presses onward and upward towards the goal (Phil. 3:12–14), she does so as a pilgrim,[73] intent on what lies

69. "nothing contributes so much to the maintenance of dignity in public worship and the cultivation of reverence and devotion among the people as the proper observance of ceremonies in the churches" (*AC*, Preface to Art. XXII–XXVIII.6, Tappert, 39).

70. Short for "Middle American Christian Church," a place for "solid suburban Americans who want a little God in their life and a place to go before brunch," its theology to be determined by surveys, but reliably inoffensive. So wrote Jack Cashill in the *Wall Street Journal*, cited in W. C. Roof, *American Mainline Religion*, 229.

71. One knowledgeable observer described the "emergent spiritual tradition" as preferring "direct experience. . . to any form of organized religion" (M. Ferguson, *The Aquarian Conspiracy: Personal and Social Transformation in the 1980s*, 367). Further: "During 'great awakenings' there is a shift from a religion mediated by authorities to one of direct spiritual experience. . . . doctrine is losing its authority, and knowing is superseding belief. . .The Radical Center of spiritual experience seems to be knowing without doctrine" (pp. 369, 371, 377).

72. *On the Councils and the Churches*, *LW* 41:170; *WA* 50:646–647.

73. Despite the laudable missionary zeal, the "village church"/"camp church" analysis in D. Luecke, *Evangelical Style and Lutheran Substance*, 51ff., is not adequate. It tends to get mired in the sociological, without noticing the underlying theology. (See also the "Review Essay" by A. Ludwig in the *Concordia Student Journal*, 4–14). Much of what is wrong with the "village church" type is really characteristic not of Lutheranism's confessional and liturgical heritage, but of the remnants of state-churchism. The solution is not the hasty

ahead, not a tourist, absorbed in the here and now. Her solidarity is not with Adam's fallen race and its "cultures," on the old plane (I Cor. 15:22ff.;II Cor. 5:16–17) but with the Second Adam and Head of the new humanity. This new humanity, the church, has her own unique identity and history, transcending this world's "cultures," which, rather, she re-shapes (Rom. 12:2). She must teach all nations (Mt. 28:19), not "mingle" with them and "adopt their customs" (Ps. 106:35, NIV). God's children and servants "take pleasure" in Zion's very "stones, and favor the dust thereof"—all on account of God's Temple which was but a shadow of things to come; "but the body is of Christ" (Col. 2:17). She of whom "glorious things are spoken" (Ps. 87:3) has no need of the tawdry, the frivolous, and the mawkish, as she shows forth the praises of Him Who called her out of darkness into His wondrous light (I Pet. 2:9). Her practice is shaped and governed—in the absence of New Testament ceremonial law—not by biblicistic proof-texting, but by her orthodox, evangelical confession. Only as she is true to her own nature can the church be true to the mission of the Good Shepherd who has compassion on the multitudes (Mt. 9:36).

"Rise, crowned with light, imperial Salem, rise!"[74]

---

scuttling of tradition in favor of the flighty, up-rooted "camp"-style of sectarianism, but a sober and deliberate reappropriation of the time-tested churchly ways, which are already trans-cultural. How our fathers resisted the "New Measures" beloved of the revivalistic "American Lutheranism" of the time (see for instance F. Pieper, *Christian Dogmatics* I:184–185, and II:523, n. 38)! It is just "parish" thinking rather than "camp" flitter-flutter that binds in one both the transient, sojourner (παροικία, I Pet. 1:17) aspect and the stable continuity of the pilgrim church. Now that the "ethnic" cultural forces no longer serve Lutherans as a unifying cement, it is all the more urgent to rally round their genuine confessional and sacramental identity, and sharpen, rather than fudge, its distinctive contours. Nor should it be overlooked that in the midst of precisely that typically American "evangelicalism" we are being asked to imitate, there is a deep longing for the very features of our Lutheran church life (not as it often is but as it can and ought to be) which are regularly denounced as obstacles to missionary work in America! See R. Webber and D. Bloesch, *The Orthodox Evangelicals*.

Finally, one must ponder Sydney Ahlstrom's 1957 observation about U.S. Lutheranism: "In retrospect, therefore, the 'Age of Definition' may be seen as a time when Lutheran doctrine came to prevail in the Lutheran Church, but also as a time when, much more than we usually realize, Reformed and Methodistic practice came to prevail" ("The Lutheran Church and American Culture: A Tercentenary Retrospect," 333). It would be fatuous to imagine that this apparently harmless yielding to sectarian "style" had nothing to do with the massive confessional and sacramental collapses which have now overtaken much of American Lutheranism.

74. *Lutheran Worship*, Mission Hymn No. 313.

EXCURSUS

"MISSOURI" AND "WISCONSIN" ON CHURCH AND MINISTRY

"Old Missouri" (Walther and Pieper) and "Old Wisconsin" (Hoenecke) did not differ over church and ministry. Both synods shared the standard Lutheran dogmatic tradition, which they reappropriated respectfully but not slavishly. The chief impetus towards "New Wisconsin" came, it seems, from the historian J. P. Koehler[1] who held that in the 19th century German disputes about church and ministry, only Höfling's position was "completely free and correct according to Scripture."[2] Modern Wisconsin's Statements on Church and Ministry[3] formally reject Höfling's stand: "It would be wrong to trace the origin of this public ministry to mere expediency (Höfling)."[4] Materially, however, the Wisconsin Statements suggest Höfling's influence, for instance in the virtual identification of priesthood and ministry,[5] and the apparent failure to distinguish the one Gospel ministry from auxiliary offices.[6] Höfling, too, admitted the "divine institution" of an abstract "public ministry" (*Predigtamt*) held in common by all. A related and very basic difficulty is the Statements' concept of "various groupings in Jesus' name for the proclamation of His Gospel," of which "all lie on the same plane. They are all church in one and the same sense. . ."[7] These "groupings" are not only local congregations and synods ("larger groupings"), but also "other groupings,"[8] of all of which it is said: "The specific forms in which believers group themselves together. . . have not been prescribed by the Lord to

1. J. Koehler, *The History of the Wisconsin Synod*, 232ff.
2. J. Koehler, *Lehrbuch der Kirchengeschichte*, 659.
3. 1967 WELS *Proceedings*, 289.
4. Ibid., II. D. 5.
5. Ibid., II.A. and D.
6. Note the use of Acts 6:1-6, *ibid.*, II.D.6.
7. Ibid., I.D.4.c., 287. Emphases in original.
8. I.D.4.b.

His New Testament Church"[9]. Church, ministry, means of grace, marks of the church, all seem to float about too abstractly here, tied too loosely to concrete divine instituting mandates.

"New Missouri," on the other hand, has tended to see the churchly nature and dignity of the local congregation and its ministry more and more in juridical or organizational, rather than theological terms. Hence T. Graebner's fateful denial that anything beyond a local congregation is really church: "We can say, synod, territorial church, a formation like the EKiD belong to Christendom, are a part of it, but are not church"[10]. This attitude, reflected also in A Statement of 1945,[11] implied that synods and their officials might behave in unchurchly ways, since they were not churches and ministers anyway. This fostered organizationalism and unionism.[12]

As for Walther and Pieper, it is not too much to say that they could not have imagined the Missouri Synod as a non-church. The whole point of the Synod's constitution was to enable "the confessing and teaching church" to attend jointly to "every particular churchly purpose," with the church's confession not a perfunctory formality, but actually shaping and permeating "the whole constitution and the church's entire way of acting" and "the discipline and governance of the church in general."[13] For Walther it was obvious that "particular churches" are not only local congregations but also entire confessional fellowships or communions, such as the Lutheran Church[14]. In his famous Iowa District essay on the chief duties of a properly Lutheran synod Walther spoke of a synod as "a living member of the Body of Christ" and of the Missouri Synod as "a true daughter of her mother, namely, of the Lutheran Church of the Unaltered Augsburg Confession."[15] Pieper too defined "churches" as both "congregations and church bodies",[16] and in his essay on "Church and Church Government"

9. Idem.

10. Y. Brilioth, ed., *World Lutheranism of Today*, 115.

11. Thesis Six wanted "questions of fellowship" shifted more to "the local congregation."

12. *The Crucible*, published briefly from London in 1939 by the brilliant W. M. Oesch, was founded to counteract especially in Missouri also "the Calvinistic and Romanistic views of the nature of the Church (as though it were essentially visible and a sector of society) and of the functions of the Church (as though it were one of its functions to assist society)."

13. *Der Lutheraner*, vol. 3, no. 1 [5 Sept. 1846], 2.

14. *Church and Ministry*, p. 111; *True Visible Church*, esp. theses IV [which cites the BC's "entire churches inside or outside the Holy Empire of the German Nation"], and V-XXV. Thesis XXIII is mistranslated as though "particular churches" meant simply local congregations.

15. 1879 LCMS Iowa District *Proceedings*, 116, 118.

16. *Christian Dogmatics*, III:422-427.

insisted on the right government of the church through synodical arrangements.[17]

Three telling counter-examples to typical "New Missouri" persuasions further illustrate the greater churchly breadth of "Old Missouri":

(1) Rather than starting with the local congregation in some exclusive sense, the 1875 North West District theses about the Power of the Keys follow this sequence: Universal church (invisible), then also all the "visible church fellowships" still retaining the Word and sacraments "essentially"—that is, not only the orthodox, Lutheran church—and "therefore also every single local congregation" has such power.[18]

(2) In 1874 the Synod held that the Convention could call teachers to its institutions since "the whole churchly power of the congregations is represented in the Synod when it is assembled."[19]

(3) Quoting an earlier *Lehre und Wehre* statement,[20] "The ministry [*Predigtamt*] goes through the world in a two-fold form, in a missionary [*missionisierenden*] and a parish-pastoral [*pfarramtlichen*] one," F. Pieper argued that missionaries called by Synod or its Districts should also be called and ordained: "This Call is not a human, but a divine Call, and those who have received and accepted this Call, have received and accepted a divine Call just as much as those called to parish-pastoral activity by already existing congregations."[21]

These are matters for friendly and level-headed discussions "with learned and sensible men, or even among ourselves" (SA III.Intro.), in the service of genuine confessional consensus.

---

17. "Kirche und Kirchenregiment," 1896 LCMS *Proceedings*, 27-46.
18. 1875 LCMS Northwest District *Proceedings*, 38-42.
19. 1874 LCMS *Proceedings*, 59.
20. *Lehre und Wehre* 9, 179.
21. Ibid., vol. 71, no. 12 [December, 1925], 425.

WORKS CITED

A Statement: Essays related to A Statement, including the text of A Statement: Speaking the Truth in Love. Chicago: Willow Press, 1945.

Adler, M. *How to Think About God*. New York: Macmillan, 1980.

Ahlstrom, Sydney E. "The Lutheran Church and American Culture: A Tercentenary Retrospect," *The Lutheran Quarterly* 9 (November 1957): 321-342.

The American Lutheran Church. *Lutheran and Presbyterian-Reformed Agreement 1986: A Study Guide*, 1986.

Anderson, H. "Gospel and Doctrine," in *The Function of Doctrine and Theology in Light of the Unity of the Church: A Report Plus 15 Papers From an Official Study Conducted by the Division of Theological Studies, Lutheran Council in the USA, During 1972-1977*. Lutheran Council in the USA, 1978.

Andrews, J. and J. Burgess, eds. *An Invitation to Action: The Lutheran-Reformed Dialogue Series III 1981-1983*. Philadelphia: Fortress Press, 1984.

Arndt, W. "The Doctrine of the Call into the Holy Ministry." *Concordia Theological Monthly* 24 (May 1954): 337-352.

Asendorf, U. and F. Kuenneth, eds. *Von der wahren Einheit der Kirche: Lutherische Stimmen zum Leuenburger Kondordienentwurf*. Berlin: Verlag Die Spur, 1973.

——— and F. Kuenneth, eds. *Leuenberg—Konkordie oder Diskordie?: Oekumenische Kritik z. Kondordie reformatorischer Kirchen in Europa*. Berlin: Verlag Die Spur, 1974.

Association of Evangelical Lutheran Churches. *Lutheran Unity: Material for Study, Discussion, and Response*. Prepared by The Committee on Lutheran Unity of the American Lutheran Church, Association of Evangelical Lutheran Churches, Lutheran Church, 1980.

Augustine. *City of God*. Translated by H. Bettenson. Pelican Classics. D. Knowles, ed. London: Penguin, 1976.

Baier, J. *Compendium theologiae positivae, adjectis notis amplioribus*. Denuo edendum curavit C. F. W. Walther. St. Louis: Luth. Concordia-Verlag, 1879.

Barclay, W. *Ethics in a Permissive Society*. London: Fontana Press, 1974.

Barrow, J. and F. Tipler. *The Anthropic Cosmological Principle*. New York: Oxford University Press, 1986.

Barth, K. *Eine Schweizer Stimme 1938-1945*. Zollikon-Zurich: Evangelischer Verlag, 1945.

———. *Theologische Studien*. Zollikon-Zurich: Evangelisher Verlag, 1950.

———. *The Word of God and the Word of Man*. Translated and with a new foreword by Douglas Horton. New York: Harper, 1957.

Bauer, W. *A Greek-English Lexicon of the New Testament and Other Early Christian Literature*. Second Edition revised and augmented by F. Wilbur Gingrich and Frederick Danker from Walter Bauer's Fifth Edition, 1958. Chicago: The University of Chicago Press, 1979.

Die Bekenntnisschriften der evangelisch-lutherischen Kirche: Herausgegeben im Gedenkjahr der Augsburgischen Konfession 1930. 10. Aufl., 41.–44. Tausend. Göttingen: Vandenhoeck & Ruprecht, 1986.

Bente, F. ed. *Triglot Concordia: The Symbolical Books of the Ev. Lutheran Church, German-Latin-English, Published as a Memorial of the Quadricentenary Jubilee of the Reformation anno Domini 1917 by resolution of the Evangelical Lutheran Synod of Missouri, Ohio, and Other States*. With *Historical Introductions to the Symbolical Books of the Evangelical Lutheran Church* by F. Bente. St. Louis: Concordia Publishing House, 1921.

Berkhof, L. *Systematic Theology*. Grand Rapids: Eerdmans, 1974.

Bird, W. *The Origin of Species Revisited*. 2 vols. New York: Philosophical Library, 1987-1989.

Blaeser, P. "Amt und Eucharistie im Neuen Testament." in P. Blaeser, ed. *Amt und Eucharistie*. Paderborn: Verlag Bonaficius-Druckerei, 1973.

Bloom, A. *The Closing of the American Mind*. New York: Simon and Schuster, 1987.

Boehme, A. "What's 'THE' Fuss All About?" *The Bride of Christ* 13 (Pentecost 1988): 5-17.

Bohlmann, R. "The Position of the LCMS on the Basis for Fellowship." *The Function of Doctrine and Theology in Light of the Unity of the Church.* A Report Plus 15 Papers from an Official Study Conducted by the Division of Theological Studies, Lutheran Council in the USA, During 1972–77, Lutheran Council in the USA, 1978, 32-39.

Braaten, C., ed. *The New Church Debate.* Philadelphia: Fortress Press, 1983.

Brand, E. "Toward a Lutheran Communion: Altar and Pulpit Fellowship." *LWF Report* (1988): 90-118.

Brauer, A. *Under the Southern Cross: History of the Evangelical Lutheran Church of Australia.* Adelaide: Lutheran Publishing House, 1956.

Brilioth, Y, ed. *World Lutheranism of Today.* Stockholm: Svenska Kyrkans Diakonistryrelses Bokforlag, 1950.

Brunner, P. *Lutherisches Bekenntnis in der Union. Festgabe fuer D. Peter Brunner.* Berlin and Hamburg: Lutherisches Verlagshaus, 1965.

———. "The Lutheran World Federation as an Ecclesiological Problem." *Lutheran World* 7 (December 1960): 237-256.

———. *The Ministry and the Ministry of Women.* St. Louis: Concordia Publishing House, 1971.

Brunotte, H. *Bekenntnis und Kirchenverfassung: Aufsaetze zur Kirchl. Zeitgeschichte.* Goettingen: Vandenhoeck and Ruprecht, 1977.

Buchrucker, A. Wort, *Kirche und Abendmahl bei Luther.* Bremen: Stelten, 1972.

Butler, C. *The Vatican Council 1869-1870.* London: Fontana, 1962.

Calov, A. *Exegema Augustanae Confessionis articulos Fidei.* Wittenberg: Johannes Borckardi, 1665.

Calvin, J. *Geneva Catechism, 1545.* Translated in *Calvin: Theological Treatises.* Translated by J. Reid. Vol. 22 *The Library of Christian Classics.* Edited by J. Baillie, J. McNeill, and H. Dusen. Philadelphia: Westminster, 1967.

———. *Institutes of the Christian Religion.* Translated and Indexed by F. Battles. Vol. 20 *Library of Christian Classics.* Philadelphia: Westminster Press, 1960.

———. *Tracts and Treatises on the Doctrine and Worship of the Church with a short life of Calvin by Theodore Beza*. Translated by H. Beveridge. Grand Rapids: Eerdmans, 1958.

Campenhausen, H. *Ecclesiastical Authority and Spiritual Power in the Church of the First Three Centuries*. Translated by I. A. Baker. Stanford: Stanford University Press, 1969.

Chemnitz, M. *Examination of the Council of Trent*. 4 vols. Translated by F. Kramer. St. Louis: Concordia Publishing House, 1971-1987.

———, John Gerhard and Polycarp Leyser. *Harmonia Quatuor Evangelistarum*. Frankfort and Hamburg, 1652.

———. *Loci Theologici*. Translated by J. A. O. Preus. 2 vols. St. Louis: Concordia Publishing House, 1989.

———. *Ministry, Word, and Sacraments: An Enchiridion*. Translated by L. Poellet. St. Louis: Concordia, 1981.

Chitty, D. J. "The Communion of Saints." Mascall, E. L., ed., *The Church of God: An Anglo-Russian Symposium by Members of The Fellowship of St. Alban and St. Sergius*. London: S.P.C.K., 1934, 157-172.

Christenson, L. *The Charismatic Renewal Among Lutherans: A Pastoral and Theological Perspective*. Minneapolis: Lutheran Charismatic Renewal Services, 1976.

Clark, S. *Civil Peace and Sacred Order*. Vol. 1 in *Limits and Renewals*. New York: Oxford University Press, 1989.

Congar, Y. , H. Kueng, and D. O'Hanlon, eds. *Council Speeches of Vatican II*. New York: Sheed and Ward, 1964.

Cord, R. *Separation of Church and State: Historical Fact and Current Fiction*. New York: Lambeth, 1982.

Cox, H. "The New Breed in American Churches: Forces of Social Activism in American Religion." *Daedalus: Journal of the American Academy of Arts and Sciences* 96 (Winter 1976): 135-150.

Craig, W. "Barrow and Tipler on the Anthropic Principle vs. Divine Design." *British Journal for the Philosophy of Science* (1988): 389-395.

Cullmann, O. *Early Christian Worship*. Translated by A. Todd and J. Torrance. Chicago: Regnery, 1953.

———. *Koenigsherrschaft Christi und Kirche im Neuen Testament*. Heft 10 in K. Barth, ed. *Theologische Studien*. Zollikon-Zurich: Evangelischer Verlag, 1950.

———. *The State in the New Testament*. New York: Scribner's, 1956.

Curtis, C. *Soederblom: Ecumenical Pioneer*. Minneapolis: Augsburg, 1967.

Darwin, C. *The Origin of Species*. New York: E. P. Dutton & Co., 1959.

Davidson, D. *Nuclear Weapons and the American Churches: Ethical Positions in Modern Warfare*. Boulder, Co.: Westview, 1983.

Declarations on the Relation of the Church to Non-Christian Religions. in *The Sixteen Documents of Vatican II with Commentaries by the Council Fathers*. Boston: Daughters of St. Paul, n.d.

Dedeken, G. *Thesaurus Consiliorum et Decisionum*. Hamburg: Michael Hering, 1623. 4 vols.

Delitzsch, K. *Vier Buecher von der Kirche*. 1847.

Denzinger, H. *The Sources of Catholic Dogma*. Translated by R. Deferrari. St. Louis: B. Herder, 1957.

Douglas, A. *The Feminization of American Culture*. New York: Alfred Knopf, 1977.

Duchrow, U. *Conflict Over the Ecumenical Movement: Confessing Christ today in the Universal Church*. Translated by David Lewis. Geneva: World Council of Churches, 1981.

———. *Christenheit und Weltverantwortung*. Stuttgart: Ernst Klett, 1970.

Dulles, A. *The Catholicity of the Church*. Oxford: Clarendon Press, 1985.

———. *Models of the Church*. Garden City, N. Y.: Doubleday, 1974.

Dummet, Michael. "A Remarkable Consensus," *New Blackfriars* 809 (October 1987): 424-431.

Dunkerley, R. and A. Headlam, eds. *The Ministry and the Sacraments. A Report of the Theological Commission appointed by the Continuation Committee of the Faith and Order Movement*. London: Student Movement Press, 1937.

Ebeling, G. *Word and Faith*. Translated by J. Leitch. London: SCM Press, 1963.

Eckhardt, E. *Homiletisches Real Lexicon*. Blair, Neb.: 1907.

Eckstrom, V. "Pluralism and Lutheran Confessionalism." *The Lutheran Quarterly* 29 (May 1977): 109-149.

Elert, W. *Der Christliche Glaube*. 5th edition. Enlarged and edited by Ernst Kinder. Translated by M. Bertram and W. Bouman as *The Christian Faith*. Columbus, Ohio: Trinity Seminary Press, 1974.

———. *Eucharist and Church Fellowship in the First Four Centuries*. Translated by N. Nagel. St. Louis: Concordia Publishing House, 1966.

———. *The Structure of Lutheranism: The Theology and Philosophy of the Life of Lutheranism especially in the Sixteenth and Seventeenth Centuries*. Volume I. Translated by W. Hansen. St. Louis: Concordia Publishing House, 1962.

Ellul, J. *False Presence of the Kingdom*. New York: Seabury, 1972.

European Supporting Documents. in the files of Concordia Historical Institute, St. Louis, Missouri.

Exon, A. *A Critical and Exegetical Commentary on the First Epistle of St. Paul to the Corinthians. International Critical Commentary*. Edinburg: T. & T. Clark, 1914.

Fagerberg, H. *Bekenntnis, Kirche und Amt in der deutschen konfessionellen Theologie des 19. Jahrhunderts*. Uppsala: A. B. Lundequistska Bokhandeln, 1952.

———. *A New Look at the Lutheran Confessions (1529-1537)*. Translated by Gene J. Lund. St. Louis: Concordia Publishing House, 1972.

Farley, E. *Ecclesial Reflection: An Anatomy of Theological Method*. Philadelphia: Fortress Press, 1982.

———. *Theologia: The Fragmentation and Unity of Theological Education*. Philadelphia: Fortress Press, 1983.

Ferguson, M. *The Aquarian Conspiracy: Personal and Social Transformation in the 1980s*. Los Angeles: Tarcher, 1980.

Flörke, W. and Brömel, A. "Das Dogma von der sichtbaren und unsichtbaren Kirche." *Zeitschrift für die gesammte lutherische Theologie und Kirche* 16 (1855): 269-292.

Florovsky, G. V. "Sobornost" in *The Church of God: An Anglo-Russian Symposium by Members of the Fellowship of St. Alban and St. Sergius*. E. L. Mascall, ed.

Fritschel, G. *Quellen und Dokumente zur Geschichte und Lehrstelleng der ev. luth. Synode von Iowa u. a. Staaten*. Chicago: Wartburg, n.d.

Fritz, J. *Pastoral Theology: A Handbook of Scriptural Principles Written Especially for Pastors of the Lutheran Church*. St. Louis: Concordia Publishing House, 1932.

Gassmann, G. *The Self-Understanding of the Lutheran World Federation*. L.W.F. Executive Committee Meeting, August 4-13, 1981.

———. "The Unity of the Church: Requirements and Structures." *LWF Report* 15 (1983).

Gerhard, J. *Loci Theologici.* Edited by J. F. Cotta. Tübingen: J. G. Cotta, 1770.

Gerrish, B. *The Old Protestantism and the New.* Chicago: University of Chicago Press, 1982.

Gillespie, N. C. *Charles Darwin and the Problem of Creation.* Chicago: University of Chicago Press, 1979.

Grane, L. *Modus Loquendi Theologicus: Luthers Kampf um die Erneuerung der Theologie.* Volume XII of *Acta Theologica Danica.* Edited by T. Christensen, E. Nielsen, R. Prenter, et. al. Leiden: Brill, 1975.

Gritsch, E. and R. Jenson. *Lutheranism: The Theological Movement and its Confessional Writings.* Philadelphia: Fortress, 1976.

Grundmann, S. "An Opinion regarding the Study Document of the Commission on Theology." *Lutheran World* 12 (April 1964): 172-185.

Hamann, H. "The New Testament and the Ordination of Women." *Lutheran Theological Journal* 9 (December 1975): 100-108.

———, ed. *Theologia Crucis: Studies in Honor of Hermann Sasse.* Adelaide, Australia: Lutheran Publishing House, 1975.

———. "The Translation of Eph. 4:12: A Necessary Revision." *Concordia Journal* 14 (January 1988): 42-49.

Harrisville, R. *Ministry in Crisis: Changing Perspectives on Ordination and the Priesthood of all Believers.* Minneapolis: Augsburg, 1987.

Hebart, S. *Wilhelm Loehe's Lehre von der Kirche, ihrem Amt und Regiment: Ein Beitrag zur Geschichte der Theologie im 19. Jahrhundert.* Neuendettelsaue: Freimund-Verlag, 1939.

———. "A Commentary on the LWF's Amended Constitution." *Lutheran World* XI, 2 (April 1964), 205-215.

Hebart, T. *Die Vereinigte Ev. Luth. Kirche in Australien (Velke): Ihr Werden, Wirken und Wesen, eine Zentenarschrift, 1838-1938.* North Adelaide: Lutheran Book Depot, 1938.

Heckel, J. *Das Blinde, undeutliche Wort 'Kirche.'* Gesammelte Aufsaetze Hrg. S. Grundmann. Köln: Böhlau, 1964.

Hedegard, D. *Ecumenism and the Bible.* Orebro: Evangeliipress, 1954.

Hein, M. *Lutherishes Bekenntnis, Kirche, und Amt, Theologie im 19. Jahrhundert*. Volume 17 of *Die Lutherische Kirche, Geschichte und Gestalten*. Guetersloh: Gerd Mohn, 1984.

Henry, C. "Church and State: Why the Marriage Must be Saved." *The Christian As Citizen. Christian Thought and Action*. Valley Stream, Ill.: Christianity Today Institute, 1985, 9-13.

———. *God, Revelation and Authority*. Waco, Tx: Word Books, 1979.

Hertz, K. H. ed. *Two Kingdoms and One World: A Sourcebook in Christian Social Ethics*. Minneapolis: Augsburg Press, 1976.

Hessel, D. *Social Ministry*. Philadelphia: Westminster Press, 1982.

Heubach, J. "Das Priestertum der Gläubigen und das Amt des Kirche." *Lutherischer Rundblick* 19 (1971): 291-300.

Hoefling, J. *Grundsaetze evangelisch-lutherischer Kirchenverfassung: Eine dogmatisch-kirchenrechtliche Abhandlung*. Erlangen: Blaesing, 1850.

Hoenecke, A. *Evangelisch-Lutherische Dogmatik*. Milwaukee: Northwestern, 1909. 4 vols.

Hoerber, R. *A Grammatical Study of Rom. 16:17*. Mankato: Lutheran Synod Book Company, 1963.

Hunter, K. "Church Growth Paper." *The Lutheran Witness—Minnesota South District Edition*, (March 1987).

———. *Foundations for Church Growth*. New Haven: Leader, 1983.

Jacobs, H. "The General Council." in *The Distinctive Doctrines and Usages of the General Bodies of the Evangelical Lutheran Church in the United States*. Philadelphia: Lutheran Publication Society, 1902.

Johnson, P. *Intellectuals*. New York: Harper & Row, 1988.

Kaesemann, E. "The Canon of the New Testament and the Unity of the Church." in *Essays on New Testament Themes*. London: SCM Press, 1961.

Kelly, J. *Early Christian Creeds*. 2nd ed. New York: David McKay, 1960.

———. *The Pastoral Epistles* in *Harper's New Testament Commentaries*. H. Chadwick, gen. ed. San Francisco: Harper & Row, 1960.

Kent, John. *End of the Line?: The Development of Christian Theology in the Last Two Centuries*. Philadelphia: Fortress Press, 1982.

Kimel, A. F., Jr. "The Holy Trinity Meets Ashtoreth: A Critique of the Episcopal 'Inclusive' Liturgies." *Anglican Theological Review,* LXXI, 1 (Winter 1989), 25-47.

Koehler, Ludwig and Walter Baumgartner. *Lexicon in Veteris Testamenti Libros*. Grand Rapids: Eerdmans, 1953.

Kirk, R. *The Conservative Mind*. Chicago: Regnery, 1986.

Kirsten, M. *"Luther und die Frauenordination," Lutherischer Rundblick* 21, 3 (1973), 139-148.

Kittel, G. ed. *Theological Dictionary of the New Testament*. Translated and Edited by G. Bromiley. Grand Rapids: Eerdmans, 1965.

Koehler, J. *The History of the Wisconsin Synod*. Edited and with an introduction by Leigh D. Jordahl. Sauk Rapids, Minn.: Faith–Life, The Protes'tant Conference, 1981, 2nd ed.

———. *Lehrbuch der Kirchengeschichte*. Milwaukee: Northwestern Publishing House, 1917.

Koehneke, P. "The Call into the Holy Ministry." Vol. I: 366-388. *The Abiding Word*. T. Laetsch, ed. St. Louis: Concordia Publishing House, 1946.

Kohls, E. and G. Muller, eds. *Kirche und Geschichte: Gesammelte Aufsaetze*. Goettingen: Vandenhoeck and Ruprecht, 1970.

Krauth, C. *The Conservative Reformation and Its Theology*. Minneapolis: Augsburg, 1963.

Lefever, E. W. *Amsterdam to Nairobi: The World Council of Churches and the Third World*. Washington: Ethics and Public Policy, 1979.

———. *Nairobi to Vancover: The World Council of Churches and the World, 1975-1987*. Washington: Ethics and Public Policy, 1987.

Lieberg, H. *Amt und Ordination bei Luther und Melanchthon*. Goettingen: Vandenhoeck and Ruprecht, 1962.

Lienhard, Marc. *Lutherisch-reformierte Kirchengemeinschaft heute*. Frankfurt: Lembeck & Knecht, 1972.

Liermann, H. "The Legal Nature and the Constitution of the L.W.F." *Lutheran World* 11 (April 1964): 185-200.

Lietzmann, H. *Handbuch zum Neuen Testament: An die Korinther I/II* Tuebingen, 1969.

———. *Handbuch zum Neuen Testament: An Die Roemer*. Tuebingen, 1928.

Lightfoot, J. B. *The Apostolic Fathers: Clement, Ignatius, and Polycarp: Revised Texts with Introductions, Notes, Dissertations and Translations*. Second Edition. New York: Macmillan, 1889-1890, reprinted Grand Rapids: Baker Book House, 1989.

Lindberg, C. *The Third Reformation: Charismatic Movements and the Lutheran Tradition*. Macon, Ga.: Mercer University Press, 1983.

Lochner, F. *Der Haupgottesdienst der evangelisch-lutherischen Kirche*. St. Louis: Concordia Publishing House, 1895.

Loehe, W. *Aphorismen Ueber die Neutestamentlichen Aemter und Ihr Verhaeltnis zur Gemeinde. Zur Verfassungsfrage der Kirche*. Nuremberg: J. R. Raw, 1849.

———. *Haus-, Schul-, und Kirchenbuch fuer Christen des Lutherischen Bekenntnisses*. Stuttgart: S. G. Liesching, 1851.

Loetscher, L. *The Broadening Church: A Study of Theological Issues in the Presbyterian Church since 1869*. Philadelphia: University of Pennysylvania Press, 1954.

Ludwig, A. "Review Essay." *Concordia Student Journal* 12 (Easter 1989); 4-14.

Luecke, D. *Evangelical Style and Lutheran Substance*. St. Louis: Concordia Publishing House, 1988.

"Lumen Gentium." *The Sixteen Documents of Vatican II with Commentaries by the Council Fathers*. Boston: Daughters of St. Paul, n. d.

Lunn, A. and G. Lean. *Christian Counter-Attack*. New Rochelle: Arlington Press, 1969.

Luther, Martin. *Luther's Works: American Edition*. 55 volumes. Jaroslav Pelikan and Helmut T. Lehmann, general editors. St. Louis: Concordia Publishing House; Minneapolis: Augsburg-Fortress Press, 1955-1986.

The Lutheran Church—Missouri Synod. *Brief Statement*.

———. *Convention Proceedings*, 1874.

———. *Convention Proceedings*, 1896.

———. *Convention Proceedings*, Detroit, 1965.

———. *Iowa District Convention Proceedings*, 1879.

———. *The Ministry: Office, Procedures, and Nomenclature*. A Report of the Commission on Theology and Church Relations of the Lutheran Church—Missouri Synod, 1981.

———. *The Nature and Implications of the Concept of Fellowship.* St. Louis: Commission on Theology and Church Relations, Lutheran Church—Missouri Synod, 1981.

———. *Northwest District Convention Proceedings,* 1875.

———. *A Statement of Scriptural and Confessional Principles,* 1973.

———. Synodical Constitution. *Concordia Historical Institute Quarterly.* 19, 1946.

———. *Thesen für die Lehrverhandlungen der Missouri Synode und der Synodalkonferenz biz zum Jahre 1893.* St. Louis: Concordia-Verlag, 1894.

———. *Women in the Church.* A report of the Commission on Theology and Church Relations of the Lutheran Church—Missouri Synod, 1985.

Lutheran Church of Australia. *Theses of Agreement.* Adelaide, 1966.

Lutheran Council in the USA. *The Function of Doctrine and Theology in Light of the Unity of the Church,* 1978.

———. *Social Ministry Affirmation: A Challenge to Lutherans Toward the Year 1990,* 1988.

Lutheran Synodical Conference. *Fellowship in Its Necessary Context of the Doctrine of the Church.* Proceedings of the Recessed Forty-sixth Convention, Lutheran Synodical Conference, 1961.

The Lutheran World Federation, *Convention Proceedings,* Minneapolis, 1957.

———. *Convention Proceedings,* Helsinki, 1963.

———. *Convention Proceedings,* Dar-es-Salaam, 1977.

———. *Convention Proceedings,* Budapest, 1984.

———. *Ecumenical Relations of the Lutheran World Federation.* Report of the Working Group on the Interrelations between the various Bilateral Dialogues. Geneva, 1977.

———. "On the Interrelation between Proclamation of the Gospel and Human Development." *Lutheran World* 2 (1973): 187-192.

Mannermaa, T. *Von Preussen nach Leuenberg: Hintergrund und Entwicklung der theologischen Methode der Leuenberger Kondordie. Arbeiten zur Geschichte und Theologie des Luthertums.* New Series, Volume I. Edited by B. Haegglund and H. Kraft. Hamburg: Lutherisches Verlagshaus, 1981.

Marquart, K. "Augsburg Confession VII Revisited" *Concordia Theological Quarterly* 45 (January-April): 17-25.

———, J. Stephenson, B. Teigen, eds., *A Lively Legacy: Essays in Honor of Robert Preus.* Ft. Wayne: Concordia Theological Seminary, 1985.

Martin, D. and P. Mullen, eds. *Unholy Warfare: The Church and the Bomb.* Oxford: Blackwell, 1983.

Mascall, E. L., ed. *The Church of God: An Anglo-Russian Symposium by Members of the Fellowship of St. Alban and St. Sergius.* London: S.P.C.K., 1934.

Maurer, W. *Historischer Kommentar zur Confessio Augustana.* Guetersloh: Guetersloher Verlaghaus, 1976. Translated by H. Anderson. *Historical Commentary on the Augsburg Confession.* Philadelphia: Fortress, 1986.

———. *Luthers Lehre von den drei Hierarchien und ihr mittelalterlicher Hintergrund.* Munich: Verlag der bayerischen Akademie der Wissenschaften, 1970.

———. *Pfarrerrecht und Bekenntnis: Ueber die Bekenntnismaessige Grundlage eines Pfarrerrechtes in der evangelisch-lutherischen Kirche.* Berlin: Lutherisches Verlaghaus, 1957.

Meyendorff, J. *The Orthodox Church: Its Past and Its Role in the World Today.* Crestwood, N. Y. : St. Vladimir's Seminary Press, 1981.

———. "Church and Ministry—for an Orthodox-Lutheran Dialogue." *Dialog* 22 (Spring 1983): 114-120.

———, A. Schmemann, N. Afanassieff, and N. Koulomzine. *The Primacy of Peter.* Leighton: 1973.

Meyer, H. "The LWF and its Role in the Ecumenical Movement. " *Lutheran World.* 20 (1973): 23-31.

Meyer, C. S., ed. *Walther Speaks to the Church.* St. Louis: Concordia Publishing House, 1973.

Miethe, T. *Did Jesus Rise From the Dead? Gary Habermas and Antony Flew: The Resurrection Debate.* San Francisco: Harper and Row, 1987.

Migne, J. P., ed. *Patrologiae Cursus Completus. Series latina.* 221 vols. *Series graeca.* 161 vols. Paris: 1857-1866.

Mileur, J., ed. *The Liberal Tradition in Crisis.* Lexington, Mass.: D. C. Heath, 1974.

Miller, E. *A Crash Course on the New Age Movement.* Grand Rapids: Baker Book House, 1989.

Mol, H. *Religion in Australia.* Melbourne, Australia: Thomas Nelson, 1971.

Moule, H. *The Epistle of Paul the Apostle to the Romans*. Cambridge: Cambridge University Press, 1925.

Muenchmeyer, A. *Das Dogma von der sichtbaren und unsichtbaren Kirche: Ein historisch-kritischer versuch*. Goettingen: Vandenhoek, 1854.

Muggeridge, M. *Jesus Rediscovered*. London: Collins, Fontana books, 1969.

Murray, W. *My Life Without God*. Nashville: Thomas Nelson, 1982.

Nagel, N. "The Office of the Holy Ministry in the Confessions." *Concordia Journal* 14 (1988): 238-299.

Nash, R. *Challenge and Response*. Washington: Ethics and Public Policy Center, 1985.

Nash, R. *Social Justice and the Christian Church*. Milfor, Mich.: Mott Media, 1989 ,i8.

Nelson, E. C. "The One Church and the Lutheran Churches." *L.W.F. Proceedings*. Helsinki, 1963.

———. "Editorial." *Lutheran World* 15 (1968): 320-324.

———. "Ecclesiology as Key to the Lutheran Future. " *Lutheran Forum* 18 (Pentecost 1984): 14-18.

———. *The Rise of World Lutheranism: An American Perspective*. Philadelphia: Fortress Press, 1982.

———, ed. in collaboration with T. Tappert. *The Lutherans in North America*. Philadelphia: Fortress Press, 1976.

Nelson, J. B. *Embodiment*. Minneapolis: Augsburg Press, 1978.

Nestle, E. et K. Aland, M. Black, C. Martini, B. Metzger, A. Wikgren, eds. *Novum Testamentum Graece*. 26. neu bearbeitete Auflage. Stuttgart: Deutsche Bibelstiftung, 1898 and 1979.

Newman, J. H. *The Arians of the Fourth Century*. Westminster, Md.: Christian Classics, 1968.

Nisbet, R. *History of the Idea of Progress*. New York: Basic Books, 1980.

Norman, E. *Christianity and the World Order*. New York: Oxford University Press, 1978.

Ochsenford, S. E. *Documentary History of the General Council of the Evangelical Lutheran Church in North America*. Philadelphia: General Council Publication House, 1912.

Oesch, W. and M. Rönsch. "Letter to President O. J. Naumann of the Wisconsin Synod." July 15, 1961.

Oesch, W. "An Open Letter to LWF President H. Lilje." *Lutherischer Rundblick* 4 (June 1956): 34-39.

———. *Die Lehre von Kirche und Amt in drei Kapiteln*. ("Three Chapters"). Private duplication, n.d.

Pearce, E. George. *The Story of the Lutheran Church in Britain Through Four Centuries of History*. London: The Evangelical Lutheran Church of England, 1969.

Persson, E. *Sacra Doctrina: Reason and Revelation in Aquinas*. Translated by J. A. R. Mackenzie. Philadelphia: Fortress Press, 1970.

Pfeffer, L. "Issues that Divide: The Triumph of Secular Humanism." *Journal of Church and State* (1977): 203-216.

Pieper, F. *Christian Dogmatics*. 3 volumes. Translated by T. Engelder, W. Albrecht, F. Mayer, and L. Blankenbuehler from *Christliche Dogmatik* (St. Louis: 1917-1924). St. Louis: Concordia Publishing House, 1950.

———. *Das Grundbekenntnis der evangelisch-lutherischen Kirche*. St. Louis: Luther Concordia Verlag, 1880.

———. *Of Unity in the Faith*. Synodical Conference Proceedings, 1888.

———. *Vortraege über die Evangelisch Lutherische Kirche die Wahre Sichtbare Kirche Gottes auf Erden*. Lectures on C. F. W. Walther's theses on the True Visible Church. St. Louis: Seminary Press, 1916.

Piepkorn, A. "What the Symbols have to say about the Church." *Concordia Theological Monthly* 26 (May 1955): 750-763.

Plummer, A. and A. Robertson. *A Critical and Exegetical Commentary on the First Epistle of St. Paul to the Corinthians*. Vol. 33. *International Crtical Commentary*. Edinburgh: Clark, 1914.

Poehlmann, H. *Abriss der Dogmatik*. Gütersloh: Gütersloher Verlagshaus Gerd Mohn, 1973.

Popper, K. *Conjectures and Refutations*. New York: Harper & Row, 1968.

Pragman, J. *Traditions of Ministry: A History of the Doctrine of the Ministry in Lutheran Theology*. St. Louis: Concordia, 1983.

Prenter, R. *Das Bekenntnis von Augsburg: Eine Auslegung*. Erlangen: Martin Luther Verlag, 1980.

———. "Die goettliche Einsetzung des Predigtamtes und das allgemeine Priestertum bei Luther." *Theologische Literaturzeitung* 86 (May 1961): 321-333.

Preus, R. "The Basis for Concord." in *Formula for Concord: Theologians' Convocation Essays*. St. Louis: Commission on Theology and Church Relations, Lutheran Church—Missouri Synod, 1977.

———. "The Confessions and the Mission of the Church." *The Springfielder* 19 (June 1975): 20-39.

Quenstedt, J. *Systema Theologicum*. Leipzig: T. Fritsch, 1715.

Rahner, K. *Concern for the Church*. Volume XX of *Theological Investigations*. New York: Crossroad, 1981.

———. *Ecclesiology, Questions in the Church: The Church in the World*. Volume XIV of *Theological Investigations*. New York: Crossroad, 1981.

———. *Faith and Ministry*. Volume XIX of *Theological Investigations*. New York: Crossroad, 1981.

———. *Jesus, Man, and the Church*. Volume XVII of *Theological Investigations*. New York: Crossroad, 1981.

Religion in Geschichte und Gegenwart. 3rd ed. Tübingen: J.C.B. Mohr (Paul Siebeck), 1957.

Rengstorf, K. H. *Apostolate and Ministry: The New Testament Doctrine of the Office of the Ministry*. Translated by P. Pahl. St. Louis: Concordia, 1969.

Reu, M. *The Augsburg Confession: A Collection of Sources with An Historical Introduction*. Chicago: Wartburg Publishing House, 1930. Reprinted in *Concordia Heritage Series*. St. Louis: Concordia Publishing House, 1983. Major portions are available in reprint. Ft. Wayne: Concordia Theological Seminary Press, n.d.

Reumann, J. *Ministries Examined: Laity, Clergy, Women, and Bishops in a Time of Change*. Minneapolis: Augsburg, 1987.

Reumann, J. "What in Scripture Speaks to the Ordination of Women?" *Concordia Theological Monthly* 44 (January 1973): 5-30.

Rieker, K. *Grundsaetze reformierter Kirchenverfassung*. Leipzig, 1899.

Roberts, A. and J. Donaldson, eds. *The Ante-Nicene Christian Library: Translation of the Writings of the Fathers Down to 325 A.D.*. 10 volumes with index plus supplement. Rev. ed. 1926. Grand Rapids: Eerdmans, 1980, reprint.

Robinson, J. *The Body: A Study in Pauline Theology*. London: SCM Press, 1957.

Roman Catechism. Translated and Annotated in Accord with Vatican II and Post-Conciliar Documents and the New Code of Canon Law by Robert I. Bradley, S. J. and Eugene Kevane. Boston: St. Paul Editions, 1985.

Roof, W. and W. McKinney. *American Mainline Religion*. New Brunswick and London: Rutgers University Press, 1988.

Rouse, R. and S. C. Neill, eds. *A History of the Ecumenical Movement 1517-1948*. London: S. P. C. K. , 1967.

Ruse, M. *The Darwinian Revolution*. Chicago: University of Chicago Press, 1979.

Sasse, H. *Holy Church or Holy Writ? The Meaning of the Sola Scriptura in the Reformation*. Sydney: IVF Graduates Fellowship (Australia), 1967.

———. *Here We Stand*. in Concordia Heritage Series. St. Louis: Concordia Publishing House, 1966.

———. *In Statu Confessionis*. Berlin: Die Spur, 1976.

———. "Theses on the Seventh Article of the Augsburg Confession. " *The Springfielder* 25 (Autumn 1961): 13-17.

———. *This is My Body: Luther's Contention for the Real Presence in the Sacrament of the Altar*. Rev. Australian ed. Adelaide: Lutheran Publishing House, 1976.

———. "Book review of E. Nelson's *The Lutherans in North America.*" *Lutheran Theological Journal* 10 (August 1976): 57-61.

———. *Was Heisst Lutherisch?* Munich: C. Kaiser, 1936.

———. *We Confess the Church*. Translated by N. Nagel. St. Louis: Concordia Publishing House, 1986.

———. *We Confess the Sacraments*. Translated and Edited by N. Nagel. St. Louis: Concordia, 1985.

Scaer, D. "The Validity of the Churchly Acts of Ordained Women." *Concordia Theological Quarterly* 53: 1–2 (January–April 1989), 3-20.

Schaeffer, F. V. Bukovsky, J. Hitchcock. *Who is for Peace?* Nashville: Thomas Nelson, 1983.

Schaff, P. *Creeds of Christendom*. 3 vols. Grand Rapids: Baker, 1977.

———. *Select Library of the Nicene and Post-Nicene Fathers of the Christian Church.* 14 vols. in each of two series. Grand Rapids: Eerdmans, 1980 reprint.

Schiotz, F. "Observations on Parts of Dr. Nelson's 'Lutheranism in North America.' " *The Lutheran Quarterly* 2 (1977): 165-168.

Schlink, E. *Theology of the Lutheran Confessions.* Translated by R. Koehnke and H. Bouman. A Translation of *Theologie der lutherischen Bekenntnisschriften.* 3rd. ed. Munich: 1948. Philadelphia: Fortress, 1975.

Schmemann, A. "The Idea of Primacy in Orthodox Ecclesiology." in *The Primacy of Peter in the Orthodox Church.* Volume I in *Library of Orthodox Theology and Spirituality.* Leighton Buzzard: Faith Press, 1973.

Schmid, H. *The Doctrinal Theology of the Evangelical Lutheran Church.* Translated by C. Hay and H. Jacobs. 3rd ed, rev. Minneapolis: Augsburg Publishing House, 1961.

Schneiders, M. "Feminist Ideology Criticism and Biblical Hermeneutics," *Biblical Theology,* Bulletin 19 (January 1989): 3-10.

Schoop, L. et al., eds. *The Fathers of the Church: A New Translation.* Washington, D. C.: The Catholic University of America Press, 1947-.

Schultz, R. C. "An Analysis of the Augsburg Confession Article VII.2 in its Historical Context, May and June, 1530. " *Sixteenth Century Journal* 11 (1980): 11-23.

Scofield, C. I., ed. *The Scofield Reference Bible.* New York: Oxford University, 1909, 1917, 1937, 1945.

Sheehan, T. *The First Coming: How the Kingdom of God became Christianity.* New York: Random House, 1986.

Sixteen Documents of Vatican II with Commentaries by the Council Fathers. Boston: Daughters of Paul, n. d.

Smith, G. S. *God and Politics: Four Views on the Reformation of Civil Government: Theonomy, Principled, Pluralism, Christian America, National Confessionalism.* Phillipsburg, New Jersey: Presbyterian and Reformed Publishing Company, 1989.

Stein, W. *Das Kirchliche Amt bei Luther.* Bd. 73 Veroeffentlichungen des Instituts fuer Europaeische Geschichte Mainz. Wiesbaden: Steiner, 1974.

Stephenson, J. "Admission to the Lutheran Altar: Reflections on Open Versus Close Communion," *Concordia Theological Quarterly*. Vol. 53, No. 1–2. (Jan–April 1989): 39-52.

———. "The Holy Eucharist: at the Centre or Periphery of the Church's Life in Luther's Thinking?" K. Marquart, J. Stephenson, B. Teigen, eds. *A Lively Legacy: Essays in Honor of Robert Preus*. Ft. Wayne: Concordia Theological Seminary, 1985, 154-163.

———. "The Two Governments and the Two Kingdoms in Luther's Thought." *Scottish Journal of Theology*. 34:321-37.

Stoeckhardt, G. "Von dem Beruf der Lehrerinnen an christlichen Gemeindeschulen." *Concordia Theological Monthly* 5 (October 1934): 764-773.

———. *Kommentar über den Brief Pauli an die Epheser*. St. Louis: Concordia, 1910.

Sundkler, B. *Nathan Soederblom: His Life and Work*. Lund: Gleerups, 1968.

Tappert, T., gen. ed. *The Book of Concord: The Confessions of the Evangelical Lutheran Church*. Trans. and ed. by T. Tappert, J. Pelican, R. Fischer, and A. Piepkorn. Philadelphia: Fortress Press, 1959, 13th printing, 1979.

Tax, S. and C. Callender, eds. *Evolution After Darwin*. Chicago: University of Chicago Press, 1960. 3 vols.

Thurian, Max, ed. *Churches Respond to BEM*. 6 vols. Geneva: WCC, 1986-1988.

Treadgold, D. W. *The West in Russia and China*. Cambridge University Press, 1973. 2 vols.

Troeltsch, E. *The Social Teaching of the Christian Churches*, tr. O. Wyon. New York: Macmillan, 1931. 2 vols.

Truemper, D. G. "The Catholicity of the Augsburg Confession: CA VII and FC X on the Grounds for the Unity of the Church. " *Sixteenth Century Journal* 11 (1980): 11-23.

———. "How Much Is Enough?" *Missouri in Perspective*. 8 Oct. 1979, 5.

———. "Concordia's Not-So-Contemporary Look at the Formula of Concord. " *The Cresset* 43 (February 1980): 22-30.

Turner, James. *Without God, Without Creed: The Origins of Unbelief in America*. Baltimore: Johns Hopkins University Press, 1985.

Turner, Nigel. *Christian Words*. Nashville: Thomas Nelson, 1981.

Vorgrimler, H. gen. ed. *Commentary on the Documents of Vatican II.* New York: Herder and Herder, 1967.

Wadensjo, B. *Toward a World Lutheran Communion: Developments in Lutheran cooperation up to 1924.* Acta Universitatis Upsaliensis 18. Uppsala: Universitet Stockholm, 1970.

Walther, C. F. W. *Amerikanisch-Lutherische Evangelien Postille.* St. Louis: Concordia Publishing House, 1875. Available in translation by D. Heck. Ft. Wayne: Concordia Theological Seminary Print Shop, 1984.

______. *Amerikanisch-Lutherische Pastoraltheologie.* 4. Aufl. St. Louis: Concordia-Verlag, 1897.

———. *Briefe.* 2 vols. Ed. L. Fuerbringer. St. Louis: Concordia-Verlag, 1915-1916.

———. *The Form of a Christian Congregation.* Printed and Published by Resolution of the Ev. Luth. Pastoral Conference of St. Louis, Mo. Second Unchanged Edition. St. Louis, Mo., 1864. Translated by J. T. Mueller. Reprinted in *Concordia Heritage Series* and bound with *The True Visible Church.* St. Louis: Concordia, 1987.

———. *Die Stimme unserer Kirche in der Frage von Kirche und Amt.* (First Edition, 1952). English translation by J. T. Mueller from the third edition (Erlangen: Andreas Deichert, 1875), as *Church and Ministry: Witnesses of the Evangelical Lutheran Church on the Question of the Church and Ministry.* St. Louis: Concordia, 1987.

———. *Theses on Communion Fellowship with the Heterodox.* An Essay Delivered at the 1870 Convention of the Western District. Translated by L. White. Edited by P. T. McCain. Fort Wayne: Concordia Theologic?l Seminary Print Shop, 1990.

———. *The True Visible Church.* An Essay for the Convention of the General Evangelical Lutheran Synod of Missouri, Ohio, and Other States for its Sessions at St. Louis, Mo., October 31, 1866. Printed at the reqest of the Synod. Translated by J. Mueller. Reprinted in the *Concordia Heritage Series* and bound with *The Form of a Christian Congregation.* St. Louis: Concordia, 1987.

———. *Walther Speaks to the Church: Selected Letters.* Ed. C. Meyer. St. Louis: Concordia, 1973.

Ward, Harry. *The Social Creed of the Churches.* Abingdon Press, 1914.

Webber, R. E. *The Church in the World.* Grand Rapids: Zondervan, 1986.

——— and D. Bloesch. *The Orthodox Evangelicals.* Nashville and New York: Thomas Nelson Press, 1978.

Whitley, W. T. , ed. *The Doctrine of Grace.* London: Student Christian Movement Press, 1932.

Wingren, G. "Ein Ungenütztes Oecumenisches Kapital." *Evangelische Kommentare* 12 (1969): 701-706.

———. *Theology in Conflict.* Philadelphia: Muhlenberg Press, 1958.

Winter, G. *How Are The Mighty Fallen: A History of the Events Leading to the Downfall of the ELCA and Formation of the ELCR.* Queensland, Australia: The Evangelical Lutheran Congregations of the Reformation, 1986.

Wisconsin Evangelical Lutheran Synod. *Convention Proceedings,* 1967.

Wolf, C. *Documents of Lutheran Unity in America.* Philadelphia: Fortress Press, 1966.

World Council of Churches. *Baptism, Eucharist, Ministry.* The Lima Statement, Geneva: 1982.

Wurmbrand, Richard. *Christ in the Communist Prisons.* New York: Coward-McCann, 1968.

SACRED SCRIPTURE INDEX

by Paul B. McCain

LUTHERAN CONFESSIONS INDEX

By Matthew Harrison

NAME INDEX

by Paul T. McCain

SUBJECT INDEX